NATIONWIDE REAL ESTATE PRE-LICENSING COURSE

Third Edition

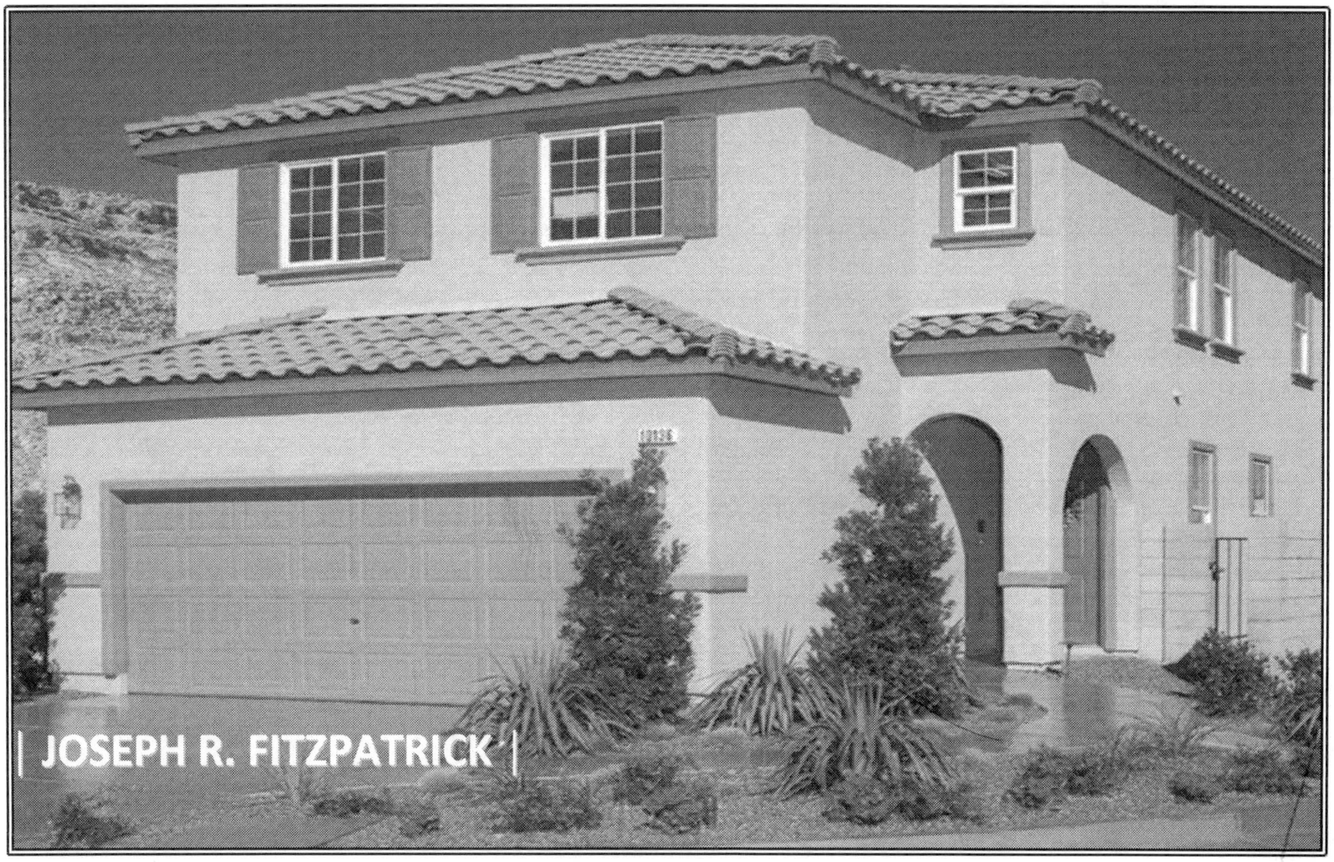

| JOSEPH R. FITZPATRICK |

Real estate licensing courses and textbooks available through RealtySchool.com:

REALTYSCHOOL.COM
NATIOWIDE REAL ESTATE PRE-LICENSING COURSE
Authored by Joseph R. Fitzpatrick
Contributing authors: Michael G. Beckner, J.D. and David Crowell
Edited by Terrance M. Fitzpatrick, Leslie Wood, and Charlotte Bentley

©2014 by RealtySchool.com LLC. All Rights Reserved. The content within this publication, or any part thereof, may not be reproduced in any manner whatsoever without the written consent of RealtySchool.com LLC.

Third Edition 2014 082715JF
ISBN-13: 978-1502443205
ISBN-10: 1502443201
cover photo courtesy of KB Home

TABLE OF CONTENTS

An Introduction to the Real Estate Business 1
    So, you want a real estate license? Introduction to Real Estate Brokerage 2
    So, *What is* Real Estate Brokerage? 3
    So, You've Considered Being a Builder? Development and Construction 7
    So, You Want To Be a REALTOR®? Professional Organizations 7
    End of Chapter Quiz 8

Chapter 1 – Contracts 11
    General Knowledge of Contract Law 12
    Contract Terminology 15
    Termination and Assignment of Contracts 16
    The Listing Agreement 18
    Buyers Brokerage Agreements 21
    Purchase Agreements 22
    The Closing Process 24
    Leases and Lease-Purchase Agreements 25
    Other Contract Issues and Vocabulary 29
    End of Chapter Quiz 31

Chapter 2 – Agency and the Practice of Real Estate 35
    Laws, Definitions, and Nature of Agency Relationships 36
    Creating Agency Relationships in Real Estate 40
    Duties of Being an Agent 41
    Terminating Agency Relationships in Real Estate 44
    Property Management 44
    Fair Housing Laws 46
    Limitations on Advertising 54
    Duties and Obligations of Brokers and Their Associates 57
    General Ethics 59
    Issues in The Use Of Technology 61
    Antitrust Laws 63
    End of Chapter Quiz 64

Chapter 3 - Appraisal and Market Analysis 71
    Appraisal 72
    The Three Appraisal Approaches to Value 75
    Market Analysis 83
    End of Chapter Quiz 86

Chapter 4 – Financing 91
    Financing Vocabulary 92
    Common Clauses Found in Mortgages or Deeds of Trust 98
    Common Types of Lending Instruments 99
    The Loan Process 102
    Sources of Money for Lending 103
    Residential Lending Programs 105
    Why Do Interest Rates Fluctuate? Government Influence on Interest Rates 109

    Finance and Credit Laws (Federal) 110
    End of Chapter Quiz 114

Chapter 5 - Property Ownership and Transfer of Title 117
    Classes of Property 118
    Land Characteristics 121
    Legal Descriptions 122
    Subdivisions 126
    Encumbrances 126
    Forms of Ownership 131
    Freehold Estates in Property 138
    Deeds 140
    Title Insurance 144
    Miscellaneous Issues in the Transfer of Title 146
    Escrow and Closing 148
    Foreclosure/Short Sales 152
    Tax Aspects of Transferring Title 153
    End of Chapter Quiz 157

Chapter 6 - Land Use Controls and Regulations 161
    Government Rights Concerning Land 162
    Public Controls and Police Powers 166
    Regulation of Environmental Hazards 169
    Private Controls 171
    Common Interest Community Properties 172
    End of Chapter Quiz 175

Chapter 7 - Real Estate Math 179
    General Math Concepts 180
    Property Tax Calculations 183
    Calculations for Transactions 184
    Mortgage and Lending Calculations 187
    Valuation Calculations 190
    End of Chapter Quiz 193

Chapter 8 - Mandated Disclosures 197
    Agency Disclosures 198
    Property Condition Disclosure Forms 199
    Home Warranties 200
    Need For Inspection and Obtaining/Verifying Information 201
    Material Facts Relating To Property Condition or Location 203
    Material Facts Relating To Public Controls, Statutes, or Public Utilities 205
    End of Chapter Quiz 206

APPENDIX A: End of Chapter Quiz Answer Keys 209
APPENDIX B: Sample Real Estate Documents from Across the Country 229
APPENDIX C: Practice Final Exams
APPENDIX D: Glossary

Introduction
An Introduction to the Real Estate Business

"I have been actively involved in the real estate business since 1984. A career in real estate sales has been exciting and financially rewarding for me. I have devoted much of my professional life to real estate education so that others may benefit as I have. With the right education as a foundation, real estate sales can provide you with the same opportunities and more!"

- Joe Fitzpatrick

DO YOU KNOW???

Do you know the five specialties of real estate licensees?
Can you explain the primary functions of a licensee?
Do you understand the difference between a *comparative market analysis* and an *appraisal*?
Are you familiar with licensing requirements of *mortgage bankers* and *mortgage brokers*?
Have you been acquainted with the phases of development and construction and can you distinguish among the three categories of residential construction?
These are some of the topics we will address in this chapter.

SO, YOU WANT A REAL ESTATE LICENSE? INTRODUCTION TO REAL ESTATE BROKERAGE

For the many of you reading this textbook, there will be a wide variety of motivations for taking this course and obtaining a real estate license. Some may wish to become real estate sales associates or brokers; some are seeking the knowledge for their own investment purposes; others may be required to obtain a license in order to legally perform the duties associated with an employment opportunity; some may be interested in property management; and a host of other reasons. Whatever avenue you wish to explore within this industry, a real estate career can provide unlimited opportunities with rewarding financial benefits.

Real estate is one of the most significant sectors of the U.S. economy serving as one of the nation's largest sources of building wealth while also employing nearly two million Americans every year. New home construction and new home starts are a common index to measure economic trends and make a direct contribution to the *Gross Domestic Product* (GDP). When the housing market is stimulated, the entire economy has historically also improved.

Just consider the careers associated with home sales in addition to real estate salespeople and brokers: appraisers, lenders, home inspectors, insurers, attorneys, tax advisors, bankers, title insurers, escrow companies, surveyors, movers, construction workers, and on and on. All of these associated industries rely heavily on real estate sales activity for their livelihoods. In addition, there are the industries that benefit from the "trickle down" effect of consumer spending associated with housing such as landscapers, pool companies, home repair, electricians, plumbers, home appliances and improvements, etc. It is easy to see how these many industries and the individuals and their families are impacted when real estate sales prosper or suffer.

SO, *WHAT IS* REAL ESTATE BROKERAGE?

Do you fancy the image of chauffeuring million-dollar home buyers around the beautiful city in your brand new, luxury automobile? Do you picture yourself at the head of a board room conference table pitching your billion dollar investment opportunity to savvy investors and entrepreneurs? Or maybe you see yourself counting all the cash you have acquired by owning several properties that have brought you great yields and dividends? That may very well be what your future holds.

Real Estate Brokerage is the matchmaking of people and bringing them together in a real estate transaction of some kind. Licensees are paid handsome commissions for the *brokering* of real estate parties such as *buyer and seller,* or *landlord and tenant.* Most states define the **services of real estate brokerage** as *buying, selling, leasing, exchanging, negotiating, offering, auctioning, and appraising* for another person, for compensation. If an individual is performing any of these services of real estate, for compensation, or even for the expectation of being compensated, a real estate license from the state where the property is located is required.

Real estate brokers and their associated salespeople are rightfully expected to be *experts in the field* whose knowledge and opinions can be reasonably relied upon. Licensees should have knowledge and expertise in:

1. **Knowledge of property transfers:** Licensees are expected to know the complete process of transferring real estate from the current owner to a new owner including the preparation and explanation of the real estate contract, making the required property disclosures, assisting the purchaser in obtaining the financing, and working through the close of escrow.

2. **Knowledge of market conditions:** Real estate market conditions change daily, even several times within a day. What is going on with property values? What about interest rates? Is it a buyer's market or a seller's market? Is the inventory shrinking or expanding? How stringent are lenders these days? How long is it taking to close? These are all very typical questions the professional is expected to answer and answer accurately.

3. **Knowledge of marketing real estate:** *Marketing* takes several forms for the real estate practitioner. When there are large inventories of homes for sale and qualified buyers are more scarce, it is said to be a *buyer's market* and the expertise to market a home for sale is

critical for the agent of the seller. I know of some licensees who have only worked in a *seller's market*, where the number of available listings is low and buyers are plentiful in a chaotic environment of multiple offers, who may very well face some serious challenges when the market turns and marketing their listings becomes essential.

But marketing also extends to a licensee marketing herself as well. In this chosen sales niche, most of the clients do not come to us; we have to find them. **Prospecting** is the marketing of yourself in order to attract real estate clients to doing business with you. Here are just some examples of the many prospecting activities successful real estate agents do to attract clients:

- *farming* a geographical area, staying in contact with all residents of a select neighborhood (the *farm*), providing information and real estate services
- door knocking
- cold calling
- conducting open houses
- visiting "for sale by owners" (FSBOs)
- contacting the sellers of expired listings that did not sell
- staying in contact with your **sphere of influence**, all the people you know
- mail and bulk mail campaigns
- internet marketing utilizing a web site, pay per click, and other methods

The list of marketing techniques to attract clients is never-ending and most agents experience success in their careers in direct proportion to the amount of marketing they do. Many new licensees are startled when they discover they have to make cold calls or knock on doors to get business. These activities are common to get your career off the ground and will eventually decline as you reap the rewards of repeat and referral business.

The primary *function*s of a real estate licensee are:

1. **Sales and leasing** – Under the direct supervision of the employing broker, licensees facilitate the sale, purchase, or rental of real estate, typically representing one of the parties while another agent represents the best interests of the opposite party. Salespersons provide any of the services of real estate to the party represented and are expected to have knowledge and expertise the client does not necessarily possess and hence, the need for hiring a real estate professional.

   There are five major sales specialties within the function of sales and leasing which include:

   - **residential** – usually defined as four or fewer residential units
   - **commercial** – income producing properties such as multi-unit dwellings, retail shopping centers, office buildings, etc.
   - **industrial** – industrial parks or lands
   - **agricultural** – lands used for farming and cultivating crops, usually 10 or more acres

- **business opportunities** – the sale or lease of existing businesses

2. **Property management** – The primary objective of a licensee hired by an owner to handle the management of the owner's income property is to maximize the owner's return on investment while also protecting the value of the property itself. Many owners do not wish to take on the day-to-day activities and hassles associated with being a landlord and hire property managers to perform those functions on the owner's behalf. Some investors are *absentee owners* and live too far from the investment to manage the property themselves. Property managers are hired to:

    - market the unit for rent
    - assess fair market rent
    - locate the tenant
    - facilitate the execution of the lease
    - coordinate the move in
    - collect deposits and rents
    - handle repair issues
    - supervise maintenance and care of the property
    - deal with late rents, non-payment of rents, and evictions
    - coordinate move outs

    There is definitely a need for the services of property managers as many owners do not have the knowledge or the inclination to take on these responsibilities themselves. When employing a property manager, the owner should use a *property management agreement* which should specify both the owner's and the property manager's duties, responsibilities, and under what conditions the property manager has the authority to make decisions or sign a contract.

3. **Real estate appraisals** – The art of estimating a property's market value is *appraisal*. It is considered an art rather than a science as the derived estimate of value is the appraiser's best *opinion* of value and therefore, two or more appraisers estimating the value on the same property could easily arrive at differing values.

    Typically, real estate agents and brokers calculate market value by preparing a *comparative market analysis (CMA)* while true appraisals are performed by state-licensed or certified appraisers. A CMA is often prepared by a real estate agent when listing property for sale and may show:

    - current, available listings for sale
    - pending sales that have not yet closed, however sale prices may not be shared
    - closed sales which represent reliable sale data where sale prices are shared
    - withdrawn listings that were taken off the market for whatever reason
    - expired listings that did not sell, typically due to being overpriced

Real estate salespeople commonly offer a CMA to a potential seller without cost in anticipation of gaining the seller's listing.

A **broker's price opinion (BPO)** is a more intricate analysis and must be performed under the supervision of the associate's employing broker. Lenders and private mortgage insurance companies will commonly request a BPO in settling a foreclosure or pre-foreclosure (short sale) transaction.

> *Neither a comparative market analysis nor a broker's price opinion may suggest it is an appraisal in any way.*

Appraisals are much more intricate in nature than a CMA and involve the utilization of the approaches to value as explained in the appraisal chapter of this textbook. Appraisers may not be compensated in proportion to the value derived due to the inherent conflict of interest that would create. Also, an appraisal for a federally related transaction must be done by a state-licensed or certified appraiser.

4. **Financing** – The majority of real estate transactions involve financing in some manner as most purchasers do not have the cash to buy property outright. The world of financing involves the process of supplying funds to purchasers to make transactions happen. Although real estate agents are not expected to be experts in the field of financing, they are expected to know enough about financing matters and how to solve related issues to be of service to their clients. The experts are mortgage bankers and mortgage brokers and these individuals will be licensed as such. There is an entire chapter in this textbook devoted to financing as it is relevant to the real estate practitioner.

5. **Counseling** – It is quite common for the real estate agent to be asked for his opinion or advice within a real estate transaction. As a licensee, you must be ever-so-cautious in the advice or counseling that you offer as those very opinions may come back to haunt you if something goes terribly wrong. There is a niche in the real estate profession for professional real estate counselors who are compensated purely for their advice regarding a sale, purchase, or investment and these individuals are extensively skilled in this area.

SO, YOU'VE CONSIDERED BEING A BUILDER? DEVELOPMENT AND CONSTRUCTION

This is yet another niche in the real estate trade and individuals who are involved in land development and the construction of homes typically have experience in this arena. Elements in development and construction are:

1. **Land acquisition** – where large parcels of vacant land are located and acquired after assuring that the land is suitable for the builder's use, is zoned accordingly, and is located in a desirable area for housing. After obtaining the necessary permits, surveys, plans for development, etc., the builder proceeds with subdividing and development.

2. **Subdividing and development** – Most municipalities require a developer, who wishes to subdivide the large parcel into lots, to file a ***subdivision plat map*** which clearly identifies the "lay of the land" identifying individual parcels, lot sizes, streets, utilities, and other information as required for approval. It is the builder's responsibility to assure there are adequate neighborhood provisions for habitability such as streets, lighting, sidewalks, parks, sewers, and such. These provisions are typically ***dedicated*** to the local government and will not be sold to the general public.

3. **Construction** – After these first two phases are complete, the builder begins the construction of homes which may be:

    - ***Speculative homes ("spec homes")*** – where the builder "speculates" what the market will do by completing a small number of homes without buyers under contract.

    - ***Tract homes*** (not "track") – where the subdivision will typically have a few models from which purchasers can choose to have the builder construct on their behalf.

    - **Custom homes** – where the builder has a buyer under contract to build a specific home that was designed and blueprinted by an architect.

SO, YOU WANT TO BE A REALTOR®? PROFESSIONAL ORGANIZATIONS

What is a REALTOR®? Is a REALTOR® a real estate licensee? Are all licensees REALTORS®? The general public uses "Agent" and "REALTOR®" interchangeably but here we will make the distinction. A REALTOR® is a member of the professional organization the ***National Association of REALTORS® (NAR)***. This organization, which has state-level and local associations under its national umbrella, promotes a higher level of professionalism, integrity, and education than non-members. NAR established the ***Code of Ethics and Standards of Practice*** which all members agree to abide by.

Real estate brokers pay dues to REALTOR® associations at the national, state, and local levels plus subscription to the ***Multiple Listing Service (MLS)*™** to access data on member broker listings. These associations provide services to their members including educational offerings including special designations for certain programs, assistance in settling broker-to-broker disputes, transaction forms, and the management of the MLS™.

INTRODUCTION:
Introduction to the Real Estate Business
End of Chapter Quiz

1. Real estate activity plays a major role in the nation's economy in that:

    a. real estate is one of largest sources of building wealth.
    b. real estate, and related industries, employ nearly two million Americans every year.
    c. new home sales make a direct contribution to the Gross Domestic Product.
    d. all of these

2. Most states define the services of real estate brokerage for compensation as all of these EXCEPT:

    a. buying and selling.
    b. leasing.
    c. engineering.
    d. negotiating and offering.

3. The general public has the right to expect that the licensee in the transaction has knowledge and expertise regarding:

    a. property transfer.
    b. market conditions.
    c. marketing.
    d. all of these

4. The prospecting activity that involves a geographical area, staying in contact with all residents of a select neighborhood and providing information and real estate services is:

    a. farming.
    b. cold calling.
    c. distributing.
    d. advertising.

5. Property managers are NOT usually expected to:

    a. locate the tenant.
    b. facilitate the execution of the lease.
    c. collect deposits and rents.
    d. repair broken household items.

6. Which of these services in assessing a property's market value is the most extensive and requires state licensing or certification?

    a. broker's price opinion
    b. appraisal
    c. comparative market analysis
    d. gross rent multiplier

7. Which of these services is a licensed real estate agent *most* likely to provide in rendering an opinion of value?

    a. appraisal
    b. broker price opinion
    c. comparative market analysis
    d. property report

8. Before a builder can begin to construct homes on subdivided lots, he must first submit and have approved a:

    a. conditional use permit.
    b. subdivision plat map.
    c. zoning variance.
    d. business plan.

9. Homes where the subdivision will typically have a few models from which purchasers can choose to have the builder construct on their behalf are called:

    a. tract homes.
    b. spec homes.
    c. custom homes.
    d. mobile homes.

10. The act of turning over ownership to subdivision amenities such as streets, sidewalks, and green areas, is:

    a. assignment.
    b. dedication.
    c. gifting.
    d. devotion.

Chapter 1

Contracts

 *There are many types of contracts and agreements used in the day-to-day business of real estate. In this chapter, we will examine the most common types such as brokerage agreements, listing agreements, and purchase agreements. Before looking at the specifics of any individual type of contract, it is necessary to familiarize with the basic principles of contract law and that body of law that governs the operation of contracts.*

DO YOU KNOW???

Do you know the differences between *valid, void, voidable,* and *unenforceable* contracts?
Are you familiar with the *Statute of Frauds*?
Can you explain how contracts can be assigned to others?
Do you know the three different types of listing contracts and how to use them?
How about different methods of assessing a commission?
These are just some of the topics covered in this chapter.

GENERAL KNOWLEDGE OF CONTRACT LAW

A *contract is a voluntary agreement between informed and capable parties to do, or to refrain from doing, something which is legal to do, and which is supported by adequate consideration.*

Five essential elements of a contract (*any* contract):

 1. **Competent Parties** – All parties must be living, of lawful age, of sound mind, and mentally competent.

  2. **Offer and Acceptance** – Sometimes referred to as "mutual assent," this element shows there is a "meeting of the minds," that an offer was made and acceptance of that offer was reached.

  3. **Legal; Legality of Object** – The purpose underlying the contract must be legal.

  4. **Informed Parties** — There can be no fraud, no misrepresentation, and no duress. The parties are fully informed, aware of the conditions of the agreement, and consent to the terms.

 5. **Consideration** – Consideration may be money, anything of value, or just a statement that consideration exists, such as "for continued love and affection" or "for good and valuable consideration."

The acronym "COLIC" is often used to remember these five essential elements of *any* contract.

Contracts for real estate have two additional elements (requirements):

1. **In writing and signed** – Real estate contracts and personal property contracts in excess of $500 require a written contract to be "enforceable." This is known as the "Statue of Frauds" requirement. The ***Statute of Frauds*** originated in England in 1677 and was known as the *Statute to Prevent Perjuries and Frauds*. It required all real estate transactions and all other transactions where the amount involved was greater than 10 pounds sterling to be in writing. If there were no writing, the courts would not hear the case if there was a dispute. In other words, such unwritten transactions would be unenforceable in court. As with our laws today, there were many exceptions, but the underlying premise was that important transactions should be reduced to writing to be enforceable in court.

   In the United States, similar laws have been adopted which require all real estate contracts, except short-term leases (less than 1 year), to be in writing. All other contracts where the amount in controversy exceeds $500 must also be in writing to be enforceable. ***Enforceable*** means a dispute between the parties will be heard in court and a judge will "enforce" the provisions of the contract.

2. **Description of the real estate** – An accurate, valid, and sufficient description of the property will depend on the nature of the transaction's documents. Deeds, Deeds of Trust, and Mortgages, together with other documents of a real estate transaction which will be *recorded in the public records*, will require a "legal description." There are three (3) forms of legal descriptions:

   - Metes and Bounds
   - U.S. Government Rectangular Survey
   - Lot, Block, and Subdivision

   Other documents containing descriptions of real property which will *NOT be recorded in the public records* simply require an adequate property description, such as:

   - Real estate purchase agreements
   - Leases
   - Listings

   An "adequate" property description has been defined as either:

   1. Address of the property
   2. Assessor's Parcel Number (APN) - This is the "account number" assigned by the county assessor to each parcel within the jurisdiction for purposes of recording payment of taxes. Although you will see this in practice, it does not give useful information concerning the location or description of the property, and it should not be used alone.

Legal concepts with real estate contracts

1. **Valid** – The contract contains visible evidence of all five essential elements of a contract (competent parties, offer and acceptance, legality of object, informed parties, and consideration) and is therefore binding and enforceable on all parties.

2. **Void** – This agreement lacks any one or more of the essential elements of a contract and has no legal effect. It is not binding on the parties.

   If the contract is for an "illegal" purpose (lacking legality of object), it is simply void. You cannot lawfully contract for an illegal purpose, such as contract for murder or contract for the purchase of an illegal substance, etc.

   If a contract is impossible to complete, then the contract will be considered void. That does not mean that it is inconvenient or too expensive to perform. This is often a factual consideration and may end up in court if the parties disagree. For example, suppose there is a contract to purchase an airplane which is scheduled to close October 2, 2013. On October 1, the airplane crashes and is totally destroyed. It is impossible to complete this contract - it will be voided.

   Likewise, illegal contracts, although void in the eyes of the law, may still be performed. For example, a contract for murder, clearly a void contract, may still take place.

3. **Voidable** – appears to be valid but may be disaffirmed because it is missing competent parties (legal capacity) such as a minor, or is missing voluntary, informed parties such as a contract executed under misrepresentation, fraud, or duress. In a voidable contract, the party suffering the legal disability has the right to void the contract, provided it is done within a reasonable time. The other party to the contract, the one who does not suffer a legal disability, does not have the right of voidability.

   General rules on "voidable" contracts

   1. A minor has up to the age of majority and for a reasonable time thereafter to avoid a contract.
   2. A person lacking mental capacity may avoid upon gaining their capacity and determining they do not want to go forward with a contract made during their period of incapacity.
   3. A person contracting under fraud, where the other party has told them an intentional falsehood or lie about a material fact concerning the subject matter of the contract, has a "reasonable period of time" after discovery of the fraud to avoid the contract.
   4. A person contracting under a misrepresentation, where the other party has carelessly or negligently misstated a material fact concerning the subject matter of the contract, has a "reasonable period of time" after discovery of the misrepresentation to avoid the contract.
   5. If both parties to the contract are truly operating under a mutual mistake, either party may avoid the contract (unenforceable). For example, I think I'm selling one property

and you think you are buying a different property. Again, the parties must act reasonably.

Note: The fact that a contract that is voidable or void does not prevent the parties from performing it. Assume that one party has perpetrated a fraud on the other party, the defrauded party discovers the fraud and has the right to void the contract, but decides to go ahead with the contract anyway. That would be the injured party's choice but the party committing the fraud would not be able to void because of his own fraud.

4. **Unenforceable** – appears to be valid, but if there is a disagreement between the parties in the performance of duties and the receipt of rights, the courts will not get involved in a resolution.

For example, we know that for a real estate contract to be "enforceable" it has to be in writing. If two parties had an oral contract, then got into a dispute over it, the courts would not hear their case as the required writing did not exist. On the other hand, if the parties did not dispute their agreement, they could perform their oral real estate agreement as they had intended.

CONTRACT TERMINOLOGY

Expressed – Expressed means the use of words, either written or oral, to show intentions of the parties to the contract.

Implied – the actions of the parties demonstrate their intent. It looks like a contracting has occurred by the appearance of things (ostensible). **Example:** You sit down at a table at a restaurant and order dinner. It looks like you have contracted with the restaurant to purchase and pay for your food. You may say, "I'll have the Surf & Turf," but your actions of being there and ordering are speaking contract much louder than words you may actually say.

Bilateral – means "two sided." Most contracts are bilateral contracts in that more than one party is making a promise to do something. **Example:** A buyer offers to buy a house for $400,000 provided the seller puts on a new roof. The seller agrees, "Okay, I'll take your $400,000 offer, and I'll have a new roof on the house before close of escrow." Both parties are making promises and are undertaking performing those promises. One promise is given in exchange for another.

Unilateral – means "one sided." Often taking the form of an option contract, a unilateral contract is binding on one party should the other party elect to perform under the agreement. It is one sided in that the party with the option does not ever have to perform. An example might be the offer of a reward. The police will pay $5,000 for information leading to the arrest and conviction of a certain criminal. The police have no obligation to do anything until someone performs by providing information that leads to the arrest and the conviction of the criminal. Then, and only then, are the police obligated to pay the $5,000.

In real estate, the "lease-option" is a unilateral contract. The owner of the property (optionor) has nothing to do and is under no obligation to perform until the prospective purchaser (optionee) decides to go forward with the purchase.

Executed: An "executed" contract is one that is fully and completely performed. "Executed," in a different context, can also mean that the contract has been fully signed by all parties.

Executory: An executory contract is not yet fully performed. For example, a 30 year mortgage is "executory" until the making of the last payment, if not paid off in full sooner. It is not "executed" until it is paid in full.

The rule of reason – Throughout the study of real estate and business in general, you will hear the term "reasonably" or "reasonable" as a requirement for the actions of real estate agents and brokers, for the conduct of parties to contracts, and for many other things. The rule of reason places an obligation on all of us to conduct ourselves as the "reasonable person" would, and to always act in a reasonable fashion. Reasonable conduct is a factual consideration given the circumstances of a particular event. In most cases, one does not know for sure if he acted reasonably until someone claims he did not and the matter is placed before a judge or jury. Ultimately, it is often the judge or jury who tells us, after the fact, if our conduct was reasonable.

TERMINATION AND ASSIGNMENT OF CONTRACTS

Once a contract has been entered, what will terminate it?

1. **Performance** – This is the most desirable outcome. The parties perform all of their duties and receive all of their rights as agreed.

2. **Mutual agreement** – The parties decide they do not want to go forward and mutually agree that each should be released from the contract. By mutual agreement, the contract is terminated. This is sometimes called a *General and Mutual Release*.

3. **Impossibility** – If it is truly impossible for the parties to perform, the contract will be terminated by impossibility. As an example, if there is a contract with the homeowner and a painter hired to paint the house, and the house burns to the ground, impossibility will terminate this contract.

4. **Operation of law** – Some contracts will be terminated by the courts or statutory prohibition. Let us assume that an Iowa corporation has a contract to sell corn to Mexico. Before the terms of the contract are performed, the U.S. government prohibits further exports to Mexico for agricultural purposes. Since it would be illegal for the Iowa corporation to carry out the terms of the contract due to the newly-passed law, the contract would be terminated by operation of law.

Assignments of contracts – Contracts are freely and fully assignable unless prohibited in the agreement. However, when one party desires to assign his rights, obligations, and benefits under the contract to a third party, that original party will remain liable for performance and obligations should the third party fail to perform. This is called *secondary liability*.

> **Example:** Ed, the owner of a shopping center leases space to Tom's bakery. As time passes, Tom decides to retire although he has 7 years left on his lease with Ed. Tom, noting there is no restriction on assignment in his lease, finds another baker and assigns the balance of his lease to the new baker. Time passes, and the new baker fails to make the rental payment required in the lease. If Ed cannot recover his losses from the new baker, Ed can hold Tom liable for the rental payment under the concept of secondary liability. Although Tom did not have a restriction on assigning his lease, Ed did not release Tom from any of the liability created in the original agreement. How could Tom have been released from all obligations under the original lease? – by a "Novation" or a "Novation of the Parties."

Novation – A novation is the substitution of a new *contract* for an old one. If Tom presented the new baker to Ed who agrees to contract with the new baker and create a new lease, then Tom is off the hook by way of a novation. "Nova" means "new" and we are dealing with a new agreement. A significant change in a provision of the original contract constitutes a novation and it is now a different agreement. The party seeking assignment is relieved from any further obligation under the new agreement.

Novation of parties – A novation of the parties is where a new *party* is substituted for an existing one. If Tom presented the new baker to Ed, who allows the new baker as a substitute tenant and allows the assignment, then Tom would be off the hook by way of a novation of parties.

Breach of contract – What if either of the parties to a contract fails or refuses to perform any duties per the contract? This is considered breach of contract and the injured party has legal remedies available.

If the *buyer* defaults, the seller may rescind (terminate) the agreement and exercise any of these option:

1. **Sue for specific performance** – This legal action will require the buyer to perform all duties as specified in the contract.

2. **Revocation** – The seller revokes the contact and *retains* the earnest money deposit. The **earnest money deposit** is typically money that accompanies an offer to show the buyer's "earnestness" in completing the contract as it is often sacrificed upon a breach of contract.

3. **Rescission** – The seller decides to call off the contract and return the earnest money deposit to the buyer. This is a complete reversal of the contract, putting everyone back to where they were before the contract.

4. **Sue for damages** – The buyer is required to pay the seller for any costs associated with the seller's hardship. The seller may possibly sue for the amount of the purchase price.

If the *seller* defaults, the buyer may rescind (terminate) the agreement and exercise these options:

1. **Sue for specific performance** – This legal action will require the seller to perform all duties as specified in the contract including going through with the sale and transferring ownership.

2. **Rescission** – The buyer decides just to call the whole thing off, get back the earnest money deposit, and be done with it. This is a complete reversal of the contract, putting the parties back to where they were before the contract.

3. **Sue for damages** – If the buyer can prove there were direct monetary damages as a result of the seller's breach, then the buyer may be entitled to a judgment against the seller for the amount of damages proved. This is quite difficult to do in residential real estate cases.

Liquidated damages – The remedies either party may recover through litigation may be limited by the terms of the contract. If the contract pre-addresses the damages that may be received in the event of default, those remedies are considered to be "liquidated damages."

Punitive damages – go above and beyond the liquidated damages and may be sought to "punish" the breaching party and compensate the injured party.

Statute of limitations – There is a legal limit to the time frame under which the injured party can legally sue the breaching party and this limit varies from state to state.

CONTRACTS IN REAL ESTATE: The Listing Agreement

The listing agreement is a contract between the seller of property and the real estate broker. Please note, while the sales agent is often the party who acts to create the listing, this activity is done on behalf of the agent's broker and the broker "owns" the listing. This is true for all agreements that salespeople prepare under the direction and supervision of their broker.

Issues to address in the listing contract:
- Identity of the Parties
- Description of the Property
- Duties and Rights of the Broker
- Broker Protection Clause
- Duties and Rights of the Seller
- Scope of Authority
- Commission
- Acceptable Price and Terms
- Personal Property Included/Excluded
- Home Warranty
- Effective Date/Expiration Date
- Any Legal Requirements
- Signatures and Dates

Three basic types of listing agreements:

1. **Open listing** – In this contract, the seller agrees to pay a commission to *any* broker who procures a ready, willing, and able buyer at list price and terms, or such other price and terms agreeable to the seller. The seller gives *no exclusivity* to the broker, and the seller may sell the property himself without owing a commission to any broker. The seller may also have several open listings in effect.

2. **Exclusive agency listing** – In this contract, the seller agrees to hire the broker on an exclusive basis, and agrees to pay a commission to the exclusive broker when the exclusive broker, or any other broker, produces a ready, willing, and able buyer at list price and terms or such other price and terms agreeable to the seller. The seller gives *exclusivity* to the broker and agrees that all other brokers must go through the exclusive broker. However, the seller may sell the property himself without owing a commission.

3. **Exclusive right to sell listing** – In this contract, the seller agrees to hire the broker on an exclusive basis and agrees to pay a commission to the exclusive broker when the exclusive broker, or any other broker, produces a ready, willing, and able buyer at list price and terms or such other price and terms agreeable to the seller. The seller gives *exclusivity* to the broker and agrees that all other brokers must go through the exclusive broker and further agrees that should the seller find a buyer on his own, he will still owe a commission to the exclusive broker.

LISTINGS	Open Listing	Exclusive Agency Listing	Exclusive Right to Sell
Seller agrees to pay a commission to the broker for producing a ready, willing, and able buyer:	Yes	Yes	Yes
Seller has an exclusive agency relationship with the broker - exclusivity:	No	Yes	Yes
Seller may sell himself without owing a commission to the broker:	Yes	Yes	No

Methods for calculating commissions – It is important to note that commissions, or the method for calculating them, are not set by law or customary practice, but are a matter for agreement between the seller and the broker in every listing transaction.

Commission as a percentage of sale price – The commission is calculated as a percentage of the gross selling price. For example, a seller agrees to pay a 7% commission to the broker. The list price is $425,000 but the buyer and seller agree to a selling price of $400,000. The seller is now obligated to pay a $28,000 commission. What the broker does with the commission money is the broker's business, but presumably, the broker will be splitting some of the commission with the broker's agent who produced the listing, and if the buyer was represented by another broker, the seller's broker will normally split the commission with the buyer's broker. Percentage commissions are the most common commission arrangements in residential real estate.

Flat fee commissions – The commission is established in the listing contract as a specific amount, regardless of what the purchase price turns out to be. If a buyer is produced, the flat fee is earned.

>**Example:** a seller agrees to pay $200,000 as a commission for the sale of a $4,500,000 office building. When the buyer is found at list price and terms or such other price and terms acceptable to the seller, the flat fee of $200,000 is earned regardless of the agreed upon price. This arrangement is more common in commercial property listings.

Net listing commission – The commission is established by what the seller must "net" from the sale. If the seller tells the broker that from the sale the seller must net $75,000 after satisfying a mortgage in the amount of $165,000, and the broker may keep anything over those amounts (there is no set commission amount or rate), the broker is likely dealing with a net listing.

The net listing commission arrangement is not permitted in many states as the arrangement inherently creates a conflict of interest between the broker and his client. If the property sells for a great deal more than required by the seller, it will appear that the broker's commission is disproportionately high and that the seller could have netted more. If the offer will bring less than, or just barely more than, the seller's required net, the broker is not likely to spend much time effort or money in marketing the property and may even fail to present such offers in the hope of finding an offer that earns him more.

Terminating real estate listings – Listings may be terminated in many ways.

1. **Performance** – The broker performs the obligations of the listing agreement by producing a ready, willing, and able buyer at list price and terms or such other price and terms agreeable to the seller. The seller pays the broker the commission. This is obviously the most desirable way to terminate a listing – the objective has been completed.

2. **Expiration** – Most all listings must have a fixed termination date. If the objective was not completed within the term of the listing, the listing will expire, and the broker and seller no longer have a contractual agreement.

3. **Revocation** – Generally, either the broker or the seller has the right to terminate the relationship by cancelling the listing. It should be noted that the party revoking the listing may be obligated to the other for expenses or hardships.

4. **Abandonment** – If the broker fails to actively market the property, it may be said that the broker has abandoned the listing. This is really a revocation by the seller with the reason (none actually being required) being the broker has ceased to represent the property.

5. **Mutual consent** – The seller and the broker cooperatively agree to terminate their relationship.

6. **Death, bankruptcy, or loss of competency** – If the seller or the broker dies during the listing term, the heirs are not bound by the listing agreement, unless the brokerage is a legal entity such as a corporation. If either party is incapacitated or not of sound mind, the party lacking competency may not go forward with the transaction and the listing is terminated. Bankruptcy of either party will be grounds for termination of the contract. Note that it is the seller or the broker's death, incapacity, or bankruptcy that is considered – not the sales agent's.

7. **Material change** – If the circumstances of the property were to change in a material way, such as zoning, placement of freeways, declaration of flood zones, or any other occurrence, which would substantially change the value, desirability, or salability of the property, these changed circumstances would permit either party to terminate the listing.

8. **Destruction of the property** – If the property were destroyed during the listing period either the seller or the broker could, and most likely would, terminate the listing.

9. **Agency coupled with an interest** – If in the listing agreement there is an obligation or personal interest, not normally undertaken by a broker, such as the broker owns a portion of the property, the seller cannot fire the broker unless the coupled interest is also terminated.

   Example: Builder Smith calls broker Jones and offers to give broker Jones an exclusive right to sell listing on her new housing subdivision, provided broker Jones will co-sign a note for builder Smith to get the financing to buy the land and build the model homes. Broker Jones agrees and co-signs the note. Time passes and builder Smith tires of paying costly commissions to broker Jones and decides to take the sales activity "in house" and attempts to fire broker Jones. Builder Smith may NOT fire broker Jones until he gets him off the note at the bank.

CONTRACTS IN REAL ESTATE: Buyers Brokerage Agreements

In recent years, the concept of buyers being represented by real estate brokers produced the need for a contract affirming the relationship. Normally, the agreement establishes an exclusive relationship where the buyer employs the broker to locate the desired property and to negotiate with the sellers on the buyer's behalf for the best available price and terms for a purchase (or a lease if a tenant representation agreement).

The buyer's brokerage agreement will generally provide for compensation to the buyer's broker based on a certain percentage of the purchase price, or for a flat fee. The agreement will normally provide that the seller's broker shares the seller's commission with the buyer's broker, and to the extent that such a sharing arrangement exists, the financial obligation of the buyer to the broker will be reduced or eliminated. However, should the buyer enter an arrangement where the seller's commission does not compensate the broker, then the buyers would owe the agreed fee to the buyer's broker.

When we covered listing agreements, the point was made that the seller employs the broker under a listing contract on an exclusive basis and agrees to pay a commission to the exclusive broker when the exclusive broker, or any other broker, produces a ready, willing, and able buyer at list price and terms or such other price and terms agreeable to the seller. A buyer's brokerage agreement is the exact same concept substituting the purpose which is to locate a property that meets the desire, price, and terms of the purchaser and to represent that buyer and negotiate on the buyer's behalf.

All of the rules covered regarding listings with respect to commission calculations, termination of the contract, exclusivity, etc. are the same with the buyer's brokerage agreement. In practice, real estate agents and brokers are slowly getting their arms around the concept of this representation agreement because the concept has only been widely practiced in more recent times while listing agreements have been used for many years.

As recent as the 1980s, it was common practice that the broker who located the purchaser was considered a "sub-agent" of the seller with a fiduciary obligation to the seller – not the purchaser. This was mostly due to the philosophy that if the seller paid the commission, the broker worked for the seller. Our society felt the buyers were just as important in the transaction and deserved fair and equal representation regardless of compensation. Today, buyer brokerage exists, giving buyers equal representation while compensation is not a relevant factor in determining the agency relationship or the fiduciary duties.

CONTRACTS IN REAL ESTATE: Purchase Agreements

This is the document that creates the agreement between the seller and buyer and clearly spells out the rights and duties of each party, the purchase price, and the terms and details of the transaction.

The purchase agreement is known by many names such as:

- Offer and Acceptance (O&A)
- Residential Purchase Agreement (RPA)
- Purchase Agreement
- Earnest Money Receipt and Purchase Agreement
- Sales Agreement
- Purchase and Sale Agreement

No matter what it is called, this is the primary transactional document. It should present the agreement between the buyer and seller with sufficient detail so that anyone reading it would understand the agreement the parties have reached. It should contain:

1. physical description of the property being purchased
2. identification of the parties
3. agreed upon purchase price
4. earnest money deposit (not legally required but requested in practice)

5. additional down payment (amount and when to be paid)
6. escrow company and escrow officer
7. general terms and conditions of the transaction
8. personal property included (if any)
9. financing contingencies (if any)
10. various required disclosures
11. specific conditions to be accomplished by the seller (usually repairs)
12. appraisal conditions (if any, also usually repairs)
13. contingencies (contract condition to be met or the contract is voidable)
14. liquidated damages
15. closing date
16. pro-rations
17. possession date
18. signatures and dates

The above is only a partial list of what is normally contained in a real estate purchase agreement. As a prospective licensee, you should review the most common forms of purchase agreements in your area.

Remember, the **statute of frauds** requires contracts for the sale of real estate to be in writing to be enforceable in court. The contract is also the complete agreement of the parties and neither party should rely on verbal representations made by anyone. The contract, as it is written, will dictate all conditions of how the transaction will close. If the parties discover a need to change or add terms later, the preparation of an **addendum** is essential to show written evidence of the agreement on those subsequent terms.

The contract process – Normally, the contracting process in real estate starts with the buyer making the seller an offer, but the original could conceivably come from the seller. To keep it clear, the proper way to refer to the parties during the offer process is to refer to them as **offeror** and **offeree**.

> *Offeror* – the party *making* the offer
> *Offeree* – the party *receiving* the offer

Not to be confusing, but rather to clarify, the buyer and seller often change roles as offeror and offeree. For example, buyer Bob makes an offer to seller Sue on Sue's 10 acre parcel of land for $210,000. Buyer Bob is the offeror and seller Sue is the offeree. If seller Sue makes a **counteroffer** to buyer Bob, raising the price to $240,000, seller Sue is in fact making a new offer to Bob. That makes Sue the offeror and Bob the offeree. If another counteroffer is made by Bob to Sue, the roles change yet again.

The offer should contain all of the elements which the offeror considers necessary. Once the offer is received, the offeree may:

1. **Accept** – An acceptance must agree to every detail of the offer as submitted no matter how small.

2. **Counteroffer** – If there is *any change,* no matter how small or large, is made to the offer, the offeree has not accepted, but has made a counteroffer. A counteroffer rejects the offer as written, but modifies what terms and conditions must be changed to make the offer acceptable.

   Each time there is a counteroffer, all of the other terms and conditions not modified by counteroffers were "preserved." For example, there is an offer and five counters which address price, loan terms, due diligence, etc. The fifth counteroffer changes the close of escrow date. Everything agreed to in the original offer and the first four counteroffers becomes part of the contract plus the change of escrow date from the fifth counteroffer.

3. **Reject** – The offeree may simply say "No," and by doing so, has rejected the offer, without counteroffering. An offeree should be aware that a rejection does not obligate the offeror to do anything whatsoever.

4. **Do nothing** – The offeree, once receiving an offer from the offeror, does not have to do anything. However, after a "reasonable time," or a date specified in the offer, if the offeree remains silent, the offeror's agent must inform the offeror that the offer is now treated as a rejection. There is no requirement that the offeror keep the offer open until the time limit expires. It may be withdrawn at any time prior to acceptance.

5. **Withdrawal or revocation** – After an offer is made, the offeror may withdraw the offer any time up to receiving notice of the offeree's acceptance. This notice of acceptance may be oral and given to the offeror directly or through his agent. Once notice of acceptance has been received, the offeror may not withdraw the offer.

> *An offer becomes a contract when the offer has been accepted by the offeree and communication of that acceptance has been received by the offeror.*

THE CLOSING PROCESS

Agents from some parts of the country refer to the closing as the ***settlement*** while others refer to being ***in escrow***. The parties to a closing are the buyer, the seller, and the escrow agent, sometimes referred to as the escrowee. Normally, the escrowee is a title insurance company, escrow company, or attorney. The function of the escrowee is to receive funds and documents under the terms of the

escrow instructions which is the escrowee's own document spelling out all the details of the transaction. Many times the purchase agreement also serves as escrow instructions.

Escrow is "opened" by placing the accepted agreement into the hands of the escrow agent along with the earnest money deposit (EMD). Although it is common for a real estate transaction to have an EMD, there are sufficient promises between the buyer and seller as to constitute "adequate consideration" and therefore an EMD is not legally required.

During the escrow period, many things are transpiring. If a new loan is involved, the financing documents are being prepared for escrow by the lender. Meanwhile, the seller's lender will be providing "pay off" information and making arrangements to satisfy that loan. The escrow officer will be settling property taxes, homeowner's association (HOA) dues, special assessments, and other charges against the property. The escrowee will calculate and prepare the closing statements, the deed, bill of sale, and any other documents that need to be executed to finalize the closing.

Equitable title – During the escrow period, the buyer is considered to have *equitable title* or an *equitable interest* because the buyer has the property under contract and no one else does. The rights associated with equitable title vary from state to state.

Legal title – is secured when the closing is completed, the deed transfers title from the seller to the buyer, and the deed is recorded.

Note that upon the death of either the seller or the buyer, death itself does not terminate a purchase agreement. The buyer's estate would have the right and obligation to purchase the property while the seller's estate would have the obligation to sell the property and the right to receive the sale proceeds.

CONTRACTS IN REAL ESTATE: Leases and Lease-Purchase Agreements

The owner of real property is considered to own a ***legal bundle of rights*** that include *possession, control, enjoyment* (use), *exclusion,* and *disposition* (sell). A lease is the temporary transfer of some of the owner's rights to another, specifically the rights of possession and enjoyment.

> *Parties to the Lease:*
> *Owner – Landlord – Lessor*
> *Non-owner – Tenant – Lessee*

Under the statute of frauds, *a lease for one year or more must be in writing to be enforceable.*

Once a lease is agreed to, the landlord is said to have a ***leased fee*** meaning the landlord still owns the property, but has surrendered the rights of possession and use to the tenant. The tenant is said to have a ***leasehold interest*** in the property, providing the right to possess and use the property, but do not own it.

While a lease temporarily transfers the rights of possession and use, it also serves as a contract for rent and other obligations.

Types of Leases: (the words *tenancy* and *estate* are interchangeable)

1. **Estate for years** – This type of lease has a definite starting and ending date. The term can be of any duration. It does not require notice by either side to terminate as the expiration date of the lease is already spelled out in the lease. In the event of the death of either party, any unexpired time on the lease is inheritable by the estate of the tenant, along with the obligations to pay rent, and is binding on the estate of the landlord. Death of either of the parties does not terminate the lease.

2. **Estate from period to period** – This lease has a stated *period of time* which will automatically renew for the same period over and over again until one party gives notice they no longer wish to continue.

    The most common example is the month-to-month lease where the parties have agreed to a lease for a month, and in the absence of either party giving notice to terminate, it shall renew for another month, and so on. But these agreements may be day-to-day, week-to-week, quarterly, year-to-year, or whatever term they agree to. The parties should provide for a definite time frame for notice of intent to terminate in the lease or the courts have ruled that where there is no specific period of notice, one period will be the required notice period.

    This type of lease is binding on the estates of the parties to the extent that there remains time left in an unexpired period.

3. **Estate at will** – This lease is an open-ended lease with no specific termination date and therefore, notice is required to terminate this lease. Should the parties have failed to specify the length of the notice period, the courts will require a "reasonable" notice be given.

4. **Estate at sufferance** – This is the status of the parties where the term of the lease has expired and the tenant remains in possession without the landlord's consent. The tenant has no right to be there and is technically a trespasser. As the name implies, the landlord is "suffering" due to the tenant's continued presence in the property.

Items to address in a lease agreement:

- rent amount and due date
- deposits and conditions under which they may be refundable
- term of lease (expiration)
- purposes for which landlord may enter the premises
- restrictions on the tenant's use

- repairs and improvements
- destruction of the premises
- assignment or subleasing
- remedies for breach
- eviction and legal costs
- terms of a lease option (if applicable)

Lease payment plans for commercial leases:

1. **Gross lease** – In this type of lease, the tenant pays a fixed monthly rent and from those funds, the landlord pays the operating expenses of the property. This is most common in residential and small office leases.

2. **Net lease** – The tenant pays a *base rent* (fixed monthly rent) and in addition to the base rent, pays some, or all of the operating expenses of the property. On a *Triple Net Lease* or *NNN* lease, the lessee pays the rent, plus all of the operating expenses including the taxes, insurance, and common area maintenance or CAM. This is most common with larger commercial and industrial leases.

3. **Percentage lease** – The tenant pays a *base rent* plus a percentage of the gross business income, normally less any payment for returned goods. The philosophy is the landlord's location, anchor tenants, and marketing contributes to the overall business income of the tenant. This lease may be gross or net.

4. **Graduated lease** – The tenant and the landlord have agreed that with the passage of time, the leased space will become more valuable and that the tenant's lease payment should increase. The lease provides the dates on which the tenant's lease payment will increase and the amount of the increase.

5. **Indexed lease** – The landlord ties the lease payment to an index for inflation, such as the Consumer Price Index (CPI), and as the index increases annually, so will the tenant's lease payment.

    Example: The rent is $1,000 per month. At the end of the year, it is determined the CPI has increased 5%. The tenant's new lease payment for the next year will be $1,000 + $50 (5% of $1,000) or $1,050. If it goes up another 5% the next year, then the new lease payment in the 3rd year would be $1,050 + $52.50 (5% of $1,050) or $1,102.50.

6. **Escalation lease** – This lease is similar to an indexed lease, except that the tenant's lease payment is increased by the actual increases in the operating expenses of the property and not directly tied to an inflation index.

7. A **ground lease** is a lease of only the land where the tenant pays for and owns any improvements including buildings. This type of lease is commonly 99 years or a very long term.

Other lease issues:

1. **Leasehold improvements** – These are improvements or alterations to the leased space. Normally they are done at the *landlord's expense* and remain a part of the leased space as the landlord's property when the tenant vacates.

2. **Trade fixtures** – These are generally items of personal property that are installed in such a fashion as to make them a fairly permanent part of the leased space. An example would be fixtures for a dentist's office.

   Normally these types of "fixtures" are installed at the *tenant's expense* with the landlord's consent. Also, normally these fixtures, although installed in such a way as to become a part of the real estate, can be removed by the tenant at the end of the lease. The tenant would be obligated to restore the landlord's property after the fixtures were removed.

3. **Options to extend or expand** – If the tenant wants the ability to extend the lease beyond the original term, or to expand into other space the landlord owns, this should be carefully spelled out in the lease.

4. **Actual Eviction** – Eviction is the lawful process of dispossessing a tenant who has either overstayed the lease term, or who is in breach of the lease, and eviction has been elected as a remedy by the landlord. The process will vary from state to state, but generally requires a written notice to the tenant giving the tenant a short period to vacate, and if the tenant does not vacate, the eviction process will allow for intervention by sheriff or police to forcibly remove the tenant.

5. **Constructive eviction** – This means the landlord has done, or failed to do, something that has had the effect of denying the tenant the use and enjoyment of the leasehold. Often this involves matters of landlord maintenance which has not been done. As an example, the outdoor temperature is 110, the landlord is responsible for maintaining the air conditioning units, but has neglected maintenance and they do not work properly. The tenant operates a candle shop and the candles are all melting and no one can stand to be in the store under these temperatures. The landlord has constructively evicted the tenant. Changing the locks is a common scenario of an unlawful constructive eviction.
The tenant, if successful in a claim of constructive eviction, may be entitled to either an abatement of rent for the period the store could not be used, or the tenant may be entitled to break the lease without further liability. The landlord may also be liable for the value of the destroyed candles.

6. **Lease options and purchases** – These agreements start out as leases but include either an *option to purchase* by the expiration of the leasehold (lease option), or include a *purchase*

agreement that will go into effect by the expiration of the leasehold (lease purchase). In either scenario, the price and terms are negotiated up front.

7. **Sale leaseback** – an arrangement whereby the buyer and seller agree to a leasehold, the seller remains in possession of the sold property under agreed upon lease terms, and compensates the buyer for that possession. This is ideal for an investor who is purchasing the property as an income producing property as the seller becomes the tenant.

OTHER CONTRACT ISSUES AND VOCABULARY

1. Option contracts – Option contracts are between the owner of the property, the *optionor*, and a purchaser who wants to have a period of time in which to decide on the purchase of the property, the *optionee*. This is a unilateral contract in that the optionor has no obligation to perform until and unless the optionee decides to purchase. At that time, the optionor would complete the sale of the property to the optionee.

The optionee must offer *option money*, better described as the agreed valuable consideration, in exchange for the option to purchase or not to purchase. If an option fee is paid, it should be clear *how* the fee paid will be applicable to the purchase price if the option is exercised and if the fee is forfeited if the option is passed over. The option contract will have all of the same terms and conditions as a typical purchase agreement. It should also be clear as to the length of time the option runs for, and what conditions, if any, might allow an extension of the option.

2. Right of first refusal – The holder of the right of first refusal has the right to match any offer made on a property. Generally these contracts are misunderstood as being a form of an "option." They are not. Instead, if a party is trying to sell a property and it is subject to a right of first refusal, the seller must fully negotiate a transaction with a prospective buyer, and before completing the contract, must contact the holder of the right of first refusal and provide an opportunity to match the transaction and exercise the right.

The existence of a right of first refusal is a material fact which must be disclosed. Presumably any informed prospective buyer would want the seller to remove the right of first refusal before negotiating a sale as the purchaser would in effect be negotiating for the other party. A quit claim deed could be used to remove the right, assuming the holder was willing to give up the right.

3. Time is of the essence – This phrase is often seen in real estate and other contracts. Simply put, it means that if a specific time period is set out in the contract, in which one of the parties is to do something, and has not done it when the allotted period of time expires, the other party may declare a breach.

Example: The buyers have agreed to make application for a new loan within 10 days of signing the contract. The 11th day comes and they have not applied; the seller now has the right to declare the buyers in breach of the contract.

4. Contingency – a clause written into a contract stating some event must be completed before all of the duties of the contract can be or will be performed. Contingencies include new loan approval, sale of current residence, inspections to be conducted, etc. If the contingency is not fulfilled or waived, the contract is voidable.

5. Parol Evidence Rule – verbal words and representations will not be binding nor overrule any written agreements

Chapter 1: Contracts
End of Chapter Quiz

1. A contract for an unlawful purpose, such as the distribution of illegal substances, would be:

   a. valid.
   b. void.
   c. voidable.
   d. unenforceable.

2. The Smithers receive an offer from the Browns who wish to purchase the Smithers home. The Smithers accept. The broker for the Browns is out of town but receives a telephone call from the Smithers' broker informing her of the Smithers' acceptance.

   a. This is still an offer and not yet a binding contract.
   b. The Smithers still have a chance to change their mind and withdraw their acceptance.
   c. Because of the phone call to Brown's broker, there is a binding contract.
   d. The Browns can still withdraw their offer as they have not received a signed contract.

3. Which of the following is FALSE regarding an open listing?

   a. The seller can have several open listings in effect at any one time.
   b. If the broker produces a ready, willing, and able buyer acceptable to the seller, the broker is entitled to a commission.
   c. The seller does not offer exclusivity to the Broker.
   d. If the seller finds his own buyer, he is still obligated for a commission.

4. A 15-year-old girl enters into a written agreement with a dance studio to take dance lessons. Her contract is:

   a. valid.
   b. void.
   c. voidable.
   d. unenforceable.

5. Contracts for the sale of real estate or for personal property over $500 must be in writing to be enforceable according to the:

   a. statute of limitations.
   b. statute of liberty.
   c. statute of frauds.
   d. parol evidence rule.

6. The type of contract that was created purely by the actions of the parties is a(n):

    a. implied contract.
    b. expressed contract.
    c. executory contract.
    d. unilateral contract.

7. Which of the following is NOT considered an essential element of ALL contracts?

    a. consideration
    b. offer and acceptance
    c. legality of object
    d. in writing and signed

8. The Smiths have an agreement with the Kellys that in the event the Kellys find a purchaser for their home, the Smiths will be given a chance to match the purchaser's offer and buy the house themselves. This is a(n):

    a. voidable contract.
    b. option contract.
    c. unenforceable contract.
    d. right of first refusal.

9. The purchasers have submitted an offer to the seller which stipulates the buyers must sell their current house before they can close on the new one. This is called a(n):

    a. addendum.
    b. contingency.
    c. backup offer.
    d. none of these

10. The sellers, Bob and Mary Decker, accepted the offer to purchase from the Nelsons but the Deckers wish to stay in the property for six months after closing in exchange for the payment of rent. This condition of the agreement is called a(n):

    a. sale-leaseback.
    b. estate for years.
    c. contingency
    d. all of these

11. Tenant Tom has not paid his rent in two months and avoids all contact with Landlord Lynn. Frustrated, Lynn enters the apartment when Tom is at work and puts all of Tom's personal property to the curb. Additionally, Lynn changes the locks. This is:

    a. legal since Tom is in breach of his lease.
    b. justified as Tom is more than 30 days late.
    c. Illegal as it is a constructive eviction.
    d. unethical as Tom will have no shelter.

12. Van Horn leases space from Perfect Properties, LLC to operate a computer repair store in a small shopping center. Van Horn pays $2,400 per month in rent and must also pay 5% of his gross sales. His lease is most likely a(n):

    a. percentage lease.
    b. gross lease.
    c. indexed lease.
    d. escalation lease.

13. Which of the following would be reasonable issues to address in *any* lease agreement?

    a. rent due date, date rent is considered late, and any penalty.
    b. the names of all occupants and the intended use.
    c. who will be responsible for repairs and repair caps.
    d. all of these

14. Buyer J makes an offer of $225,000 on Seller W's home which is listed for $227,500. While W is considering the offer, Buyer J contacts his agent requesting the offer be withdrawn. Meanwhile, Seller W has signed the contract and notified his agent. Which of these statements is TRUE if it were to occur?

    a. Buyer J cannot withdraw the offer as Seller W has already accepted and signed.
    b. Buyer J cannot withdraw the offer as the agent for Seller W was notified of the acceptance.
    c. Buyer J can withdraw the offer since there was no communication of acceptance to him or his agent.
    d. Buyer J can withdraw the offer since there is no acceptance of the offer.

15. The most accurate term to describe the person making an offer is the:

    a. buyer.
    b. seller.
    c. offeree.
    d. offeror.

16. The seller is to the listing agreement as the buyer is to the:

    a. listing agreement.
    b. buyer brokerage agreement.
    c. purchase agreement.
    d. lease.

17. Once a lease is agreed to, the tenant is said to have a:

    a. freehold estate.
    b. leased fee.
    c. leasehold interest.
    d. reversionary interest.

18. Which party is typically the optionee?

    a. seller
    b. buyer
    c. offeree
    d. broker

19. An essential requirement for any contract to be valid is the offering of money or anything of value. This is known as:

    a. currency
    b. consideration
    c. financing
    d. colic

20. Broker Adams is meeting with the seller of a duplex. Adams estimates the value of the duplex to be $195,000. Adams and the seller enter into a listing agreement with no specific commission but instead, the seller tells Adams he can have any funds above the seller's required proceeds of $75,000. What type of listing does Adams have?

    a. exclusive agency
    b. open listing
    c. flat fee listing
    d. none of these

Chapter 2
Agency and the Practice of Real Estate

Agency is one of the most important concepts in real estate brokerage. It is the primary reason that real estate agents exist to serve clients or principals. Like many present-day statutes, our modern system of agency is derived from English Common Law, and having been practiced for centuries, it is now very well defined and understood. The first section of this chapter presents the concepts of agency, responsibilities of agents, fiduciary duties of agents, dual agency, four types of agency, brokerage agreements, and termination of agency agreements.

DO YOU KNOW???

What are the duties of being the *fiduciary*?
Why do some states keep it illegal to create a dual agency?
What are the differences between *steering, blockbusting,* and *redlining*?
What is meant by the term *protected class* and how does that affect your practice?
Can you give an example of *puffing* versus a fraudulent statement?
These are just some of the topics covered in this chapter.

AGENCY

LAWS, DEFINITIONS, AND NATURE OF AGENCY RELATIONSHIPS

American concept of agency – The American concept of *agency* evolved from English Common Law and depicts the duties and obligations originally assigned to an agent of the crown, a very powerful position in English society. Today, agency refers to the fiduciary relationship between a **principal** (the employer) and an **agent** (the employee). The role of the agent is to deal with third parties on behalf of the principal. Note that when we speak of "agency," the term "agent" is NOT referring to a "real estate agent" such as a salesperson. There are many agency relationships such as the relationship of an attorney to a client or a CPA to a tax client. In real estate agency relationships, the **agent** is the **broker** and the **principal** is the buyer or seller **client**.

Key concepts of *all* agency relationships:

- **Agency** describes the fiduciary relationship between the agent and the principal.
- The **principal** delegates authority to the agent to represent the principal's interest in a transaction. The principal is obligated by contract to compensate the agent and not hinder the agent's ability to fulfill the agent's fiduciary obligations.
- The **broker** is an agent who agrees to represent the interests of the principal, who agrees to let the broker exercise authority on behalf of the principal.
- The **client** is the principal to whom the agent is expected to give advice and counsel during the period of agency.
- The **customer** is a third party for whom a service is provided by the agent.

Types of Agency – In most states, four types of agency have been defined. These are *Universal Agency*, *General Agency*, *Special Agency*, and *Subagency*.

- **Universal agency** – This form of agency is created in a written, *unlimited power of attorney* which grants the agent the authority to do anything the clients could do for themselves. Universal agency authorizes binding the client to contracts and authorizes the sale or other disposition of real and personal property.

    <u>Example:</u> A member of the military is preparing to be shipped overseas to a combat area. While the military member is overseas, the spouse is given full authority through a universal agent's power of attorney.

- **General agency** – This form of agency is created in a general agency agreement, normally in writing, and often referred to as a *limited power of attorney* or a *general power of attorney*. A general agent has the authority to negotiate contracts and to bind the client to a contract, but only within specially designated and limited areas.

    <u>Example:</u> An insurance agent is normally a general agent with the power to bind insurance companies to contracts of insurance within certain defined guidelines.

    <u>Example:</u> Property managers also act as general agents. They are authorized to represent the property owner in all matters concerning one area of interest – the property to be managed.

- **Special agency** – This form of agency is most often used in real estate. Special agency is created in an agreement, often in writing. The special agent represents the client and has all of the fiduciary duties, but has no authority to bind the client to anything. The role of the special agent is simply to represent the interests of their client, but the special agent must allow the client to make the final decision whether or not to be contractually bound.

    <u>Example:</u> Real estate brokers are special agents. They represent their clients, but have no authority to bind their clients to contract.

- **Subagent** – A subagent is a person to whom agency has been delegated, always by an agent who is responsible to a principal and always with the permission of the principal. Subagents assist in carrying out client-based functions on behalf of the principal. Note that subagents from the same company have the same fiduciary duties and responsibilities as the original agent.

    <u>Example:</u> A principal who wants to sell a home will often list the property with a particular brokerage. At this point, the principal becomes the client of the broker, and the broker becomes the special agent of the principal. Any agents associated with this broker on this transaction become subagents and represent the principal.

Fiduciary duties and responsibilities – One of the key concepts of agency is that of *fiduciary duties and responsibilities*. Originally known as duties the agent had to perform for the king or queen, they eventually found their way into English common law, and then into the law of agency that exists in every state.

In our modern system of agency, these important fiduciary duties involve "trust and confidence" and are owed by the agent to the principal in the transaction, who may be the buyer, seller, lessor, or lessee of property.

The six fiduciary duties are *care, obedience, loyalty, disclosure, accounting, and confidentiality* — often remembered by the acronym COLDAC. (Remember: "COLD Air Conditioning.")

C O L D A C

Care – The agent is required to put forth best efforts on behalf of the client and always take great care in representing the client's interests. Principals have a right to expect the level of real estate knowledge of an agent to be superior to that of an average person. Care also encompasses an agent's competency or skill and knowledge.

> **Example:** If the agent represents the *seller*, great care and skill must be applied to help the seller arrive at a realistic and appropriate listing price, to help the seller understand the local market, to discover and disclose facts that affect the seller's position, and to properly present contracts and other documents for the seller's signature.

> **Example:** If the agent represents the *buyer*, the agent is expected to help the buyer locate suitable property, evaluate the property and its value, discover and disclose property and neighborhood considerations, and properly draft offers and counteroffers.

Obedience – The agent is required to be obedient to the client. As the king or queen was the law in old England, this did not represent a problem, since there could be no real conflict between the crown's requirements and those of the third parties with whom the agent was dealing. In modern society, however, the agent is obviously not representing the crown, but another individual.

> **Important exception:** While the agent must obey the client, this obedience does not permit breaking the law or concealing material facts from others. When dealing with third parties on behalf of a client, the agent must follow the rules of fair and honest dealing and the disclosure of material facts to the third parties.

Loyalty – It is expected that the agent will always be loyal to the client and to the client's interests to the highest standards.

Disclosure – Information may reach the agent which would be significant for the client to know. The agent must keep the client informed of all material facts which may have any importance in matters where the agent is representing the client. If the agent acquires information which would cause a reasonable person to ask some questions, the agent is expected to do so. This is the **Duty of Further Inquiry**.

Accounting or accountability – The agent may receive money, property, or other things of value which belong to the client. The agent must account to the client for these items and must use great care in protecting the client's interests.

Confidentiality – An agent must keep confidential all information about the client which, if disclosed without the principal's permission, could hurt the principal's bargaining position.

> <u>Example</u>: If the agent represents a *seller*, the agent cannot reveal information about the seller's financial condition, or willingness to accept less than the list price, or urgency to accept an offer, or other similar facts.

> <u>Example</u>: If the agent represents the *buyer*, information cannot be revealed about the buyer's financial condition, willingness to pay more than list price, the tightness of the buyer's moving schedule, etc. Note that these rules are codified by statute at the state level, so it is important for you to consult your state's treatment of all six parameters (COLDAC).

> <u>Important note</u>: While a broker has a fiduciary duty to the principal, the broker or agent is obligated to disclose all known material facts about the property to the customer, including those which would potentially be detrimental to the principal. Most states have specific forms that outline these fiduciary duties and require that they be presented to the client as disclosures.

A client's duty toward the agent – As you can imagine, when an agent represented a king or queen, the relationship was pretty lopsided. A person acting as the queen's agent owed her all of those fiduciary duties, but was owed little in return. Over time, another concept has materialized, the **Duty of Indemnification**. This means should an agent suffer an injury (now most likely a financial one) while acting in the client's behalf, the client must indemnify, or secure against loss, the broker or agent.

An agent's duty to third parties – Modern agents, and particularly real estate agents, deal with third parties frequently to meet contractual responsibilities. An agent is required to deal with third parties in a truthful and honest fashion and is required to disclose all material facts which the agent knows about the property, or should know about the property or through the exercise of reasonable due diligence.

> **Definition:** *A material fact is a fact that would be important to a reasonable person in deciding whether to engage or not to engage in a particular transaction; or would affect the price paid. It is an important fact as distinguished from some unimportant or trivial detail.*

CREATING AGENCY RELATIONSHIPS IN REAL ESTATE

In most states, there are two ways that an agency relationship can be created: *expressed agency* or *implied agency*.

An *expressed agency* relationship occurs when a formal document is signed, binding the parties to an agency relationship. Once signed, a listing agreement, buyer's brokerage agreement, or similar document, creates an agency relationship.

Implied agency occurs when the parties involved "act like" or "imply" that an agreement has been reached. Once this occurs, an implied agency agreement has been created, though this may have been done accidently, inadvertently, or unintentionally.

Obviously then, an agency relationship can be created without signatures, although a signed, documented agency agreement is usually preferable because it prevents misunderstandings between the parties.

Agent of the seller – This relationship is created in the listing agreement where the seller is the client and the broker is the special agent. The sales agent involved on behalf of the broker is technically a special subagent, who owes the fiduciary duties to the seller through the broker. In most states, the listing agreement provides for exclusivity as in an exclusive brokerage agreement, or an exclusive right to sell listing.

Agent of the buyer – This relationship is created in the buyer's brokerage agreement where the buyer is the client and the broker is the special agent. The sales agent involved on behalf of the broker is technically a special subagent, who owes the fiduciary duties to the buyer through the broker.

Agent for the owner-investor – This agency relationship involves the act of managing property for the owner-investor. This relationship is created in the property management agreement, between the broker and the property owner. This relationship is a general agency, and an agent of the brokerage would be a general, subagent of the owner through the broker.

Single agency – This is the typical, agency relationship used in real estate. One agent represents the seller and another agent represents the buyer, in most cases. Every client who enters into an agency agreement with a broker has the right to know that in a single transaction, the agent exclusively represents only his side of a transaction.

Dual agency – In a situation where one agent represents both buyer and seller, the resulting arrangement is generally called *dual agency*. In some states, dual agency is not allowed. In others, it is allowed, but only with the expressed, informed consent of both represented parties.

A dual agency scenario exists for a sales agent when he has produced a ready, willing, and able buyer for one of his own listings. Because the agent will be able to receive a commission from both sides of the transaction, dual agency is attractive because of its significant monetary rewards.

Conflicts inherent in dual agency – There are inherent conflicts of interests with dual agency. Sellers typically want the highest price, with the best possible terms, and a quick closing. Buyers want the lowest possible price, with the best possible terms, and a closing date that allows for mortgage application processing and due diligence. These can be conflicting interests.

Many other conflicts can also be present. For example, the agent probably knows the reasons the sellers have for selling which the buyers would like to know. Or, the sellers have probably told the agent what the "bottom dollar" is and may also have disclosed information which, if revealed to the buyers, would be considered a breach of the agent's fiduciary duties to the sellers. The reverse is often true concerning the agency relationship with the buyers. They have probably revealed information about their buying decision and their "top dollar," which if disclosed to the sellers, would compromise the buyers bargaining position.

Even considering all of these reasons not to enter into a dual-agency relationship, there are circumstances where such a relationship makes sense. Some states, therefore, have made allowances for dual agency or *multiple party representation*, providing that the dual agency situation and its potential conflicts of interest have been fully and completely disclosed to both buyer and seller. In these situations, both buyer and seller will normally have to voluntarily consent *in writing* to the dual agency representation, after which dual agency will be permitted.

Assigned/Designated agency – In some other states, brokers are allowed to "designate" agents to represent clients. This could happen when one salesperson is designated to represent the seller and another is designated to represent the buyer in the same transaction. This could happen when a brokerage has the listing "in-house" and also has the buyers "in-house." In this situation, many of the potential problems of dual agency go away, however, the broker, in some states, remains a dual agent. In other states, the broker has no agency with the two parties.

Transaction or transactional broker – Some states deal with dual agency concerns by using the concept of a *transaction broker*. A transaction broker is an agent without fiduciary duties but who handles the transaction from start to finish. Those states adopting the transaction broker approach take the position that the real estate professionals represent the transaction and not the parties to the transaction. So, if an otherwise dual agency situation arises, the duty of fair and honest dealing with all parties remains, but no fiduciary duties exist. It is important to note that some states do not recognize the concept of transactional brokerage.

DUTIES OF BEING AN AGENT

Responsibilities of agents to customers and third parties – Even though agents are primarily responsible to the principal, agents also have duties and responsibilities to the customer and third parties. Anytime agents work with or have contact with customers or third parties, responsibilities as an agent encompass these areas:

- understand and adhere to state and federal consumer protection laws
- understand and adhere to the ethical requirements imposed by professional organizations

- exercise care in performance
- demonstrate reasonable skill as a real estate agent or subagent
- ensure honest and fair dealing with everyone
- disclose all facts that the licensee knows, or should reasonably be expected to know, that materially affect the desirability or value of the property in question

Responsibilities relative to environmental hazards – Environmental and health hazards, whether confined to a subject property or endemic to a larger area, can render a property without value, unsuitable for a client's needs, and therefore unsalable. Agents are required, often by federal law as is the case involving lead-based paint, to disclose the possible presence of environmental hazards.

These hazards may include:

- lead-based paint
- presence of mold
- asbestos
- radon gas
- toxic-waste dumping
- underground storage tanks
- contaminated soil or water
- nearby chemical or nuclear facilities

Opinion versus fact – Real estate agents are encouraged to be very careful about the statements they make, ensuring that the listener understands if the statement is an opinion or a fact. Statements of fact are always permissible if they are true; statements of opinion are permissible, if there is no intent to deceive.

One long recognized activity in business is the practice of *puffing* or *puffery*, which is the exaggeration of a property's benefits such as "This home has the best curb appeal on the block." Puffing is legal because it is based on individual opinions, but agents must make sure that none of their comments or statements about real estate can be treated as fraudulent. Fraud involves the intentional misrepresentation of a material fact.

More about fraud:

- Fraud is the intentional use of deceit, a trick, or some other dishonest means to take money, property, or a legal right from another person.
- Victims of fraud can file a lawsuit for damages, including punitive damages.
- Punitive damages serve as punishment and as a public example of the malicious nature of a fraud.
- If multiple people are involved in committing a fraud they may individually be held liable for the total damages.
- Inherent in fraud is an unjust advantage being taken over another.
- For real estate agents, fraud can include failing to point out a known mistake in a contract or for not communicating an important fact that should have been communicated.
- Perpetrators of fraud can also face criminal charges.

Negligent misrepresentations – Misrepresentations can also be negligent or just plain mistakes. *Negligent misrepresentations* occur when a broker or agent should have known that a statement about a material fact was false. The broker's lack of awareness of the fact is no excuse. Also, the concept of negligent misrepresentation extends to situations where the broker or agent simply fails to do something or follow through as expected. A broker's failing to deliver an offer from a buyer to a seller might be an example of a negligent misrepresentation.

Brokers or agents can be sued for these transgressions if their clients or customers were injured because of the broker's actions. Some practitioners and students falsely assume the difference between fraud and misrepresentation is the degree of harm or damage caused by what was said. The true difference is *intent*. If the intention of the agent was to provide false information, it is like fraud. If there were no intent, but the statement was nonetheless false, it is likely misrepresentation.

Property conditions – In years gone by, it was always incumbent on the buyer to discover all of the possible things wrong with a property before the purchase was consummated. This was referred to as *caveat emptor*, translating to "buyer beware." Federal and state laws have dramatically changed this playing field to the extent that the seller or agent must disclose defects and issues that they know to exist. Some of the categories of issues that must be disclosed are:

- *material* construction defects that have not been resolved
- *patent defects* (an archaic term, but still used in construction), which are accessible, un-hidden, visible defects
- *latent defects* – those defects that are not visible. These may be known or unknown to the seller or agent. If these are known, both the seller and the agent have a responsibility to reveal them.
- Violation of building codes must also be disclosed.

Notwithstanding, these categories of defects and the responsibility of the seller and agent to disclose them, it is still incumbent on the buyer, and often required by law, for the buyer to perform the inspections necessary to ensure that defects do not exist. For these reasons, many buyers perform a home inspection and possibly a pest inspection during the period of **due diligence**.

The term **as is** is used in many listings to communicate the fact that a property is being sold in its "known" present condition. It does not mean that a seller has been absolved of all responsibility relative to defects of which he or she is aware. Many states have adopted a specialized form and mandate that a seller disclose the condition of a property for sale on this form.

Stigmatized properties – A property may become stigmatized because of some event that has occurred at the property or nearby, or because of the presence of some negative factor in the local area. All of these factors could stigmatize a property:

- a death or a homicide
- illegal drug manufacturing

- gang activity
- a suicide
- a sex offender living in the area

The issue of stigmatization is complex and is the focus of numerous federal and state laws. Consider the regulations of two adjacent states when an owner dies in his home. In one state, this fact *must be disclosed* to a potential buyer. In the adjoining state, this fact *must NOT be disclosed* to a potential buyer. What is the law in your state?

Consider that disclosing a previous occupant of a property died of AIDS or was HIV positive constitutes illegal discrimination against the handicapped under the federal Fair Housing Act. Since there are dozens more scenarios like these two, agents should seek competent legal counsel when dealing with a stigmatized property.

TERMINATING AGENCY RELATIONSHIPS IN REAL ESTATE

There will be times when an agency relationship must be terminated, either because the need for the agency is no longer a factor, or because the principal or the agent wants to terminate the agreement. In most states there are six ways to terminate an agency relationship.

- **Expiration** – The term of the agency agreement has run out or expired. This happens frequently with listing agreements when a home fails to sell within the term of the agreement.

- **Completion** – The property was sold or transferred, so there is no further need for the agency. This is also referred to as *fulfillment* or *performance*.

- **Death/Incapacity** – the demise or incapacity of either the principal or the broker

- **Destruction** – The property was condemned, or destroyed by fire, flood, war, wind, etc.

- **Mutual agreement** – Both parties agree to cancel the agency relationship

- **Breach** – One of the parties breached the contract, failed to perform as promised, or stated performance would not occur as promised.

- **Operation of law** – The agency relationship may be cancelled by operation of law, which occurs for example, when the principal enters a bankruptcy proceeding and the property is transferred to a court-appointed receiver.

PROPERTY MANAGEMENT

Fiduciary duties of a property manager – In most states, the role of a property manager creates a *general agency*. In this relationship, the broker doing property management, or agents within the brokerage authorized by the broker to engage in the property management activity, are serving the client in a general agency relationship as there will be some authority extended from the client to the property manager to bind the client or the client's property to contract. The extent of this authority should be clearly spelled out in the property management agreement.

In most states the property management agreement must be in writing, and the broker must maintain a separate trust account for the property management activities.

The property manager will be responsible for the proper handling of rents received, for deposits made by tenants, and other funds belonging to the owner which come into the care, custody, and control of the property manager.

The property manager should be fully versed on the various federal laws dealing with the rental of property or the operation of buildings open to the public. Among these will be:

- the 1968 Fair Housing Act, as amended;
- the Americans with Disabilities Act (ADA) as it applies to public buildings and buildings open to the public;
- the Uniform Residential Landlord Tenant Act (URLTA) as it was adopted by your state. This sample law was developed in 1974 by The National Conference on Commissioners on Uniform State Laws and was adopted individually by states.

URLTA provisions – While the provisions of the URLTA vary from state to state, the following provisions are generally applicable to all states:

- deposits, including security deposits and last month rent deposits, cannot exceed 3 times the monthly rent.
- reasonable rules and regulations concerning the property and the tenant's use and enjoyment of the property can be adopted by and enforced by the landlord. However, the tenant must be provided notice of the rules and regulations at the time of renting the property. If not, they may not be enforced against the tenant, unless the tenant acknowledges in writing the new rule or regulation, or until the tenant has had a thirty-day written notice of it.
- the tenant may not deny landlord reasonable access to the premises for the purposes of inspection or making repairs.
- the landlord may not use the right of access to harass the tenant and except in the case of emergency, will give the tenant 24 hours prior notice of access. The landlord will access the premises only during normal business hours unless the tenant agrees otherwise.
- the landlord cannot retain the tenant's personal property for unpaid rent unless the landlord has been granted an order of attachment or garnishment by a court.
- the purpose of the URLTA is to *assure the parties to the lease that neither the tenant nor the landlord has unreasonable rights solely as a function of their respective positions.*

THE PRACTICE OF REAL ESTATE

The practice of real estate is a comprehensive section involving a wide range of related subject areas of interest to agents at all levels. These subjects include fair housing laws, advertising, agent supervision, commissions and fees, antitrust laws, ethics, and technology.

FAIR HOUSING LAWS

There are a number of important federal laws, dating from 1866 to the present day, that focus specifically on the rights of American citizens to buy, sell, own, and rent property. Real estate agents, among others, need a working knowledge of these laws to fulfill the responsibilities of being the agent.

As a group, these laws:

- the Civil Rights Act of 1866
- the Fair Housing Act of 1968
- the Americans with Disabilities Act

are often referred to as *Fair Housing Laws*. During the period of Reconstruction (1865-1876), several issues were addressed: the return to the Union of those southern states that had seceded, the status of ex-Confederate leaders, and the integration of the African-American freedmen; bitter controversy arose over how to accomplish it all.

Central to the success of the Reconstruction effort was the development of laws regarding the status and rights of the 4 million former slaves. Three important amendments to the U.S. Constitution began to accomplish the establishment of freedom for former slaves.

- the 13th Amendment (1865) abolished slavery
- the 14th Amendment (1868) established citizenship for all persons born in the U.S. or naturalized, and granted them federal civil rights, including due process of Law
- the 15th Amendment decreed that the right to vote could not be denied based on race, color or the "previous condition of servitude." This amendment did not grant the right to vote, as electoral policies are established by the states; however, it did limit the ability to use race, color, or slavery as reasons a state could use to deny the right to vote.

The establishment of fair housing continued with the Civil Rights Act of 1866, the 1968 Fair Housing Act, and the Americans with Disabilities Act (2005).

Civil Rights Act of 1866 (Reconstruction Act) – This legislation was passed by Congress over the veto of President Andrew Johnson who succeeded to the Presidency from vice president after the assassination of President Abraham Lincoln. This law provides that all persons born in the United States are declared to be citizens, regardless of race or color, and shall have the right to enter into contracts, to sue, inherit, acquire and dispose of property, and shall equally benefit from the law as do white citizens.

Classes protected by this law are race and color.

Notwithstanding the racial injustice prevailing in American society in the 100 years between the passage of the Civil Right act of 1866 and the mid-1960s, not much happened to improve the lot of our minority citizens. However, by the 1960s, the matter of civil rights for all citizens had again reached the status of a national crisis. Numerous acts were adopted to advance the equal treatment of people of all races, and principal among them was the Fair Housing Act of 1968.

Fair Housing Act – Formally known as Title VIII of the Civil Rights Act of 1968 as amended by Fair Housing Amendments Act, this legislation was enacted on April 11, 1968, and was amended in 1988. The federal Fair Housing Act provides the basis for fair housing rights and enforcement throughout the United States. The Act also provided for accessibility requirements for covered multi-family housing built for first occupancy after March 13, 1991.

This comprehensive legislation protects four classes or classifications of Americans. Race and color from 1866 and in 1968 covered religion and national origin. Gender was added in 1974 and family status and disability were added in 1988.

- Race (1866)
- Color (1866)
- Religion (1968)
- National Origin (1968)
- Sex/Gender (1974)
- Familial Status (1988), families with children 18 and under and pregnant women
- Disability (1988), mental or physical impairments

These seven, protected classes formed the basis of a new effort to assure the American dream of housing to all citizens.

Specific wrongs – The 1968 Fair Housing Act defined prohibited practices involving housing, which involved sales, rentals, advertising, and financing. The law's most important provisions made it unlawful to take the following actions if the prohibited behavior affected a member of a protected class:

- refusing to sell a property, or to lease a property, because the prospective buyer or tenant is a member of a protected class;

- altering terms in a contract to purchase or to lease a property because the prospective buyer or tenant is a member of a protected class;
- using discriminatory statements in advertising;
- denying service as a real estate professional because the prospective client is a member of a protected class;
- showing properties to a prospective buyer or tenant only in areas of the market which are predominantly of the same ethnicity as the prospect – ***steering***;
- attempting to create panic selling by creating a sales contract with a member of a protected class with the intent to use the sale to a protected class member as a method of inducing owners in the area to sell, before the neighborhood becomes too "mixed" or the homes lose value is called ***blockbusting***. Blockbusting contracts are void. Listings based upon a blockbusting scheme are voidable by the seller once the blockbusting scheme is discovered;
- A lender who refuses to lend in an area because it is populated with members of a protected class is ***redlining***. The term comes from lenders who would make areas on a map (often with a red line) and say they "just don't loan in areas like that."

Beyond the seven prohibited practices, the ***Fair Housing Act*** included a wide variety of parameters which were very important to real estate agents:

Wide applicability – The Fair Housing Act prohibits discriminatory conduct by many kinds of legal entities. These include individuals, corporations, associations, partnerships, legal representatives, mutual companies, labor organizations, family trusts, unincorporated organizations, trustees, receivers, fiduciaries, municipalities, local government units, as well as cities and federal agencies.

A fifth new protected class (1974) – The Housing and Community Development Act (1974) added sex/gender to the list of protected classes, bringing the total to five.

Two new protected classes (1988) – The Fair Housing Amendments Act of 1988 added two major sets of provisions that apply to *disabled persons* and *families with children 18 years old and under*, bringing the total number of protected classes to seven.

Disability – It became illegal to discriminate in the sale or rental of a dwelling because of the disability of the buyer or tenant, any disabled person who will reside in the dwelling after it is sold or rented, or any person associated with the buyer or renter.

Familial Status – It became illegal to discriminate against any buyer or renter based on the size of their family or on the pregnancy of a prospective tenant.

Refusal to Rent or Sell – It is *not* illegal to refuse to rent or sell property to an individual whose tenancy would constitute a threat to other individuals or to their health and safety, or whose tenancy would result in damage to the building or to the property of others.

Multifamily properties – Multi-family properties must be constructed so that the public portions and common-use portions are accessible to people with disabilities.

Advertising restrictions – Advertising of dwellings for sale or for lease must not disclose a "preference, limitation, or discrimination," based on any of the protected categories. Any media company that runs an offensive advertisement may be held liable for it. The advertiser may also be held liable.

Selective advertising – The act prohibits advertising programs that selectively market properties to minorities, especially housing which is segregated or over-priced. Also prohibited is the use of code words, such as "exclusive neighborhood," in the text of an advertisement to sell or rent housing.

Discriminatory statements – The law prohibits unpublished statements which include discriminatory language or encourage discriminatory conduct, such as a landlord's instruction to his property manager that she should not rent to minorities or should give white customers a preference.

"Not Available" statements – The Fair Housing Act prohibits the practice of representing, to any member of a protected class, that a dwelling is not available for sale or rental, when it actually is available. In case law, one real estate firm was found to have violated the law by its practice of putting sold signs on their listings in a white neighborhood in an attempt to discourage minorities from renting or purchasing homes in that neighborhood.

Blockbusting – The 1968 act was intended to end the practice of blockbusting. This practice, in place before 1968, tried to frighten homeowners into selling their homes at low prices, based on the "talk" that members of a particular race, ethnic group, religion, or other protected class were moving into the neighborhood. In cases that are alleged to show blockbusting activities, the court has focused on what was heard, not what was said. So, at the end of the day, if a homeowner felt threatened, it did not matter if there was no wrongful intent by the real estate agent, or explicit reference to a protected class, the agent may have violated the Fair Housing Act.

Regulation of banks – The Fair Housing Act governs the activities of the banks and financial institutions because Congress felt that lenders might discriminate in the housing and real estate industries. As a result of the act, banks and financial institutions may not discriminate when financing the purchase, construction, improvement, repair, or maintenance of a residential housing unit.

Enforcement and fines – The federal Fair Housing Act is administered by the Office of Fair Housing and Equal Opportunity and supervised by the secretary of HUD. HUD makes information available to the public regarding the process to citizens who feel they were discriminated against illegally. Substantial fines may be imposed and civil and criminal lawsuits can also be brought. HUD "testers" are sent out to determine if agents are engaging in discriminatory activities.

Handicapped persons – Under the amendment to the 1968 act adding "Status of Handicap," a new area of potential concern was opened. In short, a landlord may not deny a handicapped person access to rent a unit, even though it may pose a potential risk to the handicapped person. The handicapped individual may make such alterations to the premises as are necessary to accommodate his handicap and do so at his own expense. The landlord may not deny the right to make these alterations. When the handicapped individual vacates the property, he is required to "reasonably restore" the property to its original condition.

Service animals – Landlords who will not allow pets may not deny handicapped individuals the right to have life assisting animals, nor can the landlord charge any additional sums due to the presence of such animals (seeing eye dogs, and other such animals are considered "life assisting." Note that a provision of "No Pets" in a rental listing is invalid when the prospective renter has a service animal.

Familial status – This deals with regulations landlords used to make properties unavailable to families with children. This amendment was added in 1988 to offset the discrimination that was occurring against families who had minor children and who were seeking to rent property It was determined that often this was nothing but thinly veiled discrimination as minority families were over-represented in families with children who were seeking to rent property.

Age-restricted communities – In age-restricted or age-qualified communities, there may be a restriction which prohibits persons under the age of 18 from residing in the residence more than 3 months in any calendar year. This has been determined as permissible under the Fair Housing Act.

The "Sun City Exception" – There is an exception for rental or ownership based communities specifically for senior citizens. If the project has a specific marketing plan, and does its marketing to persons over the age of 55, then it may have a prohibition against children in the project.

Exemptions to the Act – Despite the depth of coverage of the law, Congress decided to exempt certain individuals from the provisions of the law. These included single family homeowners, multiple-family homeowners (up to four units), religious organizations, private clubs, and senior citizens. In other words, members of these groups are given limited permission to discriminate in certain ways and under certain conditions.

Exemptions include:

1. Any single-family dwelling sold or rented by the owner under the following conditions. The owner:

- cannot own more than three single-family dwellings at any one time.
- must currently reside in the dwelling or be the most previous resident of the dwelling.
- cannot use the services of a real estate agent or company for any reason.
- cannot publish or advertise in a way to violate the Act.

2. The rental of rooms or units up to four family units if the owner actually maintains and occupies one of the units as his/her residence.

    Example: A female wishing to rent a room in her house and does not desire to rent to a male. It would be *legal* to discriminate against sex under this exemption.

3. Religious or church related non-profit organizations may restrict the use of property owned by the organization by only allowing members of that religion to occupy the property.

4. Private clubs providing lodging which it owns or operates for other than a commercial purpose, may limit rental or occupancy to its members and give preference to its members.

> **NOTE:** None of the above mentioned exemptions apply to Real Estate Agents or Real Estate Companies. Those that meet the requirements above can discriminate so long as they do not use the services of Real Estate Agents in any capacity. Real Estate Agents and Companies will face significant fines and penalties for violating Fair Housing Laws.

Equal Credit Opportunity Act (ECOA) – This act prohibits creditors from discriminating against credit applicants on the basis of race, color, religion, national origin, sex, marital status, age, or because an applicant receives income from a public assistance program.

The most import application of this law is in the granting of mortgages, home improvement loans, or in the use of credit-based information in the renting of homes.

Regulatory authority for this law is spread across several federal agencies and it is based on the type of financial institution involved—national bank, state bank, credit union, mortgage broker, mortgage originator, mortgage servicer, lender offering private educational loans, and payday lender, regardless of size.

Housing and Community Development Act of 1974 – The Act's primary purpose was to end discrimination in various areas of community development. According to the Department of Housing and Urban Development (HUD), when Congress passed the Housing and Community Development Act of 1974 (HCD), it broke down the barriers of prevailing practice where under separate categorical programs, the government had made the decisions about every community development project undertaken by cities.

The HCD Act departed from this model by creating a block grant program titled the Community Development Block Grant program (CDBG). CDBG merged seven (7) categorical programs into a block of flexible community development funds distributed each year by a formula that considers population and measures of distress, including poverty, age of housing, housing overcrowding, and growth lag. Grantors now determine what activities they will fund as long as certain requirements are met.

The Housing and Community Development Act of 1974 also added a fifth protected class, that of sex/gender, to the Fair Housing Act of 1968.

Americans with Disabilities Act (The ADA) – The ADA is an anti-discrimination law that deals with physical workplace accommodations for disabled persons. While the ADA is not usually related to housing units and properties, real estate agents are advised to have some knowledge of the law and its requirements.

The ADA prohibits discrimination in employment practices against persons with disabilities. Before this law went into effect, many employers had facilities which were not "handicap accessible." They were able to claim inability to hire the handicapped because of work place limitations. The ADA banned discrimination based on the status of a person's handicap, and also addressed the issue of accessibility for "public buildings" or "buildings open to the public."

Public buildings are defined as buildings owned or operated by a public entity such as city, county or state buildings, buildings in public parks, libraries, museums and the like. Buildings open to the public but owned by private owners are covered if they are business properties open to the general public, or are residential properties consisting of five (5) or more units (apartment complexes, timeshare developments, and other similar properties).

The types of disabilities protected are:

- vision impaired
- limited mobility
- confinement to wheelchair or similar devices
- hearing impaired
- alcoholism – if the person is enrolled in a recognized treatment program
- drug Addiction – if the person is enrolled in a recognized treatment program
- HIV positive or AIDS

To insure access for handicapped persons to public buildings and buildings open to the public, a barrier-free construction requirement was phased in, starting in 1992. To be ADA compliant, hallways and doors have to be wide enough to accommodate a standard wheelchair, restrooms have to have provisions for handicapped persons, structures more than one story have to have elevators, instructions in Braille must be posted on elevator controls and on certain signs.

Handicap parking must also be provided.

Section 504 of the Rehabilitation Act (1973) – Section 504 of the Rehabilitation Act of 1973 prohibits discrimination against people with disabilities in programs and activities conducted by HUD or that receive financial assistance from HUD. This includes public housing, public university housing, government run housing programs, etc.

Housing for Older Persons Act (1995) – HOPA outlines the requirements *for the persons who are 55 years of age or older* exemption established in the Fair Housing Act. This exemption applies to the familial status provisions of the Fair Housing Act, but does not exempt the housing from the other provisions of the law.

This law states that communities can legally market themselves as "age-restricted" or "age-qualified," provided that 80 percent of the occupied units are occupied by at least one person who is 55 years of age or older. Most 55+ age-restricted, active, adult communities place an age-minimum on the residents. In most of these communities, no one under the age of 19 may reside in the community unless granted an exemption. Nearly all age-restricted and active adult communities allow people under the age minimum, such as grandchildren, to visit and stay on a limited basis. Most age-restricted communities have covenants that allow people under the age minimum to reside temporarily in the community for a period of time, ranging from two weeks to 90 days per year (varies by community).

State fair housing laws – Many states have addressed areas still not covered by federal legislation, and as a result, there are also state laws in the form of municipal laws and regulations that you will have to know about as an agent. Find out about these before you do business in your community.

The chart below illustrates the classes of individuals protected by Fair Housing Laws:

Classes of Citizens Protected by Major Civil Rights Legislation

Legislation → / Protected Class ↓	Civil Rights Act 1866	Fair Housing Act 1968 Title VIII	Fair Housing Amendments Act (1988)	Equal Credit Opportunity Act of 1974	Housing and Community Development Act (1974)	Americans with Disabilities Act (1995)	Section 504 Rehabilitation Act	Housing for Older Persons Act (1995)
Race	√	√		√				
Color	√	√		√				
Religion		√		√				
National Origin		√		√				
Sex				√	√		√	
Age				√				√
Marital Status				√				
Disability			√			√		
Familial Status			√					
Public Assistance Income				√				

Summary of Fair Housing Legislation:

The fair housing legislation can be daunting. While it is interesting to understand which laws cover which people, which properties, and which situations, it is also important to understand the combined applicability of all of this legislation. The following is a summary.

Why do we have fair housing laws?

- Fair housing is the right to choose housing without having to endure unlawful discrimination.
- Federal, state, and local fair housing laws protect from unlawful discrimination in transactions involving rentals, sales, lending, and insurance.
- Fair housing guarantees that people have the right to choose the housing that is best for their needs without discrimination.
- Fair housing laws help guarantee that no outside preferences or stereotypes will be imposed.
- Fair housing laws encourage sellers, landlords, and even neighborhoods to put out their "welcome mat."
- Fair housing laws contribute to the establishment of appealing, friendly, vibrant, dynamic neighborhoods.

Are people in protected classes who are seeking mortgage loans similarly protected?

Yes, a lender cannot:

- refuse to provide information regarding loans.
- impose different terms or conditions on a loan.
- charge different interest rates, points, or fees.
- refuse to make a mortgage loan based on class.
- discriminate in appraising property.
- refuse to purchase a loan.
- set different terms or conditions for purchasing a loan.

However, a lender may refuse a loan to anyone, regardless of protected class or any other factor, if the applicant fails the income or credit qualifications.

LIMITATIONS ON ADVERTISING

The purpose of advertising is to motivate and to inform. Real estate advertising is controlled by federal statutes, state laws, and the rules of common law and common sense. When a statement is made, the statement may contain *material facts*.

A material fact is a fact that would be important to a reasonable person in deciding whether to engage or not to engage in a particular transaction; it is an important fact as distinguished from some unimportant or trivial detail.

Opinions – Everyone has opinions, including real estate agents. Most people can state their opinions freely, but real estate agents have to be much more careful about what they say. Because agents are considered experts in real estate, agents always need to ensure that opinions are clearly stated as opinions.

> **Example:** A statement like, "In my opinion, this room will fit a round table with room to spare," an agent is expressing an opinion. Or agents may confine opinions to a trivial or unimportant area, "I think your daughter will like the purple room."

Puffing (Puffery) – Not unique to the real estate world, puffery is considered "good salesmanship" and is not a statement or misstatement of material fact. "This is the best view in town!"

Nowhere are these advertising concepts more important than in real estate sales. Over the years, a number of abuses have led to a plethora of federal, state, and local laws about advertising, as well as statements of ethics and similar devices published by professional organizations and individual brokerages. The same thing has occurred in the related industry of mortgage lending.

It is unethical, and potentially illegal conduct, for a real estate professional to engage in any form of deception concerning the condition of the property or any other material fact about the property.

Example: A real estate agent runs the following advertisement in the local paper:

> **Great Starter Home!** Beautiful condition, 3br/2ba, 2-car garage. Priced for quick sale at $287,500. A true must see! Call Bonnie at Carson Realty 702-555-5555.

On the surface this ad looks okay. "Great Starter Home," "Beautiful condition," and "A true must see" are all puffery. That the home has 3 bedrooms, 2 baths, and a 2-car garage are facts, perhaps material facts. The price being $287,500 is also a material fact.

What we did not tell you: Bonnie has had no activity on this listing because the sellers told her they will not even consider an offer under $300,000. Bonnie thinks this is too high, but was not able to convince her sellers to list at a lower price. Her plan is to get buyers to look at the house and then tell them the newspaper misprinted the price and that the price is really $300,000.

So, what's the problem? First, Bonnie is flirting with fraud if she has not already committed it. Second, Bonnie is guilty of "false advertising," and third, she has breached her fiduciary duty to her clients who have only authorized Bonnie to price the property at a minimum of $300,000.

A real estate professional must always be truthful when dealing with clients and with customers. Remember that the agency relationship requires the agent to act in accordance with the fiduciary responsibilities owed by an agent to the client. The agent also has the duty of fair and honest dealing and disclosure of all material facts to the customer.

When dealing with clients or customers, real estate professionals are often asked for opinions or advice. This is an exceptionally precarious area and some good practices in "risk aversion" or "risk management" should be developed.

If asked a question to which you know the answer, and you would not be disclosing confidential information, and it is not rendering an expert opinion or practicing law, it is probably permissible to answer the question. However, clients often want information and seem to expect the real estate professional to be able to provide it. But for many reasons, the agent should not give the answers.

Example Questions:

"What is crime like in this neighborhood?" Tell them you understand their interest but you do not keep those records. Perhaps refer them to the local police for that information.

"Why are the sellers selling?" If the reason is not confidential and the sellers have authorized you to tell, go ahead. But if the reason is they are about 30 days away from foreclosure, that is confidential information, and you should discuss with your broker how this should be handled.

"Is this lot at least 3 acres? I need that to build my store." Unless you are a registered surveyor, you cannot answer. However, you could consult the tax record and show that to the client. Or, you could suggest that if precise size is an issue, you will arrange for a survey at either party's cost.

"What is this black splotch on the bathroom wall? Is that the black mold stuff I have heard about in the news?" Unless you are a mold expert, you cannot answer. You can tell them that you understand their concern and suggest it be examined by an expert.

"We're a married couple and we want to avoid probate costs if we can. How should we take title to our home?" You might know the answer is probably "joint tenancy," but to say so would be considered giving legal advice. Unless you are also a lawyer licensed to practice law in the state, you cannot advise. You can tell them there are several ways to hold title which, based on their particular circumstances, will impact the complexity of their estate. They should really discuss this with their attorney, tax advisor, or escrow officer.

Truth in Advertising – Federal truth-in-advertising regulations are designed to protect the public, especially consumers, from advertising that is false, misleading, or both. These laws are based on the simple concepts that advertisers (including real estate agents) be required to tell the truth about products and to be able to prove the claims they make in their ads.

The **Federal Trade Commission (FTC)** is the primary enforcement body for truth-in-advertising claims, although

---

Definition: "Deceptive"

An ad is labeled deceptive if misleading statements and/or omitted items of information affect a consumer's decision to purchase or use a product. An ad is considered unfair if it causes unavoidable consumer injury that is not outweighed by a benefit.

a number of state agencies are also active in this regard. If real estate customers or clients have fallen victim to advertising violations, the law allows for the reporting of a complaint and remediation.

Generally, truth-in-advertising laws require print, TV, magazine, newspaper, Internet, and other advertising to be truthful, non-deceptive, provable by evidence furnished by the advertiser, and fair.

DUTIES AND OBLIGATIONS OF BROKERS AND THEIR ASSOCIATES

Broker responsibilities: Brokers, operating as agents of clients, must respect the laws of the state in carrying out fiduciary responsibilities. While different states have different rules concerning brokers, the following are universal. Note that many of these "broker" responsibilities also apply to associated licensees as they are "sub-agents" to the seller through their employing broker.

Affiliation – In most states, a salesperson and a broker-salesperson must be affiliated with either a licensed real estate broker or a registered owner-developer of new homes. This affiliation should be represented by a written agreement spelling out the relationship, commission splits, office or desk fee arrangements, franchise fees, if any, and the entire agreement between the broker and the agent.

Fixed place of business – Each broker must maintain a fixed place of business.

Trust accounts/commingling and conversion of funds – A busy brokerage might be holding thousands of dollars for clients as earnest money deposits. The law may require all of these funds be deposited in a trust account, or be handled in a manner to which the principal has agreed. These funds may not be *commingled* (mixed) with the broker's operating funds nor may they be spent, *conversion*.

Reasonable care – A broker must always exercise reasonable care when representing a principal.

Good faith – The broker must always act in the client's best interests and carry out the principal's legal instructions within the scope of the authority provided by the principal.

Presentation of offers – The broker must present all offers to the principal promptly when received. Note that the broker and the principal can agree on the timeframes for presenting offers, such as *"Review them Monday at 5 PM,"* or *"Hold them until the weekend,"* etc. but absent such an agreement, the broker cannot simply hold onto offers until the broker or agent feels like presenting them.

Buyer agency – Most buyers hire a broker to locate a home or particular type of property. The broker is committed to the principal, the buyer, through a buyer's agency agreement even when the entire commission is paid for by the seller. The broker in this situation must be fair and honest with the seller, but owes greater responsibility to the buyer and must work to protect the buyer's best interests. This includes disclosing pertinent facts and opinions to the buyer. These could be that the home has been listed for over a year, or that it is currently overpriced, or that the HOA is in a legal battle with the city where it operates, etc. Buyer agency also requires the broker to use bargaining and negotiating skills in the best interest of the buyer.

Cooperating brokers – This term is reserved for buyer brokers who work with (cooperate with) listing brokers to produce a buyer who is ready, willing, and able to purchase.

Salespersons – In most communities, salespersons are formally classified as subagents, although they typically call themselves "real estate agents." There activities are also regulated by statute. The following are some of the rules governing the behavior of salespersons:

Licensing – Every salesperson is licensed to a particular broker and can carry out only the activities assigned and approved by that broker.

Listings belong to brokers – All listings taken by a salesperson are taken in the name of the brokerage. The listing belongs to the broker, not the salesperson. Similarly, all salesperson's activities must be carried out in the name of their brokers.

Supervision – All salespersons must be supervised by their respective brokers.

Advertising requirement – In most states, salespersons may not place advertising without identifying their brokers. This requirement may include a provision for "Open House" or "For Sale" signs to similarly identify the brokerage.

Employment of salespersons – Salespersons may work for brokers either as employees or independent contractors. Most salespersons are employed as independent contractors.

- **Employee status** – In some states, by statute and regulation, the salespersons and broker-salespersons are employees. This is the relationship that transfers the obligation to train and supervise agents to the broker. It also is the relationship that gives the broker the authority to direct the activities of the associates.

- **Independent contractor status** - This is a tax status. The Internal Revenue Service (IRS) has agreed to allow real estate professionals to elect independent contractor status for tax purposes, even though they may legally be employees. In order to qualify for this treatment, agents must have a written employment agreement with the broker which states an agent will be treated as an independent contractor for tax purposes. As an independent contractor, agents are able to deduct those reasonable and necessary business expenses. This tax treatment often offers greater deductibility of operating expenses than if taxed as an employee.

Commissions and fees – Commissions in the real estate industry are earned by brokers (agents) who share these commissions with salespersons (subagents) with whom they are associated and with other brokers (cooperating brokers).

- **Compensation agreements** – Salespersons are compensated based on schedules or agreements signed with their brokers, most commonly referred to as *Independent Contractor Agreements*.

- **Setting commissions** – Commissions are always negotiable between a broker and the principal. They are NOT fixed nor is there an industry standard. It is a violation of the Sherman Anti-Trust Law, "price fixing," to suggest there is a standard commission rate. Commissions will always be expressed in the agency agreement as a percentage of a sale price, or as a flat fee, or both. Net listings, a concept where a broker receives any overage after a pre-determined net proceeds to the seller, is not allowed in most states.

- **Earning commissions** – To be entitled to a brokerage commission for listing or selling a property, a broker must:

    - be licensed
    - be the *procuring cause* (the cause of the chain of events that caused the sale)
    - be employed by the principal
    - act according to the laws of agency

    In most listing agreements, there is a protection clause that provides for the payment of a commission to the listing broker in those cases where, within a certain number of days after the listing agreement expires or is cancelled, the owner transfers or sells the property to someone whom the listing broker/agent had previously introduced to the seller. In other words, it prevents a principal from cancelling a listing agreement, or letting one expire, with the intent of escaping the payment of a commission.

- **Sharing commissions** – Brokers can share commissions only with the people they employ or with other licensed brokers. When sharing with other brokers, the brokers do not have to be in the same state or country, but they must be licensed in their own jurisdictions.

- **Entitlement to commissions** – When a broker, employed by a seller, successfully finds a buyer who is ready, willing, and able to complete a transaction based on the terms and conditions in the listing, the broker has earned commission – even if the sale is not completed because of a principal's default.

- **Payment of commissions** – Salespersons may not receive any compensation directly from the principals they represent. All commissions earned by the salesperson must be paid to the broker who will share the commission with the salesperson, usually according to a predefined agreement.

GENERAL ETHICS

The ethical behavior of real estate agents may be best summarized or guided by the following statements:

1. Tell the truth.
2. Tell the whole truth.

3. Don't steal the money.
4. Do your homework.
5. Don't act like an expert in areas you are not.
6. Treat your clients as you would want to be treated.
7. Keep your client's confidential information to yourself.
8. Disclose required information even if it may blow the deal.
9. Know the law and follow it.
10. Understand your ethical obligations and practice them at the highest level.

Regrettably, not all real estate professionals follow these ten simple statements and as a result, we have an enormous number of rules, regulations, and laws we must follow and for which we can be punished if we fail in our professional responsibilities.

This is a subject vital to the success of any professional, notwithstanding a specific profession. Ethics are matters of standards of conduct and moral behavior based on the concept of "doing the right thing." The author recommends agents purchase and read *Doing the Right Thing* by Deborah H. Long. Ethics are perceived as conduct which is not only legal in nature, but more than just merely legal, getting closer to terms like "justice," "fairness," "kind," "honest," "generous," and "exceeded our expectations."

The law describes the *minimum acceptable conduct.* If you go any lower, you are breaking the law and your conduct is illegal. Ethical conduct is generally above and beyond what is required to be "legal.
In real estate, the most frequent examples of unethical conduct come in the form of "taking advantage." There is nothing wrong with taking an advantage, as in seizing the moment, or exercising superior knowledge and skill for your client, but, when you take advantage of your client, or your customer, you are acting unethically.

An example of an ethical situation – You are having lunch at the local diner and the head of planning and zoning and one of the prominent county commissioners take the booth behind you. In the course of eating your lunch, you overhear their conversation which deals with the final decision on the location of a new freeway off ramp. It will be placed right next to a commercial listing you have, making that property greatly more valuable than its current list price. The commissioner tells the head of planning and zoning to keep it under wraps until the press conference set for next week. You should:

a. call a buddy of yours who is a developer and tell him you can get him a real steal on a great commercial site, if he agrees to cut you in for 25% of the deal.
b. do nothing. You weren't supposed to hear the conversation anyway.
c. call your clients, tell them what you heard, and suggest you get together to re-evaluate the pricing on the property.
d. take a "wait and see" approach until after the public announcement next week.

So, what do you do? Easy! Is it's a material fact you have to disclose. Period!

To whom do you have to disclose? You are required to disclose to both sides of the transaction any material fact that affects the value or desirability of the property. Therefore, you must do so with both your client and the buyer.

Ethical requirements for real estate licensees – *The Code of Ethics*, established by the National Association of REALTORS®, has become *the* governing guidelines of ethical behavior for real estate practitioners. Some states have even added to the NAR code in attempts for even more professionalism within the industry.

The NAR Code of Ethics can be found in Appendix B.

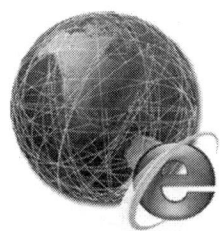

ISSUES IN THE USE OF TECHNOLOGY

The Internet has changed the real estate industry forever. Once, agents faxed or drove hard copy documents all around their town. Now, we e-mail these to clients, customers, escrow companies, and lenders, who may affix electronic signatures with their computers or smart phones and send the documents back.

Clients and customers can search MLS services and other web sites while relaxing on their patio.
This conversion has been so rapid and so complete that it would be virtually impossible for a real estate agent to work for a day without interacting with a computer.

Some of the emerging and fully emerged trends in technology are:

E-Mail – E-mail has become the preferred method of communication for real estate agents. It is quick, efficient, written, easy to use, allowing communication with many people at the same time, leaves a paper trail, and much more.

There are some preferred practices for the use of e-mail:

- use the subject line to show the address of the property
- use e-mail "strings" to group communications
- avoid spelling errors
- be careful to whom you copy
- respond promptly
- be specific and to the point
- be as brief as possible
- keep attachments small (learn how to scan properly)
- do not send unsolicited e-mails

Websites – Most real estate companies have web sites that use the powerful Internet Data Exchange (IDEX) system which allows members to search and display MLS data.

Licensees can purchase web site management tools that are extremely helpful in managing the effectiveness of Internet marketing methods and programs.

Internet advertising – State laws govern internet advertising, so before getting involved in these programs, consult the laws of your state to see what you can do and what you should avoid. For example, here is a sample of requirements from various states:

- All advertising and electronic communications by a real estate licensee must include the licensee's name, office address, and broker affiliation.
- The listing of a salesperson's name in an advertisement, without the name of the affiliated broker, is prohibited.
- Real estate professionals must disclose their status (broker or salesperson) *on every page* of their web site.
- Online real estate ads must be a true representation and must not be misleading.

National Do Not Call Registry – In 2003, a federal do-not-call law went into effect and most telephone advertisers, including real estate salespersons, must comply with this law. The law allows for consumers to add their phone numbers to a list managed by the Federal Trade Commission (FTC). Real estate agents may not call anyone on this list.

Several exceptions should be noted. Real estate agents may call consumers with whom they have had business relationship for up to 18 months after the consumer's last purchase, or three months after the consumer's last request for assistance or information. In cases where the consumer asks the licensee not to call, the licensee must stop calling immediately and not call for five years. You can learn more at www.donotcall.gov.

Electronic contracting – It is often much more convenient to handle contracts by digital, or electronic means. There are two federal laws that govern electronic commerce: the Uniform Electronic Transaction Act (UETA) and the Electronic Signatures in Global and National Commerce Act (E-Sign).  In general, UETA removes barriers in electronic commerce that would otherwise threaten or prevent the enforcement of contracts. A total of 47 States (all except Washington, Illinois, and New York), the District of Columbia, Puerto Rico, and the U.S. Virgin Islands have all adopted it into their own laws. Its overarching purpose is to bring into line the differing state laws over such areas as retention of paper records and the validity of electronic signatures, thereby supporting the validity of electronic contracts as a viable medium of agreement.

The four key provisions of UETA are as follows:

1. If a state's laws require a signature on a contract, an electronic signature is sufficient.
2. If a state's laws require a written record, an electronic record is sufficient.
3. A contract cannot be denied its intended legal effect just because an electronic record was used.
4. A record or signature cannot be denied its legal effect just because it is in an electronic format.

Even with these convenient new systems, there are still some real estate transactions that require "wet" or original signatures.

ANTITRUST LAWS

Background – Like most other industries, the real estate industry is subject to federal and state anti-trust laws. Administered by the Federal Trade Commission (FTC), these laws were designed to prevent the formation and operation of monopolies, trusts, contracts, and conspiracies that would unreasonably restrain trade. In other words, these laws were designed to prevent the behaviors which would prevent the free and fair flow of goods and services in a competitive marketplace.

The most common anti-trust violations, and those the laws were designed to prevent or mitigate, are price-fixing, group boycotting, allocation of customers or markets, and tie-in agreements.

Price-fixing – is the act of agreeing to set prices or fees at a predefined level, as opposed to allowing markets and market forces to set them. This is illegal. Real estate brokers must independently set commission rates for their own companies, and they must never discuss these with other brokers in an attempt to arrive at a standard fee.

Group boycotting – occurs when several businesses get together and agree to withhold their patronage or not use a particular organization, possibly an escrow company, or home warranty company, or lender.

Allocation of customers – This occurs when several firms agree to divide markets and refrain from competing for customers. Brokers by internal policy may, however, allocate customers or markets into geographic areas where they plan to operate exclusively.

Tie-in agreements – involve agreements to sell customers one product or service only if they purchase another product. Usually the sale of a desirable product is tied into the purchase of a less desirable product. An alarm company that will only sell its equipment to the customer if the customer also agrees to a five-year monitoring service contract, is using tie-in agreements.

The penalties for violating federal antitrust laws are severe. For example, violations of the **Sherman Antitrust Act** can range to $1 million for individuals and $100 million for corporations.

Chapter 2: Agency and the Practice of Real Estate
End of Chapter Quiz

1. A salesperson advertises a property without including the name of the broker. This practice is allowed in which of the following instances?

    a. The salesperson is the listing agent.
    b. The salesperson owns the property and is selling it as a "for sale by owner."
    c. Permission has been given by the agency to exclude the broker's name.
    d. The salesperson is paying 100% of the cost of the ad.

2. A salesperson sold a *short sale property* which was listed by her broker a year ago on an exclusive right to sell basis. The salesperson may accept her commission payment from:

    a. the buyer.
    b. the seller.
    c. the listing broker.
    d. the listing broker's attorney.

3. A real estate broker is usually which type of agent?

    a. General Agent
    b. Special Agent
    c. Universal Agent
    d. Free Agent

4. A listing broker has earned a commission because her listing was sold by a cooperating broker and his salesperson. The listing broker must pay some portion of her earned commission to which other party?

    a. The salesperson who made the sale.
    b. The broker of the salesperson who made the sale.
    c. Whoever is listed in the purchase contract as "listing broker."
    d. Only the listing salesperson.

5. In a real estate transaction, the listing broker has an agency relationship with:

    a. the seller.
    b. the buyer.
    c. all parties in the transaction.
    d. none of the parties in the transaction.

6. Broker Tiffany is a "special agent" of principal Bob. Her responsibilities to Bob are as follows:

    a. represent Bob in a specific transaction.
    b. represent Bob's interests in all real estate transactions.
    c. exercise a power of attorney for Bob.
    d. exercise authority for all of Bob's affairs.

7. A broker manages a large, busy office with over 100 salespeople, so she has had to establish policies and procedures to avoid chaos and confusion. A salesperson from another brokerage submitted a written offer on one of her listings, which she quickly e-mailed to her client. Later that day, two more offers came in: one lower and one higher than the first. According to her policy, she waited to present these two new offers until her client, the seller, has considered the first offer. Before the end of the day, the seller accepted the first offer. In this case the broker's actions were:

   a. permissible, provided that the agent formally rejected the second and third offers.
   b. not permissible, because the broker must submit all offers to the seller in a timely manner.
   c. not permissible, because the broker must notify the second and third buyers that an offer is already being considered by the seller.
   d. permissible, because the broker followed her own procedures.

8. When a broker lists a property for sale, the broker has the power to do which of the following?

   a. bind the seller to a higher-than-list contract
   b. reject a much-lower-than-list offer on the seller's property
   c. advertise the seller's property
   d. offer legal advice to the seller

9. Jean Philips, the broker for Empty Nest Realty, just took an exclusive-right-to-sell listing on Bob Williams' hilltop house in the valley. Jean will receive her commission when which of the following events occur?

   a. when the transaction closes
   b. when Bob signs an offer to purchase
   c. when all counteroffers are accepted by all parties
   d. when she finds a qualified buyer who is ready willing, and able to purchase the home under the terms advertised on the listing

10. As used in the real estate profession, the word "agency" describes:

    a. a mandatory part of the name of any company dealing in real estate transactions.
    b. the fiduciary relationship between an agent and a principal.
    c. the relationship between a real estate broker and the associated salespeople.
    d. the relationship between an agent and a customer.

11. As a real estate broker, Ann has entered into a fiduciary relationship with a buyer, John, who wants to purchase a home. Which of the following statements does NOT describe Ann's relationship with John?

    a. Ann is John's agent.
    b. Ann owes loyalty to John.
    c. Ann is a neutral third-party.
    d. Ann must conform to John's legal instructions.

12. Broker Bradley appoints Alice agent, and only Alice, to represent a seller. Alice would be:

    a. an appointed or designated agent.
    b. a dual agent.
    c. an affiliated agent.
    d. a representative agent.

13. Our modern system of agency is one of well-defined fiduciary responsibilities. These are:

    a. obedience, loyalty, disclosure, accountability, confidentiality.
    b. care, obedience, loyalty, disclosure, accountability, confidentiality.
    c. trust, care, obedience, loyalty, disclosure, confidentiality.
    d. trust, care, obedience, loyalty, disclosure.

14. A salesperson who has just listed a home for a neighbor has the following relationship with the neighbor?

    a. The neighbor is the customer.
    b. The neighbor is the client of the broker.
    c. The neighbor is the listing broker's customer and not the salesperson's.
    d. The neighbor is the salesperson's customer.

15. During the course of a showing, the seller's broker makes a number of statements. Which of these is a violation of the broker's fiduciary relationship with the seller?

    a. "The pool equipment was stolen yesterday."
    b. "This the best buy on the market at $220,000."
    c. "The lowest price that the seller will accept is $200,000."
    d. "The homeowners' association is active in school and education issues."

16. A real estate agent has the responsibility to disclose the following to third parties in a transaction:

    a. material facts
    b. buyers' preferences
    c. sellers' preferences
    d. home value stated in the latest appraisal

17. Representing both buyer and seller in a transaction may be legal in your state, but only if the following is accomplished first:

    a. full disclosure to the seller
    b. full disclosure to the buyer
    c. full disclosure to both seller and buyer
    d. never legal in any state

18. Salesperson Sam is licensed through broker Brandy. Which of the following statements is TRUE concerning their relationship?

    a. Sam is responsible to broker Brandy.
    b. Sam can work for another broker holding open houses on weekends.
    c. Sam must work for broker Brandy as an independent contractor.
    d. Broker Brandy must pay Sam the generally accepted commission rate for his work.

19. Which of the following statements is FALSE concerning a sub-agent?

    a. A sub-agent has powers that have been delegated by an agent.
    b. A sub-agent needs employment by the principal in order to perform.
    c. A sub-agent has fewer fiduciary duties to the principal than the agent.
    d. A sub-agent represents the principal.

20. The Federal Fair Housing Act (as amended) specifically addresses and prohibits discrimination on the basis of all of the following, except:

    a. race.
    b. religion.
    c. gender.
    d. sexual orientation.

21. The practice of trying to talk homebuyers of a protected group into buying in a specific area of a city, and other groups into other areas is known as:

    a. blockbusting.
    b. redlining.
    c. steering.
    d. testing.

22. Which of the following statements is FALSE concerning fraud?

    a. Fraud can involve the taking of a "legal right" from someone using a dishonest means.
    b. If multiple people are involved in a fraud, they may all be held liable for the whole amount.
    c. Perpetrators of fraud face criminal, not civil, punishment.
    d. For real estate agents, fraud can be not communicating an important fact that should have been communicated.

23. Which of the following acts would be prohibited under the federal fair housing laws?

    a. A Brazilian advertising his house for rent "to Brazilians only."
    b. A Greek Orthodox Church giving preferential treatment to parishioners in the rental of its housing.
    c. The American Legion operating a home for veterans as well as the general public.
    d. A Catholic organization renting out rooms in a guest house near one of its hospitals.

24. Which of the following rental practices would be permitted under federal fair housing laws?

    a. refusing to rent to a hearing-impaired woman with a service dog because the property does not allow dogs
    b. charging a family with a three-year old boy a higher security deposit than a family with no children
    c. refusing to rent a home to a person who was convicted of marijuana distribution
    d. a property manager disclosing to an owner that a prospective tenant is a minority

25. The first major civil rights legislation dealing with housing was passed in:

    a. 1826
    b. 1866
    c. 1875
    d. 1975

26. Which of the following types of disabled persons are not protected under the Americans with Disabilities Act (ADA)?

    a. people confined to wheelchairs
    b. HIV positive individuals
    c. alcoholics or drug users if enrolled in a recognized treatment program
    d. cancer patients

27. Dual agency is a situation where a seller and a buyer on the same transaction are represented by a single, individual agent. Which of the following statements about dual agency is INCORRECT?

    a. Dual agency is legal in all states.
    b. Dual agency is not allowed unless all represented parties agree to it.
    c. Beyond being informed, the parties must also give their written consent.
    d. Dual agency often has inherent conflicts of interest.

28. Which of the following would be classified as a latent defect?

    a. a cracked heat exchanger in the furnace
    b. a wobbly stair rail
    c. a large crack in the kitchen ceiling
    d. a chimney that is broken away from the house and leaning

29. The owner committed suicide inside the listed property, 1401 S. Elm, last year and the buyer's agent knows it. The buyer does not have any idea, however. Does the buyer's agent have an obligation to disclose this information?

    a. Yes. This is a material fact and the buyer's agent must disclose it.
    b. Yes. The suicide affects the desirability of the home.
    c. No, this is not important or material.
    d. Could be yes or no. State laws vary about disclosing facts of this nature.

30. Which of the following would probably NOT have to be disclosed as a material fact dealing with the condition of the electrical system in a home?

    a. Some copper wires have been stripped from the circuit breaker panel.
    b. Half of the bulbs in the chandelier in the foyer are burned out.
    c. The inside workings of the A/C units have been stolen.
    d. The spa tub in the master bathroom does not have a safety shut off.

Chapter 3
Appraisal and Market Analysis

Although there are many appraisal principles in performing the duties of a real estate agent, it is essential to note if you are not licensed as an appraiser, you cannot perform formal appraisals. Yet, it is important to comprehend the fundamentals of appraisal in creating market analyses, broker price opinions, and to be of assistance with the loan approval process.

DO YOU KNOW???

What is the *best* indicator of market value for any given property?
Could you explain the *principle of substitution* to a potential seller and how it affects price?
Which appraisal technique is most appropriate for an income producing property?
What is the relationship between *NOI, Rate of Return*, and *Value*?
If the subject property has a pool and the comparable does not, what adjustment is made?
These are just some of the topics covered in this chapter.

APPRAISAL

Generally considered, there are four (4) influences, or characteristics, of value. Note there are both physical as well as economic characteristics defined further in chapter five.

1. **Demand**: There must be a demand in the market for the property. If the market does not want the property, it has little or no value. *Effective Demand* refers to the market having the capacity or ability to purchase the property. If the market lacks adequate purchasing power to buy the property, the property's value is greatly diminished.

2. **Utility**: The property must be useful in the eyes of the market. If the real estate is not useful (not good for anything) it has little or no value.

3. **Scarcity**: The extent to which the supply in the marketplace will have an influence on the value. If there are vast numbers of similar properties, any one property's value is greatly diminished. Likewise, if there are few or no such properties, the value will increase.

4. **Transferability**: The property must be able to be sold (transferred) from one owner to another. If the property cannot be sold due to restrictions on its ownership, such as a burden on title, the property's value is greatly diminished.

Many refer to the acronym "DUST" to remember these four characteristics of value.

Definition of an appraiser: An individual licensed or certified by a state authority who is educated in the field of valuation and is skilled in estimating the current value of property. Appraisers must be licensed or certified to handle federally related work on residential real estate valued at $250,000 or more.

Definition of an appraisal: An estimate by an appraiser of the current price which will most probably be paid in a market consisting of informed buyers and sellers who are acting under normal and rational motivations. Such a transaction should be at *arm's length*, meaning there is no special pricing because of the relationship of the parties.

It is important to note that the appraiser is giving an *estimate* of value. The *best* indicator of market value is that price at which an informed seller and buyer ultimately agree to. This will not be known until there is an accepted offer on the property and the transaction closes.

The **Uniform Residential Appraisal Report (URAR)** is the standard format of a written appraisal as required by many institutions.

Appraisals may be ordered for any number of different and specific uses, not always just a step in the loan approval process. Appraisals may be ordered by different parties who have a present or potential future interest in the ***subject property***.

The Uniform Standards of Professional Appraisal Practice (USPAP) establishes the quality control standards applicable for real property, personal property, intangibles, and business valuation appraisal analysis and reports. USPAP was founded in the 1980s by a committee of appraisers representing the major U.S. and Canadian appraisal organizations.

Uses of Appraisals:

1. to verify value of collateral for lenders (this is the greatest use of appraisals).

2. to establish value for insurance companies using a "co-insurance" clause in their policies. In residential homeowner insurance policies, the insured is normally required to carry insurance equal to at least 80% of the property's value.

3. Internal Revenue Service – The IRS uses appraisals for "means testing" to determine if the value of property owned by a tax payer is consistent with the income reported by the tax payer.

4. Federal Institutions Reform, Recovery and Enforcement Act – Often referred to as the "Savings and Loan Bailout Act," this enactment determined that one of the causes of losses in the savings and loan industry was the absence of appraisals to verify the value of collateral securing loans made. From and after 1991, all "federally related" loans required an appraisal made by a state licensed or certified appraiser.

Appraisal principles:

1. ***Highest and best use*** – The appraiser must determine if the current use of the *subject property* (the property to be appraised) is the most profitable legal use for the property. If not, this must be

disclosed in estimating the value. Property should only be appraised considering differences, if any, between its current use and its highest and best use.

2. **Substitution** – The principle of substitution is based on the likelihood that the market will not pay substantially more for one property over another if the properties are substantially the same.

3. **Conformity** – The property should be consistent with the nature of its location and the other surrounding properties. If a property is significantly better than surrounding properties, its value will *regress* (*regression*) downward toward the value of the surrounding properties. If a property is significantly poorer than surrounding properties, the surrounding properties will tend to cause the subject property's value to *progress* (*progression*) upward as a result of the higher value of the surrounding properties.

4. **Supply and demand** – If there is an imbalance in the supply of or the demand for the subject property, this will be reflected in its market value.

$$\text{High Demand + Low Supply = Higher Values}$$
$$\text{Low Demand + High Supply = Lower Values}$$

5. **Contribution** – The appraiser must determine what the market will pay for a feature or amenity. The value the feature or amenity *contributes* is not necessarily equal to its cost.

> **Example:** If a typical swimming pool costs about $45,000 to construct, will the presence of a swimming pool add $45,000 to the value of the property when compared to similar properties without swimming pools? Normally the answer will be no.
>
> The appraiser must determine the amount of value contributed by the swimming pool. This is done by finding other properties which have recently sold and are similar to each other (not necessarily similar to the subject property) one of which has a pool, the other does not. If all other amenities are fairly equal, the difference in price paid should represent the value the market considers the pool adds. This is called a *paired sales analysis*.

6. **Increasing and decreasing returns** – Similar to the principle of contribution, the concept of increasing and decreasing returns takes a look at whether or not the cost of making an improvement or repair adds more to the value than making the improvement or repair costs. If it does not, then the improvement or repair should not be made, unless the owner is doing it for reasons other than increasing the value of the property.

> **EXAMPLE:** An owner is considering replacing the carpeting before putting the home on the market. The carpet is several years old and does show some sign of wear. The new carpet will cost $5,000. Will installing the carpet add at least $5,000 to the value of the house? If so, called the *law of increasing returns*, it should be done. If not, the *law of decreasing returns*, it should not be done.

7. **Plottage and assemblage** – If several smaller parcels could be assembled into one large parcel, often the resulting larger parcel will have a greater value than the sum of the values of the individual smaller parcels. If so, this increase in value is called **Plottage** and the act of bringing the parcels together is called **Assemblage**.

> **EXAMPLE**: A shopping center developer sees an opportunity, but the available parcel is not big enough for his shopping center. He is able to purchase several surrounding parcels and reach the needed land size. The act of assemblage brought together several small parcels which, when consolidated into the shopping center parcel, were much more valuable than they were individually. This increase in value is the plottage.

8. **Change and anticipation** – In some parts of a community, the available uses for parcels may be changing. Increased traffic may diminish the value of a property for residential, but increase its value as a commercial site. Local economic considerations may be affecting values. The opening of new industries or the closing of sources of employment can have a great effect on values, even though they may not have any direct impact on the physical property. The appraiser, in reaching a valid estimate of the market value of a property, must take these matters into consideration in reaching an estimate of value.

THE THREE APPRAISAL APPROACHES TO VALUE

There are three commonly accepted methods by which an appraisal can be performed. The method used is determined by the type of property being appraised.

I. **Cost approach** – The cost approach is based on the appraisal principle of substitution. The appraiser determines what it would cost to replace the subject property as if it were being built from the land up. Using informational sources available to the appraiser, the subject property is "rebuilt" on paper.

Normally, the appraiser uses **replacement cost** in this approach. Replacement cost represents the theoretical building of a substantially similar property, using currently available materials and construction techniques.

Reproduction cost would be used if the building were so unique that using available materials and techniques would not produce a substantially similar building. If the building were an historical structure having unique and features not commonly used in current-day construction, the appraiser would use reproduction costs.

The cost approach is used by the appraiser when the property does not produce income, and when there is not an established market for the type and use of the property.

The steps in the cost approach:

1. ***Determine the value of the land*** – This is done by looking to see what comparable parcels of land have recently sold for. This is the "land value." Remember, this approach calculates the cost to rebuild the property from the "ground" up, hence we start with the value of the land.

2. ***Determine the replacement cost of the structure*** – The appraiser would rely upon resource material to determine the cost of the materials and labor to construct a structure similar to the subject property. We acquired the land on paper and now we rebuild the structure on paper.

3. ***Determine accumulated depreciation*** – Depreciation is the reduction in value as a result of age, poor state of repair, poor design, etc. We depreciate the building of the comparable on paper to mirror the subject property. (***Appreciation*** is the increase in value.)

    In appraisal there are three (3) sources of depreciation, also referred to as ***obsolescence***:

    a. ***Physical depreciation*** – The property is in a bad state of repair, or some of the components of the property are nearly worn out.

    b. ***Functional depreciation*** – The property is out of style for the market place, or features of the property, although working properly, are inadequate for the property. As an example, the air conditioning system is too small for the property, although operating properly.

    c. ***External/Environmental/Locational/Economic Obsolescence*** – Four names for the same thing! The property is located in an "environment" or in a "location" in which the market will penalize the value, such as the subject property being adjacent to a waste facility.

    In considering the depreciation, the appraiser will determine if the depreciation is ***curable*** or ***incurable***. *Curable depreciation* consists of two (2) elements:

    1) that the depreciation can be cured (fixed or repaired), and
    2) that the added value to the property by curing the depreciation will be more than the cost to cure it

    Note that curable depreciation is not just that the depreciation can be remedied. The law of increasing returns must apply.

    Incurable depreciation dictates that the loss in value is either unfixable or not cost effective to make the repairs.

    a. ***Physical depreciation*** can be curable or incurable.
    b. ***Functional depreciation*** can be curable or incurable.
    c. *Environmental or locational obsolescence* is always incurable as you cannot move the land.

COST APPROACH		
Reproduction cost (new)		$100,000
Minus: Physical deterioration	$25,000	
Functional obsolescence	10,000	
Economic obsolescence	5,000	
Total accrued depreciation	$40,000	– 40,000
Depreciated value of improvements		$ 60,000
Add: Site value		20,000
Value indicated by *cost approach*		$ 80,000

4. *Subtract the accumulated depreciation from the replacement cost.*

5. *Add in the land value.* Land is not depreciable and is added after the structure's depreciation is subtracted.

EXAMPLE: If the appraiser were appraising a church, the cost approach would most likely be used as there are not many churches for sale in a community (market data comparison approach) and churches do not produce income (income approach). The appraiser determines that the land value for the parcel on which the church sits is $200,000. The appraiser estimates that the structure can be replaced at $185.00 per square foot and the size of the church is 10,000 square feet. The appraiser estimates the church structure has a useful life of 50 years and is not subject to any other type of depreciation other than physical depreciation due to its age. The church is 14 years old.

SOLUTION:

1. **Determine the value of the land**
   (through the market data approach): $200,000

2. **Determine the replacement cost** of the structure:
   $185 replacement cost per sq. ft. x 10,000 sq. ft. $1,850,000

3. **Determine accumulated depreciation**:
   $1,850,000 replacement cost ÷ 50 years useful life x 14 years of age
   $518,000

4. **Subtract the accumulated depreciation from the replacement cost**:
   $1,850,000 replacement cost - $518,000 accumulated depreciation $1,332,000

5. **Add in the land value**:
   $1,332,000 depreciated structure + $200,000 land $1,532,000

II. *Market data or comparable sales approach* – This approach is also based on the principle of substitution. This appraisal approach is the most common particularly for residential properties. In the market data approach, the appraiser looks for properties which have sold recently, in close proximity, and comparable in features and amenities to the subject property. What is considered proximate and recent is going to be community specific. In smaller markets, properties may not be selling as quickly as in larger markets. In some areas, proximity might be within a few miles, while in others it would be within a few blocks.

The appraiser is working with *comparables*. They are recently sold properties that resemble the subject property but are not identical, and therefore some adjustments may be required. The need for, and the extent to which adjustments are made, are judgment calls by the appraiser.

In making adjustments, the appraiser, based on the principle of contribution, determines the market value of features or amenities which differ between the comparable property and the subject. The appraiser will *adjust the price for which the comparable property sold upward*, if it lacked features or amenities which the subject property has. Conversely, if the comparable property has features or amenities which make it superior to the subject property, the appraiser will *adjust the price of the comparable downward.*

Note: The appraiser adjusts the sold price of the <u>comparable</u> upward or downward – **not the subject property**. There is no price of the subject to adjust! This is a commonly missed test item.
  If the comparable is superior, the appraiser will subtract the contribution for the amenity.
  If the comparable is inferior, the appraiser will add the contribution for the amenity.

Subject
3 bedrooms, 2 baths, and a pool

Comparable
3 bedrooms, 2.5 baths, and no pool

Sold for $387,500

EXAMPLE: The subject property has 3 bedrooms, 2 baths, and a pool. The comparable property which is 3 blocks from the subject property, sold two weeks ago for $387,500. (Note that the comparable is proximate and recent.) The "comp" has 3 bedrooms, 2.5 baths, and no pool. The appraiser, based upon a paired sales analysis, has determined the market will pay $32,000 for a pool and the value of a ½ bath is $2,200.

Subject
3 bedrooms, 2 baths, and a pool

Comparable
3 bedrooms, 2.5 baths, and no pool

Sold for $387,500

SOLUTION: The appraiser will make adjustments to the comparable to make the comparable look as much like the subject as possible. The number of bedrooms is the same with both homes, so there is no adjustment for bedrooms.

The comparable property is superior to the subject by an extra half bath, so the appraiser will subtract the contribution for a half bath, $2,200.

The comparable is inferior to the subject by having no pool. The comparable must have the contribution of the pool, $32,000, added to the sale price.

The appraiser makes the following adjustments to the comparable:
$387,500 Sale Price of Comparable + 32,000 Pool - $2,200 Half Bath = $417,300 Value

The adjustments made in this scenario were made on "physical" characteristics. It should be noted that the appraiser might make adjustments for:

- location
- financing conditions
- non-arm's length sale
- timeliness of closing date
- terms of the transaction
- distressed seller or property

> *If the comparable is superior, subtract.
> If the comparable is inferior, add.*

Here are some suggestions for choosing the best "comps":

Location, location, location – Choose comps as close to the subject property as possible. Sometimes, however, a comp on the next street might not be as good a choice as a house that is the same model and has the same amenities but is located in an adjacent subdivision. In most cases, homes should be compared against comps from the same development since these homes were usually built at the same time, by the same builder.

Use recent comps – The more recent the sale, the better the representation of the subject's value. As a general rule, try to use sales that have closed within the last three to four months, but if that is not feasible, you may have to go back further and make adjustments to the comps for time. Have prices been increasing or decreasing? Make your adjustments accordingly.

Price per square foot – This is a widely accepted concept that works well in practice. Looking at your comparables, divide the sale price by the living area square footage for each comp, and calculate an average price per square foot. Then apply that figure to the square footage in the subject property. Potential flaws with this method are location, condition, extras, upgrades, lot size, pools, etc. are not considered when using this method, so adjustments will need to be made for those differences.

Price per front foot – Whenever land dimensions are given, the *first* dimension is always the front footage – that border of the property which is adjacent to the road frontage. A lot 60' X 100' has a front footage of 60 feet. Property can be expressed as a dollar amount per front foot.

Amenities – Other factors also contribute to the subject property's value, in some instances, such as:

- curb appeal
- condition of exterior
- nearby parks and shops
- neighborhood condition
- traffic or noise
- school district

If you are a listing agent, on a listing appointment with a potential seller, remember that the seller probably already knows the value of the home and more than likely has already decided where to price it. The seller may have already met with one or more other agents, may have heard what the neighbors sold for, and may have used an online service like Zillow® to estimate the value.

III.   *The income approach*: This approach is based upon the value of an income producing property being a reflection of the Investor's required rate of return by investing in real estate. This method is most commonly utilized to determine the value of an income producing property.

The IRV circle: Commonly referred to as the "IRV circle," or sometimes the "T-bar," this helpful device helps students visualize what numbers to multiply or divide. The rule is, the part is a percentage of the total; or the smaller number is a percentage of the larger number. The beauty of the circle is, as long as you have any two of the three numbers, the circle will tell you the mathematic formula to follow.

This tool is used in several of the math problems contained throughout this textbook. As it relates to the income approach to valuation, IRV is used in the following way: "I" equals Income (net operating income); "R" equals Rate (*rate of return* or *capitalization rate*); and "V" equals Value. The theory is, if we know the net operating income of the property, and we know an investor's desired rate of return, we can plug those numbers into the IRV circle to estimate the value.

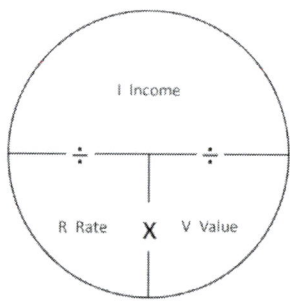

The **net operating income** (I) is the gross scheduled income of the property minus the property's annual operating expenses and also minus the annual vacancy and bad debt the property experiences. The following equation is used to determine NOI:

```
        GSI/PGI  (Gross Scheduled Income or Potential Gross Income)
      -   V/BD   (Vacancies and Bad Debts)
      =   EGI    (Effective Gross Income)
      -   OE     (Operating Expenses)
      =   NOI    (Net Operating Income)
```

Gross scheduled income, or **potential gross income**, reflects the income the property *should have earned* had there not been vacancies or bad debts and before the operating expenses were calculated.

Vacancies and bad debts are those losses to the gross income the owner incurred due to units being vacant for any length of time and for rents that should have been, but were not, collected. When expressed as a percentage, they reflect a percentage of the GSI.

Effective gross income, or *adjusted gross income*, is the income *actually collected or earned*. It is the GSI less the V/BD.

Operating expenses are costs associated with operating the building such as utilities, taxes, management fees, etc. and should not be confused with "debt service fees" which are incurred as a result of financing the original purchase of the property. When expressed as a percentage, they express a percentage of the EGI.

The "Rate (R)," also referred to as the *capitalization rate, cap rate, desired rate of return,* or *return on investment*, is the yield to the investor for investing in the income property. This rate may be determined based on the current income and value of the property, or the rate the investor demands. This rate will be compared to alternate investments such as stocks, bonds, mutual funds, and anything the investor may have an interest in.

```
GSI/PGI
 - V/BD
 =  EGI
 -  OE
 =  NOI
```

EXAMPLE: An apartment building has 300 units which rent for an average of $1400 per month. 8% of the units are vacant or represent bad debts. The operating expenses of the property are 28% of the rents received. An investor is considering the apartment but requires an annual return of 8.2% on any real estate investment he makes. How much would this investor be willing to pay for this property?

SOLUTION: Remembering this sequence of calculations will be essential in solving such problems.

GSI: 300 units x $1,400 avg. rent per month x 12 months = $5,040,000 GSI

V/BD: When expressed as a percentage, they reflect a percentage of the GSI.
$5,040,000 x .08 = $403,200 V/BD

EGI: $5,040,000 GSI - $ 403,200 V/BD = $4,636,800 EGI

OE: When expressed as a percentage, they are a percentage of the EGI. The question states, "The operating expenses of the property are 28% of the rents received." – That *is* 28% of the Effective Gross Income, the income actually collected.

$4,636,800 EGI x .28 OE = $1,298,304 Operating Expenses

$4,636, 800 EGI - $1,298,304 Operating Expenses = $3,338,496 NOI
The NOI is the "I" in IRV. NOI, when divided by the desired annual return of 8.2%, is the value of that property to that investor.
$3,338,496 NOI ÷ .082 Rate of Return = <u>$40,713,365</u> Value

If the appraiser is looking to determine the value using the income approach and there is no investor with the expectation of a certain rate of return, the appraiser will have to find the apparent rate of return required by investors in a given "class" of property. To do this, the appraiser will seek out income producing properties which have recently sold, contact the new owners and ask for the income, vacancy, and operating expense numbers to determine a market rate of return.

In our example, the appraiser would have been able to find that the property had sold for $40,713,365, and after talking with the owner or the property manager, would have been able to come up with a NOI of approximately $3,338,496. He would then divide the purchase price paid by the investor by the NOI to get an indicated return rate which the investor required (3,338,496 ÷ 40,713,365 = .082 or 8.2%).

The appraiser would find several such properties and then be able to determine what the apparent rate of return requirement was. With this information, a value for the subject property can be determined.

GRMs and GIMs: Abbreviations for *gross rent multiplier* and *gross income multiplier*, these two techniques are alternate methods for assessing the value of income producing properties from a single family home to an industrial property. The GRM is used on smaller, residential property while the GIM is used on income producing real estate on a grander scale. The appraiser knows the "multiplier" for the appraised market area through methods covered prior such as by looking at comparable sales, determining their income streams, and calculating the multipliers.

GRM = Sale Price ÷ Gross, Monthly, Rent
Value = Monthly Rental Income x GRM

> **EXAMPLE:** An appraiser is determining the value of a duplex which is generating a gross income for the seller of $450 per month per side. Using a GRM of 101, what will the appraiser determine the value to be?
>
> **SOLUTION**: Value = Monthly Rental Income x GRM
> Value = $900 (2 units at $450 per month each) x 101 = $90,900

GIM = Sale Price ÷ Gross, Annual, Rent or Income
Value = Annual Income x GIM

> **EXAMPLE:** A local toy store grosses an average monthly profit of $15,700. The assigned appraiser uses a GIM of 4 for smaller retail establishments in the area. What value will the appraiser likely assess to the toy store?
>
> **SOLUTION:** Value = Annual Income x GIM
> Value = $188,400 ($15,700 monthly gross income x 12 months) x 4 = $753,600

Note: GRMs are generally larger numbers and GIMs usually are smaller simply because GRMs are applied to monthly figures while GIMS are used for annual incomes.

SUMMARY: Appraisals are estimates of value made by persons who are skilled in making them. If possible, all three of the appraisal approaches should be used when doing an appraisal and often are. If the property is unique, the appraiser cannot use the market data approach; if the property produces no income, then the appraiser cannot use the income approach. Sometimes, the appraiser is limited to only the cost approach.

Reconciliation - There will be a difference in value between the various approaches and this is where the judgment of the appraiser comes into play. The appraiser must assign weights to the various results based on how relevant and reliable the findings under each approach proved out. Using a "weighted average" gives the appraiser a method of expressing confidence in the results given by the application of the various approaches.

MARKET ANALYSIS

A ***market analysis*** is taken from the data contained in the ***local multiple listing service***. Most MLS™ systems require member brokers to report listings as they are taken and post pertinent data such as the list price, the date of the closing of the sale, the amount of the sale price, and the days the property was on the market before it closed (the DOM). This information can then be used by both appraisers as well as other real estate professionals to complete a market analysis:

> *Sold Listings*: show recent trends in the prices of property; the comparables
> *Active Listings*: show properties currently for sale in the market; the competition
> *Expired Listings*: show properties that did not sell; usually overpriced
> *Days on Market*: shows the length of time from list date to sale

The appraiser or agent will rely on the *sold listings* most. This establishes the market value based on recent sales. Real estate professionals can use all the information above to develop a comparative market analysis (CMA) for their clients. If the market is trending up or down in price, this information is valuable to the seller and the buyer.

Active listings show sellers the current competition and suggest the range in which they should price their property for sale. Active listings show buyers what other similar properties are being offered for, and suggest the range of price they should offer. However, active listings do *not necessarily* represent market value as asking prices could be inflated.

Expired listings reflect properties which did not sell during the period of the listing. It is often because the price was too high. Sometimes the property did not sell because it did not show well or was not properly marketed.

Days on market shows sellers how long it took for the sale price to be achieved. Sellers generally want their property sold within a reasonably short period of time. DOM lets the seller know that perhaps they can attain a certain price if they are willing to wait as long as other sellers had to.

Pending sales are formerly active listings that are now under contract but not yet closed. Because they have not closed, you will likely not know the sale price to use for your analysis. Most listing agents are trained not to disclose the actual sale price until the transaction closes. If the house should go back on the market, the sellers will have a difficult time getting a better price if their prior accepted price is public knowledge. However, pending sales do indicate the direction the market is moving and the active listings that were chosen by buyers in the market.

Withdrawn listings – are properties that were taken off the market for a variety of reasons such as the seller's decision not to move, the market was not willing to meet the seller's price, or the seller terminated the listing relationship with the broker. The information from these properties could be of some use as well.

Summary of Comparable Listings

February 05, 2010

This page summarizes the comparable listings contained in this market analysis.

AGE DESC

Active listings

Address	L/S Price	Bd	Bth	Sqft	$/Sq	Age	MLS#	Date	DOM
21495 W 122Nd Street	$179,900	3	3.1			6-10 Years	1609356	04/27/2009	278
21439 W 121St Street	$185,000	4	2.1			6-10 Years	1647034	12/16/2009	51
12289 S Crest Drive	$194,500	3	2.1			3-5 Years	1650969	01/21/2010	15
21212 W 119Th Place	$197,500	3	2.1			6-10 Years	1649398	01/12/2010	24
	$189,225	3.3	2.4						92

Pending listings

Address	L/S Price	Bd	Bth	Sqft	$/Sq	Age	MLS#	Date	DOM
21233 W 119Th Place	$179,900	4	3.1	1,661	$108	6-10 Years	1639847		70
12296 S Clinton Street	$210,000	3	2.2			6-10 Years	1645314		37
	$194,950	3.5	2.7	1,661	$108				54

Sold listings

Address	L/S Price	Bd	Bth	Sqft	$/Sq	Age	MLS#	Date	DOM
21443 W 119Th Place	$187,000	3	2.1			3-5 Years	1636718	12/21/2009	48
21467 W 120Th Street	$189,950	3	2.1	1,575	$121	3-5 Years	1628598	10/15/2009	13
	$188,475	3.0	2.1	1,575	$121				31

Median: $188,475
Average: $190,469

Broker price opinion: This tool to determine value is requested by a third party such as the lender in the case of foreclosure and by a relocation company in the event of an executive transfer that will result in a buyout. "BPOs" are generally performed by licensed real estate agents and brokers for a nominal fee. The report is more detailed than a CMA generally because the party making the request is not familiar with the subject property or the area.

Broker price opinion:

ITEM	SUBJECT	CLOSED SALES					
		COMPARABLE NO. 1		COMPARABLE NO. 2		COMPARABLE NO. 3	
Address	123 MAIN ST	490 MILLER AVE		190 MAIN ST		325 CRANE ST	
Proximity to Subject		0.15 MILES		0.02 MILES		0.46 MILES	
Original List Price	$	$ 139,900		$ 144,900		$ 145,000	
List Price When Sold	$	$ 130,000		$ 128,900		$ 142,000	
Sales Price	$	$ 130,000		$ 127,000		$ 142,000	
Sales Date		01/09/10		02/08/10		12/14/09	
Days on Market		88		169		104	
VALUE ADJUSTMENTS (Use the following codes for the adjustments: S=Superior E=Equal I=Inferior U=Unknown)							
DESCRIPTION	DESCRIPTION	DESCRIPTION	ADJ	DESCRIPTION	ADJ	DESCRIPTION	ADJ
Above Grade Room Count	Total # of Rooms 6 Bdrm 2 Baths 1	Total # of Rooms 6 Bdrm 2 Baths 1.5		Total # of Rooms 6 Bdrm 2 Baths 1		Total # of Rooms 6 Bdrm 2 Baths 1.5	
Gross Living Area	Sq. Ft. 850	Sq. Ft. 890	Code	Sq. Ft. 844	Code	Sq. Ft. 950	Code
Sales or Financing Concessions		NONE	E	NONE	E	NONE	E
Location							
Site/Lot Size	.10 ACRES	.15 ACRES	S	.10 ACRES	E	.07 ACRES	E
Landscaping							
Design and Appeal	AVERAGE	AVERAGE	E	AVERAGE	E	AVERAGE	E
Age (number of yrs. since house was built)	80	70	E	81	E	77	E
Overall Condition	AVERAGE	AVERAGE	E	AVERAGE	E	AVERAGE	E
Garage/Carport	1 CAR ATT	NONE	I	1 CAR ATT	E	1 CAR ATT	E
Porch, Patio Deck, Pool, Fence	NONE	NONE	E	NONE	E	NONE	E
Overall Rating/Est. $ Value of Adjustments		$0.00	E	$0.00	E	$0.00	E
Indicate Property Most Comparable to Subject (Check One)		☐		☒		☐	
COMMENTS:							

Chapter 3: Appraisal and Market Analysis
End of Chapter Quiz

1. Outdated, square tile countertops would likely be considered:

    a. incurable physical depreciation.
    b. curable environmental depreciation.
    c. incurable functional obsolescence.
    d. curable functional obsolescence.

2. Which of the following would be a consideration in appraising property using the Market Data Approach?

    a. terms of the sale
    b. original purchase price
    c. annual income of the property
    d. depreciation

3. The first step in the income approach to valuation is:

    a. calculate the potential gross income of the property
    b. factor in the vacancies and bad debts
    c. evaluate comparable sales
    d. obtain the property's operating expenses

4. An appraiser is assessing the value of a commercial office building that earns $35,000 per quarter after vacancies and expenses. The appraiser uses a capitalization rate of 6.75% for this type of property. What is the likely valuation of the building?

    a. $518,518
    b. $2,074, 074
    c. $6,222,222
    d. There is not enough information.

5. If the appraiser in question #4 were using a gross income multiplier of 15, what would the value be?

    a. $525,000
    b. $2,100,000
    c. $6,300,000
    d. There is not enough information.

6. Depreciation is applied to:

    a. the land.
    b. the building.
    c. the land and the building.
    d. neither the land or the building.

7. Which of the following is considered economic depreciation?

    a. The interior and exterior needs painting and the carpet and padding need replacement.
    b. The home backs up to a main thoroughfare.
    c. The floor plan is strange and not desirable to buyers who see the property.
    d. all of these

8. The Harrigans write an offer of $175,000 on a home listed for $210,000 because there are two others available in the same subdivision for $179,900 and $175,900. The Harrigans are probably basing their offer on the theory of:

    a. highest and best use. (seller)
    b. conformity. — when listing a price
    c. substitution. — (buyer) when making an offer
    d. contribution.

9. Your land is valued at $240,000 an acre. It is determined by the appraiser that your building's replacement cost is $210,000. If your building sits on ¼ of an acre and the depreciation was calculated at 24%, what is the value of your property?

    a. $50,400
    b. $159,600
    c. $219,600
    d. $399,600

10. Which approach is best suited for a special purpose structure such as the local YMCA building?

    a. cost approach
    b. income approach
    c. market data approach
    d. any of these

11. Which of the following is NOT one of the generally accepted characteristics of value?

    a. demand
    b. use
    c. scarcity
    d. time

12. An out-of-state investor sees a 4-plex with you, as his agent. After you have provided him the net operating income of $677,000, he tells you he will not accept a return on his investment less than 9% annually. What is the investor's offer likely to be? (Rounded)

    a. $60,000
    b. $615,000
    c. $675,000
    d. $7.5 Million

13. With which type of income producing property would a GRM likely NOT be appropriate?

    a. shopping center
    b. free-standing office suite
    c. single family home
    d. a duplex

14. The subject property being appraised has a family room, but the comparable does not. Virtually all other aspects of the comparable are similar. What adjustment will the appraiser make?

    a. adjust the subject upward for the contribution of the room
    b. adjust the subject downward for the contribution of the room
    c. adjust the comparable upward for the contribution of the room
    d. adjust the comparable downward for the contribution of the room

15. What term would best indicate that the buyer and seller had no special relationship, such as being related, friends, or business partners, and therefore the sale reflected true market value?

    a. arm's length
    b. fiduciary
    c. unrelated
    d. competitive

16. A comparable property just sold for $395,000 and had 400 square feet more than the subject, but the subject had an additional half bath that the comparable did not. If the contribution is $100 per square foot and $5,500 for a half bath, how will the appraiser reflect the differences?

    a. Adjust the subject property upward $40,000 and then downward $5,500.
    b. Adjust the comparable property upward $40,000 and then downward $5,500.
    c. Adjust the comparable property downward $40,000 and then upward $5,500.
    d. Adjust the subject property downward $40,000 and then upward $5,500.

17. What is the name of the standard form of appraisal required by most lenders and governmental agencies?

    a. Uniform Residential Appraisal Report
    b. Uniform Reconciliation Appraisal Report
    c. Standard Real Estate Appraisal
    d. Market Valuation and Appraisal

18. Which method of valuation would factor in reproduction costs if applicable?

    a. cost approach
    b. income capitalization approach
    c. sales comparison approach
    d. none of these

19. The developer of her property intends to build a movie theatre but has assessed there is not enough property for ample parking. There are two lots immediately north of the property she can acquire for approximately $80,000 each. The process of her purchasing the properties and combining them legally with the land she currently owns is known as:

    a. plottage.
    b. progression.
    c. contribution.
    d. assemblage.

20. What might be the cause of an appraisal to be ordered?

    a. to verify value of real estate collateral for lenders
    b. to establish value for insurance companies
    c. to determine if the value of property owned by a tax payer is consistent with the income reported by the tax payer
    d. all of these

Chapter 4
Financing

A better understanding of financing will allow you to better aid and assist your clients with their real estate transactions. This unit will cover the language of financing and offer extensive explanations and examples allowing you to best assimilate the information.

DO YOU KNOW???

Are you familiar with the three basic types of mortgages?
Can you explain the workings of private mortgage insurance to a client?
Do you have an understanding of *Loan-to-Value* and *Debt-to-Income* ratios?
Are you familiar with *Fannie Mae, Freddie Mac, FHA* and *VA* and how they pertain to each different loan?
These are just some of the topics covered in this chapter.

FINANCING VOCABULARY

Financing – is simply the borrowing of money. It may be borrowing from a private party or a professional lender. The borrowing may be unsecured (no collateral, only the credit worthiness of the borrower is considered), or the borrowing may be secured (real or personal property is given to assure repayment of the loan).

Since most buyers do not have sufficient assets to pay cash for their real estate purchases, financing becomes a critical and valuable tool for the real estate professional.

Monetary lien or monetary encumbrance –giving another the right to repossess or foreclose against real or personal property and to sell the property to pay that debt or obligation owed to the lienholder.

Collateral – the real or personal property upon which the lien is given to secure the borrowing.

Purchase money mortgage – any portion of the purchase price which the seller "carries." In real estate, the owner of the property being sold may be in the position to act as the lender. In fact what is happening is the seller is willing to wait for the payment of the purchase price over time from the buyer.

This could be accomplished through the use of a ***promissory note*** and ***deed of trust*** or ***mortgage***, or by a ***contract for deed***. It may be a first mortgage, second mortgage, any ***position*** of mortgage. Whatever the "transactional documents" are, the money which the Seller is carrying is a purchase money mortgage.

Note – or a promissory note, is a legal document which creates and identifies the debt. The note will contain the following:

- borrower's name
- lender's name
- amount borrowed
- interest rate, or the method in which the interest is to be calculated if a variable rate
- date the first payment is due and the frequency of payments thereafter
- term or length of time the borrower has to repay the loan
- amount of the final payment and due date if the loan is not a fully amortizing loan
- address to which payments are to be sent
- note may reference any collateral documents such as a Mortgage or Deed of Trust
- note may contain other provisions to which the Borrower has agreed

The note is a contract and the equivalent of an I.O.U. It is the document which creates the debt between the borrower and the lender. It is the *evidence of the debt*. A note is a **negotiable instrument**, meaning the lender may sell the note without consent from the borrower in order to liquidate the lender's funds.

The note does not create a lien against property. Should the borrower default on the note, and the lender has no documents creating a lien against property of the borrower, the only recourse the lender has is a suit against the borrower for *specific performance* of the note.

Interest – the compensation paid by the borrower to the lender for the period during which the borrower has use of the lender's money.

> **EXAMPLE:** Interest is stated as a percentage of the loan and is calculated on an annual basis. If John borrows $100.00 at 10% interest to be paid in full at the end of one year. John would pay the lender the **principal** of $100.00, plus 10% of the principal ($100.00 x .10 = $10.00) for a total payment to the lender of $110.00.

When doing interest calculations, it is necessary to determine the current outstanding balance on the loan and then multiply it by the annual interest rate to calculate the interest for one year. If the question deals with the monthly interest, divide the annual interest by 12 to get the amount of interest for one month.

Long term mortgage rates are driven by the yield on the 10-year treasury bond. The relationship is not a direct one, but if the yield goes up or down, then mortgages rates will probably do the same. If you pay attention to the stock market, when the market is doing well, that usually means the opposite for mortgage rates and when the market is doing poorly, it usually means interest rates are looking good.

Prime rate – the prime rate is the interest rate charged by banks to their most creditworthy customers (usually the most prominent and stable business customers). The rate is almost always the same amongst major U.S. banks. Adjustments to the prime rate are usually made by the banks at the same time, but the prime rate does not adjust on any regular basis. Although the prime rate is probably the most widely quoted rate, it has very little to do with the residential mortgage rates being offered. Generally speaking, the only residential mortgages which are based on the prime rate are home equity lines of credit.

Usury – Many states have established the maximum amount of interest a lender may charge on certain types of loans. To the extent that the interest charged exceeds the statutory amount, it is referred to as *usurious* and cannot be collected. Not all states have such provisions.

Discount points – One point equals 1% of the loan amount. The IRS considers a point to be a form of interest paid upfront instead of over the term of the loan. As a result, points paid on a mortgage loan are generally tax deductible. According to the IRS, the following terms are often used to describe points: discount points, loan discount points, maximum loan charges, and loan origination fees.

Discount points are charged when there is a cost to receive a certain rate or to buy a rate down (***buydown***) and hence the name "discount."

Hypothecation – the pledging of property as security for a debt but retaining possession and use of the property so long as the debt is being performed as agreed. Hypothecation is the most common form of secured lending arrangements. An example would be, you buy your home using a 30-year loan. You may have possession and use of the home so long as you are performing as agreed on your home loan; this is a *hypothecation* of your home.

Mortgage – a contract which creates a ***monetary lien*** against real property. Mortgages are most frequently used in the states east of the Rocky Mountains. The westerners use deeds of trust described next. Some think of mortgages as the "what if?" document where the question "what if the borrower stops making payments?" is addressed.

There are two parties to the mortgage; the ***mortgagor*** who is the borrower, and the ***mortgagee*** who is the lender. Throughout this course and in practice, terms are used that refer to persons as either an "or" or an "ee." The best way to keep track of who is who is to remember that the "or" is person giving and the "ee" is the person receiving.

---

or : gives
ee : receives

the "*or*" is the giver (the giv"*or*")
the "*ee*" is the receiver ("the rec"*ee*"ver)

The mortgagor is the giver of the mortgage.
The mortgagee is the receiver of the mortgage.

The borrower is the mortgagor and the lender is the mortgagee.

That last sentence has confused thousands over the years: "The borrower is the mortgagor and the lender is the mortgagee." No, that is *not* a typo. The mortgage is a document that offers the property for the lender to take control of, and dispose of, to recover the lender's funds should the borrower default on the loan. Commonly misspoken in society, the borrower does *not* apply for a *mortgage;* the borrower applies for a *loan*. The borrower *gives* the mortgage in order to *receive* the financing. Therefore, the borrower is the mortgagor and the lender is the mortgagee.

The borrower, by executing a mortgage with the lender is giving the lender a *lien* against the borrower's property. If the borrower fails to perform under the note which is *secured by* the mortgage, the lender may foreclose against the property and sell it applying the proceeds from the foreclosure sale to the outstanding balance due.

Deed of Trust – is a contract which creates a *monetary lien* against real property. Deeds of trust are most frequently used in the states west of the Rocky Mountains. In a deed of trust, there are three parties:

1. the ***trustor*** (the borrower)
2. the ***trustee*** (an independent third party chosen by the lender)
3. the ***beneficiary*** (the lender)

In a deed of trust, the trustee holds **naked title** to the property and has been given the **power of sale** by the trustor (borrower). This arrangement is for the benefit of the lender who is the beneficiary of the trust and who would receive the funds obtained by the trustee should the power of sale be exercised.

Under the deed of trust, nothing happens unless the borrower fails to perform. If the borrower *defaults,* the lender may order the trustee to exercise the power of sale and commence foreclosure proceedings against the property.

The net effect of either a mortgage or a deed of trust is the same. Each creates a lien against the property and both allow the sale of the property securing the note with the proceeds being applied to the outstanding interest and principal balance.

The borrower's obligations in a mortgage or deed of trust:

- make the required payments of principal and interest when due
- pay the property taxes when due
- keep the property insured against loss through fire, windstorm, and other casualties
- keep the property in good repair
- make no alterations to the property which would decrease its value

Priority – You have, no doubt, heard people talk in terms of "carrying a second mortgage" or "applying for a second," but what does that really mean? Second to what? Why not "third" or "fourth"? With mortgages, priority refers to the order in which these mortgages were recorded. Their priority governs which lender will be paid first, then second, etc., in the event of a foreclosure sale. A second mortgage really means that it is a second mortgage on a specific property recorded after the recordation of a first mortgage.

A **subordination agreement** is an agreement between two lien holders to swap priority position.

Equity loans, or home equity lines of credit (HELOC), may be done when the homeowner has a substantial amount of equity in the property and wishes to use that equity (by borrowing against it) for some other purpose.

Impound accounts – Also called escrow accounts, an impound account is established to hold funds for the future payment of the borrower's property taxes and casualty insurance. The lender or the servicer of the loan is the holder of the account. When a mortgage transaction closes, funds will be collected by the escrow company to make the initial payments for taxes and insurance. In most cases the lender will require 15 months collected upfront for the borrower's casualty insurance and three to six months will be collected for property taxes. When these funds are collected and the transaction closes, the escrowee will prepare a check directly to the insurance company to pay the first year's premium in full. The remaining three months that was collected will begin the borrower's impound account. The funds that are collected for the property taxes will either go directly into the impound account or a portion may be paid directly to the county to cover the current taxes depending on when the next required payment is due.

From that point forward, when the borrower makes a mortgage payment, part of the payment is designated to the impound account and will continue to build a surplus so that when the next year's premium is due for insurance, there are enough funds in the account to cover that payment. The same is done with the property taxes. When each quarter's tax is due, the lender will send a check directly to the county on behalf of the borrower. The borrower will never have to pay a payment directly to the homeowner's insurance company or for property taxes if the loan is impounded.

The reason this is done is the lender wants to be absolutely sure the property taxes and casualty insurance is paid. By requiring the borrower to impound these funds, the lender makes the payments to assure they are paid. If property taxes were to go unpaid, they become a priority lien before the lender and would be paid first in a foreclosure sale creating a potential shortage for the lender. If the property were destroyed and there were no insurance, the lender's collateral is also destroyed.

Prepayment penalties – are associated with loans that are paid off early, before the end of the term. When there is a prepayment penalty, it is typically only for a designated period of time such as within the first two to three years. Prepayment penalties were very common with *sub-prime* loans. Most conventional loans in today's market do not have prepayment penalties. They are prohibited on mortgage loans that are insured by the government.

Title theory versus lien theory – In title theory states, the mortgagor (borrower) gives the mortgagee (lender) legal title and retains equitable title. Legal title is returned to the mortgagor upon full payment of the debt.

Lien theory states the mortgagor (borrower) retains legal and equitable title. The mortgagee (lender) has only a lien on the property as security for the debt. In order for the lender to take the property for sale, foreclosure proceedings must be initiated to obtain the legal title.

Naked title versus legal title vs. equitable title – *Naked title* means that the holder does not actually own the property, nor may he occupy or enjoy the right of ownership. The holder does have the *power to sell* the property under the terms of an agreement, such as the right of a trustee in a deed of trust.

Legal title means that the holder *does* legally own the property. However, if legal title has been separated from *equitable title*, the legal owner of the property does not have the right to possess and enjoy the rights of ownership unless the owner of the *equitable title* fails to do whatever is required, such as failing to perform the obligations in a contract for deed.

Equitable title means the holder has the right to possess and enjoy all of the rights of ownership, but, if all they own is equitable title, the title records will not show the holder as the owner, but will show the owner of legal title.

In most real estate transactions, legal title and equitable title are held by the same person.

Contract for deed – is a form of seller financing. In the contract for deed, sometimes called a *Land Contract*, the **vendor** (seller) retains *legal title* to the property but transfers e*quitable title* to the **vendee** (buyer). So long as the buyer performs in the making of payments and whatever else may be required, the buyer continues to enjoy equitable title. However, should the buyer fail in the required performance under the contract for deed, the seller (as holder of legal title) may declare default, dispossess the buyer from the property, and retake equitable title for himself. If the buyer does perform as required, then at the conclusion of performance, the seller is obligated to convey legal title to the buyer where it will join with the equitable title the buyer already holds.

Amortization – Amortization is the pattern in which the principal of a loan is paid.

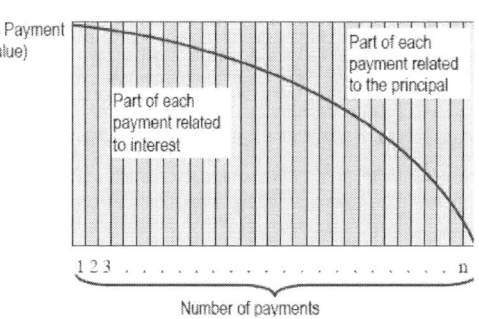

Level payment, fully amortizing loan – is the most common in residential lending. The amount of the payment remains the same over the life of the loan, however the components of principal and interest change with each payment. As the balance of the loan is reduced by payment of the principal, the amount for interest will decrease with each payment. This process causes the loan to pay off at the stated term.

Balloon Loan – amortizes at the stated interest rate and term, as if it were a fully amortizing loan, but requires an early payoff.

EXAMPLE: A loan stated as a "30 due in 5" means that the loan will amortize on a 30 year amortization schedule, but the entire outstanding principal balance will be due at the end of 5 years.

Straight loan (also called a "term loan" or an "interest only loan") – the borrower pays only interest during the life of the loan. At the end of term, the entire principal balance is paid off in full. There is no amortization.

COMMON CLAUSES FOUND IN MORTGAGES OR DEEDS OF TRUST

Acceleration clause – allows the lender to call all payments due if the borrower defaults. This allows for a foreclosure of the entire outstanding balance. This clause "accelerates" the time for which payment is due to *now*.

Assignment clause – gives the borrower notice that the lender will likely be transferring the mortgage or deed of trust to another party sometime after the closing on the loan. As a mortgage or deed of trust is a contact, the lender wants to be sure there is no problem with the borrower if the lender assigns the contract to another investor or to the *Secondary Mortgage Market*.

Due on sale clause (sometimes referred to as an *alienation clause*) – The lender informs the borrower, in advance, that the lender will not permit an assignment of the borrower's obligations under the note, or interest in the property, unless the lender is paid in full. As the name implies, the loan is due on sale – if there is a sale, the loan is due. "Alienation" refers to alienating oneself from the property.

Prepayment clause – informs the borrower under what circumstances the lender will accept payment, in whole or in part, before the due date. In some cases, the lender is happy to have the loan paid off sooner than planned such as when opportunities exist to use the capital at a higher yield. But should the Lender not want the loan prepaid, such as when such opportunities do not exist, the issue will be addressed in the prepayment clause.

Assumption clause – describes under what circumstances, if any, the lender will allow another person to assume the mortgage or deed of trust. *Assumption* of a mortgage means a person is acquiring property with an underlying loan and agrees to personally take over financial responsibility for the mortgage. Commonly found provisions of an assumption clause include no assumption permitted, assumption only with qualifying by the new party, assumption with the payment of a fee, or no restrictions – *Fully and Freely Assumable*.

Defeasance clause – requires the lender to issue a *satisfaction of mortgage* indicating the loan has been paid in full.

COMMON TYPES OF LENDING INSTRUMENTS

Each loan type will have a note and will be secured by either a mortgage or a deed of trust. *For simplicity, the terms "mortgage" and "deed of trust" will be interchangeable within this section.*

Blanket mortgage – will cover multiple parcels and is common in subdivision development financing.

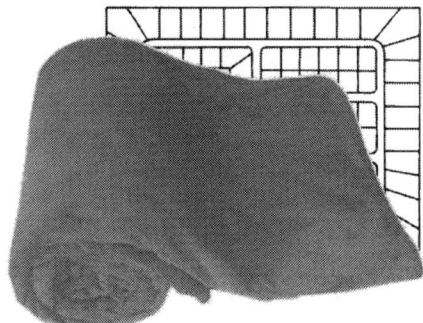

This loan will have a **partial release clause** allowing the builder to pull the parcel sold "out from under" the blanket mortgage.

In most cases, there was one loan to purchase the entire parcel of land which was later subdivided into lots and perhaps built upon. As the homes were completed and sold, the individual parcels of land had to be *released* from the blanket mortgage that encumbered them in o order to deliver clear title to the purchasers.

Package mortgage – This instrument provides financing for both the real estate and the personal property that goes with it. Common examples are loans that cover major appliances like refrigerators, washers and dryers, window treatments, equipment, furniture, etc. that are all included in the purchase price.

Open end mortgage or equity line of credit (HELOC) – The borrower establishes a line of credit secured by the real estate and can make draws against the line, much like using a credit card. In other scenarios, the loan is considered "open ended" for future advances from the lender usually to a pre-determined amount.

Construction Loan – As the name implies, a loan for construction purposes, usually a short term loan, two to five years depending on the length of time required, to build the project. It is considered *interim financing* until the builder can secure permanent financing until the project is complete. The developer makes periodic *draws* against the maximum loan amount as construction progresses. The lender normally inspects each phase of construction to assure there is enough construction to serve as collateral. Normally the funds can only be used for construction of the project which is the collateral for the construction mortgage. This is considered a riskier loan and is priced accordingly. These are usually interest-only loans.

Wrap around mortgage or all inclusive deed of trust – a form of seller financing (purchase money mortgage) available only where there is no existing *due on sale* clause in the original mortgage document. The seller still owes on the original mortgage (the **underlying mortgage**) and continues to make those payments. The buyer makes payments to the seller for the new amount financed as a purchase money mortgage.

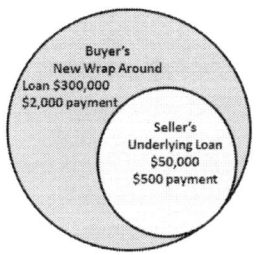

EXAMPLE: The seller has a $50,000 balance on his mortgage. He sells his house for $325,000 and takes a down payment from the buyer of $25,000

and creates a $300,000 wrap around mortgage. The buyer is paying the seller based on the $300,000 wrap, and the seller continues to make payments on the $50,000 underlying mortgage.

Why is it called a *wrap around*? The new loan given by the seller to the buyer wraps around the existing loan. Where did the seller get the $300,000 to loan to the buyer? $50,000 of it is the pre-existing lender's money. As the buyer makes the payments to the seller, the seller makes the payments to his lender. The seller is only lending $250,000 of his own money which may come from equity in the property or funds from another source. The wrap around is usually done at a higher interest rate and is ideal for a buyer who cannot obtain financing elsewhere.

If the original loan has a due on sale clause, this cannot be legally done, unless the lender were to allow it. Remember that the due on sale language says, "If the property is sold, the loan is due." This is indeed a sale.

Graduated payment mortgage – most often seen when interest rates are high and/or the borrower is not able to qualify at the higher interest rate. The lender makes the loan with a provision that the starting payments are lower than what would otherwise be required to pay the principal and interest on the loan. The borrower agrees to increase the payment amount each year for the next two or three years until reaching the required payment. 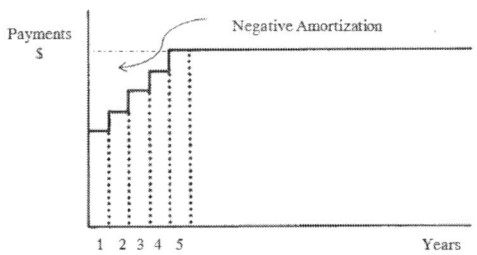 During this time, the unpaid interest is added to the unpaid balance (***negative amortization***). This will result in an increase in the size of the loan balance until the agreed increase in payment is sufficient to amortize the loan.

Adjustable rate mortgage (ARM) – First becoming widely used in the high interest era of the late 1970's, the ARM was designed to have interest rates that fluctuated with the lender's cost of funds. The ARM has the following elements:

1. **Index** – the cost of funds indicator used by the lender. This may be the prime rate, the T-Bill rate, the 10-year treasury bond rate, the 11th district federal reserve funds rate, the London Interbank Offering Rate (LIBOR), or any other gauge or benchmark the lender and borrower choose. As the index rises or decreases, the interest rate will adjust accordingly.

2. **Margin** – this represents the *profit and overhead* the lender wants to earn above the costs of funds. This will be stated in the note and will not be changed to another amount for the life of the loan. The margin is added to the index to calculate the interest rate (*Desired Pay Rate*).

INDEX + MARGIN = RATE

3. **Interval** – represents the frequency in which the interest paid by the borrower will change. Most ARMS have six month or one year intervals. The interval will be stated in the note and will not be changed to another period for the life of the loan.

4. **Cap** – the maximum the interest rate can change in any interval. This will be stated in the note and will not be changed for the life of the loan.

    EXAMPLE: The borrower of an ARM loan is currently paying 6% interest the first year. The *annual cap* is stated in the note as being 1%, meaning the rate cannot go up more than 1% in any interval. If the:

    index is 4%
    margin is 2% (4% + 2% = 6% initial interest rate)
    and the index moves up to 5.5%
    and the margin is always 2%, then the
    new interest rate *would be* 7.5%, but
    the ARM has a cap of 1%, so the most the rate can increase to is 7% (6% + 1%)

    > *In the absence of an index and a cap, borrowers could be subject to arbitrary interest rates at the whim of the lenders. The lenders are limited as to what an adjusted rate can be because of these two elements.*

5. **Ceiling and floor**: Sometimes called the *lifetime cap*, the ceiling represents the maximum interest rate the borrower can be charged anytime during the life of the loan. Likewise, the *floor* represents the minimum interest rate the borrower will have to pay anytime during the life of the loan. This will be stated in the note and will not be changed for the life of the loan. In most ARM's, this will be 5% to 6% over the initial rate.

    EXAMPLE: Working with the same prior example, the loan had an initial rate of 6%. If the ceiling were 5% and the floor were 2%, the highest the rate could *ever* go would be 11%. Likewise, the lowest the rate could ever be is 4%.

    The ceiling and floor actually protect both parties in the event the index spikes dramatically in either direction. They cap the liability the borrower will pay or the lender will receive.

6. **Conversion** – Often, an ARM will give the borrower the option of *converting* to a fixed rate mortgage at various periods during the loan. Usually, these are at 3 years, 5 years, and 7 years. If the borrower thinks it is in her best interest to convert, she may do so at any of these anniversary dates. Most ARMS allow full pre-payment without penalty, so if she chooses to, she may either convert to a fixed rate at an anniversary date or pay it off and replace it with a new loan whenever she wishes.

7. **Reverse annuity mortgage (RAM)** – designed mainly for older homeowners who own their homes free and clear, or who have very large equities, but who do not wish to sell or cash out the equity in their homes in one lump sum. The RAM lender will pay to the RAM borrower an agreed upon sum each month. In effect, the RAM borrower is drawing out equity in the home monthly. Taxes and insurance must still be paid by the homeowner.

The RAM loan will be paid off upon the occurrence of:

1. sale of the home
2. death of the borrower
3. expiration of the loan

Normally, the RAM is for a limited period of time, 5, 10 or 15 years. This loan allows the borrowers to decide when their home no longer fits their needs. With the aging population, this may become a popular loan and offer an alternative to senior citizens feeling forced to sell their homes to supplement their retirement income.

Loaning seniors money when they have no ability to repay has potential for abuse and predatory lending. These loans have also been highly scrutinized as they have led to the forced sale of the property as the borrower has no way of paying off the loan after expiration.

THE LOAN PROCESS

Pre-qualification – an interview, in person or by phone, between the lender and the borrower. The lender will typically obtain consent and run a credit report to look for red flags. Calculations as to debt to income ratios and debt to housing expense ratios are done.

Pre-approval – Assuming the lender is convinced the loan can be done, the lender will prepare a preapproval which demonstrates the borrower's ability to qualify subject to conditions being satisfied. Often done in the form of a pre-approval letter, this document strengthens the buyer's position as the buyer negotiates a purchase agreement with the seller.

Loan application (1003) – The formal loan application can only be taken when a property has been identified and the borrower is in contract. Borrowers on all types of loans in today's current mortgage market are required to provide information in order to process and determine the qualification of the loan, including:

- tax returns and W-2's or 1099's for the most recent 2 years
- provide employment information for the most recent 2-year period
- copies of identification

- most recent 30 days of pay stubs
- if properties are owned, mortgage statements and proof of insurance and taxes for each
- rental agreements of investment properties
- HOA information
- asset information
- divorce decrees, if applicable
- bankruptcy documents, if applicable

Each lender has different requirements and each borrower has unique circumstances.

Processing – The processors will verify all information provided to the loan officer, order the appraisal as well as title documentation, flood certifications, insurance, verify employment and asset account information, obtain any missing documentation, and lock the rate prior to underwriting.

Underwriting – This is the final review and decision making process pertaining to granting the loan.

Closing – Once the approval from underwriting is obtained, processing will request loan docs to be sent to title who will arrange for the borrower to sign. The borrower will deliver their funds to title. Loan documents are returned to lender for final review and then wires the loan funds to escrow. Escrow sends all documents to the county for recordation and the transaction is considered closed.

SOURCES OF MONEY FOR LENDING

Loans are a form of investment. The lender places the investment money at risk by loaning the money to the borrower. To reduce the risk taken by the lender, a mortgage or deed of trust is taken on the borrower's real estate creating collateral against which the investor may foreclose upon if the money is not paid back as agreed. To compensate the lender for the making of the loan, and to provide a *return on the lender's investment*, the note will provide for the payment of interest. In theory, this assures the lender a *return on* and a *return of* the funds invested in the loan.

THE LENDERS: The Primary Market – represents those persons or businesses who *actually make* the loan. This primary market is often called the ***loan originators***.

1. **Savings and loans** – these institutions accept funds from depositors and agree to keep the money safe and pay a return in the form of interest or dividends. The S&L then makes real estate loans secured by mortgages (or deeds of trust) to qualified borrowers. Until the 1970's, the primary source of home loans was from savings and loans.

2. **Banks** – Some banks make home loans, but generally banks are not comfortable making loans longer than three to five years. In recent years, banks have become a major source for equity lines of credit or second mortgage financing, but are not a significant source of long-term, fully amortizing home loans.

3. **Mortgage brokers** – these are the *loan originators* now most common in the market. The mortgage broker takes the application for the loan from the borrower, then "shops" the loan to find an investor who will make the loan and who will offer competitive terms. If a loan is made, the mortgage broker is paid a fee for services. Mortgage brokers do not provide **loan servicing** for the investor which would include collecting the loan payments, accounting tasks, handling escrow accounts for future payment of insurance, property taxes, etc. Once the loan is closed and funded, the job of the mortgage broker is essentially done.

4. **Mortgage bankers** – These are also loan originators and are common in the market. Some mortgage bankers work as a "middle man" between mortgage brokers and the ultimate investors. Some mortgage bankers have funds of their own with which to fund the loan, but will normally then sell the loans they have created to liquidate capital to lend again. A significant difference between a mortgage banker and a mortgage broker is that bankers often *do* provide servicing for the loans after they are made. They service their own loans and provide this service for investors at an additional charge.

THE INVESTORS: The Secondary Market – represents those persons or businesses who actually *fund* the loan. This group is where the *lenders* go to get the funds to lend.

1. **Large investors** – high wealth individuals and corporations with excess funds to invest and often find the relative safety and security of real estate loans appealing.

2. **Pension funds** – although these organizations place a majority of their funds in *equities* (stocks and bonds), many pension funds will allocate a portion of their investment portfolios to residential or commercial real estate mortgages.

3. **Insurance companies** – Due to the large amounts of money life, health, and casualty insurance companies have at their disposal to invest, the making of individual residential loans is not feasible. However, they are interested in participating in large commercial real estate loans and also are buyers of *packaged residential loans* (individual loans packaged together and then sold to a single investor).

4. **Mutual funds** – Like the pension funds, these organizations have enormous amounts of money to invest and will allocate a portion of their portfolios to residential and commercial real estate mortgages.

THE WAREHOUSES: – The purpose of the "warehouse" system is to provide the availability of mortgage money nationwide and to provide a method of allowing global funds to reach the American homeowner.

1. **Federal National Mortgage Association (FNMA "Fannie Mae")** – was created in the late 1930's to provide a method of

attracting private investment funds in Federal Housing Administration (FHA) loans. FNMA initially dealt in FHA and later, VA loans. Fannie Mae now is a major warehouse underwriter of **conventional** loans as well as U.S. government insured (FHA) or guaranteed loans (VA).

2. **Government National Mortgage Association (GNMA "Ginnie Mae")** – A descendant of the Great Depression of the 1930's, Ginnie Mae's mission was to attract the maximum available mortgage capital into the American mortgage market. By pooling individual mortgages, which were backed either by U.S. government guarantees or U.S. government insurance, Ginnie Mae was able to provide a **mortgage backed security** which was completely backed by the "full faith and credit" of the United States government. This investment instrument allowed global investment capital to be funneled into the American housing market.

3. **Federal Home Loan Mortgage Corporation (FHLMC "Freddie Mac")** – created in 1970, Freddie Mac operates under a congressional charter and is "stockholder owned." Its function is to purchase qualified residential mortgages from the originators. Freddie Mac then issues a security to private investors which represents an undivided interest in the mortgages Freddie Mac owns. These securities contain a guarantee against loss to the investor. Freddie Mac deals in residential mortgages which *do not* contain U.S. government backed loans; these are the so called *conventional* mortgages.

RESIDENTIAL LENDING PROGRAMS

Loan to value ratio (LTV) – The loan to value ratio is the ratio between the loan being made and the appraised value of the property given as collateral, or the purchase price, *whichever is less*.

> **EXAMPLE**: If the purchase price is $300,000, the appraisal comes in at $290,000, and the lender is using an 80% LTV, the lender will make a maximum loan of $232,000. ($290,000 x .80 = $232,000; not $240,000 as the appraisal was the lower figure.)

The higher the LTV ratio, the larger the loan and the smaller the down payment required.

(1) Conventional Loans – The term "conventional" is used to describe a loan that is neither FHA nor VA: made with *neither* federal government insurance nor guarantees. This loan is priced, and the lending decision is made by the lender, solely on the credit history and strength of the borrower and upon the value of the borrower's collateral.

A conventional loan can be originated by virtually any loan originator and may be sold into the secondary market, most likely to Fannie Mae or Freddie Mac.

Private mortgage insurance – With a conventional loan, the lender does not have government insurance or guarantee and has only the collateral property and the borrower's credit scores and history to rely upon in making the lending decision. As a result, most conventional lenders will only loan 80% of the purchase price or appraisal, whichever is less.

To induce lenders to raise their LTV's, a new insurance product was created in the 1960's known as *private mortgage insurance*, or PMI. The original PMI insurance company was the Mortgage Guarantee Insurance Company, known as MGIC. This concept truly was "magic" to the real estate industry. Given that a lender would loan only 80% without any further assurances, what MGIC did was to provide insurance against loss on that portion of the loan above 80%. So, if the lender made a 90% LTV loan, they were above their normal loan by 10% of the purchase price. If they made a 95% loan, they were above their normal loan by 15% of the purchase price, and so on.

The PMI company covers the amount above 80% LTV if the lender suffers a loss through a foreclosure sale which brings less than 80% of the purchase price or appraisal used at the time the loan was made.

EXAMPLE: Capital Federal Savings and Loan makes a loan of $295,000 on a property appraised at $300,000 (a 95% LTV loan). Time passes, and the borrower defaults on the loan.

$300,000 Sale Price
- 15,000 Down Payment (5%)
 285,000 Loan (95%)

Capital Federal Savings forecloses and the property sells for $275,000. The unpaid and accrued interest and costs total $10,000.

$275,000   Proceeds from Foreclosure Sale
- 285,000   Loan
  (10,000) Shortage to the Lender
- 10,000 Interest and Costs
  (20,000) Total *loss* to the lender

At the time of the foreclosure sale, the outstanding balance on the loan was $275,000. Had Capital Federal made only an 80% LTV loan, they would have loaned $240,000 and would not have suffered any loss on this transaction.

$300,000 Sale Price
- 60,000 Down Payment (20%)
$240,000 Loan (80%)

$275,000   Proceeds from Foreclosure Sale
- 240,000   Loan (80%)
   35,000   Net Proceeds
- 10,000   Interest and Costs
   25,000   Total *Gain* to the lender

As it is, because of the 95% LTV loan, the lender has suffered a loss of $20,000. This loss would be paid by the PMI insurance company to the lender.

If real estate values are appreciating, the likelihood of loss by the lender from these higher LTV loans decreases. With the reduction of the loan balance through amortization and the increase in value of the property, many borrowers reach a point where their current equity in their home equaled or exceeded 80%, making PMI no longer necessary. Federal legislation now requires the lender to inform the borrower, at the time the loan closed, the date on which their balance owed will be less than 80% LTV. This date is based solely on amortization of the mortgage balance and does not consider increase in value of the property due to inflation and no accurate estimate of that can be made.

With PMI, lenders will loan at higher LTV's making purchasing a home much easier for buyers. The cost of the PMI is paid by the borrower, often with an "up-front" charge and monthly insurance premiums which are added to the monthly payments.

(2) FHA insured loans – The Federal Housing Administration (FHA) was created in the 1930's as one of the programs intended to stimulate the economy in hopes of bringing an end to the Great Depression. Although the suffering was wide spread, many American's still had jobs and wanted to purchase homes. Lenders, given the general economic conditions, were reluctant to make home loans and the construction and related industries were in bad shape.

The idea for the FHA 203b loan was a private lender would make the loan to a qualified borrower and the FHA would insure the lender against loss on the loan. With the "full faith and credit" of the United States government standing behind the loan, it was hoped that private lenders would be willing to make the loans, thereby meeting the needs of the home buying population and stimulating the economy.

The FHA program introduced the concept of *long term, fully amortizing* loans. Prior to the FHA, most loans made by banks or other financial institutions were short term loans, ranging in length from six months to five years. If the bank did not want to renew the loan, the loan would be "called" and the borrower would have to either sell the home, find another lender, pay off the loan from their personal funds, or face the loss of their home by foreclosure. This did not make for a stable real estate market, particularly during difficult and uncertain economic times.

The FHA does not make loans directly. Loans are made through private lenders. The FHA does not set interest rates on FHA loans. The interest is determined by the lender to be competitive in the market.

> ***FHA does not make loans; they insure them.***

The FHA today: Now, many years later, the FHA continues to play a major role in our housing market. Under the ***Department of Housing and Urban Development (HUD)***, FHA loans remain viable financing alternative to home buyers, and in particular, first time home buyers.

Elements of FHA programs:

1. 1 to 4 family, owner-occupied residential properties
2. The buyer pays a ***Mortgage Insurance Premium (MIP)*** both in an up-front payment and also monthly for the life of the loan. The amount, or percentage, for these two costs changes from time to time.
3. The maximum FHA loan is set regionally.
4. 3.5% minimum cash contribution by buyer which is technically not just a down payment as a portion of these funds can be applied to certain closing costs
5. The property must be appraised by a certified FHA appraiser. The FHA appraisal is called a ***conditional commitment***. The conditional commitment may have "appraisal conditions" which must be corrected before FHA will insure the loan.
6. Discount points may be paid by either party.
7. Loans are always ***budget loans*** with principal, interest, taxes, and insurance (PITI) and the mortgage insurance premium is included in the monthly payment.
8. FHA Loans are assumable with qualifying by the assumption buyer.
9. FHA Loans have a 30-year maximum term.
10. There can be no *junior liens* (2nd mortgages) at close of escrow. You cannot finance the minimum cash contribution.

Also authorized to provide insured loans is the ***Rural Economic Community Development Administration (RECD)***, formerly known as the ***Farmer's Home Administration (FmHA)***. The RECD is permitted to operate only in communities with less than 20,000 population.

(3) Veteran's Administration (VA) guaranteed loans – As the end of World War II approached, the government needed to plan for the assimilation of returning veterans. Our soldiers, sailors, and airmen all basically wanted the same thing – to return to a normal life. Some wanted to continue their education by going to college, others wanted to learn a trade to get a good job, others wanted to marry, start their own families, and have a home of their own. Most of them shared another thing in common – they did not have the money to purchase homes.

In order to stimulate the peacetime economy and to meet the needs of our returning troops, Congress passed the "Soldiers and Sailors Readjustment Act of 1944." Among its many provisions, the creation of the "Veterans Administration Guaranteed Home Loan Program" had a major impact on jump starting the construction industry and expanding homeownership.

> *VA does not usually make loans; they guarantee them.*

The VA does not normally make loans. Loans are made through private lenders. The VA may fund the loan if there is no available lender. The VA does not set interest rates on VA loans. The interest is determined by the lender to be competitive in the market.

Elements of VA loans:

1. 1 to 4 family, owner occupied, residential properties to *qualified veterans.*
2. This is a true, 0% down payment loan. However, there are out of pocket *expenses*.
3. The buyer pays a *funding fee* of either 2.15% for first-time users, or 3.3% for subsequent users. This funding fee works much the same as the MIP in an FHA loan, but is not considered an "insurance premium" – it's a "guarantee program." The veteran buyer may pay the fee at close of escrow, but normally the veteran elects to roll the funding fee into the loan. The funding fee may be waived for veterans with service related disabilities depending on the degree of disability. Borrowers with a down payment have a reduced funding fee. This fee changes from time to time.
4. There is no maximum VA *loan amount*. There is a maximum VA *guarantee*. The guarantee is what the government promises to the lender if there is a shortage from foreclosure. The guarantee provides the lender with a guarantee for the first 25% of the loan up to $60,000.
5. The property must be appraised by a certified VA appraiser. The VA appraisal is called a **certificate of reasonable value (CRV)**. The CRV may have *appraisal conditions* which must be corrected before VA will guarantee the loan.
6. Discount points may be paid by either party.
7. VA loans are always budget loans.
8. VA loans are assumable with qualifying by the assumption buyer.
9. VA Loans have a 30-year maximum term.
10. The partial guarantee can be restored in one of two ways:
    a. The veteran sells the property and pays off the VA guaranteed loan.
    b. The veteran sells the property to another qualified veteran who agrees to substitute his entitlement for the selling veteran's entitlement.
11. If the veteran did not use all of his entitlement in the purchase of the property, he will still have a **partial entitlement** which would be his total entitlement minus the portion used. This allows a veteran who has purchased a home and decides to keep it as an investment property, to still have VA benefits in the form of the remaining partial entitlement for use in purchasing his next home.

Note: A veteran cannot use his entitlement or any portion of it to *purchase* investment property. The veteran must have a "good faith intent to occupy" the property as his residence.

WHY DO INTEREST RATES FLUCTUATE? GOVERNMENT INFLUENCE ON INTEREST RATES

Government budget deficits or surpluses – If the federal government is operating at a *surplus,* it does not need to borrow money to pay the bills of the government such as Social Security checks, payrolls for the military and other government employees, and the other costs and expenses of operating the government. During periods of surplus, nearly all excess funds in the economy would be available for private purposes, including home loans. With plentiful funds, interest rates should be low due to the lack of borrowing demand.

During periods of *budget deficits*, the government must borrow in order to pay the bills and costs of operation. When the federal government starts competing for the available funds, this increases the demand for loan funds and tends to drive the interest rates higher as a function of *supply and demand*.

Reserve requirements – One of the functions of the Federal Reserve System is to assure the nation of a sound and safe banking system and to control inflation. Should the Federal Reserve determine that the amount of available money in the system is either creating inflationary pressures on the economy, or is insufficient to sustain desired economic growth, reserve requirements may be adjusted. An increase in the reserve requirements of member banks would have the effect of reducing available funds for lending and increasing interest rates. A relaxing of reserve requirements would have the opposite effect.

Discount rate – the Federal Reserve Board from time to time establishes increases or decreases in the *discount rate*. This is the interest rate the Federal Reserve System charges its member banks. If the Federal Reserve Board of Governors feels inflationary pressures in the economy exist, they may decide to raise the discount rate, which would have the effect of making borrowing more expensive for business and consumers and in theory cooling the business economy and reducing inflationary pressure. The converse is also true. If the "Fed" thinks a little boost to the economy is needed, they might decide to reduce the discount rate making borrowing less expensive and encouraging consumers to spend more and for businesses to expand their operations, production and hiring.

FINANCE AND CREDIT LAWS (FEDERAL)

CONSUMER CREDIT PROTECTION ACT, TRUTH-IN-LENDING ACT, REGULATION "Z" – The potential for the abuse of a borrower by a lender, together with actual abuses which were occurring in the market, brought about a series of federal laws designed to protect consumers with credit matters. The Truth in Lending Act (TILA), Title I of the Consumer Credit Protection Act, is aimed at promoting the informed use of consumer credit by requiring disclosures about its terms and costs. In general, this regulation applies to each individual or business that offers or extends credit to consumers.

Transactions covered:

1. loans to individual consumers (not business loans)
2. loans with more than 4 installment payments
3. all consumer real estate loans where a lien will be placed against the residence of the consumer
4. the loan balance equals or exceeds $25,000 or is secured by an interest in real property or a dwelling

The principal purpose of these laws is to provide the consumer with complete and understandable credit information so the consumer can make informed credit decisions. The disclosures required by these laws are:

Finance charges:

1. interest charged on the loan
2. loan fees (such as the loan origination fee)
3. discount points
4. appraisal fees
5. mortgage guarantee/insurance costs
6. credit reports or other fees charged in connection with researching the borrower's credit history
7. other service charges or fees charged as a requirement for obtaining the loan

Annual Percentage Rate (APR):

1. The APR is the finance charges, expressed a percentage when applied to the unpaid balance of the loan. The total of the finance charges is the sum of all of the costs in order to obtain the loan. The APR will always be greater than the stated interest rate, unless there are no costs at all to the borrowing, in which case the loan would be a true zero interest, zero cost loan.

2. The APR must be disclosed, in writing, to the borrower as a percentage rate.

3. The APR must be disclosed, in writing, to the borrower in total dollars charged.

Advertising Restrictions: Lenders or others who are advertising credit must either refrain from stating *any* credit terms, *or* must state *all* credit terms. In advertising, lenders may not pick and choose what terms to advertise.

Vague references, or general terms, may be advertised without disclosure. The first advertisement would be permissible, as no credit terms are used, and "price" is not a ***trigger term***. A trigger term is any term of the financing and "triggers" the need to disclose *all* credit terms – all or none.

The second advertisement would NOT be permissible, as the down payment is a trigger term, and the entire credit disclosure including the APR would need disclosure in the advertisement.

The only numbers which may be used in an advertisement which do *not* trigger are "price" and the "APR."

> **Willow Way Executive Homes:** Easy, move-in pricing. Luxury which won't bust your budget! Homes starting from the low $600,000s

> **Willow Way Executive Homes:** Easy, move-in pricing. $25,000 down payment, starting from the low $600.000s

Three (3) business day right of rescission – To protect the consumer from areas in which abuse has occurred, the law provides for a *three business day right of rescission*. This right to rescind the agreement applies only to:

1. the creation of any monetary encumbrance on the personal residence of the consumer, including:

    a. second mortgages or other junior liens.
    b. refinancing.
    c. home improvement loans.
    d. transactions which create a potential mechanic's lien against the consumer's personal residence.

2. **EXCEPTION:** The loan which finances the original purchase of the consumer's personal residence (the first mortgage) does NOT have a right of rescission.

EQUAL CREDIT OPPORTUNITY ACT (ECOA)

In the attempt to open the opportunity of home ownership to all Americans, Congress determined that equal access to financing needed to be provided and discrimination in lending practices were essentially the same as discrimination in housing availability. The ECOA prohibits discrimination in lending based upon:

1. race
2. color
3. gender
4. age (provided the party is of lawful age to contract)
5. religion
6. national origin
7. marital status – it is a custom that the credit of a married couple is often kept in the name of the husband. In the event of divorce or death, many women found themselves without a credit history in their name. The ECOA allows the widow, or divorced spouse to use the credit of the husband during the husband's lifetime, or period of the marriage.
8. source of income – many lenders were denying loans to individuals if any of the income received by the prospective borrower was some form of "public assistance." Normally this was income from the "Aid to Dependent Children" programs. Congress determined that minorities were "over-represented" in the receipt of public assistance, and to not include this income in qualifying the borrower for a loan was effectively discrimination based on race, national origin, or marital status. The only requirement to be considered is that the source of income must be "legal Income."

REAL ESTATE SETTLEMENT PROCEDURES ACT (RESPA) – administered by HUD, the primary purpose of RESPA is to inform the parties to a covered real estate transaction what the closing costs and charges are, and which costs they pay for. RESPA applies to:

1. new first mortgages (also refinances if it creates a new first mortgage)
2. on 1 to 4 family homes, and,
3. are "federally related" in some way
    a. FHA, VA or RECD loans
    b. loans by a federally chartered lender
    c. loans by a federally insured lender
4. any Lender who makes $1,000,000 or more in loans

Not covered are:
1. seller financing under $1,000,000
2. land loans
3. investor or commercial loans
4. second mortgages
5. assumptions (provided there are no changes in terms)

To satisfy RESPA, the borrower must be provided with a copy of the HUD booklet *Shopping for Your Home Loan* revised in 2010 and formerly called *Settlement Costs and You*. This is normally provided by the Lender. The Lender also must provide the borrower with a *Good Faith Estimate of Closing Costs* within 3 business days from loan application.

The **Uniform Settlement Statement** (**HUD 1**) must be used for the closing. This is an easy to read form which details the amount of the closing costs and who is paying them (seller, buyer, or a third party).

A party who wants to see the actual closing costs, they may, if they request it one day prior to close of escrow. This short time period is because the closing costs are constantly changing with the effect of accruing interest on loans, and the effect of the passage of time on amounts due for things such as real estate taxes, homeowner association dues, special assessments, or any other charge which is time sensitive.

The primary motive behind RESPA is to expose any *kickbacks* which may be occurring. All payments to and from the parties to the transaction, together with the real estate professionals, the title and escrow companies, and the casualty insurance companies must be disclosed.

Chapter 4: Financing
End of Chapter Quiz

1. Mr. and Mrs. Smith are purchasing their third property. The purchase price is $250,000 and their intention is to rent this property out. What is the minimum down payment required for Mr. and Mrs. Smith if they were to obtain financing?

    a. $8,750
    b. $25,000
    c. $50,000
    d. $12,500

2. Who is able to use a loan that is guaranteed by the Veteran's Administration Home Loan Program?

    a. a veteran and his spouse
    b. a veteran's child
    c. the general public
    d. both A & B

3. Joe is purchasing a home for $150,000. He will be putting down $15,000 as his down payment. What is Joe's loan-to-value ratio?

    a. 95%
    b. 90%
    c. 80%
    d. 96.5%

4. What types of loans cannot contain pre-payment penalties?

    a. conventional
    b. FHA
    c. VA
    d. both B & C

5. What information will you find in a mortgage "note"?

    a. the interest rate
    b. the borrower's previous address
    c. the contract date
    d. the company to which the loan has been sold

6. The theory that states the mortgagor retains legal and equitable title while the mortgagee has only a lien on the property as security for the debt, is known as a:

    a. title theory state.
    b. lien theory state.
    c. both A & B
    d. none of these

7. What does RESPA stand for?

    a. Real Estate Settlement Process Act
    b. Real Estate Supplemental Protection Act
    c. Real Estate Settlement Procedure Act
    d. Real Estate Settlement Protection Action

8. The Truth in Lending Act requires that a *truth in lending form* and a *good faith estimate* must be issued to the borrower within how many days of loan application?

    a. 15
    b. 5
    c. 1
    d. 3

9. When will a conventional loan have *private mortgage insurance* included?

    a. when the borrower is putting more than 20% down
    b. when the borrower is putting less than 20% down
    c. every conventional loan has private mortgage insurance
    d. both A & B

10. Which properties do not fall under residential mortgage guidelines?

    a. duplexes
    b. condos
    c. a 6-plex apartment unit
    d. single Family

11. What is the maximum loan amount FHA will lend in a rural area?

    a. $125,000
    b. $217,500
    c. $286,300
    d. none of the Above

12. What determines if a loan is considered first or second with respect to priority?

    a. The larger amount is the first mortgage.
    b. The order in which the loans were funded will determine priority.
    c. The order in which the notes and mortgages were recorded will determine priority.
    d. The one with the higher interest rate will be the second.

13. What does FHA stand for?

    a. Fair Housing Administration
    b. Federal Housing Association
    c. Frequent Housing Acquisition
    d. Federal Housing Administration

14. Impounds for a home loan serve what purpose for the lender?

    a. assure the taxes and insurance are paid
    b. to avoid the borrower having to make lump sum payments for insurance or property taxes
    c. establish a reserve in the event of foreclosure.
    d. penalize the borrower for delinquent payments

15. Which loans are defined as *conventional* loans?

    a. federally insured loans
    b. government guaranteed loans
    c. non-FHA or VA loans
    d. loans with mortgage insurance premium (MIP)

16. Which of the terms below is considered a "trigger" term per Regulation Z?

    a % down payment
    b. interest rate
    c. loan amount
    d. All of the Above

17. What law provided financing to all qualified Americans and prohibited discrimination in lending practices?

    a. ECOA
    b. RECD
    c. RESPA
    d. MGIC

18. What is the maximum loan amount as established by the VA?

    a. $60,000
    b. $120,000
    c. $240,000
    d. VA does not set a maximum loan amount.

19. When the loan closing costs are factored in with the interest rate as if the costs were being paid over the life of the loan, lenders refer to a(n):

    a. ARM
    b. APR
    c. AARP
    d. ACT

20. *Budget loans* are loans that:

    a. are at a discounted interest rate.
    b. are specially designed for low income families on a tight budget.
    c. require impounded payments for taxes and insurance.
    d. all of these

Chapter 5

Property Ownership and the Transfer of Title

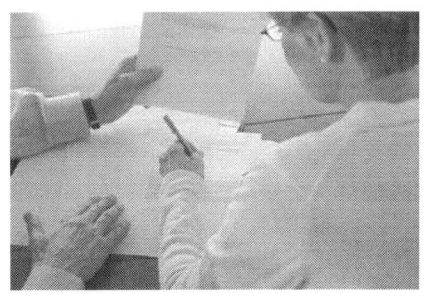

This chapter has two major sections: the concepts surrounding the ownership of property and the transfer of ownership from one party to another.

Ownership of property will explore categorizations of property and the rights of property owners. A segment on physical and economic characteristics of property as well as legal descriptions follows. The many types of encumbrances associated with real property are covered and a final unit describes the forms of ownership for both natural persons and business entities.

Transfer of title from one person or business entity to another will address the subjects of title insurance, deeds, escrow and the closing processes, special cases like foreclosures and short sales, and the tax aspects of transferring title.

DO YOU KNOW???

Do you know the five rights in the *Bundle of Rights of Ownership*?
Can you calculate the size of the land described in a U.S. Government Rectangular Survey legal description?
Can you give an example of a *monetary encumbrance*?
Are you able to distinguish the dominant tenement from the servient tenement?
What form of ownership would a corporation hold title to real estate?
These are just some of the topics covered in this chapter.

PROPERTY OWNERSHIP

CLASSES OF PROPERTY

There are three important property definitions that are very important to real estate agents: land, real estate, and real property.

Land – is defined as the surface of the earth, extending upward to infinity and downward to the center of the earth. It includes all things that are attached to the surface of the earth, like trees and shrubs, and the water that exists on and below the land. Land also includes the soil and minerals below the surface (termed the *subsurface*) and the air above the earth's surface (termed the *airspace*).

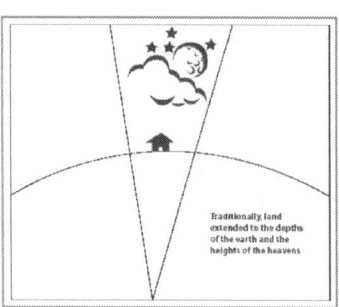

Traditionally, land extended to the depths of the earth and the heights of the heavens

Most laws that control the ownership of land are state and local in nature, especially those that cover minerals and water.

Real estate – is defined as the land, as described above, plus all *improvements*, which are the man-made artificial things attached to the land. Notice the term *artificial* describes the man-made things that we know as buildings, fences, driveways, swimming pools, etc.

Real property – Real property consists of physical land, the natural features, the man-made improvements to the land, and, the bundle of rights of ownership of real property. Real property includes both land and real estate and is defined as all of the rights, benefits, and interests that are associated with the ownership of real estate. Real property includes the earth's surface, the airspace, subsurface, plus all natural features and man-made improvements, as well as the legal rights, benefits, and benefits associated with the ownership of a parcel of real property.

Rights of real property ownership – The owner of real property is said to have the following *bundle of rights*, which come to us from old English law:

- **Possession** – the right to possess and occupy the property
- **Control** – the right to control the property; to use it for any legal purpose
- **Enjoyment** – the right to use the property in any legal way
- **Exclusion** – the right to keep others from having access to the property
- **Disposition** – the right to sell, will, transfer, or dispose of the property

The word *title* is synonymous with *ownership* of real property. It means *ownership* of real property and includes the bundle of rights listed above plus a document called the *deed* to the land which serves as evidence of ownership.

Rights relative to land:

- **Subsurface rights** are the rights to natural resources that exist below the surface of the earth. These can be sold or conveyed separately from the land, and the conveyance can be split among several buyers. Thus, a farmer with a 100 acre farm could sell the rights to subsurface oil to one buyer and the rights to subsurface coal to another buyer.

- **Air rights** can be a significant part of the land and may have great value. Many large buildings in large cities have been constructed using the air rights above other objects like railroad tracks or parking lots.

- **Water rights** can also be sold, but since water moves across the land, the sale of water rights is a complex legal process, normally regulated by the state. It wetter areas, like the Great Lake states, water is relatively plentiful and regulation is minimal. In the water-scare states in the southwest, water control and water laws are relatively more complex.

Rights relative to water:

- **Riparian rights** are common-law rights granted to owners along the course of a river or stream. They generally allow the landowner unrestricted use of the water as long as the owner does not alter the flow or contaminate the water in any way. On smaller streams that are not navigable, the owner typically owns the land under the water, out to the exact center of the stream. On larger, navigable streams and rivers, the owner owns only to the edge of the water.

- **Littoral rights** describe the rights of owners whose land borders large (commercially navigable) lakes, seas, and oceans. These owners have claim only to the high water mark of water that borders their property.

- **Changes in borders** occur when actions of nature change the border between land and water.

    - **Accretion** – The owner of a piece of property which borders water may find that the property has become a little larger due to a process of accretion, where the action of water has added to the land. Increases in land due to accretion of alluvial (washed up) deposits belong to the land owner (*accession*).

    - **Erosion** – Conversely, an owner may find that wind, rain, or flowing water has removed land through the process of erosion and replaced it with water. The missing land no longer belongs to the landowner.

    - **Avulsion** – The sudden removal of soil by an act of nature can cause a landowner's property to become much smaller very quickly.

- **Prior appropriation** means that the government has already taken and reserved the water rights for the government and can sell or lease those rights separately.

Personal property – is defined as all property which can be owned by an owner but does not fit the definition of real property. One important definitional difference is that personal property can be moved. This still leaves a broad range of personal property, from potted plants to manufactured homes. *Chattel* is another term synonymous with personal property.

- **Manufactured homes** pose an area of special interest to real estate agents. Since they are manufactured in a factory and moved to a site where they are parked or installed, manufactured or mobile homes are usually classified as personal property in most states. However, if they are permanently affixed to the land, and the land is included with the sale, manufactured homes can sometimes be classified as real property. Again, this branch of real estate law differs broadly by state.

- **Trees and crops** seem similar but they are defined differently from a real estate point of view. Trees, rocks, bushes, and other landscaping that does not require cultivation on an annual basis are considered part of the land and are therefore real property. Fruit, vegetables, nuts, grasses, grains and other annually cultivated crops are known as *emblements* or *fructus industriales*, and are considered personal property.

Fixtures are items of personal property that have been permanently attached to land or a building, so that they become part of the real property. Examples of fixtures are display racks, alarm systems, heating systems, elevators, kitchen cabinets, etc. When buildings are transferred from one owner to another, the contractual definition of an item as a fixture (real property) can be controversial. Over time a *test of intent* has been developed to help define the status of a fixture. To understand intent it is necessary to determine if the item was installed permanently on the property, or was it designed to be removed sometime in the future.

Over time, the courts have defined three legal tests to determine if an item is real property (a fixture) or personal property.

1. **Method of annexation** – How permanent is the attachment? Can the item be easily removed or will it cause damage to the building to remove the item?

2. **Adaptation to real estate** – For example, a refrigerator is usually considered personal property, but if built into the kitchen cabinetry, with panels that match the other kitchen cabinets, it is probably fixture.

3. **Have the parties agreed to its status in an offer to purchase?** If so, that will become a determinant. For example, if the buyer's offer to purchase specifically identifies and includes an item, it is probably real property.

Trade fixtures in commercial spaces – Trade fixtures are a special category of item. They are installed in a rented space by a tenant, for the tenant's use. Unlike regular fixtures, which become real property, trade fixtures are the property of the tenant and must be removed by the final day of the tenant's occupancy. Some examples are: bowling alley equipment, a pizza oven, or kitchen equipment in a restaurant. If they are not removed upon vacating the property, they become property of the landlord through *accession*.

LAND CHARACTERISTICS

Land has characteristics, three physical and four economic, that describe its nature and affect its use.

Physical Characteristics:

Immobility – While some characteristics of a parcel of land can be changed by paving, or by moving dirt around, or by digging, the parcel of land is still there, in the same place, and immobile.

Indestructibility – In addition to being immobile, land is also indestructible. It is permanent. Deterioration of buildings built on the land may decay and reduce the desirability of the land, but buildings can eventually be demolished and the land returned to its prior state.

Uniqueness – This concept refers to the idea that no two parcels of land are exactly the same. While they may seem similar, each parcel is unique and differs from its neighbors in some way (***non-homogenous/non-homogeniety***).

Economic characteristics:

Location/Area Preference – Location is often the most important characteristic affecting the value of a piece of property. Area preference refers not only to a property's geography, but to people's preference for a particular area. This characteristic has been expressed as "location, location, location."

Scarcity – There is quite a bit of land around us, but much of the earth's surface is covered by water, and a great deal of the remaining land is unused or uninhabitable, so we generally think of what's left as finite and scarce.

Improvements – The construction of a building or otherwise putting land to work in some way, can dramatically raise the value of a piece of property. Conversely, utilizing the land in an undesired manner such as establishing a dump or landfill on a property will lower its value.

Durability/Permanence of investment – Buildings, both residential and commercial, represent a large investment of capital and labor. So do the infrastructure investments in sewerage, utilities, drainage, and landscaping. We think of investments in land to be long term and relatively stable.

LEGAL DESCRIPTIONS

Types of legal property descriptions – The story is that a very long time ago, when a parcel of land changed hands, the buyer was given a bundle of sticks from one of the trees on the property as evidence that he was the new owner. One can only imagine the conflicts, misunderstandings, and errors that would have come from such a system!

> **Definition:** A *survey* is a study performed by a surveyor which determines property boundary lines. A survey will also uncover any violations of setbacks or encroachments.

We have come a long way since then, having invented the concept of *legal descriptions*, which are defined as descriptions that provide for a specific location of the parcel in question. A legal description has sufficient certainty that the courts will rely upon it in resolving disputes. Legal descriptions are necessary for documents which will be recorded, or which will convey or encumber real property, such as deeds, mortgages, deeds of trust, grants, easements, and mechanic's liens.

Vague references – We also use *vague references* like street addresses and *assessor's parcel numbers (APNs)*. Vague references are generally acceptable in documents which will not be recorded. The vague reference will give a person general information about the location of the property. Vague references are often used in listing agreements, leases, and purchase agreements and are considered to be *adequate descriptions.*

Legal descriptions – a legal description is one that describes one parcel of property so well that it cannot be confused with another parcel. (Legal descriptions were also introduced in chapter one.)

In most states, there are only three acceptable legal descriptions:

> **Definition:** A *benchmark* or *datum* is a permanent reference mark, sometimes called a "brass cap," usually embedded in streets or sidewalks and used by surveyors as a reference point for elevations.

- Metes and bounds (done by a registered surveyor or engineer)
- Reference to the United States Government Rectangular Survey
- Lot, block, and subdivision (according to an approved plat map)

A. Metes and bounds – The least common, this type of a system relies on a description of *metes* (distance and direction) and *bounds* (landmarks or boundary edges) to define the borders of a parcel of land. This system goes back several hundred years and was the first method used to convey a legal description. A metes-and-bounds description of a piece of property uses a *point of beginning (POB)*, and then directions and linear measurements to define the borders of the property, finally returning to the POB.

Example: "Commencing at the intersection of the west line of Apply Valley Road and the north line of Edison Lane; thence west 200 feet along the north line of Edison Lane; thence north 15° east to the center thread of Blue Ridge Lake, being 175 feet more or less; thence easterly along the centerline of said lake to its intersection with the west line of Apple Valley Road, being 220 feet more or less; thence southerly along the west line of Apple Valley Road to the point of beginning, being 160 feet more or less."

Notice this description starts and closes with the *point of beginning*. This is essential with a metes and bounds description.

In olden times, it was common for fixed, permanent, natural objects, such as large stones, trees, a stream, etc., to be referenced in the description. These natural objects are called **monuments**.

Beginning at the south line of Perrysburg Drive and the east line of Kalkaska Drive, then south along the east line of Kalkaska Drive 250 feet, then east 85 degrees 400 feet, more or less to the center line of the Vegas Valley wash, then northwesterly along the centerline of said wash to the old oak tree at its intersection with Perrysburg Drive, then west along the south line of Perrysburg Drive to the Point of Beginning.

Metes and bounds legal descriptions have been around for a long time and are generally presumed to be the first attempt to describe land in such a way that one parcel could not be confused with another. These descriptions also reference the *latitude* and *longitude*, use *degrees*, *minutes*, and *seconds*.

360° degrees in a circle | 60' minutes in a degree | 60" seconds in a minute
So, a boundary line's direction may be expressed as: *thence N 45°25'20" East ...*

B. **U.S. Government Rectangular Survey System** — This system was established in 1785 when America was still a new nation. The idea behind its use was to establish a system where any parcel of land in the United States could be precisely identified. Legal descriptions using the government survey system are not generally used in the original 13 states. This system references *principal meridians* and *base lines* and forming imaginary lines vertically parallel to the principal meridians called *range lines*, and lines horizontally parallel to the base lines called *township lines*. Each strip of land is 6 miles apart, creating *tiers* and *ranges*. Dividing the land by rectangles, *townships* are formed by the intersection of the ranges and tiers. Each township contains **36 sections** one mile by one mile.

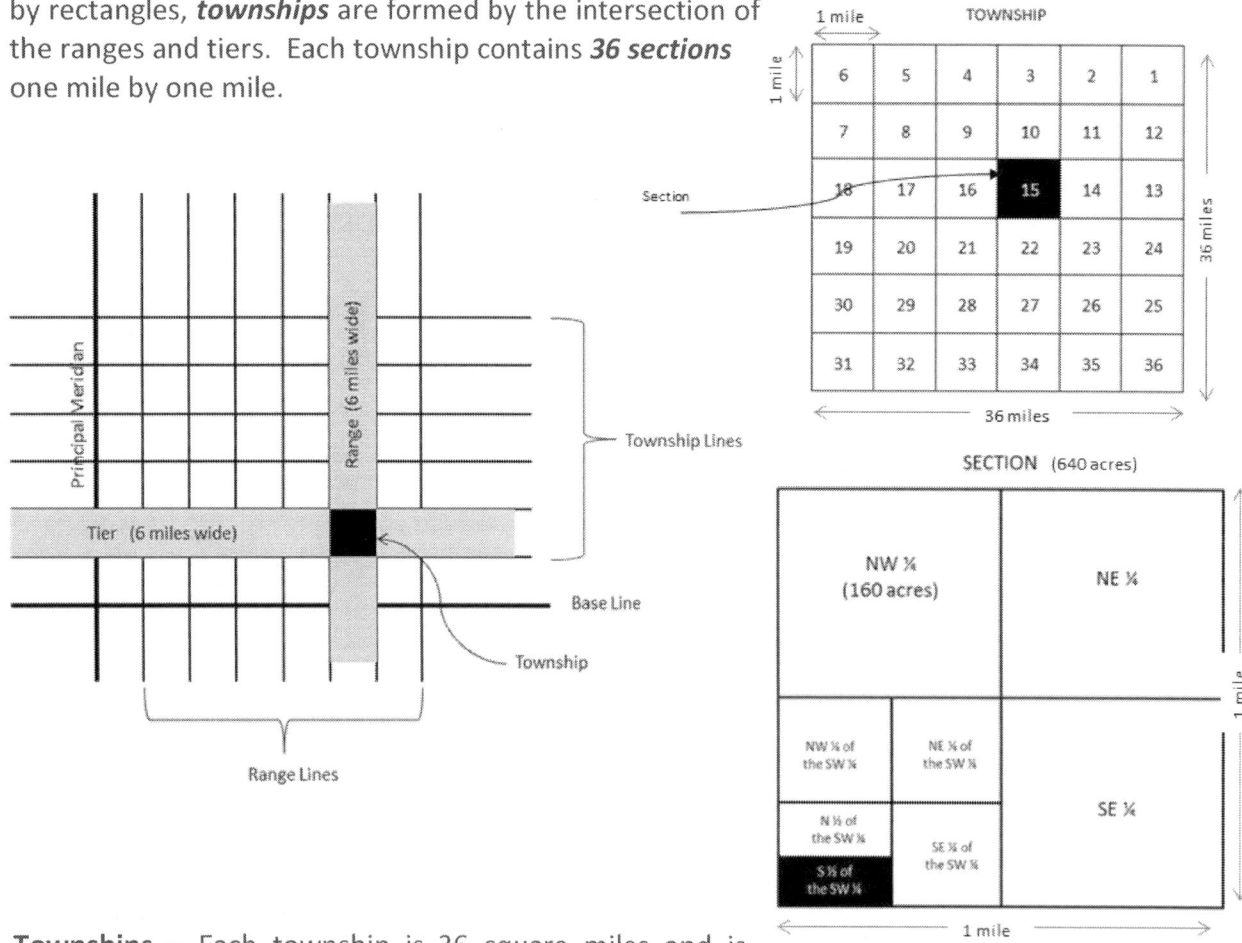

Townships — Each township is 36 square miles and is divided into 36 one-mile-wide and one-mile-high squares called sections. A township, therefore, contains 36 sections. A section contains 640 acres. An acre is 43,560 square feet.

Note that section 16 in every township shows where a school could be built, and is therefore known as the *school section*.

Sections – Each of the squares labeled 1 through 36 refers to a section of land, and each section measures 5,280 feet on a side (one mile) and contains 640 acres of land.

Parcels are described within each section as per this example:
Example: "The S 1/2 of the SW 1/4 of the SW 1/4 of Section 15, Township 14 North, Range 4 West of the 6th Principal Meridian."

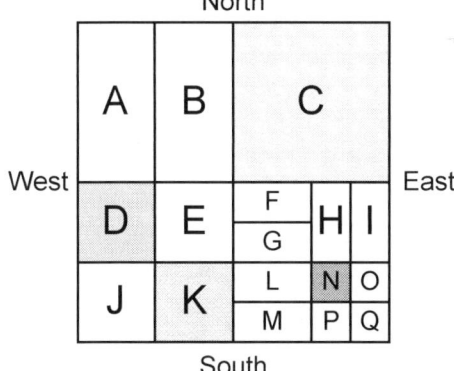

For reference purposes, sections are divided in half (320 acres), in quarters (160 acres) and then further divided into halves and quarters, producing a diagram that could look like the one here, in which the parcels of land are of several sizes and are labeled A through Q.

The entire section is 640 acres, so area C is ¼ of that, or 160 acres. Areas A and B are each 1/8 of the total, so they are each 80 acres (a sort of standard size for a farm back in the 1800s). Areas D, E, J, and K are 40 acres, and so on.

Now, early surveyors did not refer to these parcels of land as A, B, C, D and so on, because that would have been confusing. They referred first to the section:

Section 16, Township 12 North, Range 5 West of the 6th Principal Meridian..

That would have been sufficient for them to locate the section in question, anywhere in the United States. Once the section was identified, they referred to sections of our diagram as follows:

- Area C would have been . . . *the NE¼ of Section 16,*
- Area D would have been . . . *the NW¼ of the SW¼ of Section 16,*
- Area K would have been . . . *the SE¼ of the SW¼ of Section 16,*
- Area N would have been . . . *the NW½ of the SE¼ of the SE¼ of Section 16.*

Please note that the designations C, D, K, and N are used here for illustration only and were never part of the nomenclature used by surveyors. Also, as a study tip, when dealing with the rectangular survey system, it is quite difficult to form a mental picture of the "NW ¼ of the SW ½ of . . ." of anything. This will be easier if you draw a diagram on a piece of scratch paper. It also helps to work backward to find the correct parcel.

C. **Lot, block, and subdivision** – The third method and the one most used in metropolitan areas of the United States is the subdivision, lot, and block system.

In this method, a plot of land is surveyed, and then divided into blocks and lots, streets, access roads, utility easements, parks, etc. Then, the blocks and lots are assigned numbers and letters. The resultant drawing is called a *plat map* or *subdivision plat*. Once approved by the local municipality, the subdivision plat is duly recorded and becomes part of the legal description of each property. It is also the legal description used on deeds and required for homestead forms.

The legal description of a 2.5 acre property under the lot and block system may look like:
Lot 5 of Block 2 of the South Subdivision plat as recorded in Map Book 21, Page 33 at the Recorder of Deeds.

Subdivisions are created by a developer and submitted for approval to the county, city, township, or other authority having jurisdiction over development activities within the area in which the subdivision is located.

The subdivision map (called a *plat* map) will describe the subdivision. It must comply, at a minimum, with the subdivision regulations the jurisdiction has adopted. In specific cases, the subdivider may be granted relief from portions of the subdivision regulations by the approving authority.

The plat will show the location, size and shape of building lots, the roads, sidewalks, street lighting, curbs and gutters, utility easements, drainage easements, flood control easements and other components necessary to support the building lots and the structures ultimately to be constructed in the subdivision.

Once the subdivision plat has been approved by the appropriate authority, it is authorized to be recorded among the public records of the county and reference can be made to the lot number, block number and subdivision name and plat as the legal description for the property.

ENCUMBRANCES

An **encumbrance** is defined as *a burden upon the title to the property,* even though great benefits may be derived by the owner as a result of the encumbrance. An encumbrance is not an estate and does not allow possession, but it may obstruct the use or value of the property. If it is a monetary encumbrance it is referred to as a *lien*. Non-monetary encumbrances include **restrictions, easements, licenses,** *and* **encroachments** that affect the use of the property.

Monetary Encumbrances:

> **Deed of trust or mortgage** – When a purchaser needs money to buy a house, the buyer may encumber the property with a mortgage or deed of trust to receive the financing.
>
> **Property tax lien** – State and local governments have the right to assess property taxes to provide for the costs of governing and providing services such as fire and police protection, schools, streets, sewers, libraries, etc. These are the benefits the property owner theoretically receives in exchange for the encumbrance for taxes against their property.

Mechanic's lien – created by state law to protect those persons who provide labor or materials to improve another's property. This lien is effective as of the date of first work or first delivery of materials, not the date it is filed in the public records.

General lien – Once a person has sued another in court and has obtained a final judgment, in order to collect on the judgment, it is often necessary to file the judgment in the public records which then creates a *general lien* against all of the property the judgment debtor owns in the jurisdiction.

Other measures involving liens:

Lis Pendens – Sometimes, an aggrieved party wants to file a lien, but cannot do so because the law suit is still in process. Should the plaintiff discover the owner is trying to sell the home, which will likely make the attachment of a lien useless, the plaintiff may consider a *lis pendens* (lien pending). Placed in the public records the, lis pendens gives notice that litigation is pending concerning the property. Lis pendens tend to prevent the property from being sold before the dispute is resolved.

Writ of attachment – If the plaintiff in a law suit believes the defendant is disposing of his assets to avoid a possible judgment, the plaintiff may seek a *Writ of Attachment* from the court. If the court agrees, the court will issue the writ, which has the effect of preventing the transfer of the asset until the lawsuit is concluded.

Writ of Execution – If the plaintiff in a law suit obtains a final judgment against the defendant, the plaintiff may request a *writ of execution* to assist in the collection of the judgment. The court will issue the writ of execution to the sheriff, which directs the sheriff to seize all property of the defendant in the jurisdiction, sell it, and apply the proceeds against the judgment.

Use encumbrances (restrictions):

Two types of "use encumbrances" are ***deed restrictions*** and ***covenants, conditions & restrictions (CC&Rs)***.

Deed restrictions – An owner of a piece of property may want to put certain restrictions on the future use of the property. These restrictions would be put in the deed. They would have been agreed to by the prospective owner, or that person should not go forward with the transaction.

EXAMPLE: The owner of a property doesn't want the property to ever be used for the sale of alcoholic beverages. The owner, therefore, put such a restriction in the deed, and all future owners of the property would be bound by the restriction. The deed restriction is said to *run with the land*, meaning the restriction remains even after future transfers of title. This is a *limiting restriction* and could be enforced by court action.

If the owner or grantor of the deed wanted to ensure that the property would always be used in a certain way, then an *affirmative deed restriction* could be put in the deed. As an example, the property in question has a large pond which is used by migrating birds. The current owner, being a bird lover, wants to sell the property, but does not want the pond drained or otherwise altered to impede its use by migrating waterfowl. The owner or grantor could put such a restriction into the deed and future owners would have to maintain the pond for the migrating birds.

With either a limiting or affirmative deed restriction, future owners are bound by the restriction unless they can get it released by the grantor, or the grantor's successors (heirs if the grantor has died), or by court order determining that the restrictions is so onerous that it impedes the free transfer of real estate and serves no useful purpose.

Conditions, covenants and restrictions (CC&Rs) – When a developer of a restricted community, such as a gated community or a condominium project, places certain restrictions on the property, including the creation of a Common Interest Community (CIC), these restrictions bind all future owners. The restrictions are usually managed by a homeowners' association (HOA), which often hires a property management company to enforce the restrictions.

The restrictions found in such projects are often very restrictive and may be offensive to some prospective buyers. Many things which would not be so strictly regulated by city or county laws or ordinance are often found in these CC&Rs. Items such as very restrictive parking regulations, types of trash containers to be used, when the container must be put out for trash pickup and when it must be taken back in, nature of landscaping materials which can be used, color of paint, number of pets, and a host of other matters are found in the CC&Rs. These are often referred to as ***private police powers*** as in fact, the homeowners' association is the "government" for the project.

Please note that most states have a process for disclosing CC&Rs and other documents managed by the homeowners' association. Such processes often give a buyer a short period (5-10 days) to review these documents, which may be very important to a buyer. Imagine, for example, an investor buying a home to add to her rental inventory, only to find out that the CC&Rs prohibit renting or leasing to anyone.

Similar restrictions can appear in deeds.

Physical encumbrances – Easements

An easement is the right of someone other than the owner to use part of a property for a specific purpose. Easements are typically recorded with the legal description, noted on a plat map, or otherwise part of the property records. In most states, there are easements for the utility companies on almost every property. On others, there may be easements for access to other properties that would otherwise be landlocked.

> **Easement by necessity** – All owners of property have a right to access to and from their property by use of the "public way." The public way is defined as a dedicated public street or

highway open for the use of the public. Should a person find that they have purchased property which does not have *ingress* (entrance) or *egress* (exit) to the public way, they may force the creation of an *easement by necessity*. This generally will involve court action and the court will seek to find the least intrusive method to give the landlocked property owner access to the public way.

Easement appurtenant – All owners of neighboring property may decide to create an easement to allow one of the owners to cross over the land of the other. The purpose of crossing is unimportant to the concept of an easement appurtenant. Perhaps the properties are large ranches and one of the ranchers wants to cross over the other rancher's property to get his cattle to market. This is not an easement by necessity as the rancher wanting to cross is not blocked from some other route, he just wants to cross his neighbor's ranch for convenience. If he crossed without the permission of his neighbor he would be a trespasser. If his neighbor agreed to allow him to cross over his ranch, they could formalize their agreement by way of an easement. The easement would need to be in writing and should be in a form which would be accepted for recording in the public records of the county in which the ranches are located.

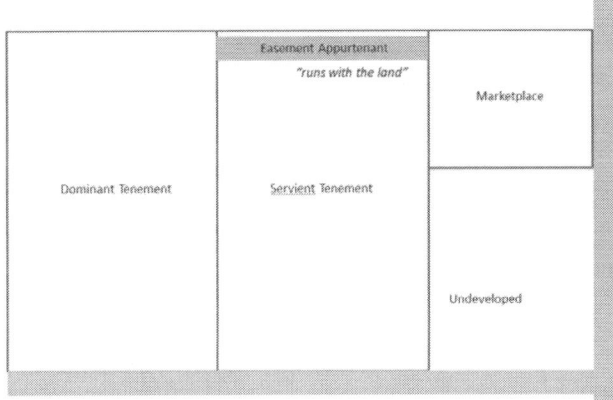

In this example, the land over which the right to cross has been given is referred to as the **servient tenement** (that which serves) and the land which enjoys the right to pass is referred to as the dominant tenement. This type of easement runs with the land. If the owner of the **dominant tenement** (that which dominates) sells his property to another, his buyer will enjoy the right of passing over the neighboring property. Likewise, if the servient tenement is sold, the buyer of it will be obligated to honor the right of the owner of the dominant tenement to cross over.

Easement in gross – This easement does not have a dominant tenement, only a servient tenement. The most common examples of an easement in gross are *utility easements*. If the property owner wants electric service to his property or gas, water, sewer, cable television, or any other service which requires the utility provider to come onto the property, the utility provider will require an easement. Normally these types of easements are created in the subdivision plat, but could be created at a later date. The easement in gross also runs with the land.

Easement by prescription – Seldom seen in modern times, these easements arose through one party's conspicuous use of a portion of another's property to cross over. The use would have to have been for a "prescribed," long period of time, normally 21 years or longer (the time period varies by state); would have to be without the permission of the landowner; would have to be continuous; and would have to be "hostile" meaning contrary to the rights of the owner of the property being crossed. If all of these requirements were met, the party crossing the property would be able to obtain a court order granting them an *easement by prescription*. This concept is based on the principle that an owner of land must exert their rights of ownership, or run the risks of losing them.

In general, easements are created by:

- granting an easement in a deed.
- reserving an easement in a deed.
- showing a landlocked condition to obtain an easement by necessity.
- taking an easement by a public entity by condemnation.
- continued long term, conspicuous, and hostile use resulting in an easement by prescription.

Easements are terminated by:

- abandonment.
- release by the easement holder (often by a quit claim deed).
- excessive use of the easement beyond what the granting party contemplated, resulting in a court order terminating the easement.
- merger. The easement holder buys the land over which the easement runs. The *doctrine of merger* says you cannot have an easement over yourself, so that would terminate the easement.

Other types of grants of access:

License – the giving of permission by the landowner to allow another to come upon the land for specific purposes. The license is a privilege and is revocable.

> **EXAMPLE:** You have a gardener who comes on your property each week to mow your yard and trim your hedges. This is known as a "business invitee" as you have given the gardener license to come on your land and render you the service. If you fired the gardener, this would revoke his license, and if he had come onto your property later, he would potentially be committing a trespass.

Profits – the giving of permission by the landowner to allow another to come onto the land for the limited purpose of removing crops, timber, soil, etc. Here the person receiving *profits* is neither a trespasser, nor a license holder, and has no easement. He is there for a very limited purpose which can be revoked at any time. Profits are not seen often in modern times, but are still found in farming areas where the public is issued a "profit" for picking up fruits or vegetables missed by the harvesters.

Encroachments – *trespass by a thing*
Encroachments exist when a thing (not a person) extends over the property line of another's property without the permission of the property owner. Encroachments can be buildings or portions thereof,

such as an overhanging second story roof line. Encroachments may be intrusions across property lines by driveways, fences or walls, trees, shrubs, or other growing things.

Methods to remedy encroachments:

- negotiations and agreements of the parties (most desirable)
- removal (either by agreement or by court order)
- suit for damages by the property owner being encroached
- utilization – agreement or court order allows the encroached upon party to have the benefit and use of the thing encroaching
- suit for easement by prescription – If the encroachment has existed for the length of time required by the state statute, has been visible and continuous, the encroaching party may be allowed either to claim an easement exists, or under the concept of "adverse possession" may be successful in a claim for ownership of the limited piece of land which is subject to the encroachment.

FORMS OF OWNERSHIP

Ownership of real estate takes many forms and can be a complex subject. Choosing the correct form of ownership affects inheritance of property, trust and estate planning, income and inheritance tax strategy, and much more. Selecting a form of ownership, or *vesting* for real estate buyers is the purview of escrow officers, attorneys, financial planners, CPAs, and professionals other than real estate brokers and agents. The real estate agent's role is to ensure that the subject area receives thoughtful consideration by the buyer.

Natural person – a human being

Non-natural person – a corporation, a limited liability company (LLC), a partnership, or a limited partnership.

Unity of title – a condition of ownership which is common to all who hold title to the property. The more unities there are, the more the owners have in common (in their ownership) with each other.

Undivided interest – When there is more than one owner to a property, they are said to hold *undivided interests* meaning that no owner can claim a specific physical portion of the property as belonging to that owner only. Multi-party ownership deals with *interests in* rather than *physical portions* of the property.

Partition – to divide out an interest where there are multiple owners. This may be done by agreement of the owners where a legal description for the agreed upon portion of the property is created and deeded out to the partitioning party by the remainder of the owners (**Physical Partition**). Or, it may be ordered by a court that may either declare a portion of the property to be owned separately by the partitioning party, or by a court-ordered sale where the property is ordered sold and the proceeds distributed based on the various percentages of ownership (*Judicial Partition*).

The following are forms of ownership. Note that not all of these are used in every state.

Tenant in severalty – There is only one owner. The title to the property has been "severed" from all others. This form of ownership is available to humans and non-humans. If a corporation bought a property it could take tile in "severalty" as the sole owner of the property. Likewise one human could acquire property in severalty. This is the concept of sole and separate property. There are no unities of title in tenant in severalty as there are no other owners.

Tenants in common – There are two or more owners. The owners of property as tenants in common have only "one unity of title." This is the right of equal access and possession. Tenants in common own undivided interests in the property and therefore may have access to any part of the property.

Tenants in common:

- may own unequal shares as long as the total interests equals 100%.
- may have acquired their individual interests at different times.
- may have acquired their individual interest in different documents.
- may sell or mortgage their interest without offering to, or gaining permission from, any of the other tenants in common.
- may be natural or non-natural.
- have interests that are inheritable.
- have interests that may be partitioned (by either physical or judicial partition).

Joint Tenancy – two or more natural owners. The owners of property as Joint Tenants have four (4) *unities of title*:

1. Equal right of access and Possession
2. Equal Interests
3. Acquired their title all at the same Time
4. Acquired their Title all in the same document.

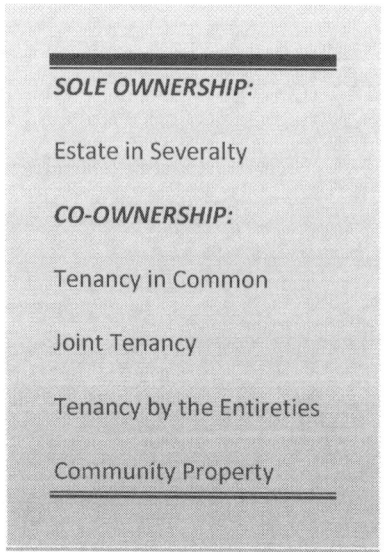

SOLE OWNERSHIP:

Estate in Severalty

CO-OWNERSHIP:

Tenancy in Common

Joint Tenancy

Tenancy by the Entireties

Community Property

Joint Tenants:

- may mortgage an individual's interest without gaining permission from the other joint tenants. This would *not* destroy the joint tenancy status.
- may sell an interest without gaining permission from the other joint tenants. This action *would* destroy the joint tenancy status because it destroys the unities of time and title. Once any of the four unities is broken, the new owner cannot be part of the

joint tenancy and enters as a tenant in common with the others. The other tenants would remain joint tenants with each other.

- may seek a physical or judicial partition if the joint tenants do not want to dissolve the relationship voluntarily. The partitioned interest would be in severalty and would terminate joint tenancy status for the parcel partitioned.

Right of survivorship – The primary significance of joint tenancy is that upon the death of one of the joint tenants, the share of the deceased joint tenant is divided equally among all of the *surviving* joint tenants. Joint tenancy is sometimes referred to as the *poor man's probate* for this reason.

If there is a question as to the intent of the parties to be joint tenants, the question will be resolved against joint tenancy and in favor of tenants in common because the inheritability of real property is presumed. For example, if John Doe and Rachel Doe take title to property simply as "John Doe and Rachel Doe," it will be presumed that they took the property as tenants in common, thereby allowing either John or Rachel's estate or heirs to inherit the property upon the death of either one of the owners.

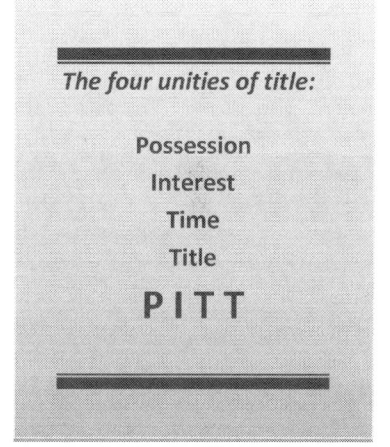

The four unities of title:

Possession
Interest
Time
Title

P I T T

In some states, this might be prevented as follows: If the couple wants to be joint tenants, by them specifying "John Doe and Rachel Doe, as joint tenants with right of survivorship" and not as tenants in common. This is sometimes abbreviated JTWROS (*Joint Tenants with Right of Survivorship*).

Tenancy by the entireties – In other states, it might be prudent for this same couple to take title using *tenancy by the entireties.* This form of ownership has the four unities of title found in joint tenancy, with the additional requirement that the parties *must be married*. Thus, there would be only two parties in a tenancy by the entireties situation but are treated as one legal person.

Tenancy by the entireties property cannot be partitioned, except in the case of divorce, and then the property would be divided according to the agreement of the parties, a court order, or a statutory requirement.

Unsecured creditors may not lien property held in tenancy by the entireties unless the unsecured debt was a joint debt of the married couple.

Once again, there are many ways to hold title to property, and choosing one is a question for an escrow officer, a real estate attorney, not a not a question for a real estate agent.

Community property statutes – The community property form of ownership requires the existence of a state statute which permits it, as not all states do. The existence of a community property statute in a state creates the possibility that a married couple may have property which belongs solely to the wife, or solely to the husband, or property which is held by them as community property.

- **Separate property** is property owned by an individual prior to a marriage or acquired after the marriage by gift or by inheritance. Property which is owned prior to the marriage, or after acquired by gift or inheritance, remains the sole and separate property of the party owning it.

- **Community property** is all other property acquired by either the husband or the wife during the marriage and each spouse is presumed to own a 50% interest in the community property. Conveyance of community property requires the signatures of both spouses. In the event of a divorce, the community property will be split 50/50, and any "sole and separate" property will be set over to its owner without marital claims from the other spouse.

Community property differs from tenancy by the entireties in that there is no right of survivorship. Upon the death of married parties in a community property state, the property would pass to the estate or to the heirs of the deceased, not automatically to the deceased party's spouse.

Trust arrangements – A trust is a device where one person transfers real property to another person for the benefit of a third, with the understanding that the real estate asset (and possibly other assets as well) will be used to care for the trustor. The individual or business entity (e.g., a corporation, LLC, etc.) who transfers the property is called the *trustor*. The person who receives the property is the *trustee*. The person who derives the benefit is called the *beneficiary*.

Trusts can be established for several reasons, but the most frequent is to ensure that should the owner (trustee) die, the property will pass directly to the beneficiary without the need for probate.

There are three types of trusts normally associated with real property:

- living trusts
- testamentary trusts
- Land Trusts

Living and testamentary trusts – are established by property owners to provide for their own financial care or for that of their family. Living trusts are established while a property owner is still alive; testamentary trusts are organized upon the principal's death. Otherwise, they are the same.

Over the last few years, living trusts have become a major tool used for tax and estate planning. They minimize the complexities, time, and costs of probate. Using a living trust, a trustor conveys property (real or personal) to a trustee, and instructs the trustee to perform certain duties, normally to care for the trust in certain ways to produce an income stream for the beneficiary. The trust may continue in this manner until the beneficiary reaches a certain age, or it may go on for a lifetime.

Land trusts – When land trusts are created, land is the only asset. Land trusts are different from living and testamentary trusts in several additional ways:

- land is the only asset in the trust

- the trust runs for a specific time (ten years, twenty years, etc.)
- public records of a land trust do not name the beneficiaries
- land trusts can be used for assembling "packages" of individual parcels
- the beneficial interest can be transferred from one beneficiary to another
- the trustee is usually the trustor

Ownership of Real Estate by Business Entities

Corporations – A corporation is a *legal person* meaning it can sue and be sued in court. A corporation consists of one or more shareholders who own stock in the corporation. As a stockholder, they do not own the property of the corporation, but have what is called a derivative interest in the equity of the corporation, some of which might be real property.

> **EXAMPLE**: If a corporation owned a property with a value of 1,000,000 and owed $250,000 against it, the property would have an equity of $750,000 (*real estate equity* is the current market value of the property minus all debt associated with the property). Assuming the corporation had no other debts or obligations, its stockholders, as a group, would have a derivative interest in the $750,000 equity of the corporation. Their percentage of ownership of the stock would determine the portion of the equity they would receive if the corporation were liquidated.

Corporations require a formal beginning. The state in which the corporation is formed will set the requirements for forming a corporation. Once formed, the corporation will be issued its Certificate of Incorporation which is essentially its birth certificate.

A corporation may own real and personal property and may participate in business arrangements where being a human is not required. In terms of real estate ownership, a corporation may hold title to property in severalty, may hold title to property as a tenant in common with others, either human or non-human, or may hold property in a partnership.

Corporations may not hold property as a joint tenant (must be human), or as tenants by the entireties (cannot marry) or as community property (same reason).

General partnerships – This form of business ownership can be an arrangement between humans or a combination of humans and other business entities such as corporations or other partnerships, where the parties agree to jointly undertake some activity. Normally the activity is a business activity for profit.

In a general partnership, no *formal beginning* is required; while it is a good idea, it is not a requirement. There is only one class of partners – **general partner**. Members of a general partnership may own equal or unequal ownership positions; however, all general partners are jointly and severally liable for the debts of the partnership. Should a creditor seek collection of a partnership obligation he can sue any or all of the partners, and each is fully liable for the debt. Likewise any general partner can participate in the business of the partnership and can create obligations for the partnership without the approval of the other partners.

Limitations on the activities of the partners can be put in place and this is what makes a formal set up of the partnership desirable, but in the absence of such restrictions, all the partners may participate.

The death of a partner typically causes the partnership to dissolve, and if the partnership is to continue, a new partnership has to be formed without the deceased partner being included.

Partners can take title to property, but some general partners take title in their individual names for convenience, flexibility, or other reasons.

Limited partnerships – Two classes of partners are created in a limited partnership. There must be at least one general partner, and there may be any number of ***limited partners***.

The general partners have the right to full participation in the activities of the partnership and are individually liable for the obligations and debts of the partnership.

The limited partners do not have any right to participate in the activities of the partnership, and are not liable beyond their initial investment in their limited partnership share for the obligations or debts of the partnership.

If a limited partner dies, his limited partnership share passes to his estate, much like a share of stock in a corporation. If a general partner dies, the partnership must usually be reformed.

The general partner can take title to property, or can take title as an individual.

limited liability company (LLC) -- a business structure that is a hybrid of a corporation and a limited partnership

Multi-unit co-ownership arrangements:

Cooperative apartments – In major cities on the eastern seaboard, developers and investors realized that apartment and other buildings with residential potential would be far more profitable if the units could be sold rather than rented. These buildings, however, were not built in such a way as to divide the units and sell them as individual dwellings.

The concept was created to form a corporation, which would own the building and sell shares of stock in the building, each share of stock entitling the owner to a ***proprietary lease***. This arrangement was approved by the Internal Revenue Service and owners of proprietary leases in a cooperative building were treated much the same as a homeowner for tax purposes.

In a *co-op* as they came to be known, the stockholder had the obligation to contribute their proportional share of the operating expenses of the building such as taxes, insurance, utilities, maintenance and other costs and expenses. The *cooperative association* often had *approval rights on the sale of a share of stock representing a unit*. If the cooperative association did not approve the buyer who was trying to buy a share of stock and thereby gain the proprietary lease on one of the units, the sale could be blocked. This would trigger the obligation on the other co-op owners to purchase the stock (at the price as would have been paid by the rejected buyer). Although the owners would later sell the unit to an approved buyer, the requirement to come up with their share of the purchase price could represent a substantial financial burden on the other co-op owners.

Condominiums – Condominium ownership differs in many from that of a co-op apartment. In a condominium, the owner owns real estate rather than a share of stock. The condo unit is, in reality, *a space in the building*, and the condo owner has ownership of only the internal walls, cabinets, fixtures, appliances, carpets, floors, etc. The land on which the condominium building sits, the parking spaces, the club house, the swimming pool, and other features or amenities of the condominium (**common elements**) are owned by all (**undivided interest**) of the condominium owners as *tenants in common*.

Condominium owners are able to obtain separate financing for their unit and are allowed the interest deduction for interest paid, the same as a homeowner. Likewise, their unit is separately taxed (deductible) and is separately insured. There will be a monthly assessment against each of the condominium units for the expenses of the common area including property taxes, insurance, maintenance, and management of the condominium. These assessments are usually called *condominium fees*.

The condominium project is created by the developer preparing, obtaining approval of the county or city authorities, and recording the *master deed*. The master deed sets out the ownership interests, creates the *condominium owners association* and the bylaws for this association, as well as the *Covenants, Conditions and Restrictions (CC&Rs)* which control the activities of the owners of the condominium units.

Townhomes – A townhome may appear to be a single family dwelling which is physically attached to adjacent structures. Each townhome is usually two-or three stories and typically sits on its own parcel of land. The owner of the townhome owns the land upon which the structure sits and also owns other common property (pools, tennis courts, parks, etc.) in the townhome project as a tenant in common with the other owners in the development.

Mixed use projects – a *mixed use development* will be designed around different but compatible users in it, such as residential, retail, restaurant, office and medical/dental facilities. Ownerships arrangements differ from project to project, but are usually similar to condominiums.

Timeshares – A timeshare may be envisioned as *the right to use and occupy a residential unit on a periodic recurring basis, according to an arrangement among the other owners, regardless if there is an additional charge for same.*

In most timeshare projects, the timeshare buyer purchases a right to use a unit (the actual room or suite where the persons will stay) for a week. Normally this week occurs annually, but depending on the timeshare plan, it could occur more or less frequently.

Most American timeshare projects are selling a real estate interest evidenced by a deed. This is referred to as a *deeded timeshare*. The other form of timeshare is based upon a lease. This is referred to as a *right to use timeshare*, and is often found on timeshares sold in foreign countries where non-citizens of that country are not permitted real estate ownership.

In most deeded timeshare projects, the deed from the project conveys an undivided interest in the common area, and most, if not all, of the project is common area.

FREEHOLD ESTATES IN REAL PROPERTY

Freehold estates – "Freehold" translates to "ownership" and provides the bundle of rights of ownership for an indeterminable period of time, either based upon someone's lifetime or forever. Freehold estates may either be **Fee Simple Estates** or **Life Estates.**

A *fee simple estate,* could be a fee simple absolute or fee simple defeasible. A *fee simple absolute* is the highest quality interest in real estate in that the holder has all the rights recognized by law. With an estate in fee simple, the estate runs forever and upon the death of the owner, the property is inheritable to the heirs. This is the ideal form of ownership.

A *defeasible fee* (or *fee simple defeasible* or *determinable fee*), has an attached stipulation such as "for as long as" or "during" and provided that condition is not broken, the holder remains in title. Upon the occurrence of that designated event, title to the property **reverts** back to the former grantor. Because the title *could* revert to the grantor, the grantor is said to have a **reversionary interest**. A defeasible fee estate is inheritable.

Freehold estates may also be classified as *life estates*, based upon the life of the owner, or some other designated person. Life estates are not inheritable so it is necessary to pre-determine to whom title shall pass upon the passing of named party.

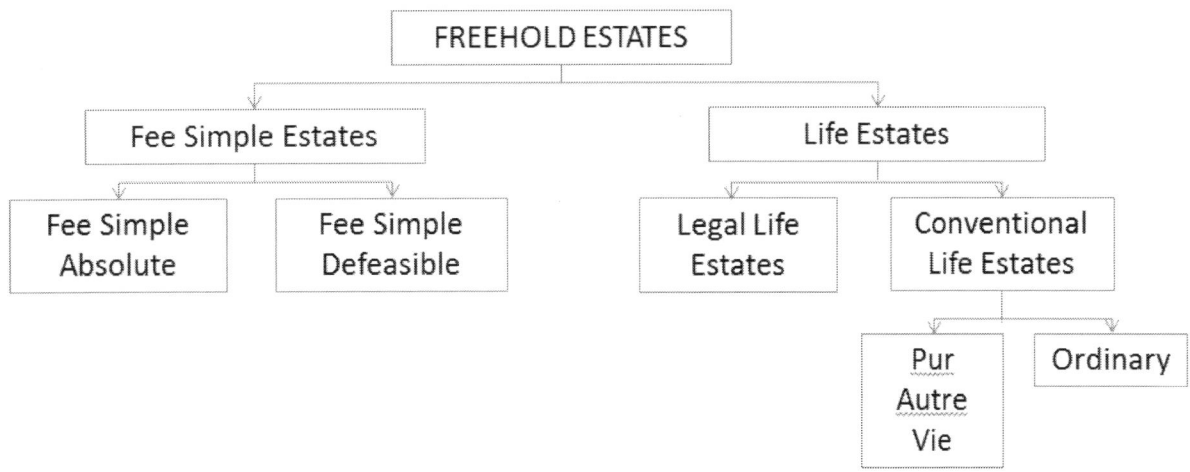

The owner of a life estate, referred to as the *life tenant* and not to be confused with "tenant" in the context of a lease agreement), can sell the property, mortgage, lease, in fact has all the rights any other property owner would with the exception that things change upon the death.

In an *ordinary life estate,* title to the property will pass upon the death of the owner. But to whom? The individual who created the life estate may name a *remainderman* who will take the title to the property as a fee simple estate. Or, the creator of the life estate may elect to elect for the property to revert to the original owner of the property who is said to have a *reversionary interest*.

Example: Tom wishes for his brother Berry to have title to an investment home that Tom currently owns, but Tom does not wish for Berry 's heirs to take title to the house upon Berry's death. Tom wants the property to revert back to Tom or to Tom's heirs if he is no longer living. Tom could create an ordinary life estate with a reversionary interest.

Example: If Tom wanted his sister Alice to take title upon Berry's death, rather than Berry's heirs, or rather than for the property to revert to Tom or his heirs, Tom could grant a life estate to Berry with Alice having a remainder interest.

A *pur autre vie*, which translates to "for another's life," life estate, dictates that title to the property that the life tenant enjoys shall transfer to another individual upon the death of some other named person.

Legal life estates, as the name implies, are created by state law. Dower, curtesy, and homestead are legal life estates used in some states. **Homestead** laws protect a homeowner's personal residence from certain creditors. The exemption offers virtually absolute protection, with no limit, from forced sale to meet the demands of creditors, except under special circumstances. The residence is not protected, however, from liens for nonpayment of property taxes, mortgage liens, construction liens, or mechanic's liens. By filing the homestead exemption in some states, property owners receive a reduction from the assessed value in the calculation of property taxes.

Elective share – protects a surviving spouse in the event the deceased spouse left the surviving spouse out of the will. The law provides the surviving spouse with a percentage of the decedent's net estate consisting of both real and personal property, a homesteaded property if any, and property owned as tenants by the entireties.

TRANSFER OF TITLE

This section deals with the transfer of title, or ownership, from one person or business entity to another. We will look at the subjects of deeds, title insurance, escrow and closing processes, special cases like foreclosures and short sales, and the tax aspects of transferring title.

DEEDS

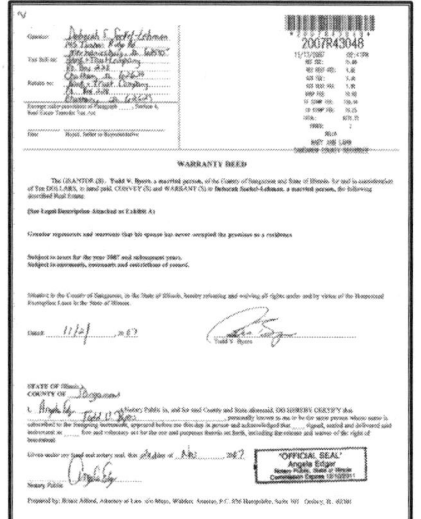

A ***deed*** is the only instrument used for the conveyance of title of real property.

The word deed comes from a ritual in English common law. If the owner of the property desired to convey it to another, *twelve men good and true* would be called out to the property from the village. In the presence of these twelve men, the party conveying the property would dig up a clump of the soil and hand it to the party to which the property was being conveyed. This was the *deed of conveyance*. Should there later be a dispute over the conveyance, the party defending title would locate one or more of the twelve men, good and true, who would then say under oath whether the deed had happened and whether it appeared to be a voluntary act.

During the time in England when this ritual was being used, very few people could read or write, so a written document concerning the conveyance was of little use. Likewise, the use of twelve men tended to ensure there would be witnesses available for a significant time into the future. These twelve men equate to our public record system of today. Today, if a conveyance occurs, it is in the form of a written instrument which is ***acknowledged*** or witnessed by a notary public, and normally recorded in the public records in the county in which the land is located.

There are three concepts common to all deeds:

- **Recordation** – Deeds are recorded in the county in which the land is located.

- **Two parties** – There are two parties to a deed – the ***grantor*** is the person making the conveyance and the ***grantee*** is the person to whom the conveyance is made.

- **Warranties and covenants** – a *warranty* or *covenant* is a promise by the grantor to the grantee concerning the title to the property, that some condition exists and will continue to exist, or, that a condition does not exist and never will.

The following paragraphs describe several types of deeds and their covenants:

General warranty deed (also known as a warranty deed, or grant, bargain, and sale deed):

This is the most commonly used form of deed and it contains five (5) warranties (covenants):

1. **Warranty of seisin** – The grantor owns the property and has the right and power to convey the property (seisin is an old French word dealing with a ceremony, the *livery of seisin*, which was an ancient ceremony used in England and France to convey real property to a new owner).

2. **Warranty against undisclosed encumbrances** – The grantor has disclosed to the grantee all encumbrances on the property, if any.

3. **Warranty of quiet enjoyment** – The grantee will be able to enjoy ownership of the property without hearing anyone make a valid claim of superior title or right to the property.

4. **Warranty of further assurances** – The grantor promises that should a claim of superior title be made, the grantor will defend against the claim and defeat it.

5. **Warranty of title forever** – The grantor promises that should another party be able to establish a superior claim to the title, the grantor will pay back to the grantee the purchase price (the *money back guarantee*).

General Warranty Deed: 5 Warranties
1. Warranty of Seisin
2. Warranty Against Undisclosed Encumbrances
3. Warranty of Quiet Enjoyment
4. Warranty of Further Assurance
5. Warranty Forever

Special warranty deed: (used by executors, trustees and universal or general agents of the grantor)

Warranty against undisclosed encumbrances – the only warranty created by the special warranty deed. With a special warranty deed, if the grantor has created any encumbrances they are disclosed. However, the grantor makes no further warranties and makes no assurances for when the property was not owned by him. If the grantor does not own the property, but is authorized to convey under a will, a trust, a power of attorney, then no warranty of seisin is made.

Quit claim deed: (the "clean-up" deed of real estate)

No warranties at all – The grantor is *quitting* any claim the grantor may have to the property, but does not assert that there is any claim at all. This deed is often used to remove liens and encumbrances from title, to surrender community property claims, or to clear *clouds on the title.*

Bargain and sale deed:

Implied warranty of seisin – This implied warranty is found in that only owners of property would normally enter into negotiations ("bargaining") about a property and then agree to sell it. There are no written warranties and is only an implication that the grantor has title and the legal right to convey it.

Requirements for a valid deed:

1. **In writing** – A deed must be in writing and signed by all owners of the interest being sold.

2. **Valid grantor** – The grantor, if a natural person, must be alive, of lawful age, and have full mental capacity. Note that a minor, or a person who lacks the mental capacity to enter a contract, cannot make a valid conveyance. If the grantor is a business entity (corporation, partnership, or LLC) it must be lawfully in existence, and the human signing on its behalf must be duly authorized to act for the entity.

3. **Identifiable grantee** – The grantee must be *identifiable.* For example, a deed to John Doe and Wife would raise the question of was John Doe married on the date of the deed and, if so, to whom?

4. **Consideration clause** – There must be a consideration clause reflecting one of these four types of consideration (anything of value):

    a. *actual consideration* – the purchase price
    b. *nominal consideration* – $1.00 and other consideration
    c. *good consideration* – for love and affection
    d. *legal consideration* – for value received

5. **Granting clause** – There must be a granting clause which states the nature and extent of the interest conveyed – *fee simple interest in . . . ,* or *25% interest in . . . ,* etc.

6. **Vesting clause** – There must be a vesting clause. Normally, vesting is a choice of the grantee, but may be stated by the grantor. The grantee or grantees would be named, followed by words that say: *in severalty,* as *a tenant in common,* as *joint tenants with right of survivorship,* etc.

7. **Habendum clause** – There may be a habendum clause (not usually required) which says "to have and to hold from this day forward." The habendum clause is not required in some states, but if there is one, its presence could be beneficial.

8. **Valid legal description** – There must be a valid legal description of the property being conveyed; either:

    a. lot, block and subdivision
    b. metes and bounds
    c. reference to the USGS survey

9. **Exceptions and reservations**:

    a. Here is where the grantor will make the grant subject to any exceptions, encumbrances, or liens on title which will not be removed by the grantor. For example, words like these could appear: "subject to encumbrances, easements and restrictions of record, if any."

    b. Here is also where the grantor may create restriction or easements. For example: "subject to an easement in favor of the grantor across the south 20 feet of the property, and subject to the right of the grantor to come upon the property at any time without notice to fish in the pond."

10. **Grantor's signature** – The grantor must sign the deed. If it is a business entity, evidence that the party signing for the business entity is authorized to sign the deed will be required. This authorization needs to be in "recordable form," meaning that the signatures on it must be notarized.

11. **Attestation** – The *attestation* in a deed is the notary public's attestation that the signing parties appeared before the notary, swore they were who they said they were, were authorized to sign the deed and did so as their free act, and actually signed the deed in the presence of the notary public. Attestation is required in most states if the deed will be filed in the public records, however, it is not necessary for the validity of the deed between the grantor and grantee.

12. **Acknowledgement** – This is the *witnessing* by witnesses of the grantor signing the deed. Like the attestation, acknowledgement is not required for the validity of the deed between the grantor and grantee. Acknowledgement would be important if the deed were not notarized and not placed in the public records. Any challenge to the deed would have to be defended by producing one or more of the witnesses who would testify as to the circumstances they observed concerning the grantor's apparent capacity and whether it was an act of free will.

13. **Delivery and acceptance** – This is the actual point or act of conveyance. Delivery and acceptance must be:

a. intended by the grantor. A deed delivered by accident or under fraudulent or coercive circumstances would not be a valid conveyance.

b. commenced during the lifetime of the grantor. For example, the grantor is taking the deed to the post office in an envelope with proper address and postage on it. As he enters the post office, he has a massive stroke and dies on the spot. A bystander thinking he's helping takes the envelope out of the dead grantor's hands and drops it in the mail slot. This is not a valid delivery because it was not commenced during the grantor's lifetime.

Recording deeds – The purpose of recording the deed is to establish the priority of the grantee over others who may claim or contend they have a claim to title to the property. Recording will establish the grantee's priority as of the date the deed is recorded. For notice to be effective, the deed must be recorded in the county in which the property is located.

TITLE INSURANCE

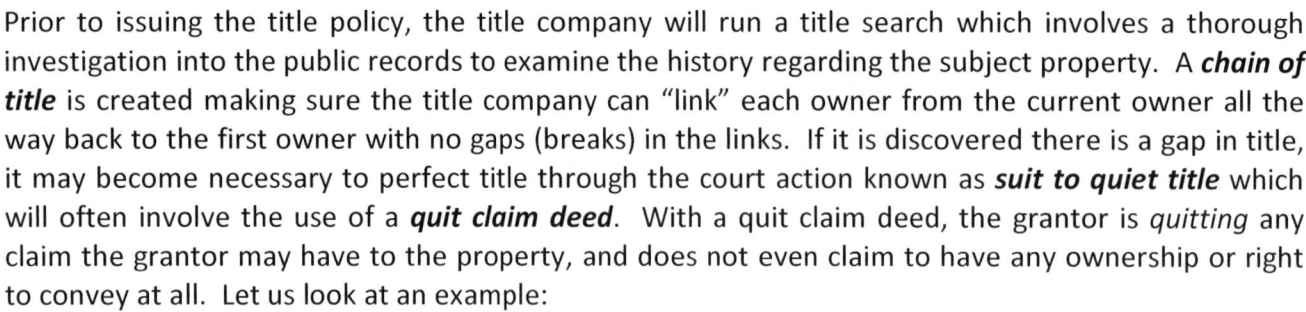

The primary purpose of a title insurance policy is to:

- assure the grantee that the status of the title is as the grantor warrants;
- provide the financial assurance that title will be defended if necessary by the title insurance company;
- pay the grantee the purchase price should the grantee's title be defeated by another who is able to make a superior claim.

Prior to issuing the title policy, the title company will run a title search which involves a thorough investigation into the public records to examine the history regarding the subject property. A **chain of title** is created making sure the title company can "link" each owner from the current owner all the way back to the first owner with no gaps (breaks) in the links. If it is discovered there is a gap in title, it may become necessary to perfect title through the court action known as **suit to quiet title** which will often involve the use of a **quit claim deed**. With a quit claim deed, the grantor is *quitting* any claim the grantor may have to the property, and does not even claim to have any ownership or right to convey at all. Let us look at an example:

In doing the title search, the title company found the transfer of title from A to B, from B to C, and then somehow, E ended up in title. The title company could not explain how E took title, but then E transferred title to F. In order to clear this gap in title (sometimes called a "cloud"), they may request a court order requiring C to issue a quit claim deed to E.

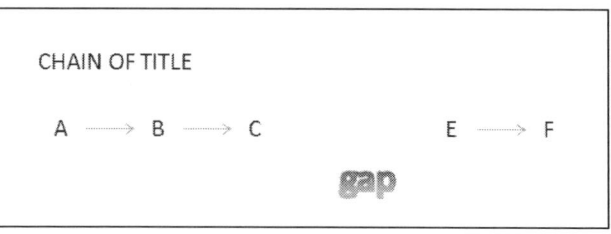

CHAIN OF TITLE

A → B → C   E → F

gap

The title company will then prepare an *abstract of title* summarizing everything found in the public records which will include recorded encumbrances and liens. Unrecorded matters will not be noted as they will not be found. An attorney may provide a similar service called an *opinion of title* after reviewing the abstract of title and rendering an opinion as to whether the title is *marketable* (good).

If the title company feels the title is marketable it will be willing to issue title insurance. Two commonly-used types of title insurance policies are the CLTA and the ALTA policies. Purchasers of residential property typically have the opportunity to choose which type of policy they want to purchase (or have the seller purchase on their behalf).

CLTA title insurance policy – This is a policy written to the standards of the California Land Title Association.

Coverage of a CLTA policy – A CLTA policy provides coverage up to the amount of the purchase price and provides coverage against:

1. forgery of the deed.

2. declaration of a marital status which is incorrect. For example, the deed refers to the grantees as John Doe and Rachel Doe, as husband and wife, when in fact they are brother and sister; or it refers to the grantee as Renee Roe, a single woman, when in fact she is married. Under some circumstance these incorrect declarations of marital status could have legal significance.

3. lack of mental capacity of the grantor. Generally, there is no way to determine the mental capacity of the grantor at the time the deed is signed. However, should it be proven that the grantor was not of sound mind, the deed could be set aside and the title insurance company would have to defend on behalf of the grantee and pay the grantee's loss up to the policy limit.

4. improper delivery. If the delivery of the deed was made by mistake or under circumstances of fraud, or not commenced during the lifetime of the grantor, the deed would be invalid. Proper delivery normally could not be discovered just by examining the deed. However, should it be proven that the delivery was improper, the deed could be set aside, and the title insurance company would have to defend on behalf of the grantee and pay the grantee's loss up to the policy limit.

Exclusions to coverage of a CLTA policy – No coverage is provided under the typical CLTA policy for:

1. specific exceptions. The policy will list any specific exceptions against which there is no insurance. These are items which will have been disclosed in the preliminary title report and have not been corrected by the seller.

2. unrecorded defects in title. This exception exempts the title insurance company from having to pay for any claims which had never been recorded. If they were not recorded, the title

company would not have been able to find them. If they had been recorded and the grantor did not correct them, then they would have become specific exceptions listed in the policy.

3. matters which would be discovered through a survey. The title insurance company is not going to go out to the property to see if there are any encroachments, or to verify the size of the property. That is all up to the parties as a part of their contracting process. So if encroachments exist, or the size is not what the grantee wanted, the title insurance company will have no liability for those disputes.

4. rights of persons in possession. It is possible that there are persons in possession of the property, perhaps under a lease with the grantor, or are on the property as licensees, or for the purpose of taking profits, or may just be trespassers? The title insurance company is not going to go out and look for these persons, or try to determine what, if any, claim they may really have. The title insurance company, by way of the exclusion, will not have liability for those disputes.

ALTA title insurance policy – This is a policy written to the standards of the American Land Title Association.

Coverage of an ALTA policy – This policy is written to the more stringent standards of the *American Land Title Association* and is designed to protect the lender. This policy is normally purchased by the buyer for the lender. It provides *extended* coverage beyond the CLTA coverage. This is a *stacking coverage*, meaning it is on top of the coverage provided in the CLTA policy. The additional coverages in an ALTA policy are:

1. survey issues; matters which would be disclosed by an examination of a survey of the property.

2. matters which would be discovered upon an inspection of the property. These matters would include "encroachments," and rights of "persons in possession." NOTE: title insurance does not insure the "condition" of the structures or other improvements, only matters which might challenge title. So the fact that the property needs a new roof is not a concern of the title insurance company.

3. unrecorded defects in title. The lender is very sensitive to the status of title of its collateral and will want some additional assurances against claims that may exist, but are not discoverable by a title search. Since a search of the title is about all the insurance company can do, the insurance company will have to calculate its risk and adjust its premium accordingly.

MISCELLANEOUS ISSUES IN THE TRANSFER OF TITLE

Voluntary vs. Involuntary Alienation – "Alienation" refers to "alienating" or separating one's self from the property. One can have his property transferred to another in either a voluntary or involuntary way. Examples of voluntary alienation usually involve a deed where the owner voluntarily transfers his title to another person. Examples of involuntary transfers are a transfer by will upon his death, foreclosure, adverse possession, condemnation, and erosion or avulsion (wearing away of the land).

Conveyance after death – When a property owner dies, the process of transferring real property to others is dependent on whether or not the deceased person had prepared a will. Those who have a will are said to have died *testate*. Those who have not are said to have died *intestate.*

Transfer of title for an intestate person – If a person dies intestate, the state in which the property is located has laws to ensure that the real and personal property transfer to the decedent's heirs according to the state's *statute of descent and distribution*. Essentially, the state is making a will for the decedent.

Transfer of title by will – A will is a legal document initiated by a person, while alive, to transfer real and personal property upon his death. A will is effective only upon death, and the persons named in the will have no rights to the property until death occurs. A person who makes a will, the *testator,* can give away three classes of assets:

- real property – a *devise*, given to a *devisee*
- personal property – a *bequest*
- money – a *legacy*

For title to pass from a decedent to another person, state laws require that the will be filed with a court and probated. Probate is the formal process or making sure the will is valid and making an accounting of the assets of the deceased. As a formal judicial process, probate can take months to complete.

Some real property, primarily that held by joint tenancy or by tenancy in the entirety, will distribute itself. The probate process will not be involved.

Some states have laws relating *dower* (a wife's legal interest, upon her husband's death, to property her husband has or acquired during their marriage) and *curtesy* (similar to dower, but dealing with the wife's property) which protect the rights of a surviving spouse, and a will cannot supersede these laws. If a will fails to provide for a surviving spouse, the spouse may demand it from the estate.

The right to inherit under laws of descent varies from state to state and property is distributed under these laws.

Legal requirements for making a will:

- Follow state law. Only a will that follows state law in the state where the property is located can be used to transfer the title to real estate.

- A testator must have legal capacity. Absent any hard rules, this usually means being of legal age and sound mind. It also refers to a voluntary act on the part of the testator.

- The will must be signed, and in most states it must also be witnessed by two additional people, not named in the will, who also sign the document. Many states do not recognize or allow property to be transferred by handwritten *(holographic)* or oral *(nuncupative)* wills.

- A testator may alter a will at any time. This is done with another document called a **codicil**. The original will is not physically altered.

- Under the law of decent and distribution in most states, the primary heirs of a decedent are the spouse and close blood relatives, like children, parents, brothers, sisters, aunts, uncles, and in some cases even cousins.

Probate process – A formal judicial process that had developed to ensure that assets are distributed properly. Probate accomplishes three things:

1. confirms that a particular will is valid if there is a will
2. adds up or accounts for all of a decedent's assets
3. identifies the people who will receive the assets

Probate takes place in the county of residence of the decedent and also in every other county where the decedent owned property.

The steps of the probate process are typically as follows:

1. The person in possession of the will, normally the **executor** of the will, presents it to the court, which files the will.
2. If anyone is in possession of a second or third will, et al, they present it to the court as well. The court will uphold one of the wills.
3. The court will approve the person to distribute the assets, including the real property. The executor will be approved to distribute the assets if there is a will. If there is no will, an **administrator** will be named.

ESCROW AND CLOSING

When you buy a used car, you give your money to the seller and the seller hands over the car, title, and the keys. That's about it.

Buying real property is a lot more complex and normally requires an *intermediary* to manage and close the transaction. The process of closing may be accomplished either with the use of attorneys, by the brokerages involved, or through the use of an escrow company or agent, referred to as an **escrowee**.

The number of real estate transactions has dramatically increased in recent years and as the closing process has become more specialized, closings with the use of the escrow agent have become the norm in most areas of the country.

Most of the time, the escrow function is performed by a company affiliated with a title insurance company or agency. The individual who actually conducts the closing is referred to as the escrow agent and is acting on behalf of the escrow company to perform the obligations in the escrow instructions. The escrow contract, often referred to as the ***escrow instructions***, is a three-party agreement between the seller, the buyer and the escrow agent. This agreement authorizes the escrow agent to collect certain monies, documents, obtain signatures, and deliver the completed documents when all of the conditions in the escrow instructions have been met. When all has been done, the escrow agent ensures that all monies have been disbursed and the proper documents (deeds, etc.) have been recorded in the public record.

Escrow process – The following steps will explain the normal steps of an escrow process:

- The escrow company will begin the escrow process when they receive the complete purchase contract and the good faith funds, also called the earnest money deposit. An escrow officer will be assigned to manage the escrow process and an escrow account number will be assigned. At this point, the parties say that *escrow has been opened*.

- The escrow company will conduct a title search to determine the ownership and status of the subject property. At this point, the title company (which may be the same company as the escrow company, or may be a different company) will issue a title report and start the process of deleting or recording items to provide clear title to the property. At the end of this process, the title company will issue a commitment to provide a policy of title insurance on the property.

- The escrow agent will request payoffs for all of the financial items that are currently encumbering the title. These might include mechanic's liens, unpaid HOA fees or fines, trash collection bills, unpaid sewer charges, IRS liens, seller's loans, etc. Sometimes these payoff requests are referred to as *demands* for information.

- The escrowee will work with the buyer's lender to understand and monitor the progress of the loan application and underwriting activities.

- Based on the close of escrow date, the escrowee will prorate all taxes, HOA charges, interest charges, etc., and other items that will have to be divided or prorated between buyer and seller.

- The escrowee will prepare the settlement statement, typically referred to as the ***HUD-1.***

- The escrowee will set up separate appointments just before the close of escrow, for the seller and buyer to sign the documents required to transfer title. For the seller, these include the deed, several disclosures, and a few other items. For the cash buyer, the total number of documents is limited. For the buyer obtaining financing, these documents will include the buyer's loan documents, which may be a substantial quantity.

- The escrow agent will collect the buyer's funds at this time, and in all probability, these will be wire transferred to the escrow agent's bank.

- After all funds have been deposited, the escrow agent will record various documents with the county recorder to transfer the property from seller to buyer. After *recordation* is confirmed, the agent will disburse funds to the seller, the seller's lender (if applicable), HOAs, taxing authorities, home warranty companies, real estate brokers, and others. Also, in most states, after recordation has taken place, the keys are provided to the buyer.

- The escrow agent will distribute the final documents to the seller's broker, the seller, the buyer's broker, the buyer, and others. Closing has taken place.

It is important to note that there are operational differences between any two escrow companies and these are due to two factors.

- Escrow companies charge for their services and these escrow fees are a large part of their income. So, each company strives to serve its customers well. They all develop different ways of doing so.

- State laws for real estate transactions, mortgages and lending, and many other factors create different environments in every jurisdiction. Escrow processes, even those of national firms, must address these differences, so they are different in each state.

Closing costs – Among the more important aspects of the closing process are the costs associated with selling or purchasing, appropriately termed *closing costs* because they are collected at the time of closing. It is important to know that closing costs are handled and treated differently by escrow companies across the country based on:

- **local laws and customs** – It may be customary in one city for the seller to pay the transfer tax (as an example), while 100 miles away, it is the buyer who normally pays this tax.
- **foreclosures** – It is included in the charter of various federal agencies that own foreclosed homes that they cannot pay taxes to a local jurisdiction. Since they are effectively the "seller" in some transactions, this responsibility shifts to the buyer.
- **short sales** – Some short sale banks (the lender who has suffered the buyer's default) will not pay certain closing costs that would normally be paid by the seller, so these costs fall to the buyer to pay.

- **VA loans** – These loans require the seller to pay certain closing costs, and the buyer may be prohibited by law from paying these charges.
- **agreement of the parties** – Buyers are free to ask, in their offers, that the sellers pay for any number of things as a condition of the sale. If the other terms of the contract are beneficial to the seller, the seller may opt to pay some of these items or even provide the buyer with a cash amount to help the buyer pay for closing costs.

For these reasons, it is somewhat difficult to determine whether the buyer or the seller will pay for any particular closing cost. This chart is meant to give a general (not exact) picture of this complex cost breakdown:

"Closing Costs" and Other Costs Paid at the Time of Closing	Buyer Usually Pays	Seller Usually Pays	Negotiable (Contract)
Title policy premium	Lender's	Owner's	
Escrow fee (seller pays all if VA loan)	½	½	
Document preparation fee	X		
Notary fees (if applicable)	X		
Recording charges for all documents in buyers' names	X		
Homeowners association transfer fee			X
Two months homeowners association fee	X		
All new lender's loan and loan origination charges	X		
Points to reduce interest rate	X		
Interest on new loan, date of funding to 30 days prior to first payment	X		
Assumption fees for takeover of existing loan	X		
Home warranty fee per contract			X
Hazard insurance premium for first 12-14 months	X		
All prepaid items for loan escrow account	X		
Courier fees	X		
Professional Home Inspection			X
Appraisal fee	X		
Owner's title insurance premium		X	
Realtor commission		X	
Any loan fees required by buyer's lender (FHA and VA)		X	
All loans in seller's name		X	
Interest accrued on the loan being paid off		X	
Transfer taxes		X	
Termite inspection and termite repairs (per contract)			X
Homeowner association disclosure document fee		X	
Unpaid homeowner association dues		X	
Judgments, tax liens, mechanic's liens against seller		X	
Recording charges to clear any documents against seller		X	
Property taxes, prorated to the day of closing, plus any in arrears		X	
Bonds or assessments			X
Courier fees if applicable		X	
Septic fees per contract			X
Any repairs per contract			X

Remember, these expenses, including who incurs their cost, varies from location to location. As a practicing licensee, you should research the closing costs in your area and who generally pays for each expense.

FORECLOSURES/SHORT SALES

Foreclosures – involve a process which ensues when a property which has been used as security for a debt (typically a mortgage) and the debtor has defaulted on the promise to pay the debt. The foreclosure process is designed to protect the rights of all parties, bring them to a conclusion, and to pass title to the holder of the mortgage or to a third party, usually known as a *trustee*, who will arrange for the property to be sold at auction, free of all encumbrances.

> *Did you know??? Should the proceeds of sale, whether a foreclosure sale or short sale, be insufficient to satisfy the loan, the lender can sue the borrower for the shortage? This is a "deficiency judgment."*

These organizations guarantee loans and often wind up as the owners or trustees of a parcel of real estate:

- **Banks, credit unions, etc.** – these organizations often foreclose on properties under their control. These would represent instances where the bank or credit union has not yet sold the loan on the secondary market.

- **The Federal Housing Administration (FHA)** – a government agency that insures home loans or mortgages.

- **Fannie Mae (FNMA)** and **Freddie Mac (FHLMC)** – government-sponsored companies that buy mortgages on the secondary market.

- **Veterans Administration (VA)** – a government agency that guarantees loans made to eligible veterans.

- **Private mortgage insurance companies (PMI)** – privately-owned companies which insure home loans against borrower defaults.

From time to time, these organizations become owners of foreclosed homes which are put on the market for sale, usually through the real estate community. It is useful that each organization has developed its own set of rules and procedures for selling and transferring title of these homes.

The FHA turns to another government agency, the Department of Housing and Urban Development (HUD), to market their foreclosed homes. HUD uses an online bidding system, found at www.hudhomestore.com to market these homes to the public, with the assistance of the real estate community.

Fannie Mae and Freddie Mac place their inventories with real estate brokers, but, as owners, control most aspects of the sale.

Short sales – A *short sale*, also known as a *pre-foreclosure*, is the sale of a mortgaged or secured property for less than is owed to the lender. Lenders agree to short sales when there is little hope that the borrower can make adequate payments on the mortgage loan. This often occurs when the borrower experiences a hardship of some kind, such as loss of employment, large medical bills, divorce, or something equally significant.

The lender may prefer to take the route of a short sale, rather than pursue a foreclosure, if the short sale, with the payment from the PMI company, yields a better result to the lender.

The process of transferring title is almost the same as it is for a standard resale, with these major differences:

- The lender must approve the buyer, who may not be a relative of the seller or anyone known to the seller.
- The lender must approve the contract terms.
- The lender must approve the sale amount and will often demand a sale price higher than the price cited in the contract.
- The lender will demand a certain net amount from the sale.
- A close of escrow date must be met.
- The seller must vacate the home and not live there again.
- The seller cannot walk away with proceeds.

Tax treatment of foreclosures and short sales – It has long been the position of the IRS that debt which is forgiven counts as income. Thus, all forgiven debt from foreclosures and short sales will generate a 1099-C (The C stands for cancellation of debt) in the year it was forgiven.

It will be necessary for taxpayers to account for this forgiven debt on their tax returns for the appropriate years. However, the *Mortgage Forgiveness Debt Relief Act of 2007* essentially forgives this debt and the seller's tax liability. This legislation was passed in 2007, at the beginning of the short sale and foreclosures boom that struck the United States and has been extended for 2008, 2009, 2010, 2011, 2012, and 2013.

TAX ASPECTS OF TRANSFERRING TITLE

A real estate transaction may have many tax considerations. A real estate professional should be aware of general tax matters, but unless specifically skilled and educated in taxation, should not render tax advice or opinions.

The following subjects are presented for general awareness and so agents can understand the language and some of the concerns of clients and customers.

Capital gain – When a real property asset is sold there is often a *capital gain*. If the asset is sold for more than its original basis, the *profit* realized may represent a capital gain. If the property is an investment property, the capital gain can probably be treated under the capital gain provisions in the tax code.

The rate of taxation will depend on the length of time the taxpayer owned the asset. Profits from assets held for a number of years are classified as long-term capital gains and receive favorable tax treatment. Assets held for shorter periods are short-term capital gains and are taxed at higher rates.

In determining the amount of the capital gain (long or short-term) the investor will determine the adjusted basis he has in the investment property and add the costs of sale to that. The adjusted basis plus the costs of sale are subtracted from the sale price of the investment property. If the resulting number is "positive" the investor has a capital gain, if the number is "negative" the investor has suffered a capital loss. The holding period will determine if the gain or loss is long or short-term.

Deductible – Certain costs of home ownership are generally tax deductible and may be deducted from the owner's gross income. These costs include the interest on the loan, local property taxes, and certain loan origination fees.

Depreciation – This is the reduction in value of a structure over time, according to schedules and methods applied by accountants and CPAs. Generally speaking, an investor buys a building and leases it to a tenant. The tenant pays rent to the owner who puts the money in a bank account and uses a portion to pay taxes, maintenance, utilities, and other expenses. The portion remaining after expenses is gross profit. Before paying taxes on these profits, the owner deserves to recoup the cost of the building, and he does this through depreciation, applying 3% (or so) of the cost of the building (but not the land) each year. This is like an extra expense, which has the net effect of reducing the owner's tax bill.

Capital improvement – a major or significant improvement to investment property which will add value to the investment property and is of a durable nature and which will or is expected to last several years.

Adjusted basis – the original purchase price of an investment property plus any capital improvements made, less any depreciation previously taken.

Costs of sale – those reasonable and necessary costs of selling an investment property which would include real estate commissions and closing costs paid in connection with the sale.

Other investment tax considerations – Real estate investments often have two components to consider. If the property produces current income, normally in the form of rents, this income may be subject to federal and state income taxes. Also, when the investment property is sold, there may be the matter of a capital gain or loss.

In order to produce income, the investor often must incur *ordinary and necessary expenses.* These are the so called *operating expenses* and are normally deductible by the investor from the *gross rental income.* The investor may have a loan against the income producing property, if so, he may deduct the interest paid on the loan, but may not deduct the principal reduction. The investor also may deduct property taxes paid on the investment property. After the deductions for operating expenses, property taxes and loan interest, (the *cash expenses* of the property) the investor may deduct the annual allowed depreciation (a *non-cash expense* of the property) to determine if he has taxable income from the investment property.

EXAMPLE: An investor has a 20 unit apartment building which is fully rented. The units rent for $900 each per month. He has paid the following:

Interest on the loan	$99,300
Property taxes	$19,500
Advertising	$14,500
Insurance	$ 9,200
General repairs	$18,000
Utilities	$ 4,300
Leasing commissions	$12,500

He has calculated his depreciation according the IRS Code and it equals $49,300. What, if any, income did he receive from this investment this year?

SOLUTION: Rental Income: ($900 x 20 units x 12 months) = $216,000
– Less Operating Expenses:

Advertising	14,500	
Utilities	4,300	
Insurance	9,200	
Repairs	18,000	
Commissions	12,500	
Property Taxes	19,500	
Interest	99,300	
		($177,300)
= Net Operating Income		38,700
– Less depreciation		(49,300)
= Operating loss after depreciation		(10,600)

This example shows the impact of the non-cash expense of depreciation. Had the investor not been able to deduct depreciation, he would have had a taxable income of $38,700; but, as a result of the non-cash deduction for depreciation he "sheltered" $38,700 from taxation and had an additional loss of $10,600 which he may be able to use to offset other income.

Taxation on gain from sale of personal residence – In recent years, the tax treatment on any gains from the sale of the personal residence has been changed significantly. Provided you meet the requirement that you have owned the property for two out of the last five years and have occupied it as your personal residence for two out of the last five years, if you sell it and realize a gain on the sale, you may be exempt from the gain based upon your filing status.

If you are single and filing as an unmarried person, you will be exempt for the first $250,000 of gain. If you are a married couple and either of you have owned the property for two out of the last five years and both of you have occupied the property for two out of the last five years, and you are filing jointly, $500,000 of the gain will be exempt.

For personal residences, the gain is the difference between sale price and the original purchase price plus capital improvements and selling expenses. Note that a personal residence cannot be depreciated.

Foreign Investor in Real Property Tax Act (FIRPTA) – This tax issue applies to the sale of properties in the United States by foreign nationals or foreign corporations. At close of escrow, 10% of the gross sale price will be withheld and transmitted to the IRS. This is done as many foreign nationals and foreign corporations were enjoying capital gains and other profits on their purchases of US properties, but were taking the profits back to their country without paying any tax to the US Government. (There is an exclusion for residential property less than $300,000 in sale price.)

Tax deferred exchanges under section 1031 of the IRS code – To encourage investment in investment real estate, investors are permitted to *exchange or trade* their property for other U.S. investment property and may be able to do so without having a current taxable event. The general rules are:

- must be U.S. Property
- must be *like kind* property (real estate exchanged for real estate)
- must trade equal or up in value (no **boot** added to make up the difference in value)
- must trade equal or up in debt on property

If any of these rules are broken the exchange treatment may be lost.

Remember that the purpose of the tax deferred exchange is to delay the payment of taxes on the capital gain to some point into the future when the actual cost of the taxes may be lower as a result of inflation. If future dollars will buy less as a result of inflation, those dollars are worth less. If the deferred taxes are paid with "cheaper" dollars the effective tax is less.

Chapter 5: Property Ownership and Transfer of Title
End of Chapter Quiz

1. Which of the following is NOT a physical characteristic of land?

    a. indestructibility
    b. immobility
    c. beauty
    d. uniqueness

2. Notice that a lien or other encumbrance may soon be filed on a parcel of property is known as a:

    a. writ of attachment.
    b. writ of association.
    c. lis pendens.
    d. abstract of judgment.

3. Three unrelated owners took title to a warehouse building as joint tenants. One of the owners died testate. The remaining two owners now own the building:

    a. as joint tenants.
    b. under the state's laws of descent.
    c. in severalty.
    d. subject to the terms of the deceased person's will.

4. An acre of land contains:

    a. 42,560 square feet.
    b. 43,560 square feet.
    c. 44,560 square feet.
    d. 46,560 square feet.

5. Your client bought ¼ of a section of land. Approximately how many acres did the client buy?

    a. 120 acres
    b. 140 acres
    c. 160 acres
    d. 180 acres

6. An electrician sells his home in which he had installed programmable thermostats. After the contract was signed, but before the home inspection or appraisal has been completed, he replaces these with standard thermostats. Which of the following is TRUE?

    a. The seller can be held liable for replacing the programmable thermostats which were present before the contract was signed.
    b. There is really no problem as both standard and programmable thermostats work well.
    c. The seller has the right to make this change as long as it is done before the home inspection and appraisals have taken place.
    d. The question should be decided by the broker who listed the house.

7. Which of the following types of property ownership (title) is limited to husbands and wives?

    a. joint tenancy
    b. tenancy in common
    c. tenancy by the entirety
    d. tenancy at will

8. Robert, a single man, owned a building that he leased to a restaurant owner, Pete. Robert married Kathy, and then a few years later, decided to sell the building to Pete, the owner of the restaurant. The buyer's attorney demanded that before the sale could take place, Kathy would have to sign a quit claim deed. What was the attorney concerned about?

    a. Robert dying intestate
    b. Kathy dying intestate
    c. common law issues
    d. a community property claim

9. Arlene sold her house. It included a water softener that she had purchased the previous year for $1,000 (installed). What is the legal status of the water softener and can Arlene take it with her?

    a. chattel; she could remove it
    b. chattel; she could NOT remove it
    c. fixture; she could remove it
    d. fixture; she could NOT remove it

10. A tenant failed to remove her restaurant equipment before her lease expired, so her landlord acquired title to the fixtures by a method known as:

    a. partition.
    b. expulsion.
    c. accession.
    d. novation.

11. Vague property descriptions, such as addresses and assessor's parcel numbers are:

    a. used on recordable documents like deeds.
    b. considered legal descriptions.
    c. acceptable only when used in documents that will not be recorded.
    d. not approved for sales contracts.

12. An investor made an offer on a piece of land described as the N ½ of the SE ¼ and the S ½ of the NE ¼ of section 12. How much land is he buying?

    a. 160 acres
    b. 320 acres
    c. 80 acres
    d. 100 acres

13. Two cousins would like to purchase and take title to an investment property. Gary will own ¾ share and Larry will have a ¼ share. To do so, they must take title under which one of the following methods?

    a. severalty
    b. tenants by the entirety
    c. joint tenants
    d. tenants in common

14. Twelve individuals own an apartment complex as tenants in common. One of them, Lola, decides to liquidate her holdings. She may legally:

    a. sell. Lola has an undivided, transferable interest.
    b. sell. Lola can sell her interest if another owner agrees to sell too.
    c. not sell. Lola's interests always remain encumbered.
    d. not sell. Lola's interests include survivorship.

15. Which of the following is NOT an encumbrance upon the title of a property?

    a. IRS lien
    b. mortgage
    c. mechanic's lien
    d. setback

16. William and Wanda, who are married and file jointly, bought a principal residence in Malibu for $250,000 in 1998. In 2013, they sold the property and moved to New York. Their capital gain was $700,000. On how much of their capital gain will they pay tax?

    a. $0
    b. $200,000
    c. $250,000
    d. $700,000

17. When a seller of real property appears before a notary public with a deed that will convey the property to a buyer, the grantor may be asked to:

    a. provide a social security card as positive identification.
    b. appear with the deed and other papers signed.
    c. make a verbal statement that their signing is voluntary.
    d. All of the above

18. A 1031 exchange allows taxpayers to defer the capital gains tax on the sale of a property, only when the exchange of property is "of like kind." Which of the following would represent a "like-kind" exchange?

    a. a single family residence for a single family residence
    b. a bowling alley for a warehouse
    c. a condo for a four-plex
    d. All of the Above

19. A quit claim deed must be signed by a:

    a. vendor.
    b. grantor.
    c. grantee.
    d. buyer.

20. Which statement is INCORRECT as to a properly executed will?

    a. It specifies who will inherit the owner's property.
    b. It takes effect only after the death of the devisee.
    c. It must conform to state law in the state where the owner lives.
    d. It must be compatible with state law regarding dower and curtesy.

Chapter 6
Land Use Controls and Regulations

In this chapter we examine how individual ownership rights of land and property are subject to certain powers of various government entities, including federal, state, and local governments. These powers supersede individual rights. We will view government rights in land, police powers used to enact public controls, the regulation of environmental hazards, and private controls.

DO YOU KNOW???

Can you name and explain some of the government's controls on our private ownership of real estate?

Are you familiar with the concepts of *zoning, variance, non-conforming use, grandfathering*, and *spot zoning*?

Are you aware of the many hazardous materials that relate to housing with which agents should be familiar and could you summarize what they are to a client?

Can you overcome a buyer's objection to a CIC and explain the benefits of living within the strict parameters of CC&Rs?

These are just some of the topics to be covered within this chapter.

GOVERNMENT RIGHTS CONCERNING LAND

Background – The feudal system was introduced to England following the invasion and conquest of the country by William I, known as William the Conqueror. The system had been used in France by the Normans from the time they first settled there in about 900 A.D. It was a simple, but effective system, where all land was owned by the king. One quarter was kept by the king as his personal property, some was given to the church and the rest was leased out under strict controls

The king was in complete control under the feudal system. He owned all the land in the country and decided who he would lease land to. He only allowed those he could trust to lease land from him, however, before they were leased any land they had to swear an oath to remain faithful to him at all times. Those who leased land from the king were known as *barons*. They were wealthy, powerful, and had complete control of the land they leased.

The land that the barons leased was known as a *manor*. The barons were known as the *lords* of the manor. They established their own system of justice, minted their own money, and set their own taxes. In return for the land they had been leased by the king, the barons had to serve on the royal council, pay rent, and provide the king with knights for military service when he demanded it. They also had to provide lodging and food for the king and his court when they traveled around the country. The barons kept much of their land for their own use and then divided the rest among their knights.

Knights were given land by a baron in return for military service when demanded by the king. They also had to protect the baron and his family, as well as the manor, from attack. The knights kept as much of their land as they wished for their own personal use and distributed the rest to villeins or serfs. The villeins had to provide the knight with free labor, food, and service whenever it was demanded. Villeins had no rights. They were not allowed to leave the manor and had to ask their lord's permission before they could marry. They were poor and little more than slaves.

There were a few "freemen," peasants who were not bound to the land. These freemen were normally tradesmen. They paid a fixed rent to the lord of the manor or to the knight. The freemen had more legal rights and fewer obligations to the lord of the manor, but in reality there was little difference between the freemen peasants and the serfs.

This method of government control over the land and the population was widespread and by the twelfth century was in use throughout England and most of Western Europe. You can still see left-over vestiges of this arrangement in some castles today, where a whole village works on the castle grounds, perhaps giving tours, hosting paying guests, working farms, or running stores and shops. They are not, however, considered *serfs* today.

The Allodial System

In America, land is considered held in an allodial system of ownership. Technically, allodial title means that the ownership is inalienable or that it cannot be taken by *operation of law* for any reason. Were that true, then the government would have no control over the land or its ownership at all. The form of ownership used in America is a modified form of allodial title. While land is considered private and free from any claims of the central government, in reality, the government, whether federal, state, or local, has considerable control over land.

Prior to 1774, all land in the American colonies could be traced to royal grants, usually one grant creating each colony. The original grantees then sold or granted parcels of land within their grant to private citizens and other legal entities. However, when the colonies won the Revolutionary War, colonists did not want to retain a feudal system of land ownership. The Treaty of Paris (1783), which ended formal hostilities and recognized American independence, also had the effect of ending any residual rights held by the original grantees or the crown. Essentially, this merely recognized that no person holding land in the new United States owed any allegiance or duty to the crown or any English noble.

While our government recognizes the basic concept of an allodial title system, it still subjects all land in the United States to certain basic governmental controls. As the country expanded, the legislatures of the states also began to put into place various controls or regulations affecting either the land or the ownership of the land.

One of the most well-known government rights is the right of various governmental entities to tax its citizenry. Basically, taxation is the raising of revenue by the federal, state, or local governments from the private citizen by taxing income, or value of property owned, or by taxing various business transactions. Many states have some type of transfer tax when a parcel of real estate is sold.

Transfer tax – Transfer taxes are sometimes referred to as *conveyance taxes, revenue stamps, documentary stamps,* or *deed stamps*. A transfer tax is a *state* tax, collected locally, based upon the value of real property when it is sold. It is normally paid by the seller at closing and is based upon a declaration of value.

> **EXAMPLE:** If the transfer tax in the state is $2.55 per $500.00 of value (or any portion thereof), the sale of a $300,000 home would result in a transfer tax of $1,530.00.
>
> **SOLUTION:** $300,000 ÷ 500 = 600 "taxable units" x $2.55 = $1,530.00
>
> If the price were $300,200, the calculation would be:
> $300,200 ÷ 500 = 600.4 taxable units becomes 601 x $2.55 = $1,532.55

Recording fees – Recording fees represent a state established charge for the recording of documents in the public records of the county. For example, a county recorder might charge $14.00 for the first page of a document and $1.00 for each additional page. Each document is considered and priced separately.

Property tax – Property taxes are also a state tax, collected locally, based upon the assessed value of the real estate (land + improvements). An *ad valorem* tax is a tax levied based upon the property value. First, the county assessor determines the value of the property and informs the property owner of the market value of the property. The state establishes an *assessment ratio* which is an *artificial lowering* of the market value. In an example state, the market value as established by the county assessor is multiplied by the assessment ratio of 35%, yielding the *assessed value*. Land is usually appraised separately from improvements (the home or structures). Moreover, land does not appreciate or depreciate as the improvements do. The tax rate is applied against the assessed value. Many states also have an *equalization factor* which may be applied to adjust for assessors who either tend to be high or low in their assessments.

After the assessed and equalized value, if applicable, is established it is multiplied by the tax rate to determine the taxes due from that property.

$$\$MV \times AR\% = \$AV$$
$$\$AV \times TR\% = \$Tax$$

> **EXAMPLE:** The market value of the property is $360,000. The state assessment ratio is 35% and the tax rate in the taxing district for the home is $2.9299 per $100 of assessed value. What are the annual taxes?

SOLUTION: $360,000 market value x .35 assessment ratio = $126,000 assessed value
$126,000 ÷ 100 = 1,260 units of $100.00
1,260 units x $2.9299 tax rate per $100 of value = $3,691.67 annual tax

Note that property taxes are always calculated annually. If you need to know the semi-annual tax amount, divide by 2; for quarterly tax divide by 4; or if you need to know what the monthly tax is, you would divide by 12.

Special assessments – are levied against property for special improvements, such as sidewalks, street lights, landscaping of public areas, and other such improvements. The special assessment is charged against the properties which *directly benefit* from the improvements and are not a general tax levied against all properties in the taxing district. Property taxes are deductible on income taxes, but special improvement assessments are not.

Under most state laws, property owned by any entity of government, religious organizations, hospitals, or educational institutions is exempt from having to pay tax. Additionally, many states have special tax statutes that can reduce taxes for certain groups, such as veterans and some senior citizens, depending on income.

Further, government entities have the right to lien a property for non-payment of taxes. Tax liens are given priority over other liens against a property, which means they must be satisfied first. In addition to the levying of taxes, there are several other government rights in land, including escheat and eminent domain.

Escheat – The concept of escheat is based on the fact that all land within the boundary of a state needs to be owned by someone, either the federal, state, county, township, or city government, or by a private owner.

As the right to inherit real and personal property has long been a founding principle, a process had to be formulated as to what happened if a person died owning real or personal property, but who had left no will directing its disposal and had no heirs living at their death. The solution is the concept of escheat.

If a person dies with no will, and after a reasonable search no heirs are found, the property will pass to the state by escheat.

In some states, if the property were taken by escheat, and the deceased had a spouse living at the time of death, the property would pass to the spouse, although the spouse is not an "heir," a person related by blood. If there are no heirs, and no living spouse, and the state receives the property by escheat, the property is sold and the proceeds of the sale are placed in the General Education Fund.

Eminent Domain – The fifth amendment to the U.S. Constitution, which is best known as prohibiting self-incrimination (as in "I take the fifth"), and as the due process clause, also contains the following language *"...nor shall private property be taken for public use without just compensation."*

It is this fifth amendment language, together with the due process provisions, which provides for the power of eminent domain at the federal, state, and local governments. Provided the tests of proof of a public use and payment of just compensation are met, private property can be taken by the government. The private owner must be afforded due process which means notice and the right to be heard. The notice must be sufficient to inform the citizen as to what is going to happen. The right to be heard means the citizen may have a hearing in court to determine the propriety and validity of the proposed action against his property. In most states, a party facing a taking by eminent domain has a right to trial by jury.

Condemnation – The process of *taking the property* is normally referred to as **condemnation**, while the *payment for the property* is normally referred to as a **condemnation award**. It is interesting to note that in some states, local city governments are taking "underwater" homes (where the loan is more than the current value) through eminent domain from the banks or investors and partnering with mortgage companies to refinance the homes for the current owners. As one can imagine, there are many legal battles over this process. With ***inverse condemnation***, a suit is brought by the land owner alleging the government has acquired an interest in his or her property without giving compensation, such as when the government floods a farmer's field or pollutes a stream crossing private land. An inverse condemnation proceeding is often brought by a property owner when it appears that the taker of the property does not intend to bring eminent domain proceedings.

PUBLIC CONTROLS AND POLICE POWERS

Police powers – Police power represents the government's right to regulate for the benefit of the general health and welfare of its citizens. Traditionally, police powers describe those activities of the state which regulate real estate such as the enacting of zoning regulations, building codes, health and safety regulations, traffic laws, and family law.

Enabling acts – The general rule is that the regulation of the land within its borders is the function of the state. However, as time has passed and population has spread, it became ineffective for the regulation of the use of land within the state to be done from the central state government. By way of the enabling acts, the state government delegated this power to local governments where decisions were made for the individual circumstances of a community.

Master plan – Each local government, be it county or city, typically develops a master plan for the community. The master plan should take into consideration the needs of the community, the location of various uses of land, the potential for conflict between uses, and the orderly growth of the community. A person considering the purchase of land should be able to look at the master plan and get a good idea what land uses will be available in which area and if conflicting or undesirable uses exist or are planned for the future. Implementation of the master plan is accomplished by the zoning process.

Zoning – The zoning of a property establishes what uses are available for a given parcel. The categories of uses generally found in zoning ordinances are:

- agricultural
- residential
- commercial
- industrial
- governmental

Each category will have several different layers dealing with either the density of the population permitted, as in residential, or the potential for conflict as in agricultural, commercial, or industrial.

Residential zoning contains many density levels which describe the number of dwellings per size of parcel, normally stated as so many housing units per acre. R-1 zoning may provide for 4 units per acre, or about ¼ acre lots, while R-2 might require a minimum lot size of 7,000 square feet or about 6 units per acre.

There are several terms that are important in zoning.

Non-conforming use (NCU) – Generally, a NCU happens when a property is put to a given use, perhaps a small "Mom & Pop" grocery store with a gas pump out in the rural area of a community where there are no zoning ordinances. Time passes and now the community has grown beyond the store with residential development. In this case, a commercial use would not be permitted in the residential area, but as the store and gas pump were there first, and is otherwise a legal use, Mom and Pop would be *grandfathered* in as non-conforming use. They could continue their operation until one of the following happened:

> 1. the use is discontinued (it could not be restarted without zoning approval)
> 2. the structure is destroyed (it could not be rebuilt without zoning approval)
> 3. the use is expanded (expansion of the existing use would require zoning approval)
> 4. the ownership changes (the new owner would have to get zoning approval)

Variances – A variance is a request for some leeway in using a parcel which violates the zoning regulations.

> **EXAMPLE**: A family wants to add a room on to their home. The zoning for their parcel says there can be no structure built closer than 15 feet from the back property line (a distance termed the *setback*). In order to make the plans for the room work, they need to be able to build within 13 feet of the back property line. They may apply for a variance. If the zoning authority felt that granting the variance was appropriate, the family could go forward with their building and exceed the rear property line setback.

Conditional use permit (CUP) – Many uses do not have a specific zone in which they are to be put. If the use does not conflict with the surrounding area, then a CUP could be granted.

EXAMPLE: A hospital wants to build on a vacant parcel located in a predominantly residential area. After a public hearing, if the zoning authorities find that the parcel's use as a hospital site would provide greater benefit than harm for the area, a CUP would be granted.

Spot zoning – is often labeled by opponents to the proposed use as being illegal. Spot zoning is not illegal; it represents the zoning authority's decision to rezone a small area in a zone different from the surrounding parcels. While this is not an illegal act by the zoning authority, it should be done sparingly; otherwise, there would be little value to having a master plan, especially if rezoning is made too easily and too frequently through spot zoning.

Setback – The required distance between structures is referred to as a setback. Typically, single family dwellings will have a 5 to 7 foot side yard setback requirement. This is largely a life-safety matter. If one house catches on fire, with the total setback between the burning house and the next door neighbor of 10 to 14 feet, chances are improved that the neighbor's house will not catch on fire. Front yard setbacks improve view lines for traffic and improve life-safety. Rear yard setbacks serve the fire protection issue as well as providing some additional privacy to the homeowners.

Buffer zones – are required separations between conflicting uses. They are often an area of land zoned for a use that smoothly *transitions* from one use to another. As an example, a housing development is separated from a commercial shopping center by a park. Or a school is separated from a bar by a minimum of 1,500 feet. In each case, the buffer zone provides separation from conflicting uses and promotes life-safety and the general welfare of the community.

Up zoning or down zoning – If additional uses are *added* to those already available for a property, this is considered an *up zone* and would normally add value to the property. If uses which a property already had are *taken away*, this would represent a *down zone* and may reduce the value of the property. Down zoning could be considered a taking under eminent domain, thus requiring compensation to the property owner who has lost value due to the down zone.

Height and density zoning – The height of a structure can be regulated by zoning. Zoning can also regulate the density of population on a parcel. The density of structures can be regulated on a parcel. Normally, this regulation would be to assure adequate areas for parking.

Planned Unit Development (PUD) – In a PUD, one will find a combination of housing, recreational amenities, and commercial uses all in one "planned development."

In addition to zoning, there are several other important police power matters, including ***subdivision regulations***, ***building codes***, and ***health codes***.

Subdivision regulations – The community will normally adopt minimum standards for subdivisions. These would contain regulations such as street widths, provisions for sidewalks and street lights, drainage provisions, lot size, house size, house styles, roof material, exterior finishes, and a host of other matters which the community chooses to regulate. So long as the requirements are reasonable, they would normally withstand any court challenge.

Building codes – In the absence of building regulations and codes, it would be left to the integrity of the builder to determine the quality and safety of the construction in a community. Experience has proved that this should not be left to the owner or the builder. Building codes will vary from one region of the country to another based upon the circumstance of the area. California, for example, has strict provisions in its building codes to deal with earthquakes, while Florida has strict provisions in its building codes to deal with hurricanes. Building codes are enforced by requiring the builder to submit plans before a ***building permit*** will be issued and construction can be commenced. Once the permit is issued, periodic inspections are conducted to be sure the construction is following the approved plans and is being done in a workman like manner. The building will not be given a final inspection and certificate of occupancy unless the builder has passed the inspections and corrected any deficiencies.

Health codes – Like building codes, the health and safety of the community is not going to be left in the hands of the business community. Health codes provide for minimum standards regarding a wide variety of matters, ranging from food handling and preparation standards, to general sanitation standards, to various forms of signage like "Wash Your Hands Before Returning to Work," and other similar matters. The citizen expects the food and water supply to be safe and healthy and that public facilities such as restaurants, theaters, hotels, hospitals and other facilities offer safe environments.

REGULATION OF ENVIRONMENTAL HAZARDS

People desire to live and work in an environment that is safe and free from certain kinds of health risks. Therefore, environmental issues have become important in the practice of real estate.

Much of the legal burden for disclosure or elimination of hazards arises when properties are transferred and so real estate salespeople must be alert to environmental hazards and familiar with local, state, and federal environmental laws.

The burden of disclosure falls heavily on the homeowners who are selling their property, as most states have a requirement for sellers to disclose the condition of their home prior to selling. Buyers also have a due diligence period in which to further check the condition of the home they are purchasing, including the presence of any environmental issues.

When confronted with any of the following environmental issues, it is wise to involve professional specialists. They have knowledge of abatement processes and the associated costs. In some instances, the abatement of mold can be done by a homeowner only if the affected area is two feet by two feet or less. Larger areas require professional assistance, which in this case, is very expensive.

Environmental protection laws – In general, environmental protection laws come from the federal government. Local and state agencies may also promote a clean and safe environment through local laws and regulations.

CERCLA and SARA – the *Comprehensive Environmental Response, Compensation, and Liability Act* (1980), CERCLA, established a *Superfund* to clean up hazardous waste sites and to collect the costs from certain responsible persons associated with the sites. The *Superfund Amendment and Reauthorization Act* (1986), SARA, clarified regulations regarding hazardous waste and limited liability for some parties, including innocent landowners and real estate brokers.

Federal clean air and clean water acts – Providing clean air and water is a fundamental role for the national government. As early as 1273, when King Edward I banned burning coal in London, the quality of air and water directly impacted the quality of life of the citizens and, more importantly, the willingness of the citizen to be governed. If the government is not able to provide clean air or water, the citizens may well conclude that government will be unable to provide other services and may determine a different government should be put in place.

In more modern times, as industry and the expansion of the population have placed strains on natural resources, the quality of water and air has taken on economic as well as political importance. Applied to real estate, the major concerns are the availability of adequate supplies of clean water to support existing populations and proposed growth. Clean air has also had a major impact on real estate and real estate development. As cities grow and residential areas are developed further away from sources of employment, traffic increases bring about issues concerning air quality.

Growth in the demand for power, combined with the general aversion to nuclear power, has caused a proliferation of natural gas and coal burning power plants, each presenting additional pollution challenges. Each new project brings with it an impact on the surrounding environment, including traffic impacts, water, gas and electric demands, potential damage to natural habitats, and possible pollution of streams, lakes, and subsurface water resources. In balancing the need for development and the desire for clean air, clean water, and safe, pleasant places to live and work, developers are required to submit impact statements to planning and zoning officials demonstrating the effect of their proposed project on existing resources and facilities. The purpose of an **Environmental Impact Statement (EIS)** is to identify the anticipated effects of developing a new project as they pertain to the safety and health of the public.

There are many hazardous materials that relate to housing with which agents should be familiar:

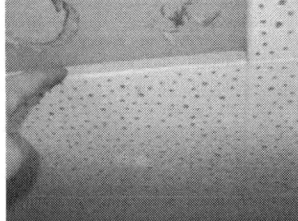

1. **Asbestos** – Asbestos is found in insulation and in ceiling and floor tiles. For many years, it was widely used in residential and commercial buildings. Removal is very expensive, and inhalation of asbestos can lead to serious, often fatal lung disease. In a state of disintegration, it is considered friable (easily crumbled or pulverized) and thus easily airborne.

2. **Lead** – Lead is found in plumbing pipes in older homes. Lead-based solder and lead-based seals could, over time, place harmful quantities of lead in the water.

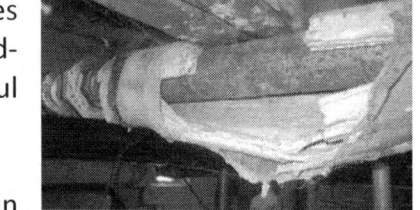

3. **Lead-based paint** – can be found in homes built prior to 1978. Federal law banned the use of lead-based paint in

residential properties after January 1, 1978. It was often used to paint cabinets and baseboards or other areas of significant wear. Discovery was made that lead-based paint was often eaten by small children as they chewed on cabinet doors and trim. Lead-based paint, if ingested, can result in brain damage and death.

Review the *"Disclosure of Information on Lead-Based Paint and/or Lead-Based Paint Hazards"* in the forms appendix to gain a better understanding of the information that must be disclosed and the agent's obligations to do so. Also note that disclosures about lead-based paint, mold, radon, and other hazards are very common in many jurisdictions. These may be separate documents signed by the buyer or a longer document that contains several disclosures.

4. **Urea formaldehyde foam insulation** (UFFI) – This has been used as an insulation in residential and commercial buildings. Ingestion and inhalation present significant health hazards.

5. **Leaking underground storage tanks (LUST)** – these tanks are found in older gas stations and other facilities where gasoline and other petroleum products were stored in steel or iron underground tanks. The primary hazard is leaking and the contamination of ground water as the petroleum product leaches further into the soil.

6. **Mold** - Recent interest in mold in homes has increased. Mold is a fungi that thrives on moisture. While some molds are benign or even beneficial, others can cause allergic reactions when inhaled or touched.

7. **Radon** - Radon is an odorless, colorless, radioactive gas produced naturally by the radioactive materials in the ground. It represents another environmental hazard and has been linked to lung cancer.

8. **Electromagnetic fields (EMFs)** - These are fields generated by the movement of electrical currents, such as in power transmission lines.

9. **Carbon monoxide (CO)** - Carbon monoxide is a colorless and odorless gas that occurs as a byproduct of burning certain types of fuels. It can pose a significant health hazard if not properly ventilated.

PRIVATE CONTROLS

The use of the land can be controlled by private parties and owners in a variety of ways.

Deed restrictions – are conditions placed in the deed by the grantor, or the grantor's successor, which limit use.

> **EXAMPLE:** "The property may only be used for residential purposes and no sale of alcoholic beverages at wholesale or retail may be made from the property."

> **EXAMPLE:** "All homes are to be occupied by the owner of record. No owner may rent or lease a home to another person."

COMMON INTEREST COMMUNITY PROPERTIES

Common interest communities (CICs) have been formed in many communities across the nation. Their purpose, within a community of homes (often one organized by a new home builder), is to set standards of behavior and living for a defined community. This is done through the establishment of ***conditions, covenants & restrictions (CC&Rs)*** that all homeowners agree to follow when they buy a new or previously-owned home in the community.

CC&Rs outlaw the most egregious behaviors (e.g., starting an auto salvage business in your front yard, or not cutting your grass all summer, etc.). All CICs have homeowners associations, which consist of an elected **board of directors**. While this board could probably manage the common interest community, most boards hire a community management company to handle this specialized responsibility.

Sometimes it is obvious that a particular community is a common interest community because it has a traffic gate, or a community pool, or a private park, etc. On other occasions, it may not be as obvious. No buyer should ever purchase a residential property only to be surprised to find out later that it has a common interest community with CC&Rs that restrict the buyer's lifestyle. For this reason and others, agents must disclose the presence of a common interest community and require the buyer to read and sign a disclosure document.

In most states, the disclosure document informs the potential buyer about these aspects of the common interest community.

1. By buying a home in this common interest community, the buyer is agreeing to restrictions on how the property can be used. These restrictions are contained and explained by the CC&Rs.

2. The buyer is told that he will have to pay owner assessment fees as long as they own the property. These could be monthly "dues" that fund general operations, pool maintenance, entrance gate maintenance, and so on. They may also be periodic assessments for sealing or paving streets, putting a new roof on a recreation center, etc.

3. If the buyer fails to pay owners' assessments, the CIC has a right to foreclose and take the owners home. Yes, you read that correctly. The CIC or Homeowners' Association has the right to foreclose when collection efforts fail – even if the unpaid amount is small.

4. By buying a home in the common interest community, you may become a member of a homeowners' association that can further limit how you enjoy your property. Like the CC&Rs, this is another force that can limit how you use your property. Unlike the CC&Rs, which were developed by the new home builder, the homeowners' association meets monthly and has the power to make new rules, e.g. New Rule: On Tuesdays and Wednesdays, the tennis courts are off limits to anybody under 18.

5. The owners, should they decide to sell their home, are required to tell prospective buyers that the community is a common interest community.

6. As a homeowner in a common interest community, the owner has certain rights that are guaranteed by the state. These might include the right to be notified of all meetings, the right to audit the homeowners' financial records, and many other similar rights.

In many cases, the rules of disclosure are even more stringent when a contract has been signed. The seller is often required to purchase a resale package, which is given to the buyer, who has five or ten days to read it and approve the contents. This resale packet could run 200-300 pages and contains CC&Rs, rules and regulations, summary of litigation, budget, financials, and five or six more items. Once placed in the hands of the buyer, the buyer has five days or so to look these over and either proceed with the transaction or cancel the contract.

Master planned communities – In some communities, subdivisions have been superseded by master planned communities, which take the subdivision idea one step further. Many of these master planned communities develop plans that include recreation centers, parks, playgrounds, and other amenities, as well as reserved spaces for schools, churches, retail establishments, and other facilities. Many master planned communities are gated, so as to restrict access to residents.

In some cases in the southwest United States, master planned communities are nested together. In other words, there may be a master planned community within a master planned community within a master planned community.

Covenants, conditions, and restrictions (CC&RS) – are restrictions created in either the planned use development documents, the homeowner association controlled projects, the townhome owners association controlled projects, or in condominium association controlled projects.

These can be very restrictive and the existence of CC&R's is a material fact which must be disclosed to any prospective purchaser before any contract is signed or money paid. Usually the time frames for turnover, receipt, and decisions based on these documents are controlled by statute. In many states, the association having control of the CC&R's must make current copies of them, together with other documents relating to the project, within 10 days of request. They can and do charge a nominal fee for the "demand" for these documents and another fee for the actual production and delivery of the documents. Sometimes these documents are referred to as the *common interest community (CIC) resale package*.

Home owner association (HOA) regulations – Originally associated with condominium ownership, homeowner associations can now exist at several levels within the real estate community. Many newer planned developments have HOAs that control even more aspects of a community than the CC&Rs. The additional HOA documents are part of the CIC resale package. These typically include the community's governing documents, the association by-laws, a current financial statement and operating budget, information regarding pending litigation, a copy of the minutes from a recent board meeting of the association, as well as the CC&Rs. Review the receipt of the CIC resale package in the forms appendix to see the types of documents that must be provided to the buyer prior to purchase in a community that has an HOA.

Chapter 6: Land Use Controls and Regulations
End of Chapter Quiz

1. All of the following are examples of public land use controls EXCEPT:

    a. environmental protection laws.
    b. subdivision regulations.
    c. zoning.
    d. deed restrictions.

2. An odorless gas produced by the decay of radioactive materials in the ground is which of the following?

    a. lead
    b. asbestos
    c. radon
    d. UFFI

3. Your city has a zoning ordinance covering what type of buildings can be built in specific areas. The basis for this is:

    a. eminent domain.
    b. police power.
    c. escheat.
    d. riparian rights.

4. Licensees often handle the possibility of hazardous substances on a property being sold. Which of the following does NOT describe what a licensee should do?

    a. A licensee should not disclose the problem as it might harm the seller.
    b. A licensee should ask the client about the possibility of hazardous substances on the property.
    c. A licensee should be scrupulous in considering environmental issues.
    d. A licensee should consider the possibility of potential liability.

5. All of the following are examples of a governmental restriction on land EXCEPT:

    a. taxation.
    b. deed restriction.
    c. eminent domain.
    d. police power.

6. Mike, a builder-developer, built an office building on a piece of land that later is re-zoned by his city to residential. Mike will likely:

    a. get the land and building re-zoned.
    b. close his building.
    c. get a conditional-use permit.
    d. be able to continue with a non-conforming use permit.

7. An electromagnetic field (EMF) is created by which of the following?

   a. contaminated groundwater
   b. peeling paint
   c. decay of radioactive substances underground
   d. none of these

8. Which of the following statements pertaining to a homeowners' association is FALSE?

   a. All homeowners must abide by the association restrictions.
   b. The HOA has the power to impose fines.
   c. All homeowners must agree with the CC&Rs.
   d. The HOA has the power to levy assessments.

9. When a county adversely acquires land for a freeway, it is exercising the power of:

   a. eminent domain.
   b. escheat.
   c. zoning.
   d. environmental protection laws.

10. The potential buyers of a property should have an inspector check around sinks, showers, basement walls, and toilets to detect which of the following problems?

    a. radon
    b. mold
    c. methane gas
    d. EMFs

11. Sarah purchased a home with a partial block wall between her property and her neighbor James' property. After she had the block wall completed, James realized it extended almost a foot onto his property. This is called:

    a. easement by prescription.
    b. license.
    c. encroachment.
    d. easement by necessity.

12. Radon generally enters a house through:

    a. doors and windows left open.
    b. the floors or foundation.
    c. the roof or patio covers.
    d. the chimney.

13. Kayla and Michael want to buy a home in Pleasant Valley, so they are looking into the property taxes on one property. The tax rate in Pleasant Valley is $3.900 per $100 of assessed value. The Market value of the home is $310,000, and the state assessment ratio is 40%. Approximately how much will they pay annually?

    a. $1,240
    b. $4,836
    c. $7,254
    d. $12,090

14. Which of the following requirements would NOT be covered by building codes?

    a. electrical wiring.
    b. sanitary equipment.
    c. fire prevention standards.
    d. minimum number of square feet of land area per house.

15. Which of the following best describes a buffer zone?

    a. a recreational area between a residential area and an office area.
    b. a sound barrier along a portion of a major highway that is near a residential area.
    c. a high-rise residential complex between a commercial area and a townhome complex.
    d. an industrial park between a strip mall and a residential neighborhood.

16. Lauren wants to build a front porch onto her house, but it is not allowed under the zoning for her area. In order to build the porch, Lauren will first have to submit an appeal for a:

    a. building permit.
    b. non-conforming use permit.
    c. variance.
    d. certificate of occupancy.

17. In which of the following situations would building codes need to be taken into account?

    a. The subdivision of a large tract of land.
    b. The construction of a new structure.
    c. The development of a master plan.
    d. The demolition of a partially destroyed building.

18. Police powers can regulate all of the following EXCEPT:

    a. building ownership.
    b. the number of buildings.
    c. building occupancy.
    d. the size of buildings.

19. The Johnson family wants to buy property on a new road to build a restaurant. To determine whether or not the property can be used as a site for a restaurant, they would need to examine:

    a. building codes for that location.
    b. a list of obtainable variances.
    c. lists of permitted non-conforming uses.
    d. zoning ordinances for that location.

20. A new zoning ordinance is enacted that prohibits horse barns from being built within the city limits. Thomas has a horse barn on his property that has been there for many years. He has been told by the city that he can be "grandfathered" in and that he does not have to tear down his barn. This is an example of

    a. eminent domain
    b. a variance
    c. a non-conforming use
    d. inverse condemnation

Chapter 7
Real Estate Math

Many students become apprehensive when "math" comes up in the course. Although we understand those nervous tendencies, we assure you that you are probably making a larger issue of the real estate math than you need to.

The "concepts" are what you need to grasp. The math is simple addition, subtraction, multiplication and division. It is knowing "what" to do with the numbers and "why" that is the real challenge. The math questions on an exam are testing your conceptual knowledge more than your ability to perform arithmetic functions. The calculation questions are based on common situations you will face in the practice of real estate so if you have mastered the "concept," the math is rather simple.

DO YOU KNOW???

Can you calculate the area of an irregular shape?
Could you convert the number of square feet of a property to acres?
Do you know how to calculate the property taxes given the assessed value and the mills?
Are you able to estimate the transfer tax for your potential seller client?
Can you figure a proration and determine to whom it is a credit or a debit?
These are just some of the topics covered in this chapter.

GENERAL MATH CONCEPTS

It is a "pre-requisite," so to speak, that candidates for completion of the licensing course and passing required exams to become a real estate practitioner, should already have the skills necessary to perform general mathematical functions such as addition, subtraction, multiplication, and division. You will generally be permitted to use a calculator for the exam provided it is the inexpensive, basic type calculator that is not a programming or financial calculator. Performing these general math functions should therefore be simple enough for any student.

Percentages, fractions, and decimals: Any one of the three, percentages, fractions, or decimals, can be expressed in any of the other two formats.

To convert a percentage to a decimal, ignore the percentage symbol and put the number over 100; divide

EXAMPLE: 90% = 9/10 = .90

To convert a percentage to a fraction, ignore the percentage symbol and put that number over 100. Reduce to the smallest fraction.

EXAMPLE: 90% becomes 90   90/100   9/10 when reduced

To reduce a fraction to the smallest fraction, find the largest number that *both* the top and bottom numbers can be reduced by. In this case, 10 is the highest factor for both 90 and 100. Divide 90 by 10 to get 9; divide 100 by 10 to get 10. 9/10 is 90% converted to a fraction.

To convert a fraction to a decimal, put the numbers in your calculator exactly as they appear and divide. 9/10 would be 9 ÷ 10 = .90 or .9

To convert a decimal to a percentage, move the decimal two places to the right and replace it with a percentage symbol. .90 becomes 90%. 5.5 becomes 550%. Notice when moving the decimal to places to the right we create a "hole." Replace that hole with a zero.

Finding the area of a square or rectangle: To find the area of a square or rectangle, multiply the width by the height (one side by the other). The order makes no difference; such as 2 x 4 or 4 x 2. Both equal 8.

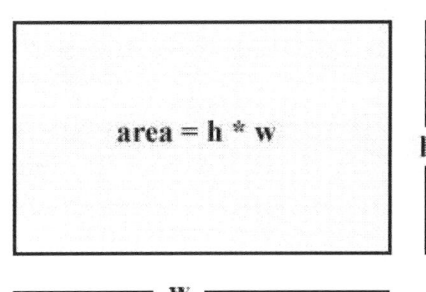

EXAMPLE: You are taking a listing on a property which measures 340 feet by 600 feet and the owner wants to list it at $3.52 per square foot, what is the list price?

In real estate, land area is referenced with the terms "frontage" and "depth," much like the example where "width" and "height" were used. As a rule, when land dimensions are listed, such as 340 feet by 600 feet, the first number is the frontage and the second number is the depth.

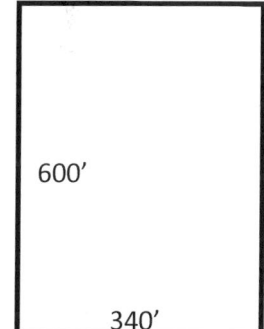

SOLUTION: 340 feet x 600 feet = 204,000 square feet. Note this is a calculation of area which will result in square units. In this case, our measurements are in feet, so we get square feet. Always pay attention to the unit used and be sure both units are the same. If one measurement is in feet and the other in yards, as an example, you will have to convert so the measurement unit is the same.

With 204,000 square feet as our area, and pricing at $3.52 per square foot, our list price will be:
204,000 square feet x $3.52 price per square foot = $718,080

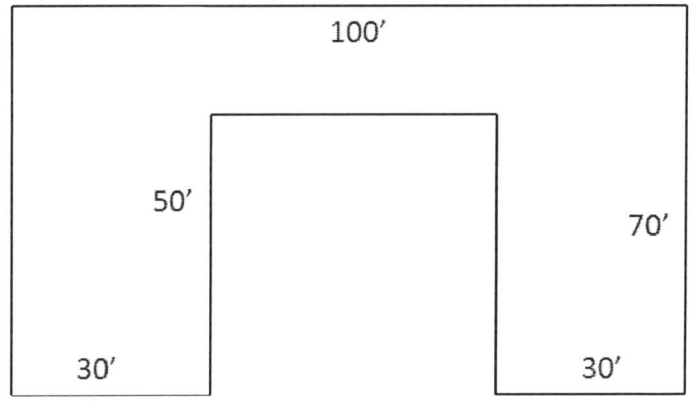

Finding the area of an irregular shape: As long as you are dealing with squares and rectangles, the area of an irregular shape can be calculated using two techniques: "Subtract a Piece" or "Add Up the Pieces."

EXAMPLE: Calculate the area of the figure.

To subtract a piece, you could look at the drawing and realize if it were a perfect rectangle, the dimensions would be 100' X 70' for a total of 7,000 square feet.

But, since the piece in the middle is "missing," you need to calculate the square footage of that missing piece, 40' X 50'. This might be a challenge to see at first. The width of the missing piece is 40 feet (100' less 30' less 30'). The depth of the missing piece is given, 50'.

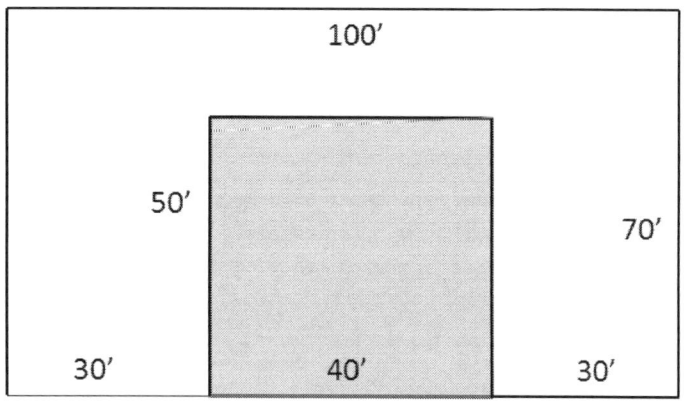

The area of the missing piece is 40' X 50' or 2,000 square feet.

SOLUTION:

Full rectangle: 7,000 sf
less missing piece: 2,000 sf =
Total Area 5,000 sf

Or, this could be calculated by adding up the pieces. The original shape can be split into three rectangles for which calculating the area is simple. Again, what may be difficult at first is to see the width of the center piece of 40' which is calculated by starting with the entire length of 100' and subtracting the two given lengths of 30' and 30', leaving 40'. Likewise, the depth of the entire piece is 70', and we are given the partial depth on the left side of 50', leaving us another 20' to the back line.

SOLUTION: The three rectangles have areas of 2,100 SF, 800 SF, and 2,100 SF for an added up total of 5,000 SF.

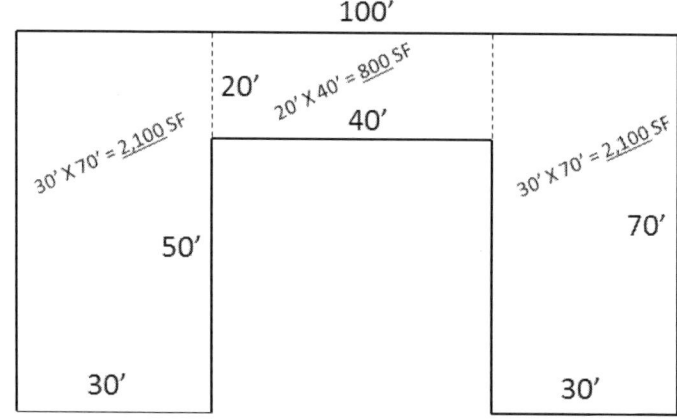

Finding the acreage of a parcel: An acre is a measurement of area. It comes from 8th Century England when King Ethelbert of Kent decided it was time to come up with some measurements for land. The "acre" represents the area a team of oxen could plow before lunch, without tiring the oxen. An acre has been defined as 43,560 square feet. This is a number a real estate professional must commit to memory!

Add 'em up
43,560
↓ ↓
7 - 11

This author has always taught, "if you forget the number of square feet in an acre, run down to 7-11 and ask them – they'll know!" If you look at the 4 and the 3 to the left of the comma, they add up to 7. If you look at the 5, 6 and 0 to the right of the comma, they add up to 11: 7-11! Then, remember it is kind of like counting: 3, 4, 5, and 6 except the first two digits are reversed. Well it isn't a perfect mnemonic device, but it works for many.

182

EXAMPLE: Your listing is 600 feet x 800 feet. You have a client who needs a parcel with a minimum of 10 acres. Should you show him this parcel?

SOLUTION: 600 x 800 = 480,000 square feet
1 acre = 43,560 square feet
480,000 ÷ 43,560 = 11.0193 acres   <u>Yes, show the property!</u>

EXAMPLE: Your listing is 600 feet x 800 feet and the market value is $125,000 per acre. What is the value of the land?

SOLUTION: Similarly, 600 x 800 = 480,000 square feet
1 acre = 43,560 square feet.
480,000 ÷ 43,560 = 11.0193 acres
11.0193 acres x $125,000 value per acre = <u>$1,377,412.50</u> value of the land

PROPERTY TAX CALCULATIONS

The information you must have to calculate property tax questions includes the *market value*, the *assessment ratio*, and the *tax rate*. You would multiply the market value by the assessment ratio which will give you the assessed value. Next, you would multiply the assessed value by the tax rate, this will give you the annual taxes.

$$MV \times AR\% = AV$$
$$AV \times TR\% = T$$

Tax rates: This is an area which causes much confusion, as tax rates are expressed in variety of ways:

Tax rate is stated as $0.016   multiply the assessed value by .016

Tax rate is stated as $1.60 per hundred
$1.60 ÷ 100 = 0.16   multiply the assessed value by .016

Tax rate is stated as $16.00 per thousand
$16.00 ÷ 1000 = 0.16   multiply the assessed value by .016

Tax rate is stated as 16 mills. A ***mill*** is one-tenth of a penny or 1/1000th of a dollar. Put the mill number in your calculator and divide by 1000.

16 mills ÷ 1000 =. 016   multiply the assessed value by .016

EXAMPLE: The property is valued at $800,000 and the Assessment Ratio is 35%. The Tax rate is 24 mills, what is the monthly tax?

SOLUTION: Remember:

> MV x AR% = AV
> AV x TR% = T

$800,000 (MV) x 35% (AR%) = $280,000 (AV)
$280,000 (AV) x .024 (TR%) = $6,720 (T)

Some students might stop there with an answer of $6,270 and might even see $6,270 as a distractor (wrong answer). Read the question. "What is the monthly tax?"
$6,720 ÷ 12 = $560 monthly tax

CALCULATIONS FOR TRANSACTIONS

These are "deal calculations" and are often calculations regarding commissions, seller's net proceeds, buyer's cash to close, transfer tax, and prorations. Always read the question carefully and draw a picture if needed to solve for the right answer.

Commission example: You have just sold a house for $585,000. The commission was 6% which was split 50/50 between the seller's broker and the buyer's broker. You represented the Buyer and are on a 60% split. How much is your commission?

This problem represents a typical residential, real estate commission scenario. The commission of 6%, presumably and typically paid by the seller, is compensation being offered to both brokerages involved. This is a "co-broke," meaning a cooperating broker found the buyer and has sold the listing broker's property. The 50/50 split between the seller's broker and buyer's broker tells us that of the 6% total commission, the listing brokerage is paying 3% to the selling firm and keeping 3% for themselves (50/50 split). You, one of the two agents, are representing the buyer. Your firm is being paid the 3% co-broke commission and of that 3%, you as an agent are compensated 60% of that 3%, the split. The question asks, what is "your" commission?

SOLUTION: $585,000 sale price x .06 total commission rate = $35,100 the total commission
$35,100 ÷ 2 = $17,550 Your Brokerage's Side of the Commission
$17,550 x .60 Your Split = $10,530 Your Commission

Seller's net proceeds example: Your seller client needs to "net" $140,000 after paying off the mortgage of $327,000 and closing costs of $8,000. He has agreed to pay a 7% commission. What is the minimum selling price to accomplish what your client needs?
This one takes a little thought. We know the client's needs:

	$327,000	Mortgage pay off
+	$ 8,000	Closing Costs
+	$140,000	Seller's Net
	$475,000	Amount need after commission has been paid

If the commission is going to be 7% and is coming out of the total sales price, then the $475,000 represents the other 93% that is not the 7% commission. 93% of the total sales price must equal $475,000, or our numbers won't work. So the question is what number is $475,000 93% of? Here's a rule: if you know a number, and you know the number that other number represents, divide.

SOLUTION: Divide $475,000 by 93%

475,000 ÷ .93 = $510,753 total sale price (rounded)

That is a tough concept for some students and you may wish to check that. If the sale price were in fact $510,753, and we deduct a 7% commission, there better be $475,000 left. Let us check.

$510,753 x .07 = 35,753 (rounded)
$510,753 – 35,753 = $475,000

This illustrates a principle of arithmetic of "If you divide a number by a number smaller than 1, you will get a larger number. If you multiply a number by a number smaller than 1 you will get a smaller number."

Buyer's cash to close example: Given information regarding the loan amount, deposit, down payment, and closing costs, students are asked to calculate the total funds needed to close the given transaction. Note: "LTV" abbreviates "Loan to Value" ratio and expresses the loan amount as a percentage of the sale price.

The Johnsons have purchased a home from the Browns for $210,000 and placed a $5,000 earnest money deposit into escrow upon acceptance. They have been approved for a new 90% LTV loan with an interest rate of 6.5%. The lender and title company have informed the Johnson they will have total closing costs of $3,800. What is the remaining cash to close for the Johnsons?

SOLUTION: It may be best to start a list of all items the Johnsons will have to fund. Follow the paragraph from beginning to end to make certain you leave nothing off your list:

(Earnest Money is not listed as the buyers have already paid that amount)
10% Down Payment (this is a 90% LTV Loan) $210,000 Price x 10% $21,000
Less Earnest Money already paid (part of 10% down)   - 5,000
Closing Costs $3,800   + 3,800
                                      Remaining cash required to close $19,800

Transfer tax example: Depending on terminology in your area, this may be referred to as *transfer tax, conveyance tax* (or fee)," or *tax revenue stamps*. They all refer to the tax the seller must pay to the state upon the transfer of title to another party. About two thirds of the states assess this tax and tax rates vary from state to state.

The tax is calculated on the entire sale price, regardless if there is financing, and you will likely be given the rate in a problem you are asked to solve. Taxable Increments such as "per $100" or "per $1,000" are rounded up to the next increment.

A property is sold for $251,200 and the buyer qualified for new loan in the amount of $201,000 with a 4.75% ARM (adjustable rate mortgage). The transfer tax rate is $5.10 per $1000. What is the transfer tax owed by the seller?

SOLUTION: Take the purchase price (loan information is completely a distraction) and divide by the taxable increment, $1000. Round that number to the next $1,000 increment and multiply by the rate, $5.10.

$251,200 purchase price ÷ $1,000 taxable increment = 251.2

Round 251.2 up to the next $1,000 equals 252. Note these are different rounding rules than what you were taught in school.

252 x $5.10 rate = $1,285.20 transfer tax

Note: Some test item writers will purposely include irrelevant data, like this question had, deliberately to test to see if you can sort through information and gather what is actually needed.

Prorations: Many expenses associated with a property are "ongoing" despite the seller is turning over ownership to the buyer. The seller is only obligated to pay for his fair share of expenses while he owned it and the buyer must pay for her share after the closing. These expenses have to be prorated between the parties. Some expenses have been paid in advance, such as homeowner's insurance premiums, causing the buyer to owe the seller for the buyer's share. Others are paid in arrears, such as utilities, meaning the buyer will receive a future bill which includes expenses that the seller will owe to the buyer.

Here are some rules to remember when calculating a proration:

1. Some areas of the country use a 360 day year (not 365) with 30 days in every month while other areas use a true, 365 day year, 366 days in a leap year, and 28 to 31 days in a month.

2. Some areas prorate with the seller paying for the day of closing while others pro-rate with that date belonging to the buyer and therefore her expense.

Taking an exam, you will likely be told which method to use, and if not told, you should not worry. If this is the case, test item writers will not prepare distractors where the only difference between the right answer and a wrong one is based on which method you used. The choices should be far enough apart such that there is only one, clear choice.

EXAMPLE: The homeowner has a paid homeowner's annual insurance policy in the amount of $680 that expires November 30th. The closing will take place July 15th. What is the amount of the proration and to whom will it be a credit?

SOLUTION: We recommend you go about a proration problem in the following way. Who paid for the item and to whom should there be a credit?

Who paid for the item? In this case, the seller paid a year in advance. To whom should there be a credit? Since the seller paid a year in advance to November 30th but will not have title as of July 15, the seller should receive a credit for that period between July 15 and November 30. If this is a credit to the seller, it must be a debit to the buyer.

You may find it helpful to draw a timeline and label it to help you visualize the scenario.

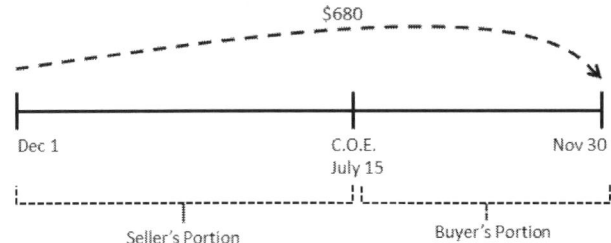

In every proration, the question to ask is, "Does the buyer need to credit the seller for the buyer's portion on the right? Or does the seller need to credit the buyer for the seller's portion on the left?"

In this problem, the buyer owes a credit to the seller for the buyer's portion on the right. Using a 360 day year, with 30 days in every month, the proration will be for 135 days: 15 days in July, plus 30 days for each of August, September, October, and November.

The math function is:

$680 annual premium ÷ 360 days = $1.8889 insurance cost per day (per diem)
Leave the infinite number on your calculator.
$1.8889 x 135 days = <u>$255.00</u>   <u>Credit to the Seller, Debit to the Buyer</u>

MORTGAGE AND LENDING CALCULATIONS

You may be asked to solve for a variety of financial type questions including the calculation of loan-to-value ratios, loan amounts and down payments, qualifying buyers, seller's equity, discount points on a loan, amortization, interest on a loan, and monthly payments.

Loan-to-value example: You have sold a property and the buyers are obtaining a loan which is a 95% loan to value (LTV). The property you sold has been appraised at $550,000. How much will the buyer's loan be?

SOLUTION: The loan amount will be based on the lesser of the contract purchase price or the appraisal. In our problem, we are just given the appraisal so that is what we will use. The loan will be a 95% LTV, meaning that the lender will be loaning 95% of the appraised amount.

$550,000 x .95 = $522,500 loan amount

Had the question asked for the required down payment, we would solve:

$550,000 purchase price - $522,500 loan amount = $27,500 down payment; or
$550,000 purchase price x .05 (100% - 95%) % down payment = $27,500 down payment

Interest example: Interest is the compensation the lender receives for making the loan and waiting for payments over time. To calculate the annual interest you would multiply the loan amount by the interest rate stated in the note.

What is the annual interest at 8% on a $165,000 loan?

SOLUTION: $165,000 loan x .08 interest rate = $13,200 annual interest

Note: If the loan is an amortizing loan, the amount of interest will change each month as the loan is paid down. In a fixed rate mortgage, the interest _rate_ will stay the same, but each month the balance decreases slightly thus less interest is due as the balance declines. In a fully amortizing loan, the principal and interest payment is constant, but the internal components change each month.

Amortization example: What is the next month's loan balance after the payment is received by the lender if the current loan balance is $110,900, the monthly principal and interest payment is $562.88, and the annual interest rate is 4.5%?

SOLUTION: Because interest rates are expressed as an *annual* rate, the interest calculated on a loan will at first be *annual* interest. Realizing that most loans are amortized, each month's payment will have different principal portions and interest portions when compared to other monthly payments.

To solve this problem:

$110,900 current loan balance x .045 annual interest rate = $4990.50 annual interest
$4990.50 annual interest ÷ 12 months in a year = $415.88 (rounded) new month's interest
$562.88 principal and interest payment - $415.88 interest portion = $147.00 principal portion
$110,900 loan balance - $147.00 principal reduction = $110,753 new loan balance

Discount points example: A discount point is a fee the lender will charge the borrower to increase the lender's yield and offer a lower interest rate for the borrower. These "points" are sometimes referred to as a "buy down" as the payment of points "buys down" the interest rate.

A discount point is simply 1% of the loan amount. Do not be fooled into calculating a percentage of the purchase price. The point is a percentage of the loan as it is the rate on the loan that is being "discounted."

EXAMPLE: Higgins purchases a property for $130,000 and puts 10% down. What is the cost to Higgins for three discount points?

SOLUTION: Remember, discount points are a percentage of the loan amount.
$130,000 purchase price - $13,000 down payment (10% down) = $117,000 loan amount
$117,000 loan amount x .03 (three discount points) = $3,510 discount points

The "IRV Circle":
Commonly referred to as the "IRV Circle," or sometimes the "T-Bar," this helpful device helps students visualize what numbers to multiply or divide. The rule is, the part is a percentage of the total; or the smaller number is a percentage of the larger number. The beauty of the circle is, as long as you have any two of the three numbers, the circle will tell you the mathematic formula to follow.

Commission example (from earlier): ... what number is $475,000 93% of? Simply by putting the smaller number, $475,000, in the part section (we know 475,000 is only a part of the total) and the 93% in the percentage section, the IRV Circle indicates we should take 475,000 ÷ .93 = 510,753.

Loan-to-value ratio examples: IRV can come in handy on calculating any one of the three elements of these questions which may ask for the loan amount, the value or purchase price of the property, and the loan-to-value ratio.

EXAMPLE: What is the loan-to-value ratio if the purchase price is $425,000 and the down payment will be $25,000?

SOLUTION: IRV tells us to put the loan amount in top portion of the circle (the smaller number) and the purchase price in the bottom right portion (the larger number). Once we have two of the three numbers plugged into the circle, IRV tells us the mathematical function to perform.
$400,000 Loan ($425,000 Purchase Price - $25,000 Loan) ÷ $425,000 Purchase Price = 94% LTV

EXAMPLE: What is the purchase price if the buyer is qualifying for an 80% LTV loan in the amount of $78,000?

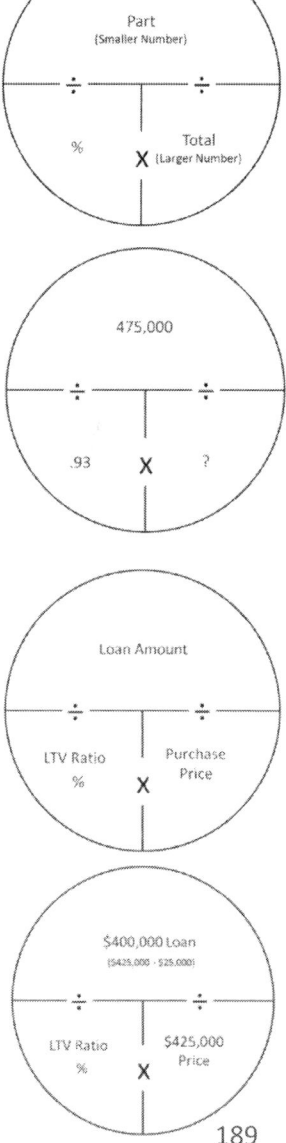

SOLUTION: Inserting the LTV ratio and loan amount in the circle as shown, IRV tells us to divide $78,000 by .80 which equals $97,500 Purchase Price.

VALUATION CALCULATIONS

Why do they call it "IRV"? The same circle is used in the valuation and appraisal of income producing property where "I" equals *income* (*net operating income*); "R" equal *rate* (*rate of return* or *capitalization rate*); and "V" equals *value*. The theory is, if we know the net operating income of the property and we know an investor's desired rate of return, plug those numbers into the IRV circle to estimate the value.

Appreciation and depreciation problems: The IRV circle helps with these problems too.

EXAMPLE: It is known that a neighborhood gained 4.2% in appreciation the last 12 months. Mr. and Mrs. Smith bought their home one year ago and paid $145,000 for it. What is the home's approximate value now?

Sure, you might be able to do this in your head, but even the best students make mistakes in their heads. As described, the IRV circle is a great visual to make sure everything is labeled correctly and the correct mathematical calculation is performed.

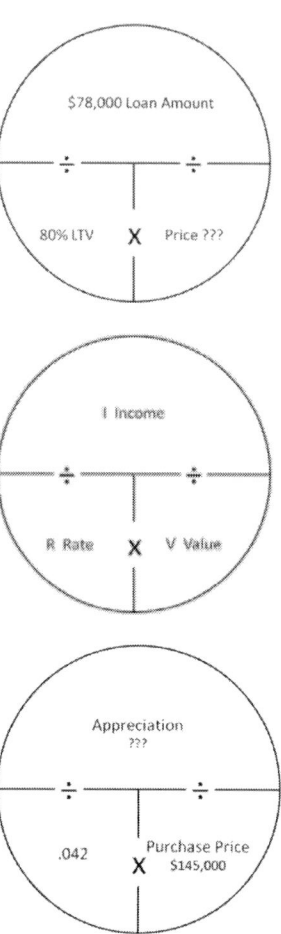

SOLUTION: .042 appreciation x $145,000 original purchase price = $6,090 appreciation
$6,090 appreciation + $145,000 original purchase price = $151,090 current value

Note: If the question asked for the current value after *two years*, you would need to repeat the process, taking the first year's appreciated value of $151,090 and calculating another 4.2% of appreciation, adding it to the $151,090 for the current value after two years.

EXAMPLE: An investor purchased a parcel of land for $40,500 one year ago which is now worth $37,200. What rate of depreciation did she suffer?

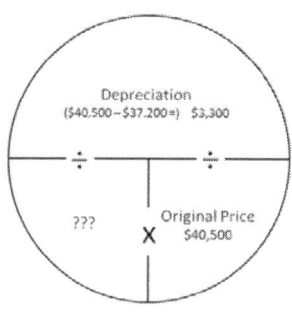

SOLUTION: Using the IRV Circle, simply plug in the smaller number, depreciation, over the larger number, purchase price, and IRV tells you to divide. $3,300 ÷ $40,500 = .08 or 8%

Math Conversions:

> 12 inches = 1 foot
> 3 feet = 1 Yard
> 5,280 feet = 1 mile
> 16.5 feet = 1 rod
> 320 rods = 1 mile
> 9 square feet = 1 square yard
> 43,560 square feet = 1 acre
> 640 acres = 1 sections = 1 square mile

Math Tips:

1. Carefully read each question to be certain you understand what the question is truly asking for. There are several components to any one mathematical question such as a purchase price, loan amount, interest rate, payment amount, principal portion, or interest portion. As an example, if the question asks that you find the loan amount, do not get misled into answering with the loan rate or payment.

2. Watch out for daily, monthly, quarterly, or annually type questions. You may have to divide by 12 or multiply by 30 as examples.

3. Beware the distractors. Distractors are the A, B, C, and Ds written to *distract* you from the real answer in a multiple-choice question. Excellent test item writers know to make those distractors as tempting as possible. With a math question, many of the wrong distractors were calculated based on mistakes you are likely to make and are not just random numbers. You may very well calculate and arrive at an answer that is incorrect, but when you see it among the choices, you mistakenly assume it is correct.

4. Another trick to watch out for is items of information that have no bearing on the problem.

    EXAMPLE: A vacant lot measures 110' x 130' with 10' setbacks on all four sides. The purchaser intends to build a 2,400 square foot home on the property. What is the total square footage of the lot?

    Tip #1 suggests you read the question carefully to really ascertain what the question is asking. In the example, the goal is the total square footage of the lot. So what do the setbacks or the square footage of the house to be built have to do with calculating the total square footage of the lot? Absolutely nothing, but many students take the bait and start subtracting the setbacks or square footage of the house simply because the information is there, in the question.

    SOLUTION: The answer is simply 110' x 130' = 14,300 square feet

5. If you are allowed scratch paper, use it. Use it and be neat and organized. If you write numbers down, label them, "purchase price," "commission rate," etc. Draw pictures and label what is what. A quick scribble can confuse you quite easily by the time you are done.

6. Avoid doing math in your head.

7. Check your work. In the net proceeds the seller needed in a prior example, we checked our work by working the math from the other direction. Once we calculated what we thought the sales price would need to be, we used that sales price and calculated the commission to check our work.

8. Whatever calculator you plan to use on the test, use it from the beginning and stay with it. You do not need to place undue stress on yourself with learning an unfamiliar calculator. We suggest you take a backup calculator just in case.

Chapter 7: Real Estate Math
End of Chapter Quiz

1. The seller has decided to replace the sod in the yard to make the home more appealing to potential buyers. The 20,000 square foot home is situated on a 150' x 250' lot with a 20' x 30' driveway. How many square feet of sod will be needed (assuming no waste and ignoring the landscaping)?

    a. 37,500 square feet
    b. 16,900 square feet
    c. 2,600 square feet
    d. There is not enough information.

2. What is the total acreage of a lot containing 54,450 square feet?

    a. .25 acres
    b. 1 acre
    c. 1.25 acres
    d. 1.5 acres

3. One half of one percent is expressed as:

    a. .1/2
    b. .012
    c. .005
    d. .0005

4. The foundation of a one-story home must contain 1,400 square feet total. Which of the following could be the dimensions of the slab?

    a. 35' x 55'
    b. 30' x 40'
    c. 25' x 56'
    d. 26' x 55'

5. Properties in Heavenly Fields subdivision, on average, are assessed at 32% of the market values. If the Walton's estate is worth $525,000, and the area's millage rate is 19 mills, what are the Walton's property taxes per quarter?

    a. $7,980
    b. $3,192
    c. $798
    d. $266

6. What is the assessed value on a property if the annual taxes are $1,800, the assessment ratio is 45%, and the tax rate is 11.5%? (rounded)

    a. $15,650
    b. $34,780
    c. $75,000
    d. none of these

7. What is your share of the brokerage fee if the sale price is $279,500, the total commission is 7%, the co-broke is 3.5%, and you are on a 40% split?

    a. $274
    b. $3,913
    c. $7,826
    d. $19,565

8. What was the transfer tax on a property that sold for $410,500 and the state charges $9.75 per thousand for the tax?

    a. $4,002.38
    b. $4,007.25
    c. $4,105.00
    d. None of the Above

9. Seller Stone has not yet received the sewer bill which estimates to be $127.00 for the quarter July 1 through September 30. If buyer Benson closes the sale on September 10th, what is the amount of the sewer bill proration and to whom will it be a credit?

   a. $24.69 Credit to the Seller
   b. $24.69 Credit to the Buyer
   c. $98.78 Credit to the Seller
   d. $98.78 Credit to the Buyer

10. What loan-to-value ratio is the lender using if the sale price is $177,000 and the loan amount is $150,450?

    a. 17%
    b. 45%
    c. 85%
    d. 95%

11. What is the new balance on Greg's loan if the balance before the payment is $210,900 and Greg makes a principal and interest payment of $1,400, on a 30 year, fully amortizing loan at 7% annual interest?

    a. $196,137.00
    b. $209,669.75
    c. $210,730.25
    d. A financial calculator is needed to solve this amortization problem.

12. The lender reflects $4,200 on the HUD 1 for discount points on a home closing that sold for $185,000 with a $17,000 down payment. How many points is the lender charging?

    a. 2 ½ points
    b. 2 points
    c. 1 ½ points
    d. 1 point

13. What is the cost of the discount points if the buyers are qualifying for a 90% LTV loan on a sale price of $235,000?

    a. $2,115
    b. $2,350
    c. 2 points
    d. There is not enough information.

14. An appraiser has determined the average, annual rate of appreciation in the community is 4%. The Brown's bought their home two years ago for $162,000 and they are now considering selling. What is a reasonable estimate of value for the Brown's home?

    a. $155,520
    b. $162,000
    c. $168,480
    d. $175,219

15. Lorraine measures the distance from the side of her house to the common wall with her neighbor to be 54 inches to determine if the landscaper can get a Bobcat backhoe through the side yard. The landscaper tells Lorraine he needs 4 feet of clearance. Will it fit?

    a. No, there needs to be six more inches width for the Bobcat to fit.
    b. Yes, but only with six inches to spare.
    c. Yes, but only with five inches to spare.
    d. Yes, there is plenty of room and Lorraine does not need to measure.

16. Lorraine also needs to order decorative rock for her front and rear yards. She measures the front to be 30 feet x 12 feet while the rear is 60 feet x 15 feet. A ton of rock covers 30 square yards of ground. How many tons should she order?

    a. 4 tons
    b. 5 tons
    c. 6 tons
    d. 35 tons

17. What is the value to Investor Iverson of a four-plex if each unit nets the owner $650 in monthly rent after operating expenses and Iverson's desired rate of return is 11% (rounded)?

    a. $285,000
    b. $70,000
    c. $25,000
    d. none of these

18. A seller wants to net $150,000 after closing. His total closing costs are estimated to be 9% which includes a 6.5% brokerage commission. What must he sell his house for (rounded)?

    a. $150,000
    b. $160,500
    c. $163,500
    d. $165,000

19. 90 acres of vacant land are purchased by a spec builder. 1/10 of the land is required to be dedicated to the roads and the builder plans to get 420 lots out of the parcel after subdividing. What will be the average square footage of the lots (rounded)?

    a. 8,400
    b. 9,330
    c. 12,700
    d. 37,800

20. The sellers have agreed to replace the carpet in the den at their expense per the request of the buyers. If the carpet bid came in at $22.00 a square yard plus $4.00 per square yard for labor, what will the carpet job cost the sellers if the room measures 200 square feet?

    a. $685.00
    b. $750.00
    c. $580.00
    d. $485.00

Chapter 8
Mandated Disclosures

To be fair and ethical, the practice of real estate requires that real estate licensees provide clients certain, mandated disclosures and even that sellers disclose information about the property being conveyed. These disclosures might include the presence of mold, pests, and lead-based paint, as well as the overall condition of the property. While some disclosures are used because they are in the best interests of the clients, others, like the group presented in this chapter, are mandated by state law and are a blend of ethics, fiduciary responsibilities, and legal requirements.

DO YOU KNOW???

As a licensee acting as a principal, do you have further obligations of disclosure?
What is the agent's role in the preparation of a property condition disclosure?
Can you explain your *duty of further inquiry*?
How do the parties to a contract proceed if unexpected repairs arise?
These are just some of the topics covered in this chapter.

AGENCY DISCLOSURES

All agents have a duty to inform their clients of their agency relationship. This requirement is defined in the law of every state, along with a requirement that it occur early in an agent's interaction with clients and customers usually at the time of the first meaningful contact with a client, or to be among the first documents signed by a buyer or seller.

Dual agency, or multiple party representation, is not legal anywhere in the country unless the multiple parities are informed in writing that such a relationship exists and they offer their consent. Even then, it may still be illegal in some states. The reason for this prohibition is that it is difficult to represent both parties in negotiations with each other and to keep each party's confidential information confidential.

Responding to non-client inquiries – Much has been said about the role of agents while working with their clients – those with whom they have an agency relationship. However, a good deal of any agent's time is spent in the presence of customers. These are people with whom the agent does not have an agency relationship.

- When representing the seller, the agent's customer is the buyer.
- When representing the buyer, the agent's customer is the seller.

Most states have reduced to writing the responsibilities of real estate agents. Here is an example gleaned from one state. What are they in your state?

1. **Disclosure** – An agent must disclose any *material and relevant facts, data, or information* which the agent knows, or which by the exercise of reasonable care and diligence, the agent should have known, relating to the property that is the subject of a transaction.

2. **Puffery** – Reasonable puffery is allowed, but only if expressed as an opinion. "In my opinion, this home has the best curb appeal on the block."

3. **Compensation** – An agent should disclose the source of any compensation that the agent will receive.

4. **Principal status** – A licensee must disclose any ownership or is otherwise a principal in a transaction, or has an interest in a principal in a transaction. "I wanted you to know that my daughter is the listing agent for this property." Many states require this disclosure to be in writing.

Agent's personal interest in a transaction – If an agent has a personal interest in a transaction, that fact must be disclosed. This could occur if the agent has an ownership interest in the property being sold, or is closely related to a party involved in the transaction. That fact must be disclosed as soon as practical and it is recommended it be included in the sales contract.

PROPERTY CONDITION DISCLOSURE FORMS

Most states mandate that the seller disclose property conditions or defects associated with the property which adversely affects its use or value. This form is a **standardized condition form**, and has a variety of names in a variety of states. Some states call this form a *Seller's Real Property Disclosure* (SRPD).

On an SRPD form, the seller is typically required to disclose defects in the structure of a home, and in its components (gas, electrical, plumbing, air conditioning, heating, etc.), to the best of the seller's knowledge. Also required by the standardized condition disclosure form are disclosures about soil conditions, construction defects, water and sewer service, flood zones, insect infestation, the existence of a homeowner's association, and a host of other items which would affect the use, enjoyment, and value of the property.

The standardized condition disclosure form is typically turned over to the buyer at the start of the due diligence period, but if the seller agrees, it can be done before that time.

Agent's role in preparation – The *agent* has *no role* in filling out the SRPD. It is a seller's disclosure form, not an agent's disclosure. The agent does not live in, or maintain the home, and has no knowledge about maintenance issues. The SRPD must be filled out by the owner. The role of the real estate professional is to furnish the form and request the seller prepare the form, or if representing the buyer, request the seller's agent provide the form.

However, real estate professionals must be aware of conditions at the property and with the exercise of their superior knowledge and skill, determine if conditions exist which should be further inspected.

When the seller's disclosure misrepresents the condition of the property – Sellers sometimes misrepresent the condition of a property. This might occur because:

1. the defect was a latent defect (not visible), and the seller had no knowledge that it existed. Remember the story of the sinkhole enveloping a home in Florida?

2. the seller wasn't "technical," and did not understand the significance of the problem. This might be a scenario like that of lead-based paint, where homes built after 1978 had no problem, because by then lead-based paint had been declared illegal and removed from stores.

3. the sellers really wanted to sell the house but did not want any complications to arise because of defects, so they kept a few defects off the SRPD.

Examples number one and two can probably be considered "careless misrepresentations." They would probably lead to a situation where a buyer could cancel the purchase contract if it was felt the condition that was misrepresented was significant, or expensive to repair, or both. The buyer might also opt to have these conditions inspected by a qualified and licensed home inspector, or an inspector with specialized skills (HVAC, roof, pool, etc.).

Example number three describes an instance of possible fraud. While the same remedies are available to the buyer as in examples number one and two, this situation is more serious and could result in allegations of fraud, and if the buyer felt injured by not having the true and valid information, might seek relief from a court.

HOME WARRANTIES

Home warranty types – A number of different companies offer *home warranties*, which are essentially an insurance policy taken out by a homeowner or home buyer against the failure of some of the many systems in a home such as heating, air conditioning, plumbing, electrical, etc. while also providing coverage for appliances like refrigerators, stoves, dishwashers, washers, and dryers.

Most home warranty policies require the homeowner to pay a service charge for each claim they make. Ostensibly, these $50-75 charges prevent homeowner abuse of their coverage.

It is common practice in some areas for buyer's agents to write into the purchase contract a requirement that the seller will buy a home warranty for the buyer. Sometimes these home warranties become effective at the close of escrow, but some providers make them effective as soon as they are written, which could be a month or more before the close of escrow and during the listing period.

NEED FOR INSPECTION AND OBTAINING/VERIFYING INFORMATION

Imagine an agent saying, in response to an attorney's question regarding disclosing a property defect, "Well, that subject never came up." That might be an unfortunate answer because agents have a "duty of further inquiry."

The duty of further inquiry – When representing a seller or a buyer, an agent is required to "discover and disclose" any material fact or material defect of which the agent knows or *should have known*. When do you find out if you should have known? This point deals with the role of being a professional in a fiduciary relationship. The professional is expected to be able to "spot" potential problems or issues and then pursue the answer until it is found.

> **EXAMPLE:** While showing a two-story home, the agent notices a pale, but visible, tan spot on the ceiling of a room on the first floor. Knowing that small tan spots on the ceiling are not generally normal, the agent has just been subjected to the *duty of further inquiry*.
>
> If the agent is representing the sellers, he should ask the sellers about the spot as this suggests a possible plumbing leak and the potential for the presence of mold. If the sellers tell the agent that they had not noticed it previously, the agent needs to tell the sellers that the source should be determined.
>
> If the sellers agree to research and resolve the incident, all is well. If the sellers decide they will paint the spot to match the ceiling, but do not want to incur any additional expense, there is a big problem. The agent has to deal with the other obligation of being a professional and must disclose to the customers (the customers are the persons not represented by the agent in a client/agent relationship) all material facts concerning the property, including any material defects. The agent may want to discuss this with his broker to see if the representation of the seller should be continued. Who knows what other problems the seller is planning to "paint over."

Agent responsibility to inquire about "red flag" issues – From time to time, an agent will see, or should see, one or more issues that are obvious only if the agent is trained into look for them. These might be called "red flag" issues because of their importance, and agents should construct a mental checklist to ask about these when listing a property or showing a property to a buyer.

A major home inspection company reports that 40% of previously owned homes have one or more of these serious defects. Virtually every home needs some sort of repair, improvement, modification, etc., either to function properly or to be in compliance with building codes.

Here are some of the "red flag" issues that agents should be aware of, and ready to point out and follow up on with buyers and sellers:

- moisture or water in the basement
- cracks in foundation or basement walls; evidence of settling
- failing air-conditioning compressor; sounds noisy or won't start
- environmental hazards including radon, water contamination, asbestos, or lead paint
- underground storage tanks; pipes sticking out of the ground
- defective roofing or flashings; several colors of roofing materials on one roof
- signs of water damage on ceilings or walls
- insect infestation
- standing water outside the structure; evidence of drainage issues
- undersized electrical system
- chimney settling or separation from house; leaning, missing bricks
- evidence of dry-rot damage
- unpermitted structures of any kind

Most of the above conditions can be repaired. It is simply a matter of cost and of whether the buyer or seller does the fixing. Or, it might result in a situation where the seller refuses to fix the issue, and the buyer thinks it too expensive and decides to move on to another property.

A new roof repair of dry-rot damage, and a few foundation issues, could cost $25,000 on a home worth $200,000, which would scare many buyers off unless the listing price had been discounted by the price of these repairs.

The best protection for your client, even if you represent the seller, is to have a structural inspection or home inspection done by a qualified home inspector, which will cost $200 to $500, depending on the inspector and the size of the home. It is good practice to provide your client with a list of qualified inspectors and let them select one to use. If you give them only one choice, and that engagement fails to go well, it could reflect poorly on you.

If repairs are needed, there are three ways to proceed:

- the buyer can ask the seller to fix one, two, or all of the issues.
- the buyer can buy the home "as is," if the price is right.
- the buyer can ask for a price reduction.

The key for the agent is to make a mental checklist of "red flag" issues and look for them when listing or showing a property.

Technical details – Agents must always be alert to the quality of information they are working with and must be sure that representations made to either clients or customers are correct.

> **EXAMPLE:** An agent is taking a listing and asks the seller if there have been any additions to the home, and if so, were proper permits and inspections obtained. The seller says no, they have not enlarged the home or done anything to it since they bought it. The agent takes

measurements of the property and finds that it is approximately 2,800 square feet and this is the number the client has furnished.

While verifying the property tax amount, the agent notices that the tax assessor has the property listed in the tax records at 2,370 square feet. The agent is now subject to the duty of further inquiry. The seller does not have any idea why there is a difference and is happy to just let the matter alone, as it might increase the taxes. What must be done?

Again, the agent should discuss the situation with the broker because there is a potential liability if nothing is done. At the very least, the agent should inform a buyer that there appears to be a discrepancy between the actual square footage and the square footage carried on the tax rolls. This *could* represent the following problems:

- The tax information is wrong and, when corrected, the taxes will probably go higher than either party may be expecting.

- An addition has been made by a previous owner who may not have obtained permits, or who may have used incompetent licensed contractors.

The agent's best solution is to make the disclosure, in writing, to both the seller and the buyer. A future problem, if there is one, should not be the responsibility of agent because the agent has made a full and complete disclosure.

Remember that while the rule of *caveat emptor* (let the buyer beware) is still applicable in some situations, all of the parties in a transaction expect the professionals to look out for them.

Remember that the agent's role as a fiduciary does not turn the agent into an insurance company. The agent has discharged her duty when she has provided the parties with a disclosure of *patent defects* (visible) and has honored her duty of further inquiry when she has done all that is reasonable to discover the answer regarding *latent defects* (hidden or non-visible).

MATERIAL FACTS RELATING TO PROPERTY CONDITION OR LOCATION

As described earlier, an agent must disclose any *material and relevant facts, data or information* which the agent knows, or which by the exercise of reasonable care and diligence, the agent should have known, relating to the property that is the subject of a transaction

We can articulate a list of seven types of material facts and some associated red flags:

1. Land/soil conditions – An individual agent may be knowledgeable of various land and soil conditions, and therefore be obligated to disclose these facts. Some examples are as follows:

    - Homes in this section of the county have trouble with septic tank leach fields.

- The well water here is unpalatable.
- This location is right under the flight path of the air force base.
- This site used to be a chemical plant that made dioxin.

2. Pest infestation, toxic mold, and other interior environmental hazards:

    - There are mousetraps all around the home.
    - Roof rats are known to infest homes in this area.
    - This is the worst area in the county for mosquitoes.

3. Accuracy of lot or improvement size, encroachments, or easements affecting use:

    - Electrical wires cross over the swimming pool.
    - The size of the yard is listed at 8,000 square feet in a subdivision where all of the other lots are 6,000 square feet.

4. Condition of electrical and plumbing systems, and of equipment or appliances that are fixtures:

    - Some copper wire has been stolen from the circuit breaker panel.
    - The inside workings of the A/C units have been stolen.
    - The glass panel in the oven door is cracked (and probably leaking).

5. Structural issues, including roof, gutters, downspouts, doors, windows, foundation:

    - The chimney, which rises from a ground-level pad, has separated from the house and is leaning toward the driveway. The windows are all single pane (before 1960).
    - The door between the house and garage has a pet door; this is a fire code violation.

6. Known alterations or additions:

    - This garage has been converted to a bedroom, but the additional area is not reflected on the tax records.
    - One bedroom seems to be added. It has no heating or cooling vents.

7. Location within natural hazard or specially regulated area (potentially uninsurable property):

    - There have been some sinkholes appear down the street.
    - This neighborhood floods each January.

MATERIAL FACTS RELATING TO PUBLIC CONTROLS, STATUTES, OR PUBLIC UTILITIES

Besides those facts related to property condition and location, an agent must disclose any *material and relevant facts, data, or information* relative to public controls, statutes, and public utilities. These could encompass five additional categories.

1. Local tax assessment districts, special county or municipal assessments, and other liens:

    - This home has an unpaid assessment against it for the Landscape Improvement District (LID) for $8,300, payable at $800 per year.
    - There is a personal IRS lien on this home for $22,000.

2. Local zoning and/or planning information, including the existence of master plans drawn up by municipalities:

    - The city of Charlottesville will revise its master plan next year.
    - This parcel backs up to R-12 zoning.
    - The city of Canyonville is financially broke, so fire department services are being taken over by the county.

3. Stigmatized or psychologically impacted property, including Megan's Law issues:

    - Back in the seventies, three people were attacked in this home.
    - Charles Manson once rented a room over the garage.
    - A registered sex offender lives next door (if allowed to disclose in your area).

4. External environmental hazards, which could be any of the following:

    - asbestos
    - urea formaldehyde foam insulation
    - groundwater contaminations
    - hazardous waste
    - high-voltage power lines
    - lead
    - radon
    - soil contamination
    - underground storage tanks
    - waste disposal sites

5. Boundaries of schools, utilities, taxation districts, flight paths:
    - The school attendance areas for most of the homes in the county are changing for the new school year.
    - Liberty High School is closing.

Chapter 8: Mandated Disclosures
End of Chapter Quiz

1. Dual agency is a situation where a seller and a buyer on the same transaction are represented by a single, individual agent. One of the following statements about dual agency is FALSE?

   a. Dual agency is legal in all states.
   b. Dual agency is not allowed unless all represented parties agree to it.
   c. Disclosure of dual agency must be made as practicable but no later than when presenting an offer.
   d. Disclosure of dual agency should be made prior to closing a real estate transaction.

2. Which of the following would be classified as a latent defect?

   a. a cracked heat exchanger in the furnace
   b. a wobbly stair rail
   c. a large crack in the kitchen ceiling
   d. a chimney that is broken away from the house and leaning

3. Which of the following statements is FALSE concerning the practice of agency disclosure?

   a. Disclosure is required at the time of the first meaningful contact with the seller.
   b. Disclosure is required at the first meaningful contact with the buyer.
   c. Disclosure is required in some states.
   d. Disclosure is always required, in every state.

4. Agent Sally is writing an offer on behalf of her mother, Alice. What disclosures must Sally make?

   a. Sally is an agent representing Alice.
   b. Sally is the daughter of Alice.
   c. A Only
   d. both A & B

5. An owner had a fire that spread to a portion of the attic. The area was floored without replacing or strengthening the charred floor joists. When the property is listed for sale next month, the ceiling joists:

   a. should be disclosed as latent defects.
   b. are discoverable defects.
   c. fall under "caveat emptor."
   d. need not be disclosed as the damage was repaired.

6. The owner died inside 1401 S. Elm last year and the buyer's agent knows it. The buyer doesn't have any idea. Should the buyer's agent spill the beans?

   a. Yes, this is a material fact and the buyer's agent must disclose it.
   b. Yes, the buyer will want to know.
   c. No, this is not important or material
   d. No, check with your broker first. State laws vary about disclosing facts of this nature.

7. Sellers often have to prepare a disclosure of facts about the condition of the property of the home they wish to sell. Typically, this is referred to as something like a "sellers' real property disclosure." This document should be filled out:

    a. by the seller's agent, so he can make sure it gets done correctly.
    b. by the seller's agent, with the harder parts being filled out by the seller.
    c. by the seller, with explanations coming from the seller's agent.
    d. by the seller, with little to no input from the licensee.

(There are only 7 questions in this quiz.)

Appendix A
Answer Keys to End of Chapter Quizzes

Introduction to the Real Estate Business

End of Chapter Quiz: ANSWER KEY

1. D
2. C
3. D
4. A
5. D
6. B
7. C
8. B
9. A
10. B

Chapter 1: Contracts
End of Chapter Quiz: Answer Key

1. B: If the contract is for an illegal purpose, lacking legality of object, it is simply void.

2. C: Notice of acceptance may be oral and given to the offeror directly or through his agent.

3. D: In an open listing or with an exclusive agency listing, the seller reserves the right to sell the property himself and not be obligated to the broker for a commission.

4. C: Contracts with a minor are voidable up to the age of majority by the minor.

5. C: Real estate contracts and personal property contracts in excess of $500 require a written contract to be enforceable, under the Statute of Frauds requirement.

6. A: With an implied contract the actions of the parties demonstrate their intent. It looks like a contracting has occurred by the appearance of things. There is no evidence in the question to suggest the agreement was also executory or executed; or unilateral or bilateral.

7. D: The requirement for the contract to be in writing and signed in order to be enforceable only applies to contracts for the sale of real estate and personal property over $500. Contracts outside this scope are enforceable without being in writing although it is more prudent to put the agreement in writing.

8. D: The holder of the right of first refusal has the right to match any offer made on a property. Generally these contracts are misunderstood as being a form of an "option." They are not.

9. B: A contingency is a clause written into a contract stating some event must be completed before all of the duties can be or will be performed.

10. D: This is *all of these* because the question represents an example of all three terms. This is a sale-leaseback as the sellers wish to close with the buyers and then "lease" the property "back." Because it is a six month lease agreement, this is also an estate for years – a fixed start date and fixed termination date. Because it is a stipulation in the contract that the buyers agree to rent it back, it is also a contingency.

11. C: When the landlord makes it impossible for the tenant to access or live in the leased property, it is considered a constructive eviction and is illegal. The landlord must follow the local, legal process for eviction.

12. A: In a percentage lease, the commercial tenant pays a *base rent* plus a *percentage of the gross business income* as the landlord's location, anchor tenants, and marketing is considered to contribute to the overall business income of the tenant. Although the lease *may* also be a gross lease or escalated lease as well, there is no evidence in the question that such is the case.

13. D: All of these issues are pertinent to address in any lease, regardless if the lease is for residential or commercial purposes, and regardless of the lease structure.

14. C: After an offer is made, the offeror may withdraw the offer any time up to receiving notice of the offeree's acceptance. This notice of acceptance may be oral and given to the offeror directly or through his agent. "A" has no communication of acceptance back to the buyer. "B" is incorrect in that the agent for Seller W was notified of the acceptance which is not communication to the buyer or his agent which is why "C" is correct. "D" is incorrect because there is acceptance of the offer but there was no communication of that acceptance to the other side.

15. D: The offeror is the party to a contract making the offer. The offeror could be the buyer or the seller. The offeree is the recipient of the offer.

16. B: The seller is the client under a listing agreement as the buyer is the client under a buyer brokerage agreement.

17. C: Once a lease is agreed to, the tenant is said to have a leasehold interest. The landlord has a leased fee.

18. B: The optionee is the one receiving the option to buy or not to buy and is therefore the buyer.

19. B: Consideration may be money, anything of value, or just a statement that consideration exists, such as "for continued love and affection" or "for good and valuable consideration."

20. D: The listing described is a net listing which is predicated on what the seller must "net" from the sale. There is no set commission amount or rate, the broker is entitled to any overage from the seller's desired net proceeds.

Chapter 2: Agency and the Practice of Real Estate
End of Chapter Quiz: Answer Key

1. B: Agents are prohibited by law from advertising a property without including the name of the brokerage. In this case "advertising" applies to newspaper ads, yard signs, open house signs, etc. The one exception occurs when the salesperson is advertising a property that he or she owns personally, however the ad must contain "Owner-Licensee."

2. C: A salesperson may only accept a commission payment from the broker with which the salesperson is affiliated. In this example, it doesn't matter if the salesperson represented the seller or the buyer. The commission could come from the salesperson's broker.

3. B: A real estate broker is a *special agent*. A *general agent* has wider responsibility, like a property manager. A *universal agent* has nearly unlimited authority.

4. B: In this situation, the listing broker can pay a commission to the cooperating broker whose brokerage made the sale. The listing broker may not pay the salesperson who made the sale. That salesperson can only be compensated by the selling broker. The listing salesperson can only be compensated by the listing broker.

5. A: The listing broker's agency relationship is with the lister or seller, and not with the buyer or anyone else who becomes involved in the transaction.

6. A: A special agent is hired to represent the client in one specific transaction – a real estate transaction, for example. Bob would not expect Tiffany to represent him in *all real estate transactions*, just this one. As a special agent, she would not have power-of-attorney, nor would she have the authority to represent Bob in all matters.

7. B: Brokers have a fiduciary responsibility to submit all offers to the seller in a timely manner. It is improper for the broker to insert any artificial sequencing plan or to select certain offers to be seen first, or to introduce anything of a similar nature, regardless of any internal policies and procedures.

8. C: From the list shown, the broker's only responsibility and power is to advertise the property. The broker would not "bind the seller" nor would he accept or reject any offers, and never would he offer legal advice, since he is not qualified to do so.

9. A: The commission will be *paid* when the transaction closes, but it has been *earned* when the buyer is found which could be choices B, C, or D.

10. B: *Agency* describes the fiduciary relationship between a real estate salesperson or broker and the principal, who can be a buyer or a seller. Answer A is incorrect. A real estate firm can be named anything the owner wants to name it. Answer C is also wrong. The relation between

the agent and a broker could be *employee* or *independent contractor*. Answer D describes a *customer* relationship with a third party (the agent and the principal).

11. C: Ann is all of the things enumerated in answers A, B, and D. She is *NOT a neutral third-party* as suggested by Answer C (the correct choice). She owes definite fiduciary responsibilities to her buyer, John.

12. A: In states which allow it, Alice would be an appointed agent—appointed by broker Bradley to singularly represent a seller, to the exclusion of all of the other agents in the office.

13. B: The six correct set of fiduciary responsibilities are *care, obedience, loyalty, disclosure, accountability, confidentiality.* These can be remembered by the acronym COLD A/C, and the only answer that has all six of the six correct duties is answer B.

14. B: The only answer that fits is B; the neighbor is actually the client of the listing broker and the salesperson. This precludes the neighbor being a "customer" of either the salesperson or his broker, making Answers A, C, and D incorrect.

15. C: The broker has a fiduciary responsibility to keep confidential the facts surrounding the seller's selling strategy, minimum acceptable price, etc. The statement which is a violation of these fiduciary responsibilities is C, the comment about the lowest price the seller will accept. Once the buyer knows, that is surely what he will offer. Comments about the pool equipment being stolen and the activity of the Homeowners Association are both material facts and should be disclosed. B is puffing and it only helps the seller's position.

16. A: The salesperson has the responsibility to disclose material facts to third parties, buyers and their agents, and others who may have an interest. They have no responsibility to discuss buyer's needs, seller's needs, appraisals, etc., with any third parties.

17. C: Some states allow dual agency and some do not. Some states give it a different name, like *multiple representation.* One common element, however, among those that allow it, is that the dual agency situation must be fully disclosed to both seller and buyer.

18. A: Only answer A is correct—Sam is responsible to Broker Brady. He cannot do open houses for another broker. The nature of his employment contract or status is independent of his status as a salesperson in Brady's brokerage. Broker Brady can pay Sam anything they both agree to. There is no *generally agreed to* accepted commission rate in any community.

19. C: Answers A, B, and D are all true, making statement C the one that is NOT True and the correct answer. A sub-agent's responsibilities to the principal are the same as (not a subset) of the fiduciary responsibilities between the agent and the principal.

20. D: While some states protect against discrimination on the basis of sexual orientation, the federal fair housing laws are currently limited to protection on the basis of race, religion, and gender.

21. C: The practice of trying to interest buyers in a certain area, to the exclusion of most others, is known as *steering* and it is illegal.

22. C: Answer C is NOT true. Perpetrators of fraud face *both* civil and criminal penalties. All other statements are correct and true.

23. A: An individual homeowner may NOT generally discriminate by excluding any particular ethnic group or nationality, in this case everyone except Brazilians. The Greek Orthodox Church may discriminate, given some conditions. The American Legion and the Catholic Church do not seem to be discriminating in any way.

24. C: All parties named in this question are protected parties, except the marijuana distributor who is not. Convicted drug dealers would never be protected by fair housing laws. The other three choices are forms of illegal discrimination.

25. B: The first major civil rights legislation dealing with housing was the *Civil Rights Act of 1866*.

26. D: All of the individuals mentioned in the answers to this question are members of protected classes or groups, with the exception of cancer patients who are not protected by federal fair housing laws.

27. A: Dual agency is NOT legal in all states. All other statements are correct.

28. A: A cracked heat exchanger is an internal metal structure inside a gas furnace. It separates the burner from the plenum that delivers heated air to the rooms of the house. It can be seen only during a thorough inspection of the furnace. It is therefore *latent* in nature. It is a dangerous condition because it might allow the leakage of combustion products, including carbon monoxide, into the warm air system of the house. All of the other defects could be seen easily during the walk through of the house.

29. D: Always check with the broker about disclosing facts which might stigmatize a building. Many states *require agents to disclose facts* like a death or a homicide, while other jurisdictions *restrict disclosures* of this nature. If there is a specific state law that prevents disclosure, it may trump the general laws that require the disclosure of material facts.

30. B: Answers A, C, and D are important *material facts, so they must be disclosed*. Answer B, burned out light bulbs, is easily and inexpensively resolved, so it does not rise to the level of a material fact.

Chapter 3: Appraisal and Market Analysis
End of Chapter Quiz: Answer Key

1. D: The cost of replacing the outdated tile countertops with a current product such as granite countertops will most likely recover the cost (increasing returns) by the property being more attractive to buyers who are willing to pay more for the property with the more modern kitchens and baths.

2. A: Terms of the sale, physical characteristics, location, and the timeliness of closing date are all areas in which the appraiser will make an adjustment. The original purchase price is irrelevant in determining a property's current value. The annual income of the property will come into play in the income approach, but not the Market Data Approach. Likewise, depreciation is used in the cost approach, but not the market data approach.

3. A: GSI – V/BD = EGI – OE = NOI; therefore the first step in the income approach to valuation is to calculate the potential gross income of the property.

4. B: If the office building earns $35,000 per quarter after vacancies and expenses, it earns an NOI of $140,000 annually. I ÷ R = V; $140,000 ÷ .0675 = $2,074, 074.

5. D: A gross income multiplier is used with gross annual income, not net operating income. The income provided in question #4 is net, not gross, therefore there is not enough information.

6. B: Depreciation is only applied to the building. Land does not depreciate.

7. B: Economic, locational, or environmental obsolescence are all terms to represent a decrease in property value because of the property's location. Location, location, location.

8. C: The theory of substitution states that if there are other, similar properties available, a buyer's willingness to pay a certain price will be limited based on there being more reasonably priced alternatives.

9. C: This requires the use of the cost approach:

Determine the value of the land ($240,000 per acre ÷ 4):	$60,000 for the ¼ acre
Determine the replacement cost of the structure:	$210,000 given
Determine accumulated depreciation	
($210,000 replacement cost x .24 depreciation)	$50,400
Subtract accumulated depreciation from replacement cost	
($210,000 replacement cost - $50,400 depreciation)	$159,600
Add in the land value:	
($159,600 depreciated structure + $60,000 land value)	<u>$219,600</u>

10. A: Market data does not work as we cannot find buildings that have just sold comparable to the YMCA that have just sold. The income approach is not a good fit as the property is not truly an income generating investment property. The cost approach is therefore the most appropriate.

11. D: Characteristics of value are *demand*, utility (or use), *scarcity* (or supply) and *transferability*. DUST

12. D: I ÷ R = V; $677,000 NOI, 9% annual rate of return; $677,000 ÷ .09 = $7,522,222. $7.5 million rounded.

13. A: A shopping center is more commercialized than the other residential choices and a GIM would be most appropriate for the shopping center.

14. C: The comparable is always adjusted, never the subject property. In this case, the comparable is inferior to the subject. It does not have a family room. So, a family room has to be added. Adjust the comparable upward (addition).

15. A: The wording in the question is actually the definition of arm's Length; that the parties are distant from one another – at an arm's length.

16. C: Adjustments are always made to the comparable; not the subject. The comparable is 400 square feet more than the subject, so the extra square footage has to be *subtracted* from the comparable so it looks like the subject. The comparable is short a half bath, so the half bath has to be *added* to the comparable.

$395,000 Sale Price - $40,000 (400 sq. ft. X $100 sq. ft.) for the square footage + $5,500 (given) half bath
Adjust the comparable property downward $40,000 and then upward $5,500.
Adjust the comparable downward $34,500. ($360,500 reflects the adjusted price of the comparable.)

17. A: Uniform Residential Appraisal Report (URAR)

18. A: Reproduction cost in the cost approach to valuation is used if the building were so unique that using available materials and techniques would not produce a substantially similar building.

19. D: Assemblage is the process of adding the parcels together. If you selected plottage, plottage is the increase in value as a result of the assemblage.

20. D: All of the items are reasons for an appraisal to be ordered and utilized.

Chapter 4: Financing
End of Chapter Quiz: Answer Key

1. C: 20% down payment is required as this is an investment, non-owner occupied, purchase.

2. A: The eligibility is only for the veteran.

3. B: The down payment is $15,000 on a $150,000 purchase which is 10% down. With 10% down, the loan must be the other 90%.

4. D: Government backed loans cannot contain prepayment penalties. Conventional loans are much more loosely regulated and may.

5. A: The information in choices B, C, and D will not be stated in the note. Remember the promissory note creates and is evidence of a debt. The note will contain borrower's name, lender's name, amount borrowed, interest rate, date the first payment is due and the frequency of payments thereafter, term or length of time the borrower has to repay the loan, amount of the final payment and due date if the loan is not a fully amortizing loan, address to which payments are to be sent.

6. B: Lien theory states the mortgagor (borrower) retains legal and equitable title. The mortgagee (lender) has only a lien on the property as security for the debt. In order for the lender to take the property for sale, foreclosure proceedings must be initiated to obtain the legal title.

7. C: Simply, RESPA stands for *Real Estate Settlement Procedure Act*. RESPA requires lenders to inform the parties to a covered real estate transaction what the closing costs and charges are, and which costs they pay for.

8. D: The requirement is 3 days.

9. B: When the borrower is putting less than 20% down PMI is required.

10. C: 1-4 family dwellings are considered residential properties.

11. D: FHA does not lend money for loans; they insure loans made by lenders.

12. C: The order the documents are recorded determines priority; not when they were funded or terms of the loan.

13. D: FHA stands for *Federal Housing Administration.*

14. A: Impounds set aside amounts for the future payments of taxes and insurance. The lender wants to be sure these are paid as taxes take priority over the lender in the event of foreclosure; and if there

is a catastrophic event to the property, the lender's collateral will be significantly diminished. "B" might be a benefit to the borrower, but not the lender.

15. C: Loans that are "conventional" are loans that are non-government loans, specifically non-FHA or VA. Loans with MIP are FHA loans and not conventional loans.

16. D: All of the terms are trigger terms, and if advertised, require the disclosure of all loan terms as well as the APR.

17. A: Equal Credit Opportunity Act

18. D: VA does not set a maximum loan amount. Lenders may choose to individually, but not VA.

19. B: Annual Percentage Rate (APR)

20. C: Budget loans require the borrower to impound for the future payments of taxes and insurance.

Chapter 5: Property Ownership and Transfer of Title
End of Chapter Quiz: Answer Key

1. C: Answer C, beauty, is NOT a physical characteristic of land, as are indestructibility, immobility, and uniqueness, which apply to every parcel of land. Beauty, on the other hand applies to some parcels, but certainly not to others.

2. C: A lis pendens is a notice that a lawsuit affecting land has been filed in a federal or state court and, depending on the outcome of the legal action, a lien or other encumbrance may affect the land.

3. A: The two remaining owners now own the building as joint tenants, so answer A is correct. The laws of descent do not play a role because the three owners are not related, and answer B does not come into play. If one of them dies, the remaining owner would own the land in severalty, answer C. The will of the decedent also does not play a role because the rules of joint tenancy automatically distribute ownership to the two remaining joint tenants, so answer D is also incorrect.

4. B: An acre of land is 43,560 square feet.

5. C: A section of land is 640 acres (more or less), so ¼ of a section would be 160 acres.

6. A: In a situation like this, the programmable thermostats are fixtures that were in the home when it was listed, when it was shown, and when a contract was signed. So, the electrician/owner can be held liable for putting them back in.

7. C: Tenancy by the entirety, answer C, is the only form of ownership in this list of answers which is restricted to married persons. Joint tenancy and tenants in common do not have to be related. There is no such form of ownership as tenancy at will.

8. D: The attorney is worried about a community property claim, answer D. The attorney is specifically concerned that Kathy would make a claim of community property at some time in the future, even though she was never named on the deed that Robert received when he originally bought the property. Having Kathy sign a quit claim deed releases any potential future claim that she might have.

9. D: The water softener is a fixture that must be left with the house that Arlene had already sold, answer D. Arlene could have listed the property, excluding the water conditioner, but since there is no reason to believe she did, it has to go with the house. Answer C is wrong because she couldn't just remove it. Answers C and D are incorrect because the water conditioner has been permanently installed. It is no longer chattel (personal property) but a fixture (part of the real property).

10. C: The correct answer is C, accession. Trade fixtures, if not removed upon vacating the property, become property of the landlord through *accession*. Novation (D) is the transfer of liability from one debtor to another, Partition (A) is a court procedure to divide co-tenants in real property when the parties do not agree to terminate. Expulsion (B) is incorrect.

11. C: Vague descriptions are fine when used in documents that *will not be recorded*. These could include MLS listings, offers to purchases, and similar documents (answer C). Recordable documents like deeds require a legal address, which a vague address is definitely not.

12. A: 160 acres is the correct answer. Looking closely at the question, you will see that it is describing a portion of a section of land AND a second portion of a section of land. The first portion specifies the N ½ of the SE ¼ of a section. We know that a ¼ of a section is 640 divided by 4 = 160, and half of that is 80 acres. The next part of the legal description is similar, the S ½ of the NE ¼. Again, it is ½ of a ¼ section or ½ of 160 acres or another 80 acres. Added together then, we have 80 acres + 80 acres = 160 acres or answer A.

13. D: Tenants in common is the correct answer if they want to take ownership with unequal shares. Severalty limits title to one owner. Tenancy by the entirety requires the owners to be *married*. Joint tenancy requires equal shares of ownership (PITT).

14. A: If Lola holds ownership of a property as a tenant in common, she may sell or transfer her ownership, at any time, with or without the permission of the other owners.

15. D: A setback is the outer portion of the property on which building is prohibited, but it is not considered an encumbrance. All the other items listed are encumbrances.

16. B: The Internal Revenue Service allows a $500,000 deduction on the sale of a home for a married couple filing jointly. In this case, the capital gain is stated to be $700,000 minus the allowable deduction of $500,000 which equals a remainder of $200,000 which is the amount taxable as a long-term capital gain.

17. C: The notary public is responsible for ensuring that the grantor is signing voluntarily and is not under duress. A social security card is not a legal form of identification. Appearing with the deed signed would compromise the notary's responsibility to see the signature being affixed to the document.

18. D: Although it is a little bit counter intuitive, the 1031 exchange allows exchanges to be made within very broad-based categories. According to the IRS, real estate is real estate, so one could exchange one property for any other property, residential for commercial, vacation property for industrial property. It just does not matter. Therefore all three cases are allowable, and answer D is correct.

19. B: The grantor must sign the deed. The grantee neither has to be present nor sign any documents. As used in real estate, the terms vendor and vendee have to do with land contracts.

20. B: Statements A, C, and D are all correct. Statement B is INCORRECT. A devise is a gift of real property by will. The giver is the devisor, so the gift would take place after the devisor's death, not the devisee's death.

Chapter 6: Land Use Controls and Regulations
End of Chapter Quiz: Answer Key

1. D: All of the others, environmental protection laws, subdivision regulations, and zoning, are examples of *public* land use controls. Deed restrictions are private controls.

2. C: Lead impedes water flow; asbestos was used as insulation; UFFI also refers to insulation.

3. B: Eminent domain and escheat both refer to the right to take property; riparian rights refer to water.

4. A: This represents a material fact that a licensee should disclose, so "A" is the correct answer. All the other answers refer to how a licensee should handle a transaction that might deal with hazardous substances.

5. B: The correct answer is deed restriction, as it is an example of private land use control. All of the other answers refer to governmental controls.

6. D: Zoning ordinances are not retroactive, thus Mike will be able to continue operating his business.

7. D: EMFs are created by the movement of electrical currents.

8. C: The correct answer is "C" as the homeowners do not have to agree with the CC&Rs but must abide by them nonetheless. The HOA has the power to levy assessments and impose fines.

9. A: Eminent domain is the right of the government to take public land or property for public use or benefit.

10. B: Mold results from a moisture problem and can cause health issues to those allergic to the mold spores.

11. C: Encroachment refers to the situation when a part of a building, fence, or driveway extends onto another's property. It is not a license, as James did not give his permission; it is not an easement by necessity, as the block wall could have been moved or built in a different location; and it is not an easement by prescription as it is not long standing.

12. B: Radon comes from radioactive materials underground.

13. B: You can determine the taxes by using the following formula:

Taxes = market value x state assessment ratio x tax rate
Taxes = $310,000 x 40% x ($3.90 per $100 in valuation)
Taxes = $310,000/100 x .40 x $3.90 = $4.836

14. D: The minimum number of square feet per housing unit would be regulated by a local zoning ordinance, not by building codes.

15. A: The correct answer is "A" as a buffer zone separates one type of land use from another, such as a park or recreational area separating a residential area from an office park. The other answers represent one type of land use next to a different type, but without a true buffer zone between them.

16. C: Variance applies to the zoning ordinances, not the building codes. She will need a variance to allow permission and *vary* from the zoning ordinances.

17. B: Building codes regulate the construction of new buildings and structures.

18. A: Police powers can regulate all of the other items, as it is the government's right to enact regulations that protect the public health, safety, and welfare.

19. D: The other choices may well come into play later, but they first must determine if the property has been zoned to allow a restaurant to be built.

20. C: A non-conforming use applies when a use has pre-dated the zoning ordinance. A variance allows the owner to use the property in a manner normally prohibited; eminent domain refers to the government's right to take the property under certain circumstances; and inverse condemnation refers to the property owner seeking just compensation when land is taken for public use, but eminent domain is not being applied.

Chapter 7
Real Estate Math
End of Chapter Quiz: Answer Key

1. B: Start by calculating the area of the full lot. 150' x 250' (both dimensions are given) = 37,500 square feet. Next, calculate the area of the structure. The house is 20,000 square feet. The driveway is 20' x 30' = 600 square feet. Therefore, the total area NOT under sod is 20,600 square feet (house plus driveway). If the total lot is 37,500 sq. ft. and the total area not taking sod is 20,600 sq. ft., then the square footage needed for sod is 16,900 square feet.

2. C: There are 43,560 in an acre. Since this lot is 54,450 square feet, 54,450 ÷ 43,560 = 1.25 acres.

3. C: One percent is expressed as .01 (1 ÷ 100). One half of .01 = .005 (.5 ÷ 100).

4. C: The only slab measurements, when multiplying width by the depth, that totals 1,400 square feet is "C," 25' x 56'.

5. C: The formula for property taxes is:
market value x assessment ratio = assessed value x tax rate = annual tax
$525,000 MV x .32 AR = $168,000 AV x .019 (19 mills) = $3,192 Annual Taxes ÷ 4 quarters = $798 quarterly tax.

6. A: Again the formula for property taxes is:

market value x assessment ratio = assessed value x tax rate = annual tax; here we are given:
   ? MV   x   .45 AR   = ? AV (item asked) x .115 Tax Rate = $1,800 Annual Taxes
$1,800 ÷ .115 = $15,650 Assessed Value (rounded)

7. B: $279,500 sale price x .07 brokerage fee x .5 your brokerage's half x .40 your split = $3913. If you chose "A," $274, you multiplied the total brokerage fee by 3.5% and then applied your split and this is incorrect. By the problem telling us the co-broke share is 3.5%, we know that the listing brokerage kept half the total commission and paid the co-broke the other half. If you selected "C," $7,826, you applied your split to the total commission, which is "D" $19,565. Notice how all four choices can be derived mathematically as is often the case with a math multiple choice item.

8. B: $410,500 sale price ÷ 1,000 = 410.5; rounded up is 411 x $9.75 = $4,007.25. Transfer tax is paid on every $1,000 of value and any fraction thereof.

9. D: The sewer bill is paid in arrears and will cover a portion of the time Seller Stone was in title to the property. Therefore, Seller Stone owes Buyer Benson Stone's portion of the bill. This will be a debit to Seller Stone and a credit to Buyer Benson. Using a 30 day month, the proration will be based on the 30 days in July, the 30 days in August, and the 10 days in September that Stone owned the

property. $127 total bill ÷ 90 days in a quarter = $1.41 cost per day x 70 days = $98.78. If you chose either of the $24.69 answers, you took the quarterly tax of $127 and mistakenly divided by 360 days.

10. C: The loan is a percentage of the value. Taking the smaller number, the loan $150,450, and dividing it by the larger number, the sale price $177,000, we see that the loan represents .85 or 85% of the value.

11. C: $210,900 loan balance x .07 annual interest = $14,763 twelve months interest ÷ 12 = $1,230.25 that month's interest. A principal and interest payment of $1,400 less $1,230.25 interest = $169.75 principal reduction. $210,900 original balance less $169.75 principal reduction = $210,730.25 new balance.

12. A: The discount points are a percentage of the loan amount, not the sale price. The loan amount is $168,000 and the cost of the points is $4,200. $4,200 ÷ $168,000 = .025 or 2 ½ points.

13. D: There is not enough information as we don't know the number of points or the cost of the points. If we knew the number of points, we could calculate the loan amount and apply the points to the loan to determine the cost.

14. D: $162,000 x .04 = $6,480 first year appreciation + $162,000 = $168,480 value first year. $168,480 x .04 = $6,739 second year appreciation + $168,480 = $175,219 after two years.

15. B: 54 inches ÷ 12 inches in a foot = 4.5 feet. 4.5 feet = 4 feet, 6 inches. If the Bobcat needs 4 feet, then there is a total of 6 inches to spare.

16. B: The front yard measures 30' x 12' or 360 square feet. The rear yard is 60' x 15' or 900 square feet, for a total of 1,260 square feet of ground area. There are 9 square feet in 1 square yard. 1,260 square feet ÷ 9 = 140 square yards. Since a ton of rock covers 30 square yards, 140 ÷ 30 = 4.67 tons of rocks, rounded to 5.

17. A: Four units that net the owner $650 monthly after operating expenses is a monthly NOI of $2,600 x 12 = $31,200 annual NOI. If Iverson's desired rate of return is 11%, we divide the NOI by the Rate: $31,200 ÷ .11 = $283,636 ($285,000 rounded).

18. D: $150,000 net proceeds represents the *other* 91% if his total closing costs are estimated to be 9%. The brokerage fee is included in the 9% and therefore irrelevant. $150,000 ÷ .91 = $164,835 ($165,000 rounded).

19. A: There are a few ways to go about this, but if only 9/10 of the 90 acre parcel is available for lots, then 90 x .9 = 81 acres for building. 81 acres x 43,560 square feet in an acre is 3,528,360 square feet ÷ 420 lots = 8,400 square feet (rounded).

20. C: We are given the room measures 200 square feet to be carpeted. Since there are 9 square feet in a square yard, 200 square feet ÷ 9 = 22.22 square yards. The carpet is $22.00 per square yard and the labor is $4.00 per square yard, or $26.00 combined. $26.00 x 22.22 = $577.77 ($580 rounded).

Chapter 8: Mandated Disclosures
End of Chapter Quiz: Answer Key

1. A: Dual agency is NOT legal in all states. All other statements are correct.

2. A: A cracked heat exchanger is an internal metal structure inside a gas furnace. It separates the burner from the plenum that delivers heated air to the rooms of the house. It can be seen only during a thorough inspection of the furnace. It is therefore *latent* in nature. It is a dangerous condition because it might allow the leakage of combustion products, including carbon monoxide, into the warm air system of the house. All of the other defects could be seen easily during the walk through of the house.

3. C: The false statement is that disclosure is required in *some* states. It is accurate to say that agency disclosure is required in all states, making answer D a true statement. Answers A and B are also true, as agency needs to be disclosed to a client as soon as possible, whether the client is a buyer or a seller.

4. D: Sally must disclose BOTH who she represents and the familial relationship that exists.

5. A: These defects should be considered latent defects and disclosed. Doing so ensures that the buyer understands the situation and has an opportunity to inspect the damage and the repair. Doing nothing, or treating the situation as *buyer beware*, could lead to major problems if found later.

6. D: Always check with the broker about disclosing facts which might stigmatize a building. Many states *require agents to disclose facts* like a death or a homicide, while other jurisdictions *restrict disclosures* of this nature. If there is a specific state law that prevents disclosure, it may trump the general laws that require the disclosure of material facts.

7. D: This should be completed and disclosed by the seller. The agent should not be involved.

Appendix B

Sample Real Estate Documents and Forms from Across the Country

CONTAINED IN THIS APPENDIX:

- **Purchase Agreement** (Chapter 1)
- **Listing Contract** (Chapter 1)
- **Buyer Brokerage Agreement** (Chapter 1)
- **Lease Agreement** (Chapter 1)
- **Consent to Act to Dual Agency** (Chapter 2)
- **NAR Code of Ethics** (Chapter 2)
- **Mortgage** (Chapter 4)
- **Promissory Note** (Chapter 4)
- **Deed of Trust** (Chapter 4)
- **HUD 1 Settlement Statement** (Chapter 4)
- **Deed** (Chapter 5)
- **Real Property Disclosure Statement** (Chapter 8)

CALIFORNIA RESIDENTIAL PURCHASE AGREEMENT AND JOINT ESCROW INSTRUCTIONS
For Use With Single Family Residential Property — Attached or Detached (C.A.R. Form RPA-CA, Revised 4/10)

Date _____

1. **OFFER:**
   A. **THIS IS AN OFFER FROM** _____ ("Buyer").
   B. **THE REAL PROPERTY TO BE ACQUIRED** is described as _____
   _____, Assessor's Parcel No. _____, situated in
   _____, County of _____, California, ("Property").
   C. **THE PURCHASE PRICE** offered is _____
   _____ (Dollars $ _____).
   D. **CLOSE OF ESCROW** shall occur on _____ (date) (or ☐ _____ **Days** After Acceptance).

2. **AGENCY:**
   A. **DISCLOSURE:** Buyer and Seller each acknowledge prior receipt of a "Disclosure Regarding Real Estate Agency Relationships" (C.A.R. Form AD).
   B. **POTENTIALLY COMPETING BUYERS AND SELLERS:** Buyer and Seller each acknowledge receipt of a disclosure of the possibility of multiple representation by the Broker representing that principal. This disclosure may be part of a listing agreement, buyer representation agreement or separate document (C.A.R. Form DA). Buyer understands that Broker representing Buyer may also represent other potential buyers, who may consider, make offers on or ultimately acquire the Property. Seller understands that Broker representing Seller may also represent other sellers with competing properties of interest to this Buyer.
   C. **CONFIRMATION:** The following agency relationships are hereby confirmed for this transaction:
   Listing Agent _____ (Print Firm Name) is the agent
   of (check one): ☐ the Seller exclusively; or ☐ both the Buyer and Seller.
   Selling Agent _____ (Print Firm Name) (if not the same as the Listing Agent) is the agent of (check one): ☐ the Buyer exclusively; or ☐ the Seller exclusively; or ☐ both the Buyer and Seller. Real Estate Brokers are not parties to the Agreement between Buyer and Seller.

3. **FINANCE TERMS:** Buyer represents that funds will be good when deposited with Escrow Holder.
   A. **INITIAL DEPOSIT:** Deposit shall be in the amount of . . . . $ _____
   (1) Buyer shall deliver deposit directly to Escrow Holder by personal check, ☐ electronic funds transfer, ☐ Other _____ within **3 business days** after acceptance (or ☐ Other _____
   OR (2) (If checked) ☐ Buyer has given the deposit by personal check (or ☐ _____)
   to the agent submitting the offer (or to ☐ _____
   made payable to _____. The deposit shall be held
   uncashed until Acceptance and then deposited with Escrow Holder (or ☐ into Broker's trust account) within _____
   business days after Acceptance (or ☐ Other _____
   B. **INCREASED DEPOSIT:** Buyer shall deposit with Escrow Holder an increased deposit in the amount of . . . . $ _____
   within _____ **Days** After Acceptance, or ☐
   If a liquidated damages clause is incorporated into this Agreement, Buyer and Seller shall sign a separate liquidated damages clause (C.A.R. Form RID) for any increased deposit at the time it is deposited.
   C. **LOAN(S):**
   (1) **FIRST LOAN:** in the amount of . . . . $ _____
   This loan will be conventional financing or, if checked, ☐ FHA, ☐ VA, ☐ Seller (C.A.R. Form SFA), ☐ assumed financing (C.A.R. Form PAA), ☐ Other _____. This loan shall be at a fixed rate not to exceed _____ % or, ☐ an adjustable rate loan with initial rate not to exceed _____ %. Regardless of the type of loan, Buyer shall pay points not to exceed _____ % of the loan amount.
   (2) ☐ **SECOND LOAN:** in the amount of . . . . $ _____
   This loan will be conventional financing or, if checked, ☐ Seller (C.A.R. Form SFA), ☐ assumed financing (C.A.R. Form PAA), ☐ Other _____. This loan shall be at a fixed rate not to exceed _____ % or, ☐ an adjustable rate loan with initial rate not to exceed _____ %. Regardless of the type of loan, Buyer shall pay points not to exceed _____ % of the loan amount.
   (3) **FHA/VA:** For any FHA or VA loan specified above, Buyer has **17 (or** ☐ _____) **Days** After Acceptance to Deliver to Seller written notice (C.A.R. Form FVA) of any lender-required repairs or costs that Buyer requests Seller to pay for or repair. Seller has no obligation to pay for repairs or satisfy lender requirements unless otherwise agreed in writing.
   D. **ADDITIONAL FINANCING TERMS:** _____
   E. **BALANCE OF PURCHASE PRICE OR DOWN PAYMENT:** in the amount of . . . . $ _____
   to be deposited with Escrow Holder within sufficient time to close escrow.
   F. **PURCHASE PRICE (TOTAL):** . . . . $ _____

Buyer's Initials (_____) (_____)   Seller's Initials (_____) (_____)

The copyright laws of the United States (Title 17 U.S. Code) forbid the unauthorized reproduction of this form, or any portion thereof, by photocopy machine or any other means, including facsimile or computerized formats. Copyright © 1991-2010, CALIFORNIA ASSOCIATION OF REALTORS®, INC. ALL RIGHTS RESERVED.

RPA-CA REVISED 4/10 (PAGE 1 OF 8)   949.748.1113   949.748.1112   Reviewed by _____ Date _____

CALIFORNIA RESIDENTIAL PURCHASE AGREEMENT (RPA-CA PAGE 1 OF 8)

Agent:	Phone:	Fax:	Prepared using zipForm® software
Broker:			

Property Address: _____ Date: _____

G. **VERIFICATION OF DOWN PAYMENT AND CLOSING COSTS:** Buyer (or Buyer's lender or loan broker pursuant to 3H(1)) shall, within **7 (or** ☐ _____ **) Days** After Acceptance, Deliver to Seller written verification of Buyer's down payment and closing costs. (If checked, ☐ verification attached.)

H. **LOAN TERMS:**
   (1) **LOAN APPLICATIONS:** Within **7 (or** ☐ _____ **) Days** After Acceptance, Buyer shall Deliver to Seller a letter from lender or loan broker stating that, based on a review of Buyer's written application and credit report, Buyer is prequalified or preapproved for any NEW loan specified in 3C above. (If checked, ☐ letter attached.)
   (2) **LOAN CONTINGENCY:** Buyer shall act diligently and in good faith to obtain the designated loan(s). Obtaining the loan(s) specified above **is a contingency** of this Agreement unless otherwise agreed in writing. Buyer's contractual obligations to obtain and provide deposit, balance of down payment and closing costs **are not contingencies** of this Agreement.
   (3) **LOAN CONTINGENCY REMOVAL:**
       (i) Within **17 (or** ☐ _____ **) Days** After Acceptance, Buyer shall, as specified in paragraph 14, in writing remove the loan contingency or cancel this Agreement;
       OR (ii) (if checked) ☐ the loan contingency shall remain in effect until the designated loans are funded.
   (4) ☐ **NO LOAN CONTINGENCY** (If checked): Obtaining any loan specified above is NOT a contingency of this Agreement. If Buyer does not obtain the loan and as a result Buyer does not purchase the Property, Seller may be entitled to Buyer's deposit or other legal remedies.

I. **APPRAISAL CONTINGENCY AND REMOVAL:** This Agreement is (or, if checked, ■ is NOT) contingent upon a written appraisal of the Property by a licensed or certified appraiser at no less than the specified purchase price. If there is a loan contingency, Buyer's removal of the loan contingency shall be deemed removal of this appraisal contingency (or■ if checked, Buyer shall, as specified in paragraph 14B(3), in writing remove the appraisal contingency or cancel this Agreement within **17 (or** _____ **) Days** After Acceptance). If there is no loan contingency, Buyer shall, as specified in paragraph 14B(3), in writing remove the appraisal contingency or cancel this Agreement within **17 (or** _____ **) Days** After Acceptance.

J. ■ **ALL CASH OFFER** (If checked): Buyer shall, within **7 (or** ☐ _____ **) Days** After Acceptance, Deliver to Seller written verification of sufficient funds to close this transaction. (If checked, ☐ verification attached.)

K. **BUYER STATED FINANCING:** Seller has relied on Buyer's representation of the type of financing specified (including but not limited to, as applicable, amount of down payment, contingent or non contingent loan, or all cash). If Buyer seeks alternate financing, (i) Seller has no obligation to cooperate with Buyer's efforts to obtain such financing, and (ii) Buyer shall also pursue the financing method specified in this Agreement. Buyer's failure to secure alternate financing does not excuse Buyer from the obligation to purchase the Property and close escrow as specified in this Agreement.

4. **ALLOCATION OF COSTS** (If checked): Unless otherwise specified in writing, **this paragraph** only determines who is to pay for the inspection, test or service ("Report") mentioned; it **does not determine who is to pay for any work recommended or identified in the Report.**

   A. **INSPECTIONS AND REPORTS:**
      (1) ■ Buyer ■ Seller shall pay for an inspection and report for wood destroying pests and organisms ("Wood Pest Report") prepared by _____ a registered structural pest control company.
      (2) ☐ Buyer ☐ Seller shall pay to have septic or private sewage disposal systems pumped and inspected _____
      (3) ☐ Buyer ☐ Seller shall pay to have domestic wells tested for water potability and productivity _____
      (4) ☐ Buyer ☐ Seller shall pay for a natural hazard zone disclosure report prepared by _____
      (5) ☐ Buyer ☐ Seller shall pay for the following inspection or report _____
      (6) ☐ Buyer ☐ Seller shall pay for the following inspection or report _____

   B. **GOVERNMENT REQUIREMENTS AND RETROFIT:**
      (1) ■ Buyer ■ Seller shall pay for smoke detector installation and/or water heater bracing, if required by Law. Prior to Close Of Escrow, Seller shall provide Buyer written statement(s) of compliance in accordance with state and local Law, unless exempt.
      (2) ■ Buyer ■ Seller shall pay the cost of compliance with any other minimum mandatory government retrofit standards, inspections and reports if required as a condition of closing escrow under any Law. _____

   C. **ESCROW AND TITLE:**
      (1) ☐ Buyer ☐ Seller shall pay escrow fee _____
          Escrow Holder shall be _____
      (2) ☐ Buyer ☐ Seller shall pay for **owner's** title insurance policy specified in paragraph 12E _____
          Owner's title policy to be issued by _____
          (Buyer shall pay for any title insurance policy insuring Buyer's **lender**, unless otherwise agreed in writing.)

   D. **OTHER COSTS:**
      (1) ☐ Buyer ☐ Seller shall pay County transfer tax or fee _____
      (2) ☐ Buyer ☐ Seller shall pay City transfer tax or fee _____
      (3) ☐ Buyer ☐ Seller shall pay Homeowner's Association ("HOA") transfer fee _____
      (4) ☐ Buyer ☐ Seller shall pay HOA document preparation fees _____
      (5) ☐ Buyer ☐ Seller shall pay for any private transfer fee _____
      (6) ☐ Buyer ☐ Seller shall pay the cost, not to exceed $ _____ , of a one-year home warranty plan, issued by _____ , with the following optional coverages:
          ☐ Air Conditioner ☐ Pool/Spa ☐ Code and Permit upgrade ☐ Other: _____
          Buyer is informed that home warranty plans have many optional coverages in addition to those listed above. Buyer is advised to investigate these coverages to determine those that may be suitable for Buyer.
      (7) ☐ Buyer ☐ Seller shall pay for _____
      (8) ☐ Buyer ☐ Seller shall pay for _____

Buyer's Initials (_____) (_____)   Seller's Initials (_____) (_____)

Copyright © 1991-2010, CALIFORNIA ASSOCIATION OF REALTORS®, INC.

Reviewed by _____ Date _____

CALIFORNIA RESIDENTIAL PURCHASE AGREEMENT (RPA-CA PAGE 2 OF 8)

blank forms

Property Address: _____ Date: _____

5. **CLOSING AND POSSESSION:**
   A. Buyer intends (or ☐ does not intend) to occupy the Property as Buyer's primary residence.
   B. **Seller-occupied or vacant property:** Possession shall be delivered to Buyer at 5 PM or (☐ _____ ☐ AM ☐ PM), on the date of Close Of Escrow; ☐ on_____; or ☐ no later than _____ **Days** After Close Of Escrow. If transfer of title and possession do not occur at the same time, Buyer and Seller are advised to: **(i)** enter into a written occupancy agreement (C.A.R. Form PAA, paragraph 2); and **(ii)** consult with their insurance and legal advisors.
   C. **Tenant-occupied property:**
      (i) Property shall be vacant at least **5 (or** ☐ _____ **) Days** Prior to Close Of Escrow, unless otherwise agreed in writing. **Note to Seller: If you are unable to deliver Property vacant in accordance with rent control and other applicable Law, you may be in breach of this Agreement.**
      OR (ii) (if checked) ☐ **Tenant to remain in possession.** (C.A.R. Form PAA, paragraph 3)
   D. At Close Of Escrow, **(i)** Seller assigns to Buyer any assignable warranty rights for items included in the sale, and **(ii)** Seller shall Deliver to Buyer available Copies of warranties. Brokers cannot and will not determine the assignability of any warranties.
   E. At Close Of Escrow, unless otherwise agreed in writing, Seller shall provide keys and/or means to operate all locks, mailboxes, security systems, alarms and garage door openers. If Property is a condominium or located in a common interest subdivision, Buyer may be required to pay a deposit to the Homeowners' Association ("HOA") to obtain keys to accessible HOA facilities.

6. **STATUTORY DISCLOSURES (INCLUDING LEAD-BASED PAINT HAZARD DISCLOSURES) AND CANCELLATION RIGHTS:**
   A. **(1)** Seller shall, within the time specified in paragraph 14A, Deliver to Buyer, if required by Law: **(i)** Federal Lead-Based Paint Disclosures (C.A.R. Form FLD) and pamphlet ("Lead Disclosures"); and **(ii)** disclosures or notices required by sections 1102 et. seq. and 1103 et. seq. of the Civil Code ("Statutory Disclosures"). Statutory Disclosures include, but are not limited to, a Real Estate Transfer Disclosure Statement ("TDS"), Natural Hazard Disclosure Statement ("NHD"), notice or actual knowledge of release of illegal controlled substance, notice of special tax and/or assessments (or, if allowed, substantially equivalent notice regarding the Mello-Roos Community Facilities Act and Improvement Bond Act of 1915) and, if Seller has actual knowledge, of industrial use and military ordinance location (C.A.R. Form SPQ or SSD).
      (2) Buyer shall, within the time specified in paragraph 14B(1), return Signed Copies of the Statutory and Lead Disclosures to Seller.
      (3) In the event Seller, prior to Close Of Escrow, becomes aware of adverse conditions materially affecting the Property, or any material inaccuracy in disclosures, information or representations previously provided to Buyer, Seller shall promptly provide a subsequent or amended disclosure or notice, in writing, covering those items. **However, a subsequent or amended disclosure shall not be required for conditions and material inaccuracies** of which Buyer is otherwise aware, or which are **disclosed in reports provided to or obtained by Buyer or ordered and paid for by Buyer**.
      (4) If any disclosure or notice specified in 6A(1), or subsequent or amended disclosure or notice is Delivered to Buyer after the offer is Signed, Buyer shall have the right to cancel this Agreement within **3 Days** After Delivery in person, or **5 Days** After Delivery by deposit in the mail, by giving written notice of cancellation to Seller or Seller's agent.
      (5) Note to Buyer and Seller: Waiver of Statutory and Lead Disclosures is prohibited by Law.
   B. **NATURAL AND ENVIRONMENTAL HAZARDS:** Within the time specified in paragraph 14A, Seller shall, if required by Law: **(i)** Deliver to Buyer earthquake guides (and questionnaire) and environmental hazards booklet; **(ii)** even if exempt from the obligation to provide a NHD, disclose if the Property is located in a Special Flood Hazard Area; Potential Flooding (Inundation) Area; Very High Fire Hazard Zone; State Fire Responsibility Area; Earthquake Fault Zone; Seismic Hazard Zone; and **(iii)** disclose any other zone as required by Law and provide any other information required for those zones.
   C. **WITHHOLDING TAXES:** Within the time specified in paragraph 14A, to avoid required withholding, Seller shall Deliver to Buyer or qualified substitute, an affidavit sufficient to comply with federal (FIRPTA) and California withholding Law, (C.A.R. Form AS or QS).
   D. **MEGAN'S LAW DATABASE DISCLOSURE:** Notice: Pursuant to Section 290.46 of the Penal Code, information about specified registered sex offenders is made available to the public via an Internet Web site maintained by the Department of Justice at www.meganslaw.ca.gov. Depending on an offender's criminal history, this information will include either the address at which the offender resides or the community of residence and ZIP Code in which he or she resides. (Neither Seller nor Brokers are required to check this website. If Buyer wants further information, Broker recommends that Buyer obtain information from this website during Buyer's inspection contingency period. Brokers do not have expertise in this area.)

7. **CONDOMINIUM/PLANNED DEVELOPMENT DISCLOSURES:**
   A. **SELLER HAS: 7 (or** ☐ _____ **) Days** After Acceptance to disclose to Buyer whether the Property is a condominium, or is located in a planned development or other common interest subdivision (C.A.R. Form SPQ or SSD).
   B. If the Property is a condominium or is located in a planned development or other common interest subdivision, Seller has **3 (or** ☐ _____ **) Days** After Acceptance to request from the HOA (C.A.R. Form HOA): **(i)** Copies of any documents required by Law; **(ii)** disclosure of any pending or anticipated claim or litigation by or against the HOA; **(iii)** a statement containing the location and number of designated parking and storage spaces; **(iv)** Copies of the most recent 12 months of HOA minutes for regular and special meetings; and **(v)** the names and contact information of all HOAs governing the Property (collectively, "CI Disclosures"). Seller shall itemize and Deliver to Buyer all CI Disclosures received from the HOA and any CI Disclosures in Seller's possession. Buyer's approval of CI Disclosures is a contingency of this Agreement as specified in paragraph 14B(3).

8. **ITEMS INCLUDED IN AND EXCLUDED FROM PURCHASE PRICE:**
   A. **NOTE TO BUYER AND SELLER:** Items listed as included or excluded in the MLS, flyers or marketing materials are **not** included in the purchase price or excluded from the sale unless specified in 8B or C.
   B. **ITEMS INCLUDED IN SALE:**
      (1) All EXISTING fixtures and fittings that are attached to the Property;
      (2) EXISTING electrical, mechanical, lighting, plumbing and heating fixtures, ceiling fans, fireplace inserts, gas logs and grates, solar systems, built-in appliances, window and door screens, awnings, shutters, window coverings, attached floor coverings, television antennas, satellite dishes, private integrated telephone systems, air coolers/conditioners, pool/spa equipment, garage door openers/remote controls, mailbox, in-ground landscaping, trees/shrubs, water softeners, water purifiers, security systems/alarms; (If checked ☒ stove(s), ☒ refrigerator(s); and
      (3) The following additional items: _____ .
      (4) Seller represents that all items included in the purchase price, unless otherwise specified, are owned by Seller.
      (5) All items included shall be transferred free of liens and without Seller warranty.
   C. **ITEMS EXCLUDED FROM SALE:** Unless otherwise specified, audio and video components (such as flat screen TVs and speakers) are excluded if any such item is not itself attached to the Property, even if a bracket or other mechanism attached to the component is attached to the Property; and _____

Buyer's Initials (_____) (_____)   Seller's Initials (_____) (_____)

Copyright © 1991-2010, CALIFORNIA ASSOCIATION OF REALTORS®, INC.

Reviewed by _____ Date _____

RPA-CA REVISED 4/10 (PAGE 3 OF 8)

CALIFORNIA RESIDENTIAL PURCHASE AGREEMENT (RPA-CA PAGE 3 OF 8)

blank forms

Property Address: _____ Date: _____

9. **CONDITION OF PROPERTY:** Unless otherwise agreed: **(i) the Property is sold (a) in its PRESENT physical ("as-is") condition as of the date of Acceptance and (b) subject to Buyer's Investigation rights; (ii)** the Property, including pool, spa, landscaping and grounds, is to be maintained in substantially the same condition as on the date of Acceptance; and **(iii)** all debris and personal property not included in the sale shall be removed by Seller by Close Of Escrow.
   A. Seller shall, within the time specified in paragraph 14A, DISCLOSE KNOWN MATERIAL FACTS AND DEFECTS affecting the Property, including known insurance claims within the past five years, and make any and all other disclosures required by law.
   B. Buyer has the right to inspect the Property and, as specified in paragraph 14B, based upon information discovered in those inspections: (i) cancel this Agreement; or (ii) request that Seller make Repairs or take other action.
   C. **Buyer is strongly advised to conduct investigations of the entire Property in order to determine its present condition. Seller may not be aware of all defects affecting the Property or other factors that Buyer considers important. Property improvements may not be built according to code, in compliance with current Law, or have had permits issued.**

10. **BUYER'S INVESTIGATION OF PROPERTY AND MATTERS AFFECTING PROPERTY:**
    A. Buyer's acceptance of the condition of, and any other matter affecting the Property, is a contingency of this Agreement as specified in this paragraph and paragraph 14B. Within the time specified in paragraph 14B(1), Buyer shall have the right, at Buyer's expense unless otherwise agreed, to conduct inspections, investigations, tests, surveys and other studies ("Buyer Investigations"), including, but not limited to, the right to: **(i)** inspect for lead-based paint and other lead-based paint hazards; **(ii)** inspect for wood destroying pests and organisms; **(iii)** review the registered sex offender database; **(iv)** confirm the insurability of Buyer and the Property; and **(v)** satisfy Buyer as to any matter specified in the attached Buyer's Inspection Advisory (C.A.R. Form BIA). Without Seller's prior written consent, Buyer shall neither make nor cause to be made: **(i)** invasive or destructive Buyer Investigations; or **(ii)** inspections by any governmental building or zoning inspector or government employee, unless required by Law.
    B. Seller shall make the Property available for all Buyer Investigations. Buyer shall **(i)** as specified in paragraph 14B, complete Buyer Investigations and, either remove the contingency or cancel this Agreement, and **(ii)** give Seller, at no cost, complete Copies of all Investigation reports obtained by Buyer, which obligation shall survive the termination of this Agreement.
    C. Seller shall have water, gas, electricity and all operable pilot lights on for Buyer's Investigations and _____ through the date possession is made available to Buyer.
    D. **Buyer indemnity and Seller protection for entry upon property:** Buyer shall: **(i)** keep the Property free and clear of liens; **(ii)** repair all damage arising from Buyer Investigations; and **(iii)** indemnify and hold Seller harmless from all resulting liability, claims, demands, damages and costs of Buyer's investigations. Buyer shall carry, or Buyer shall require anyone acting on Buyer's behalf to carry, policies of liability, workers' compensation and other applicable insurance, defending and protecting Seller from liability for any injuries to persons or property occurring during any Buyer Investigations or work done on the Property at Buyer's direction prior to Close Of Escrow. Seller is advised that certain protections may be afforded Seller by recording a "Notice of Non-responsibility" (C.A.R. Form NNR) for Buyer Investigations and work done on the Property at Buyer's direction. Buyer's obligations under this paragraph shall survive the termination or cancellation of this Agreement and Close of Escrow.

11. **SELLER DISCLOSURES; ADDENDA; ADVISORIES; OTHER TERMS:**
    A. **Seller Disclosures (if checked):** Seller shall, within the time specified in paragraph 14A, complete and provide Buyer with a:
       ☐ Seller Property Questionnaire (C.A.R. Form SPQ)   **OR**   ☐ Supplemental Contractual and Statutory Disclosure (C.A.R. Form SSD)
    B. **Addenda (if checked):**   ☐ Addendum # _____ (C.A.R. Form ADM)
       ☐ Wood Destroying Pest Inspection and Allocation of Cost Addendum (C.A.R. Form WPA)
       ☐ Purchase Agreement Addendum (C.A.R Form PAA)   ☐ Septic, Well and Property Monument Addendum (C.A.R. Form SWPI)
       ☐ Short Sale Addendum (C.A.R. Form SSA)   ☐ Other
    C. **Advisories (if checked):**   ☑ Buyer's Inspection Advisory (C.A.R. Form BIA)
       ☐ Probate Advisory (C.A.R. Form PAK)   ☐ Statewide Buyer and Seller Advisory (C.A.R. Form SBSA)
       ☐ Trust Advisory (C.A.R. Form TA)   ☐ REO Advisory (C.A.R. Form REO)
    D. **Other Terms:**

12. **TITLE AND VESTING:**
    A. Within the time specified in paragraph 14, Buyer shall be provided a current preliminary title report, which shall include a search of the General Index. Seller shall within 7 Days After Acceptance give Escrow Holder a completed Statement of Information. The preliminary report is only an offer by the title insurer to issue a policy of title insurance and may not contain every item affecting title. Buyer's review of the preliminary report and any other matters which may affect title are a contingency of this Agreement as specified in paragraph 14B.
    B. Title is taken in its present condition subject to all encumbrances, easements, covenants, conditions, restrictions, rights and other matters, whether of record or not, as of the date of Acceptance except: **(i)** monetary liens of record unless Buyer is assuming those obligations or taking the Property subject to those obligations; and **(ii)** those matters which Seller has agreed to remove in writing.
    C. Within the time specified in paragraph 14A, Seller has a duty to disclose to Buyer all matters known to Seller affecting title, whether of record or not.
    D. At Close Of Escrow, Buyer shall receive a grant deed conveying title (or, for stock cooperative or long-term lease, an assignment of stock certificate or of Seller's leasehold interest), including oil, mineral and water rights if currently owned by Seller. Title shall vest as designated in Buyer's supplemental escrow instructions. THE MANNER OF TAKING TITLE MAY HAVE SIGNIFICANT LEGAL AND TAX CONSEQUENCES. CONSULT AN APPROPRIATE PROFESSIONAL.
    E. Buyer shall receive a CLTA/ALTA Homeowner's Policy of Title Insurance. A title company, at Buyer's request, can provide information about the availability, desirability, coverage, survey requirements, and cost of various title insurance coverages and endorsements. If Buyer desires title coverage other than that required by this paragraph, Buyer shall instruct Escrow Holder in writing and pay any increase in cost.

13. **SALE OF BUYER'S PROPERTY:**
    A. This Agreement is NOT contingent upon the sale of any property owned by Buyer.
    OR B. ■ (If checked): The attached addendum (C.A.R. Form COP) regarding the contingency for the sale of property owned by Buyer is incorporated into this Agreement.

Buyer's Initials (_____)(_____)   Seller's Initials (_____)(_____)

Copyright © 1991-2010, CALIFORNIA ASSOCIATION OF REALTORS®, INC.

RPA-CA REVISED 4/10 (PAGE 4 OF 8)   Reviewed by _____ Date _____

CALIFORNIA RESIDENTIAL PURCHASE AGREEMENT (RPA-CA PAGE 4 OF 8)   blank forms

Property Address: _____ Date: _____

14. TIME PERIODS; REMOVAL OF CONTINGENCIES; CANCELLATION RIGHTS: The following time periods may only be extended, altered, modified or changed by mutual written agreement. Any removal of contingencies or cancellation under this paragraph by either Buyer or Seller must be exercised in good faith and in writing (C.A.R. Form CR or CC).

   A. **SELLER HAS: 7 (or ■___) Days After Acceptance** to Deliver to Buyer all Reports, disclosures and information for which Seller is responsible under paragraphs 4, 6A, B and C, 7A, 9A, 11A and B, and 12. Buyer may give Seller a Notice to Seller to Perform (C.A.R. Form NSP) if Seller has not Delivered the items within the time specified.

   B. (1) **BUYER HAS: 17 (or ■_____) Days** After Acceptance, unless otherwise agreed in writing, to:
      (i) complete all Buyer Investigations; approve all disclosures, reports and other applicable information, which Buyer receives from Seller; and approve all other matters affecting the Property; and
      (ii) Deliver to Seller Signed Copies of Statutory and Lead Disclosures Delivered by Seller in accordance with paragraph 6A.
   (2) Within the time specified in 14B(1), Buyer may request that Seller make repairs or take any other action regarding the Property (C.A.R. Form RR). Seller has no obligation to agree to or respond to Buyer's requests.
   (3) Within the time specified in 14B(1) (or as otherwise specified in this Agreement), Buyer shall Deliver to Seller either (i) a removal of the applicable contingency (C.A.R. Form CR), or (ii) a cancellation (C.A.R. Form CC) of this Agreement based upon a contingency or Seller's failure to Deliver the specified items. However, if any report, disclosure or information for which Seller is responsible is not Delivered within the time specified in 14A, then Buyer has **5 (or ■___) Days After** Delivery of any such items, or the time specified in 14B(1), whichever is later, to Deliver to Seller a removal of the applicable contingency or cancellation of this Agreement.
   (4) **Continuation of Contingency:** Even after the end of the time specified in 14B(1) and before Seller cancels this Agreement, if at all, pursuant to 14C, Buyer retains the right to either (i) in writing remove remaining contingencies, or (ii) cancel this Agreement based upon a remaining contingency or Seller's failure to Deliver the specified terms. Once Buyer's written removal of all contingencies is Delivered to Seller, Seller may not cancel this Agreement pursuant to 14C(1).

   C. **SELLER RIGHT TO CANCEL:**
   (1) **Seller right to Cancel; Buyer Contingencies:** If, within time specified in this Agreement, Buyer does not, in writing, Deliver to Seller a removal of the applicable contingency or cancellation of this Agreement then Seller, after first Delivering to Buyer a Notice to Buyer to Perform (C.A.R. Form NBP) may cancel this Agreement. In such event, Seller shall authorize return of Buyer's deposit.
   (2) **Seller right to Cancel; Buyer Contract Obligations:** Seller, after first Delivering to Buyer a NBP may cancel this Agreement for any of the following reasons: (i) if Buyer fails to deposit funds as required by 3A or 3B; (ii) if the funds deposited pursuant to 3A or 3B are not good when deposited; (iii) if Buyer fails to Deliver a notice of FHA or VA costs or terms as required by 3C(3) (C.A.R. Form FVA); (iv) if Buyer fails to Deliver a letter as required by 3H; (v) if Buyer fails to Deliver verification as required by 3G or 3J; (vi) if Seller reasonably disapproves of the verification provided by 3G or 3J; (vii) if Buyer fails to return Statutory and Lead Disclosures as required by paragraph 6A(2); or (viii) if Buyer fails to sign or initial a separate liquidated damage form for an increased deposit as required by paragraphs 3B and 25. In such event, Seller shall authorize return of Buyer's deposit.
   (3) **Notice To Buyer To Perform:** The NBP shall: (i) be in writing; (ii) be signed by Seller; and (iii) give Buyer at least **2 (or ■___)** Delivery (or until the time specified in the applicable paragraph, whichever occurs last) to take the applicable action. A NBP may not be Delivered any earlier than **2 Days** Prior to the expiration of the applicable time for Buyer to remove a contingency or cancel this Agreement or meet an obligation specified in 14C(2).

   D. **EFFECT OF BUYER'S REMOVAL OF CONTINGENCIES:** If Buyer removes, in writing, any contingency or cancellation rights, unless otherwise specified in a separate written agreement between Buyer and Seller, Buyer shall with regard to that contingency or cancellation right conclusively be deemed to have: (i) completed all Buyer Investigations, and review of reports and other applicable information and disclosures; (ii) elected to proceed with the transaction; and (iii) assumed all liability, responsibility and expense for Repairs or corrections or for inability to obtain financing.

   E. **CLOSE OF ESCROW:** Before Seller or Buyer may cancel this Agreement for failure of the other party to close escrow pursuant to this Agreement, Seller or Buyer must first give the other a demand to close escrow (C.A.R. Form DCE).

   F. **EFFECT OF CANCELLATION ON DEPOSITS:** If Buyer or Seller gives written notice of cancellation pursuant to rights duly exercised under the terms of this Agreement, Buyer and Seller agree to Sign mutual instructions to cancel the sale and escrow and release deposits, if any, to the party entitled to the funds, less fees and costs incurred by that party. Fees and costs may be payable to service providers and vendors for services and products provided during escrow. **Release of funds will require mutual Signed release instructions from Buyer and Seller, judicial decision or arbitration award. A Buyer or Seller may be subject to a civil penalty of up to $1,000 for refusal to sign such instructions if no good faith dispute exists as to who is entitled to the deposited funds (Civil Code §1057.3).**

15. REPAIRS: Repairs shall be completed prior to final verification of condition unless otherwise agreed in writing. Repairs to be performed at Seller's expense may be performed by Seller or through others, provided that the work complies with applicable Law, including governmental permit, inspection and approval requirements. Repairs shall be performed in a good, skillful manner with materials of quality and appearance comparable to existing materials. It is understood that exact restoration of appearance or cosmetic items following all Repairs may not be possible. Seller shall: (i) obtain receipts for Repairs performed by others; (ii) prepare a written statement indicating the Repairs performed by Seller and the date of such Repairs; and (iii) provide Copies of receipts and statements to Buyer prior to final verification of condition.

16. FINAL VERIFICATION OF CONDITION: Buyer shall have the right to make a final inspection of the Property within **5 (or_____) Days** Prior to Close Of Escrow, NOT AS A CONTINGENCY OF THE SALE, but solely to confirm: (i) the Property is maintained pursuant to paragraph 9; (ii) Repairs have been completed as agreed; and (iii) Seller has complied with Seller's other obligations under this Agreement (C.A.R. Form VP).

17. PRORATIONS OF PROPERTY TAXES AND OTHER ITEMS: Unless otherwise agreed in writing, the following items shall be PAID CURRENT and prorated between Buyer and Seller as of Close Of Escrow: real property taxes and assessments, interest, rents, HOA regular, special, and emergency dues and assessments imposed prior to Close Of Escrow, premiums on insurance assumed by Buyer, payments on bonds and assessments assumed by Buyer, and payments on Mello-Roos and other Special Assessment District bonds and assessments that are a current lien. The following items shall be assumed by Buyer WITHOUT CREDIT toward the purchase price: prorated payments on Mello-Roos and other Special Assessment District bonds and assessments and HOA special assessments that are a current lien but not yet due. Property will be reassessed upon change of ownership. Any supplemental tax bills shall be paid as follows: (i) for periods after Close Of Escrow, by Buyer; and (ii) for periods prior to Close Of Escrow, by Seller (see C.A.R. Form SPT or SBSA for further information). TAX BILLS ISSUED AFTER CLOSE OF ESCROW SHALL BE HANDLED DIRECTLY BETWEEN BUYER AND SELLER. Prorations shall be made based on a 30-day month.

Buyer's Initials (_____)(_____) Seller's Initials (_____)(_____)

Copyright © 1991-2010, CALIFORNIA ASSOCIATION OF REALTORS®, INC.
RPA-CA REVISED 4/10 (PAGE 5 OF 8)

Reviewed by _____ Date _____

CALIFORNIA RESIDENTIAL PURCHASE AGREEMENT (RPA-CA PAGE 5 OF 8)

blank forms

Property Address: _____ Date: _____

18. **SELECTION OF SERVICE PROVIDERS:** Brokers do not guarantee the performance of any vendors, service or product providers ("Providers"), whether referred by Broker or selected by Buyer, Seller or other person. Buyer and Seller may select ANY Providers of their own choosing.
19. **MULTIPLE LISTING SERVICE ("MLS"):** Brokers are authorized to report to the MLS a pending sale and, upon Close Of Escrow, the sales price and other terms of this transaction shall be provided to the MLS to be published and disseminated to persons and entities authorized to use the information on terms approved by the MLS.
20. **EQUAL HOUSING OPPORTUNITY:** The Property is sold in compliance with federal, state and local anti-discrimination Laws.
21. **ATTORNEY FEES:** In any action, proceeding, or arbitration between Buyer and Seller arising out of this Agreement, the prevailing Buyer or Seller shall be entitled to reasonable attorney fees and costs from the non-prevailing Buyer or Seller, except as provided in paragraph 26A.
22. **DEFINITIONS:** As used in this Agreement:
    A. **"Acceptance"** means the time the offer or final counter offer is accepted in writing by a party and is delivered to and personally received by the other party or that party's authorized agent in accordance with the terms of this offer or a final counter offer.
    B. **"C.A.R. Form"** means the specific form referenced or another comparable form agreed to by the parties.
    C. **"Close Of Escrow"** means the date the grant deed, or other evidence of transfer of title, is recorded.
    D. **"Copy"** means copy by any means including photocopy, NCR, facsimile and electronic.
    E. **"Days"** means calendar days. However, After Acceptance, the last **Day** for performance of any act required by this Agreement (including Close Of Escrow) shall not include any Saturday, Sunday, or legal holiday and shall instead be the next Day.
    F. **"Days After"** means the specified number of calendar days after the occurrence of the event specified, not counting the calendar date on which the specified event occurs, and ending at 11:59PM on the final day.
    G. **"Days Prior"** means the specified number of calendar days before the occurrence of the event specified, not counting the calendar date on which the specified event is scheduled to occur.
    H. **"Deliver", "Delivered" or "Delivery",** regardless of the method used (i.e. messenger, mail, email, fax, other), means and shall be effective upon (i) personal receipt by Buyer or Seller or the individual Real Estate Licensee for that principal as specified in paragraph D of the section titled Real Estate Brokers on page 8; OR (ii) if checked, ■ per the attached addendum (C.A.R. Form RDN).
    I. **"Electronic Copy" or "Electronic Signature"** means, as applicable, an electronic copy or signature complying with California Law. Buyer and Seller agree that electronic means will not be used by either party to modify or alter the content or integrity of this Agreement without the knowledge and consent of the other party.
    J. **"Law"** means any law, code, statute, ordinance, regulation, rule or order, which is adopted by a controlling city, county, state or federal legislative, judicial or executive body or agency.
    K. **"Repairs"** means any repairs (including pest control), alterations, replacements, modifications or retrofitting of the Property provided for under this Agreement.
    L. **"Signed"** means either a handwritten or electronic signature on an original document, Copy or any counterpart.
23. **BROKER COMPENSATION:** Seller or Buyer, or both, as applicable, agrees to pay compensation to Broker as specified in a separate written agreement between Broker and that Seller or Buyer. Compensation is payable upon Close Of Escrow, or if escrow does not close, as otherwise specified in the agreement between Broker and that Seller or Buyer.
24. **JOINT ESCROW INSTRUCTIONS TO ESCROW HOLDER:**
    A. **The following paragraphs, or applicable portions thereof, of this Agreement constitute the joint escrow instructions of Buyer and Seller to Escrow Holder,** which Escrow Holder is to use along with any related counter offers and addenda, and any additional mutual instructions to close the escrow: 1, 3, 4, 6C, 11B and D, 12, 13B, 14F, 17, 22, 23, 24, 28, 30, and paragraph D of the section titled Real Estate Brokers on page 8. If a Copy of the separate compensation agreement(s) provided for in paragraph 23, or paragraph D of the section titled Real Estate Brokers on page 8 is deposited with Escrow Holder by Broker, Escrow Holder shall accept such agreement(s) and pay out of Buyer's or Seller's funds, or both, as applicable, the respective Broker's compensation provided for in such agreement(s). The terms and conditions of this Agreement not specifically referenced above, in the specified paragraphs are additional matters for the information of Escrow Holder, but about which Escrow Holder need not be concerned. Buyer and Seller will receive Escrow Holder's general provisions directly from Escrow Holder and will execute such provisions upon Escrow Holder's request. To the extent the general provisions are inconsistent or conflict with this Agreement, the general provisions will control as to the duties and obligations of Escrow Holder only. Buyer and Seller will execute additional instructions, documents and forms provided by Escrow Holder that are reasonably necessary to close the escrow.
    B. A Copy of this Agreement shall be delivered to Escrow Holder within **3** business days after Acceptance (or ☐ _____). Escrow Holder shall provide Seller's Statement of Information to Title company when received from Seller. Buyer and Seller authorize Escrow Holder to accept and rely on Copies and Signatures as defined in this Agreement as originals, to open escrow and for other purposes of escrow. The validity of this Agreement as between Buyer and Seller is not affected by whether or when Escrow Holder Signs this Agreement.
    C. Brokers are a party to the escrow for the sole purpose of compensation pursuant to paragraphs 23 and paragraph D of the section titled Real Estate Brokers on page 8. Buyer and Seller irrevocably assign to Brokers compensation specified in paragraphs 23, respectively, and irrevocably instruct Escrow Holder to disburse those funds to Brokers at Close Of Escrow or pursuant to any other mutually executed cancellation agreement. Compensation instructions can be amended or revoked only with the written consent of Brokers. Buyer and Seller shall release and hold harmless Escrow Holder from any liability resulting from Escrow Holder's payment to Broker(s) of compensation pursuant to this Agreement. Escrow Holder shall immediately notify Brokers: **(i)** if Buyer's initial or any additional deposit is not made pursuant to this Agreement, or is not good at time of deposit with Escrow Holder; or **(ii)** if either Buyer or Seller instruct Escrow Holder to cancel escrow.
    D. A Copy of any amendment that affects any paragraph of this Agreement for which Escrow Holder is responsible shall be delivered to Escrow Holder within **2** business days after mutual execution of the amendment.

Buyer's Initials (_____)(_____)   Seller's Initials (_____)(_____)

Copyright © 1991-2010, CALIFORNIA ASSOCIATION OF REALTORS®, INC.

RPA-CA REVISED 4/10 (PAGE 6 OF 8) Print Date

Reviewed by _____ Date _____

CALIFORNIA RESIDENTIAL PURCHASE AGREEMENT (RPA-CA PAGE 6 OF 8)

blank forms

Property Address: _____ Date: _____

25. LIQUIDATED DAMAGES: If Buyer fails to complete this purchase because of Buyer's default, Seller shall retain, as liquidated damages, the deposit actually paid. If the Property is a dwelling with no more than four units, one of which Buyer intends to occupy, then the amount retained shall be no more than 3% of the purchase price. Any excess shall be returned to Buyer. Release of funds will require mutual, Signed release instructions from both Buyer and Seller, judicial decision or arbitration award. **AT TIME OF THE INCREASED DEPOSIT BUYER AND SELLER SHALL SIGN A SEPARATE LIQUIDATED DAMAGES PROVISION FOR ANY INCREASED DEPOSIT. (C.A.R. FORM RID).**

Buyer's Initials _____ / _____ Seller's Initials _____ / _____

26. DISPUTE RESOLUTION:

  A. MEDIATION: Buyer and Seller agree to mediate any dispute or claim arising between them out of this Agreement, or any resulting transaction, before resorting to arbitration or court action. **Buyer and Seller also agree to mediate any disputes or claims with Broker(s), who, in writing, agree to such mediation prior to, or within a reasonable time after, the dispute or claim is presented to the Broker.** Mediation fees, if any, shall be divided equally among the parties involved. If, for any dispute or claim to which this paragraph applies, any party (i) commences an action without first attempting to resolve the matter through mediation, or (ii) before commencement of an action, refuses to mediate after a request has been made, then that party shall not be entitled to recover attorney fees, even if they would otherwise be available to that party in any such action. THIS MEDIATION PROVISION APPLIES WHETHER OR NOT THE ARBITRATION PROVISION IS INITIALED. **Exclusions from this mediation agreement are specified in paragraph 26C.**

  B. ARBITRATION OF DISPUTES:
  Buyer and Seller agree that any dispute or claim in Law or equity arising between them out of this Agreement or any resulting transaction, which is not settled through mediation, shall be decided by neutral, binding arbitration. Buyer and Seller also agree to arbitrate any disputes or claims with Broker(s), who, in writing, agree to such arbitration prior to, or within a reasonable time after, the dispute or claim is presented to the Broker. The arbitrator shall be a retired judge or justice, or an attorney with at least 5 years of residential real estate Law experience, unless the parties mutually agree to a different arbitrator. The parties shall have the right to discovery in accordance with Code of Civil Procedure §1283.05. In all other respects, the arbitration shall be conducted in accordance with Title 9 of Part 3 of the Code of Civil Procedure. Judgment upon the award of the arbitrator(s) may be entered into any court having jurisdiction. Enforcement of this agreement to arbitrate shall be governed by the Federal Arbitration Act. Exclusions from this arbitration agreement are specified in paragraph 26C.

  "NOTICE: BY INITIALING IN THE SPACE BELOW YOU ARE AGREEING TO HAVE ANY DISPUTE ARISING OUT OF THE MATTERS INCLUDED IN THE 'ARBITRATION OF DISPUTES' PROVISION DECIDED BY NEUTRAL ARBITRATION AS PROVIDED BY CALIFORNIA LAW AND YOU ARE GIVING UP ANY RIGHTS YOU MIGHT POSSESS TO HAVE THE DISPUTE LITIGATED IN A COURT OR JURY TRIAL. BY INITIALING IN THE SPACE BELOW YOU ARE GIVING UP YOUR JUDICIAL RIGHTS TO DISCOVERY AND APPEAL, UNLESS THOSE RIGHTS ARE SPECIFICALLY INCLUDED IN THE 'ARBITRATION OF DISPUTES' PROVISION. IF YOU REFUSE TO SUBMIT TO ARBITRATION AFTER AGREEING TO THIS PROVISION, YOU MAY BE COMPELLED TO ARBITRATE UNDER THE AUTHORITY OF THE CALIFORNIA CODE OF CIVIL PROCEDURE. YOUR AGREEMENT TO THIS ARBITRATION PROVISION IS VOLUNTARY."

  "WE HAVE READ AND UNDERSTAND THE FOREGOING AND AGREE TO SUBMIT DISPUTES ARISING OUT OF THE MATTERS INCLUDED IN THE 'ARBITRATION OF DISPUTES' PROVISION TO NEUTRAL ARBITRATION."

  Buyer's Initials _____ / _____ Seller's Initials _____ / _____

  C. ADDITIONAL MEDIATION AND ARBITRATION TERMS:
  (1) **EXCLUSIONS:** The following matters shall be excluded from mediation and arbitration: (i) a judicial or non-judicial foreclosure or other action or proceeding to enforce a deed of trust, mortgage or installment land sale contract as defined in Civil Code §2985; (ii) an unlawful detainer action; (iii) the filing or enforcement of a mechanic's lien; and (iv) any matter that is within the jurisdiction of a probate, small claims or bankruptcy court. The filing of a court action to enable the recording of a notice of pending action, for order of attachment, receivership, injunction, or other provisional remedies, shall not constitute a waiver or violation of the mediation and arbitration provisions.
  (2) **BROKERS:** Brokers shall not be obligated or compelled to mediate or arbitrate unless they agree to do so in writing. Any Broker(s) participating in mediation or arbitration shall not be deemed a party to the Agreement.

27. TERMS AND CONDITIONS OF OFFER:
This is an offer to purchase the Property on the above terms and conditions. The liquidated damages paragraph or the arbitration of disputes paragraph is incorporated in this Agreement if initialed by all parties or if incorporated by mutual agreement in a counter offer or addendum. If at least one but not all parties initial such paragraph(s), a counter offer is required until agreement is reached. Seller has the right to continue to offer the Property for sale and to accept any other offer at any time prior to notification of Acceptance. If this offer is accepted and Buyer subsequently defaults, Buyer may be responsible for payment of Brokers' compensation. This Agreement and any supplement, addendum or modification, including any Copy, may be Signed in two or more counterparts, all of which shall constitute one and the same writing.

28. TIME OF ESSENCE; ENTIRE CONTRACT; CHANGES: Time is of the essence. All understandings between the parties are incorporated in this Agreement. Its terms are intended by the parties as a final, complete and exclusive expression of their Agreement with respect to its subject matter, and may not be contradicted by evidence of any prior agreement or contemporaneous oral agreement. If any provision of this Agreement is held to be ineffective or invalid, the remaining provisions will nevertheless be given full force and effect. Except as otherwise specified, this Agreement shall be interpreted and disputes shall be resolved in accordance with the laws of the State of California. **Neither this Agreement nor any provision in it may be extended, amended, modified, altered or changed, except in writing Signed by Buyer and Seller.**

Buyer's Initials (_____)(_____)   Seller's Initials (_____)(_____)

Reviewed by _____ Date _____

Property Address: _____ Date: _____

29. EXPIRATION OF OFFER: This offer shall be deemed revoked and the deposit shall be returned unless the offer is Signed by Seller and a Copy of the Signed offer is personally received by Buyer, or by _____, who is authorized to receive it, by 5:00 PM on the third Day after this offer is signed by Buyer (or, if checked, ☐ by _____ ☐ AM ☐ PM, on _____ (date)).
Buyer has read and acknowledges receipt of a Copy of the offer and agrees to the above confirmation of agency relationships.

Date _____ Date _____
BUYER _____ BUYER _____
(Print name) _____ (Print name) _____
(Address) _____

☑ Additional Signature Addendum attached (C.A.R. Form ASA).

30. ACCEPTANCE OF OFFER: Seller warrants that Seller is the owner of the Property, or has the authority to execute this Agreement. Seller accepts the above offer, agrees to sell the Property on the above terms and conditions, and agrees to the above confirmation of agency relationships. Seller has read and acknowledges receipt of a Copy of this Agreement, and authorizes Broker to Deliver a Signed Copy to Buyer.
☑ (If checked) **SUBJECT TO ATTACHED COUNTER OFFER (C.A.R. Form CO) DATED:**_____.

Date _____ Date _____
SELLER _____ SELLER _____
(Print name) _____ (Print name) _____
(Address) _____

☐ Additional Signature Addendum attached (C.A.R. Form ASA).
(_____/_____) **CONFIRMATION OF ACCEPTANCE:** A Copy of Signed Acceptance was personally received by Buyer or Buyer's authorized
(Initials) agent on (date) _____ at _____ ☐ AM ☑ PM. **A binding Agreement is created when a Copy of Signed Acceptance is personally received by Buyer or Buyer's authorized agent whether or not confirmed in this document. Completion of this confirmation is not legally required in order to create a binding Agreement. It is solely intended to evidence the date that Confirmation of Acceptance has occurred.**

REAL ESTATE BROKERS:
A. Real Estate Brokers are not parties to the Agreement between Buyer and Seller.
B. Agency relationships are confirmed as stated in paragraph 2.
C. If specified in paragraph 3A(2), Agent who submitted the offer for Buyer acknowledges receipt of deposit.
D. **COOPERATING BROKER COMPENSATION:** Listing Broker agrees to pay Cooperating Broker **(Selling Firm)** and Cooperating Broker agrees to accept, out of Listing Broker's proceeds in escrow: **(i)** the amount specified in the MLS, provided Cooperating Broker is a Participant of the MLS in which the Property is offered for sale or a reciprocal MLS; or **(ii)** ☐ (if checked) the amount specified in a separate written agreement (C.A.R. Form CBC) between Listing Broker and Cooperating Broker. Declaration of License and Tax (C.A.R. Form DLT) may be used to document that tax reporting will be required or that an exemption exits.

Real Estate Broker (Selling Firm) _____ DRE Lic. # _____
By _____ DRE Lic. # _____ Date _____
Address _____ City _____ State _____ Zip _____
Telephone _____ Fax _____ E-mail _____

Real Estate Broker (Listing Firm) _____ DRE Lic. # _____
By _____ DRE Lic. # _____ Date _____
Address _____ City _____ State _____ Zip _____
Telephone _____ Fax _____ E-mail _____

ESCROW HOLDER ACKNOWLEDGMENT:
Escrow Holder acknowledges receipt of a Copy of this Agreement, (if checked, ☐ a deposit in the amount of $_____),
counter offer numbered _____, ☐ Seller's Statement of Information and ☐ Other _____
_____, and agrees to act as Escrow Holder subject to paragraph 24 of this Agreement, any supplemental escrow instructions and the terms of Escrow Holder's general provisions if any.
Escrow Holder is advised that the date of Confirmation of Acceptance of the Agreement as between Buyer and Seller is _____.
Escrow Holder _____ Escrow # _____
By _____ Date _____
Address _____
Phone/Fax/E-mail _____
Escrow Holder is licensed by the California Department of ☑ Corporations, ☑ Insurance, ☑ Real Estate. License # _____

PRESENTATION OF OFFER: (_____) Listing Broker presented this offer to Seller on _____ (date).
Broker or Designee Initials

REJECTION OF OFFER: (_____) (_____) No counter offer is being made. This offer was rejected by Seller on _____ (date).
Seller's Initials

THIS FORM HAS BEEN APPROVED BY THE CALIFORNIA ASSOCIATION OF REALTORS® (C.A.R.). NO REPRESENTATION IS MADE AS TO THE LEGAL VALIDITY OR ADEQUACY OF ANY PROVISION IN ANY SPECIFIC TRANSACTION. A REAL ESTATE BROKER IS THE PERSON QUALIFIED TO ADVISE ON REAL ESTATE TRANSACTIONS. IF YOU DESIRE LEGAL OR TAX ADVICE, CONSULT AN APPROPRIATE PROFESSIONAL.
This form is available for use by the entire real estate industry. It is not intended to identify the user as a REALTOR®. REALTOR® is a registered collective membership mark which may be used only by members of the NATIONAL ASSOCIATION OF REALTORS® who subscribe to its Code of Ethics.

Published and Distributed by:
REAL ESTATE BUSINESS SERVICES, INC.
a subsidiary of the California Association of REALTORS®
525 South Virgil Avenue, Los Angeles, California 90020
REVISION DATE 4/10

Reviewed by
Broker or Designee _____ Date _____

CALIFORNIA RESIDENTIAL PURCHASE AGREEMENT (RPA-CA PAGE 8 OF 8)

blank forms

BUYER'S INSPECTION ADVISORY
(C.A.R. Form BIA-A, Revised 10/02)

Property Address: _____ ("Property").

A. IMPORTANCE OF PROPERTY INVESTIGATION: The physical condition of the land and improvements being purchased is not guaranteed by either Seller or Brokers. For this reason, you should conduct thorough investigations of the Property personally and with professionals who should provide written reports of their investigations. A general physical inspection typically does not cover all aspects of the Property nor items affecting the Property that are not physically located on the Property. If the professionals recommend further investigations, including a recommendation by a pest control operator to inspect inaccessible areas of the Property, you should contact qualified experts to conduct such additional investigations.

B. BUYER RIGHTS AND DUTIES: You have an affirmative duty to exercise reasonable care to protect yourself, including discovery of the legal, practical and technical implications of disclosed facts, and the investigation and verification of information and facts that you know or that are within your diligent attention and observation. The purchase agreement gives you the right to investigate the Property. If you exercise this right, and you should, you must do so in accordance with the terms of that agreement. This is the best way for you to protect yourself. It is extremely important for you to read all written reports provided by professionals and to discuss the results of inspections with the professional who conducted the inspection. You have the right to request that Seller make repairs, corrections or take other action based upon items discovered in your investigations or disclosed by Seller. If Seller is unwilling or unable to satisfy your requests, or you do not want to purchase the Property in its disclosed and discovered condition, you have the right to cancel the agreement if you act within specific time periods. If you do not cancel the agreement in a timely and proper manner, you may be in breach of contract.

C. SELLER RIGHTS AND DUTIES: Seller is required to disclose to you material facts known to him/her that affect the value or desirability of the Property. However, Seller may not be aware of some Property defects or conditions. Seller does not have an obligation to inspect the Property for your benefit nor is Seller obligated to repair, correct or otherwise cure known defects that are disclosed to you or previously unknown defects that are discovered by you or your inspectors during escrow. The purchase agreement obligates Seller to make the Property available to you for investigations.

D. BROKER OBLIGATIONS: Brokers do not have expertise in all areas and therefore cannot advise you on many items, such as soil stability, geologic or environmental conditions, hazardous or illegal controlled substances, structural conditions of the foundation or other improvements, or the condition of the roof, plumbing, heating, air conditioning, electrical, sewer, septic, waste disposal, or other system. The only way to accurately determine the condition of the Property is through an inspection by an appropriate professional selected by you. If Broker gives you referrals to such professionals, Broker does not guarantee their performance. You may select any professional of your choosing. In sales involving residential dwellings with no more than four units, Brokers have a duty to make a diligent visual inspection of the accessible areas of the Property and to disclose the results of that inspection. However, as some Property defects or conditions may not be discoverable from a visual inspection, it is possible Brokers are not aware of them. If you have entered into a written agreement with a Broker, the specific terms of that agreement will determine the nature and extent of that Broker's duty to you.
YOU ARE STRONGLY ADVISED TO INVESTIGATE THE CONDITION AND SUITABILITY OF ALL ASPECTS OF THE PROPERTY. IF YOU DO NOT DO SO, YOU ARE ACTING AGAINST THE ADVICE OF BROKERS.

E. YOU ARE ADVISED TO CONDUCT INVESTIGATIONS OF THE ENTIRE PROPERTY, INCLUDING, BUT NOT LIMITED TO THE FOLLOWING:
1. **GENERAL CONDITION OF THE PROPERTY, ITS SYSTEMS AND COMPONENTS:** Foundation, roof, plumbing, heating, air conditioning, electrical, mechanical, security, pool/spa, other structural and non-structural systems and components, fixtures, built-in appliances, any personal property included in the sale, and energy efficiency of the Property. (Structural engineers are best suited to determine possible design or construction defects, and whether improvements are structurally sound.)
2. **SQUARE FOOTAGE, AGE, BOUNDARIES:** Square footage, room dimensions, lot size, age of improvements and boundaries. Any numerical statements regarding these items are APPROXIMATIONS ONLY and have not been verified by Seller and cannot be verified by Brokers. Fences, hedges, walls, retaining walls and other natural or constructed barriers or markers do not necessarily identify true Property boundaries. (Professionals such as appraisers, architects, surveyors and civil engineers are best suited to determine square footage, dimensions and boundaries of the Property.)
3. **WOOD DESTROYING PESTS:** Presence of, or conditions likely to lead to the presence of wood destroying pests and organisms and other infestation or infection. Inspection reports covering these items can be separated into two sections: Section 1 identifies areas where infestation or infection is evident. Section 2 identifies areas where there are conditions likely to lead to infestation or infection. A registered structural pest control company is best suited to perform these inspections.
4. **SOIL STABILITY:** Existence of fill or compacted soil, expansive or contracting soil, susceptibility to slippage, settling or movement, and the adequacy of drainage. (Geotechnical engineers are best suited to determine such conditions, causes and remedies.)

The copyright laws of the United States (Title 17 U.S. Code) forbid the unauthorized reproduction of this form, or any portion thereof, by photocopy machine or any other means, including facsimile or computerized formats. Copyright © 1991-2004, CALIFORNIA ASSOCIATION OF REALTORS®, INC. ALL RIGHTS RESERVED.

BIA-A REVISED 10/02 (PAGE 1 OF 2)

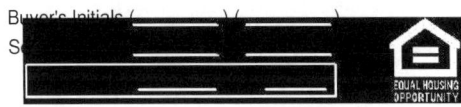

Agent:

Broker:

Prepared using zipForm® software

Property Address: _____ Date: _____

5. **ROOF:** Present condition, age, leaks, and remaining useful life. (Roofing contractors are best suited to determine these conditions.)
6. **POOL/SPA:** Cracks, leaks or operational problems. (Pool contractors are best suited to determine these conditions.)
7. **WASTE DISPOSAL:** Type, size, adequacy, capacity and condition of sewer and septic systems and components, connection to sewer, and applicable fees.
8. **WATER AND UTILITES; WELL SYSTEMS AND COMPONENTS:** Water and utility availability, use restrictions and costs. Water quality, adequacy, condition, and performance of well systems and components.
9. **ENVIRONMENTAL HAZARDS:** Potential environmental hazards, including, but not limited to, asbestos, lead-based paint and other lead contamination, radon, methane, other gases, fuel oil or chemical storage tanks, contaminated soil or water, hazardous waste, waste disposal sites, electromagnetic fields, nuclear sources, and other substances, materials, products, or conditions (including mold (airborne, toxic or otherwise), fungus or similar contaminants). (For more information on these items, you may consult an appropriate professional or read the booklets "Environmental Hazards: A Guide for Homeowners, Buyers, Landlords and Tenants," "Protect Your Family From Lead in Your Home" or both.)
10. **EARTHQUAKES AND FLOODING:** Susceptibility of the Property to earthquake/seismic hazards and propensity of the Property to flood. (A Geologist or Geotechnical Engineer is best suited to provide information on these conditions.)
11. **FIRE, HAZARD AND OTHER INSURANCE:** The availability and cost of necessary or desired insurance may vary. The location of the Property in a seismic, flood or fire hazard zone, and other conditions, such as the age of the Property and the claims history of the Property and Buyer, may affect the availability and need for certain types of insurance. Buyer should explore insurance options early as this information may affect other decisions, including the removal of loan and inspection contingencies. (An insurance agent is best suited to provide information on these conditions.)
12. **BUILDING PERMITS, ZONING AND GOVERNMENTAL REQUIREMENTS:** Permits, inspections, certificates, zoning, other governmental limitations, restrictions, and requirements affecting the current or future use of the Property, its development or size. (Such information is available from appropriate governmental agencies and private information providers. Brokers are not qualified to review or interpret any such information.)
13. **RENTAL PROPERTY RESTRICTIONS:** Some cities and counties impose restrictions that limit the amount of rent that can be charged, the maximum number of occupants; and the right of a landlord to terminate a tenancy. Deadbolt or other locks and security systems for doors and windows, including window bars, should be examined to determine whether they satisfy legal requirements. (Government agencies can provide information about these restrictions and other requirements.)
14. **SECURITY AND SAFETY:** State and local Law may require the installation of barriers, access alarms, self-latching mechanisms and/or other measures to decrease the risk to children and other persons of existing swimming pools and hot tubs, as well as various fire safety and other measures concerning other features of the Property. Compliance requirements differ from city to city and county to county. Unless specifically agreed, the Property may not be in compliance with these requirements. (Local government agencies can provide information about these restrictions and other requirements.)
15. **NEIGHBORHOOD, AREA, SUBDIVISION CONDITIONS; PERSONAL FACTORS:** Neighborhood or area conditions, including schools, proximity and adequacy of law enforcement, crime statistics, the proximity of registered felons or offenders, fire protection, other government services, availability, adequacy and cost of any speed-wired, wireless internet connections or other telecommunications or other technology services and installations, proximity to commercial, industrial or agricultural activities, existing and proposed transportation, construction and development that may affect noise, view, or traffic, airport noise, noise or odor from any source, wild and domestic animals, other nuisances, hazards, or circumstances, protected species, wetland properties, botanical diseases, historic or other governmentally protected sites or improvements, cemeteries, facilities and condition of common areas of common interest subdivisions, and possible lack of compliance with any governing documents or Homeowners' Association requirements, conditions and influences of significance to certain cultures and/or religions, and personal needs, requirements and preferences of Buyer.

> Buyer and Seller acknowledge and agree that Broker: **(i)** Does not decide what price Buyer should pay or Seller should accept; **(ii)** Does not guarantee the condition of the Property; **(iii)** Does not guarantee the performance, adequacy or completeness of inspections, services, products or repairs provided or made by Seller or others; **(iv)** Does not have an obligation to conduct an inspection of common areas or areas off the site of the Property; **(v)** Shall not be responsible for identifying defects on the Property, in common areas, or offsite unless such defects are visually observable by an inspection of reasonably accessible areas of the Property or are known to Broker; **(vi)** Shall not be responsible for inspecting public records or permits concerning the title or use of Property; **(vii)** Shall not be responsible for identifying the location of boundary lines or other items affecting title; **(viii)** Shall not be responsible for verifying square footage, representations of others or information contained in Investigation reports, Multiple Listing Service, advertisements, flyers or other promotional material; **(ix)** Shall not be responsible for providing legal or tax advice regarding any aspect of a transaction entered into by Buyer or Seller; and **(x)** Shall not be responsible for providing other advice or information that exceeds the knowledge, education and experience required to perform real estate licensed activity. Buyer and Seller agree to seek legal, tax, insurance, title and other desired assistance from appropriate professionals.

By signing below, Buyer and Seller each acknowledge that they have read, understand, accept and have received a Copy of this Advisory. Buyer is encouraged to read it carefully.

Buyer Signature _____ Date _____ Buyer Signature _____ Date _____

Seller Signature _____ Date _____ Seller Signature _____ Date _____

THIS FORM HAS BEEN APPROVED BY THE CALIFORNIA ASSOCIATION OF REALTORS® (C.A.R.). NO REPRESENTATION IS MADE AS TO THE LEGAL VALIDITY OR ADEQUACY OF ANY PROVISION IN ANY SPECIFIC TRANSACTION. A REAL ESTATE BROKER IS THE PERSON QUALIFIED TO ADVISE ON REAL ESTATE TRANSACTIONS. IF YOU DESIRE LEGAL OR TAX ADVICE, CONSULT AN APPROPRIATE PROFESSIONAL.

This form is available for use by the entire real estate industry. It is not intended to identify the user as a REALTOR®. REALTOR® is a registered collective membership mark which may be used only by members of the NATIONAL ASSOCIATION OF REALTORS® who subscribe to its Code of Ethics.

Published and Distributed by:
REAL ESTATE BUSINESS SERVICES, INC.
a subsidiary of the California Association of REALTORS®
525 South Virgil Avenue, Los Angeles, California 90020

Reviewed by _____ Date _____

EQUAL HOUSING OPPORTUNITY

TEXAS ASSOCIATION OF REALTORS®

RESIDENTIAL REAL ESTATE LISTING AGREEMENT
EXCLUSIVE RIGHT TO SELL

USE OF THIS FORM BY PERSONS WHO ARE NOT MEMBERS OF THE TEXAS ASSOCIATION OF REALTORS® IS NOT AUTHORIZED.
©Texas Association of REALTORS®, Inc. 2003

1. **PARTIES:** The parties to this agreement (this Listing) are:

   Seller: _____
   Address: _____
   City, State, Zip: _____
   Phone: _____ Fax: _____
   E-Mail: _____

   Broker: _____
   Address: _____
   City, State, Zip: _____
   Phone: _____ Fax: _____
   E-Mail: _____

   Seller appoints Broker as Seller's sole and exclusive real estate agent and grants to Broker the exclusive right to sell the Property.

2. **PROPERTY:** "Property" means the land, improvements, and accessories described below, except for any described exclusions.

   A. <u>Land:</u> Lot _____, Block _____, _____
   _____ Addition, City of _____,
   in _____ County, Texas known as _____
   _____ (address/zip code),
   or as described on attached exhibit. *(If Property is a condominium, attach Condominium Addendum.)*

   B. <u>Improvements:</u> The house, garage and all other fixtures and improvements attached to the above-described real property, including without limitation, the following permanently installed and built-in items, if any: all equipment and appliances, valances, screens, shutters, awnings, wall-to-wall carpeting, mirrors, ceiling fans, attic fans, mail boxes, television antennas and satellite dish system and equipment, heating and air-conditioning units, security and fire detection equipment, wiring, plumbing and lighting fixtures, chandeliers, water softener system, kitchen equipment, garage door openers, cleaning equipment, shrubbery, landscaping, outdoor cooking equipment, and all other property owned by Seller and attached to the above-described real property.

   C. <u>Accessories:</u> The following described related accessories, if any: window air conditioning units, stove, fireplace screens, curtains and rods, blinds, window shades, draperies and rods, controls for satellite dish system, controls for garage door openers, entry gate controls, door keys, mailbox keys, above-ground pool, swimming pool equipment and maintenance accessories, and artificial fireplace logs.

   D. <u>Exclusions:</u> The following improvements and accessories will be retained by Seller and excluded: _____

   E. <u>Owners' Association:</u> The property ❏ is ❏ is not subject to mandatory membership in an owners' association.

(TAR-1101) 10-16-03   Initialed for Identification by Broker/Associate _____ and Seller _____, _____

Residential Listing concerning _____

3. **LISTING PRICE:** Seller instructs Broker to market the Property at the following price: $ _____ (Listing Price). Seller agrees to sell the Property for the Listing Price or any other price acceptable to Seller. Seller will pay all typical closing costs charged to sellers of residential real estate in Texas (seller's typical closing costs are those set forth in the residential contract forms promulgated by the Texas Real Estate Commission).

4. **TERM:**

   A. This Listing begins on _____ and ends at 11:59 p.m. on _____.

   B. If Seller enters into a binding written contract to sell the Property before the date this Listing begins and the contract is binding on the date this Listing begins, this Listing will not commence and will be void.

5. **BROKER'S FEE:**

   A. <u>Fee</u>: When earned and payable, Seller will pay Broker a fee of:

   ☐ (1) _____% of the sales price.

   ☐ (2) _____

   B. <u>Earned</u>: Broker's fee is earned when any one of the following occurs during this Listing:
   (1) Seller sells, exchanges, options, agrees to sell, agrees to exchange, or agrees to option the Property to anyone at any price on any terms;
   (2) Broker individually or in cooperation with another broker procures a buyer ready, willing, and able to buy the Property at the Listing Price or at any other price acceptable to Seller; or
   (3) Seller breaches this Listing.

   C. <u>Payable</u>: Once earned, Broker's fee is payable either during this Listing or after it ends at the earlier of:
   (1) the closing and funding of any sale or exchange of all or part of the Property;
   (2) Seller's refusal to sell the Property after Broker's Fee has been earned;
   (3) Seller's breach of this Listing; or
   (4) at such time as otherwise set forth in this Listing.

   Broker's fee is <u>not</u> payable if a sale of the Property does not close or fund as a result of: (i) Seller's failure, without fault of Seller, to deliver to a buyer a deed or a title policy as required by the contract to sell; (ii) loss of ownership due to foreclosure or other legal proceeding; or (iii) Seller's failure to restore the Property, as a result of a casualty loss, to its previous condition by the closing date set forth in a contract for the sale of the Property.

   D. <u>Other Fees</u>:

   (1) <u>Breach by Buyer Under a Contract</u>: If Seller collects earnest money, the sales price, or damages by suit, compromise, settlement, or otherwise from a buyer who breaches a contract for the sale of the Property entered into during this Listing, Seller will pay Broker, after deducting attorney's fees and collection expenses, an amount equal to the lesser of one-half of the amount collected after deductions or the amount of the Broker's Fee stated in Paragraph 5A. Any amount paid under this Paragraph 5D(1) is in addition to any amount that Broker may be entitled to receive for subsequently selling the Property.

   (2) <u>Service Providers</u>: If Broker refers Seller or a prospective buyer to a service provider (for example, mover, cable company, telecommunications provider, utility, or contractor) Broker may receive a fee from the service provider for the referral. Any referral fee Broker receives under this Paragraph 5D(2) is in addition to any other compensation Broker may receive under this Listing.

Residential Listing concerning _____

    (3) <u>Transaction Fees or Reimbursable Expenses</u>: _____
_____
_____

  E. <u>Protection Period</u>:

    (1) "Protection period" means that time starting the day after this Listing ends and continuing for _____ days. "Sell" means any transfer of any interest in the Property whether by oral or written agreement or option.

    (2) Not later than 10 days after this Listing ends, Broker may send Seller written notice specifying the names of persons whose attention was called to the Property during this Listing. If Seller agrees to sell the Property during the protection period to a person named in the notice or to a relative of a person named in the notice, Seller will pay Broker, upon the closing of the sale, the amount Broker would have been entitled to receive if this Listing were still in effect.

    (3) This Paragraph 5E survives termination of this Listing. This Paragraph 5E will not apply if:
        (a)   Seller agrees to sell the Property during the protection period;
        (b)   the Property is exclusively listed with another broker who is a member of the Texas Association of REALTORS® at the time the sale is negotiated; and
        (c)   Seller is obligated to pay the other broker a fee for the sale.

  F. <u>County</u>: All amounts payable to Broker are to be paid in cash in _____
_____ County, Texas.

  G. <u>Escrow Authorization</u>: Seller authorizes, and Broker may so instruct, any escrow or closing agent authorized to close a transaction for the purchase or acquisition of the Property to collect and disburse to Broker all amounts payable to Broker under this Listing.

6. LISTING SERVICES:

❑ A. Broker will file this Listing with one or more Multiple Listing Services (MLS) by the earlier of the time required by MLS rules or 5 days after the date this Listing begins. Seller authorizes Broker to submit information about this Listing and the sale of the Property to the MLS.

<u>Notice</u>: MLS rules require Broker to accurately and timely submit all information the MLS requires for participation including sold data. Subscribers to the MLS may use the information for market evaluation or appraisal purposes. Subscribers are other brokers and other real estate professionals such as appraisers and may include the appraisal district. Any information filed with the MLS becomes the property of the MLS for all purposes. **Submission of information to MLS ensures that persons who use and benefit from the MLS also contribute information.**

❑ B. Broker will not file this Listing with a Multiple Listing Service (MLS) or any other listing service.

7. ACCESS TO THE PROPERTY:

A. <u>Authorizing Access</u>: Authorizing access to the Property means giving permission to another person to enter the Property, disclosing to the other person any security codes necessary to enter the Property, and lending a key to the other person to enter the Property, directly or through a keybox. To facilitate the showing and sale of the Property, Seller instructs Broker to:
    (1) access the Property at reasonable times
    (2) authorize other brokers, their associates, inspectors, appraisers, and contractors to access the Property at reasonable times; and
    (3) duplicate keys to facilitate convenient and efficient showings of the Property.

B. <u>Scheduling Companies</u>: Broker may engage the following companies to schedule appointments and to authorize others to access the Property: _____.

Residential Listing concerning _____

C. Keybox: **A keybox is a locked container placed on the Property that holds a key to the Property. A keybox makes it more convenient for brokers, their associates, inspectors, appraisers, and contractors to show, inspect, or repair the Property. The keybox is opened by a special combination, key, or programmed device so that authorized persons may enter the Property, even in Seller's absence. Using a keybox will probably increase the number of showings, but involves risks (for example, unauthorized entry, theft, property damage, or personal injury). Neither the Association of REALTORS® nor MLS requires the use of a keybox.**

(1) Broker ❏ is ❏ is not authorized to place a keybox on the Property.

(2) If a tenant occupies the Property at any time during this Listing, Seller will furnish Broker a written statement (for example, TAR No. 1411), signed by all tenants, authorizing the use of a keybox or Broker may remove the keybox from the Property.

D. Liability and Indemnification: When authorizing access to the Property, Broker, other brokers, their associates, any keybox provider, or any scheduling company are not responsible for personal injury or property loss to Seller or any other person. Seller assumes all risk of any loss, damage, or injury. **Except for a loss caused by Broker, Seller will indemnify and hold Broker harmless from any claim for personal injury, property damage, or other loss.**

8. **COOPERATION WITH OTHER BROKERS:** Broker will allow other brokers to show the Property to prospective buyers. Broker will offer to pay the other broker a fee as described below if the other broker procures a buyer that purchases the Property.

    A. MLS Participants: If the other broker is a participant in the MLS in which this Listing is filed, Broker will offer to pay the other broker:
       (1) if the other broker represents the buyer: _____% of the sales price or $_____
       (2) if the other broker is a subagent: _____% of the sales price or $_____

    B. Non-MLS Brokers: If the other broker is not a participant in the MLS in which this Listing is filed, Broker will offer to pay the other broker:
       (1) if the other broker represents the buyer: _____% of the sales price or $_____
       (2) if the other broker is a subagent: _____% of the sales price or $_____

9. **INTERMEDIARY:** *(Check A or B only.)*

❏ A. Intermediary Status: Broker may show the Property to interested prospective buyers who Broker represents. If a prospective buyer who Broker represents offers to buy the Property, Seller authorizes Broker to act as an intermediary and Broker will notify Seller that Broker will service the parties in accordance with one of the following alternatives.

(1) If a prospective buyer who Broker represents is serviced by an associate other than the associate servicing Seller under this Listing, Broker may notify Seller that Broker will: (a) appoint the associate then servicing Seller to communicate with, carry out instructions of, and provide opinions and advice during negotiations to Seller; and (b) appoint the associate then servicing the prospective buyer to the prospective buyer for the same purpose.

(2) If a prospective buyer who Broker represents is serviced by the same associate who is servicing Seller, Broker may notify Seller that Broker will: (a) appoint another associate to communicate with, carry out instructions of, and provide opinions and advice during negotiations to the prospective buyer; and (b) appoint the associate servicing the Seller under this Listing to the Seller for the same purpose.

(3) Broker may notify Seller that Broker will make no appointments as described under this Paragraph 9A and, in such an event, the associate servicing the parties will act solely as Broker's intermediary representative, who may facilitate the transaction but will not render opinions or advice during negotiations to either party.

Residential Listing concerning _____

❏ B. <u>No Intermediary Status</u>: Seller agrees that Broker will not show the Property to prospective buyers who Broker represents.

Notice: **If Broker acts as an intermediary under Paragraph 9A, Broker and Broker's associates:**
- **may not disclose to the prospective buyer that Seller will accept a price less than the asking price unless otherwise instructed in a separate writing by Seller;**
- **may not disclose to Seller that the prospective buyer will pay a price greater than the price submitted in a written offer to Seller unless otherwise instructed in a separate writing by the prospective buyer;**
- **may not disclose any confidential information or any information Seller or the prospective buyer specifically instructs Broker in writing not to disclose unless otherwise instructed in a separate writing by the respective party or required to disclose the information by the Real Estate License Act or a court order or if the information materially relates to the condition of the property;**
- **may not treat a party to the transaction dishonestly; and may not violate the Real Estate License Act.**

10. **CONFIDENTIAL INFORMATION:** During this Listing or after it ends, Broker may not knowingly disclose information obtained in confidence from Seller except as authorized by Seller or required by law. Broker may not disclose to Seller any confidential information regarding any other person Broker represents or previously represented except as required by law.

11. **BROKER'S AUTHORITY:**

A. Broker will use reasonable efforts and act diligently to market the Property for sale, procure a buyer, and negotiate the sale of the Property.

B. In addition to other authority granted by this Listing, Broker may:
   (1) advertise the Property by means and methods as Broker determines, including but not limited to creating and placing advertisements with interior and exterior photographic and audio-visual images of the Property and related information in any media and the Internet;
   (2) place a "For Sale" sign on the Property and remove all other signs offering the Property for sale or lease;
   (3) furnish comparative marketing and sales information about other properties to prospective buyers;
   (4) disseminate information about the Property to other brokers and to prospective buyers, including applicable disclosures or notices that Seller is required to make under law or a contract;
   (5) obtain information from any holder of a note secured by a lien on the Property;
   (6) accept and deposit earnest money in trust in accordance with a contract for the sale of the Property;
   (7) disclose the sales price and terms of sale to other brokers, appraisers, or other real estate professionals;
   (8) in response to inquiries from prospective buyers and other brokers, disclose whether the Seller is considering more than one offer, provided that Broker will not disclose the terms of any competing offer unless specifically instructed by Seller;
   (9) advertise, during or after this Listing ends, that Broker "sold" the Property; and
   (10) place information about this Listing, the Property, and a transaction for the Property on an electronic transaction platform (typically an Internet-based system where professionals related to the transaction such as title companies, lenders, and others may receive, view, and input information).

C. Broker is not authorized to execute any document in the name of or on behalf of Seller concerning the Property.

Residential Listing concerning _____

12. **SELLER'S REPRESENTATIONS:** Except as provided by Paragraph 15, Seller represents that:
    A. Seller has fee simple title to and peaceable possession of the Property and all its improvements and fixtures, unless rented, and the legal capacity to convey the Property;
    B. Seller is not bound by a listing agreement with another broker for the sale, exchange, or lease of the Property that is or will be in effect during this Listing;
    C. any pool or spa and any required enclosures, fences, gates, and latches comply with all applicable laws and ordinances;
    D. no person or entity has any right to purchase, lease, or acquire the Property by an option, right of refusal, or other agreement;
    E. there are no delinquencies or defaults under any deed of trust, mortgage, or other encumbrance on the Property;
    F. the Property is not subject to the jurisdiction of any court;
    G. all information relating to the Property Seller provides to Broker is true and correct to the best of Seller's knowledge; and
    H. the name of any employer, relocation company, or other entity that provides benefits to Seller when selling the Property is: _____.

13. **SELLER'S ADDITIONAL PROMISES:** Seller agrees to:
    A. cooperate with Broker to facilitate the showing, marketing, and sale of the Property;
    B. not rent or lease the Property during this Listing without Broker's prior written approval;
    C. not negotiate with any prospective buyer who may contact Seller directly, but refer all prospective buyers to Broker;
    D. not enter into a listing agreement with another broker for the sale, exchange, or lease of the Property to become effective during this Listing;
    E. maintain any pool and all required enclosures in compliance with all applicable laws and ordinances;
    F. provide Broker with copies of any leases or rental agreements pertaining to the Property and advise Broker of tenants moving in or out of the Property;
    G. complete any disclosures or notices required by law or a contract to sell the Property; and
    H. amend any applicable notices and disclosures if any material change occurs during this Listing.

14. **LIMITATION OF LIABILITY:**

    A. If the Property is or becomes vacant during this Listing, Seller must notify Seller's casualty insurance company and request a "vacancy clause" to cover the Property. Broker is not responsible for the security of the Property nor for inspecting the Property on any periodic basis.

    B. **Broker is not responsible or liable in any manner for personal injury to any person or for loss or damage to any person's real or personal property resulting from any act or omission not caused by Broker's negligence, including but not limited to injuries or damages caused by:**
        (1) other brokers, their associates, inspectors, appraisers, and contractors who are authorized to access the Property;
        (2) acts of third parties (for example, vandalism or theft);
        (3) freezing water pipes;
        (4) a dangerous condition on the Property; or
        (5) the Property's non-compliance with any law or ordinance.

    C. **Seller agrees to protect, defend, indemnify, and hold Broker harmless from any damage, costs, attorney's fees, and expenses that:**
        (1) are caused by Seller, negligently or otherwise;
        (2) arise from Seller's failure to disclose any material or relevant information about the Property; or
        (3) are caused by Seller giving incorrect information to any person.

Residential Listing concerning _____

15. SPECIAL PROVISIONS:

16. **DEFAULT:** If Seller breaches this Listing, Seller is in default and will be liable to Broker for the amount of the Broker's fee specified in Paragraph 5A and any other fees Broker is entitled to receive under this Listing. If a sales price is not determinable in the event of an exchange or breach of this Listing, the Listing Price will be the sales price for purposes of computing Broker's fee. If Broker breaches this Listing, Broker is in default and Seller may exercise any remedy at law.

17. **MEDIATION:** The parties agree to negotiate in good faith in an effort to resolve any dispute related to this Listing that may arise between the parties. If the dispute cannot be resolved by negotiation, the dispute will be submitted to mediation. The parties to the dispute will choose a mutually acceptable mediator and will share the cost of mediation equally.

18. **ATTORNEY'S FEES:** If Seller or Broker is a prevailing party in any legal proceeding brought as a result of a dispute under this Listing or any transaction related to or contemplated by this Listing, such party will be entitled to recover from the non-prevailing party all costs of such proceeding and reasonable attorney's fees.

19. **ADDENDA AND OTHER DOCUMENTS:** Addenda that are part of this Listing and other documents that Seller may need to provide are:
    - ☐ A. Information About Brokerage Services;
    - ☐ B. Seller Disclosure Notice (§5.008, Texas Property Code);
    - ☐ C. Seller's Disclosure of Information on Lead-Based Paint and Lead-Based Paint Hazards (required if Property was built before 1978);
    - ☐ D. MUD, Water District, or Statutory Tax District Disclosure Notice (Chapter 49, Texas Water Code);
    - ☐ E. Request for Information from an Owners' Association;
    - ☐ F. Request for Mortgage Information;
    - ☐ G. Information about On-Site Sewer Facility;
    - ☐ H. Information about Special Flood Hazard Areas;
    - ☐ I. Condominium Addendum to Listing;
    - ☐ J. Keybox Authorization by Tenant;
    - ☐ K. Seller's Authorization to Release and Advertise Certain Information; and
    - ☐ L. _____

20. AGREEMENT OF PARTIES:

A. <u>Entire Agreement</u>: This Listing is the entire agreement of the parties and may not be changed except by written agreement.

B. <u>Assignability</u>: Neither party may assign this Listing without the written consent of the other party.

Residential Listing concerning _____

    Binding Effect: Seller's obligation to pay Broker an earned fee is binding upon Seller and Seller's heirs, administrators, executors, successors, and permitted assignees.

    Joint and Several: All Sellers executing this Listing are jointly and severally liable for the performance of all its terms.

    Governing Law: Texas law governs the interpretation, validity, performance, and enforcement of this Listing.

    Severability: If a court finds any clause in this Listing invalid or unenforceable, the remainder of this Listing will not be affected and all other provisions of this Listing will remain valid and enforceable.

    Notices: Notices between the parties must be in writing and are effective when sent to the receiving party's address, fax, or e-mail address specified in Paragraph 1.

21. ADDITIONAL NOTICES:

    A. Broker's fees or the sharing of fees between brokers are not fixed, controlled, recommended, suggested, or maintained by the Association of REALTORS®, MLS, or any listing service.

    B. Fair housing laws require the Property to be shown and made available to all persons without regard to race, color, religion, national origin, sex, disability, or familial status. Local ordinances may provide for additional protected classes (for example, creed, status as a student, marital status, sexual orientation, or age).

    C. Seller may review the information Broker submits to an MLS or other listing service.

    D. Broker advises Seller to remove or secure jewelry, prescription drugs, and other valuables.

    E. Statutes or ordinances may regulate certain items on the Property (for example, swimming pools and septic systems). Non-compliance with the statutes or ordinances may delay a transaction and may result in fines, penalties, and liability to Seller.

    F. If the Property was built before 1978, Federal law requires the Seller to: (1) provide the buyer with the federally approved pamphlet on lead poisoning prevention; (2) disclose the presence of any known lead-based paint or lead-based paint hazards in the Property; (3) deliver all records and reports to the buyer related to such paint or hazards; and (4) provide the buyer a period up to 10 days to have the Property inspected for such paint or hazards.

    G. Broker cannot give legal advice. READ THIS LISTING CAREFULLY. If you do not understand the effect of this Listing, consult an attorney BEFORE signing.

_____   _____
Broker's Printed Name   License No.   Seller   Date

By:_____   _____
Broker's Associate's Signature   Date   Seller   Date

CHICAGO ASSOCIATION OF REALTORS®
EXCLUSIVE BUYER - BROKER AGREEMENT
Rev. 01/2008

1. **BROKER.** This Exclusive Buyer-Broker Agreement ("Agreement") is entered into by and between _____ ("Broker") and _____ ("Buyer"). Broker agrees to appoint a sales associate affiliated with Broker to act as the Buyer's designated agent ("Buyer's Designated Agent") for the purpose of assisting Buyer in identifying and negotiating the acquisition of residential real estate ("Property") and Buyer agrees to grant Buyer's Designated Agent the exclusive right ("Exclusive Right") to represent Buyer in such acquisition per the terms and conditions set forth in this Agreement. The terms "acquire" or "acquisition" shall mean the purchase (title transfer or Articles of Agreement for deed), lease, exchange, or contract for the option to purchase Property by Buyer or anyone acting on Buyer's behalf.

2. **TERM.** Broker's Exclusive Right shall extend from the Effective Date, as set forth on page 3 ("Commencement Date"), until 11:59 P.M. on _____, 20___, at which time this Agreement shall automatically terminate ("Termination Date").

3. **COMPENSATION.** Broker shall seek to be paid a commission from the listing broker under a cooperative brokerage arrangement or from the seller if there is no listing broker. In the event that the seller or listing broker does not pay Broker a commission, then Buyer shall pay Broker at the time of closing, compensation equal to _____% [percent] of the purchase price of the Property which Buyer acquires during the Term of this Agreement ("Acquisition Commission"), whether or not the Property has been identified by Broker to Buyer. If Buyer leases Property or enters into a lease/purchase contract during this Agreement, and the landlord does not agree to pay Broker a leasing commission, then Buyer shall pay to Broker for the duration of the lease, including all renewals and extensions, a commission of 5% of each rental payment paid by Buyer to landlord ("Rental Commission"). The Rental Commission and the Acquisition Commission are together referred to as "Compensation". Furthermore, if Buyer acquires (or enters into an agreement to acquire) Property that was identified to Buyer by Broker during the Term of this Agreement within _____ days / months (strike one) following the Termination Date ("Compensation Deadline"), then Buyer shall pay Broker at closing or upon the commencement of any lease, as the case may be, the Compensation set forth above. If Buyer enters into an agreement to acquire Property and the closing does not occur because of any fault on the part of Buyer, then Broker shall still be entitled to the Compensation set forth above. In no event shall Broker be obligated to advance funds to Buyer to facilitate the closing of any acquisition. (strike the following sentence if NOT applicable) Buyer shall pay Broker's Designated Agent a non-refundable retainer fee of $_____ which shall be due and payable to, and shall be considered earned by, Broker upon signing this Agreement. Buyer's obligations under this Paragraph 3 shall survive the termination of this Agreement.

4. **MINIMUM SERVICES.** Pursuant to the Real Estate License Act of 2000, as amended, Broker must provide, at a minimum, the following services: (a) accept delivery of and present to the Buyer offers and counteroffers to sell or lease any Property that Buyer seeks to acquire; (b) assist the Buyer in developing, communicating, negotiating and presenting offers, counteroffers and notices that relate to the offers and counteroffers until a lease or agreement for the acquisition of the Property is signed and all contingencies have been satisfied or waived; and (c) answer the Buyer's questions relating to the offers, counteroffers, notices and contingencies.

5. **BUYER'S DESIGNATED AGENT.** Broker and Buyer agree that (a) _____, a sponsored licensee of Broker, is Broker's Designated Agent under this Agreement with Broker, and (b) neither Broker nor other sponsored licensees of Broker will be acting as agent for Buyer. Buyer understands and agrees that Broker and any of Broker's other sponsored licensees may enter into agreements with other prospective purchasers and sellers of Property as agents of those purchasers and sellers.

6. **BUYER'S DESIGNATED AGENT'S DUTIES.** Buyer's Designated Agent shall: (a) use best efforts to identify Properties available for acquisition that meet the Buyer's specifications relating to location, purchase price, features and amenities; (b) arrange, to the extent available, inspections of Properties identified by Buyer as potentially appropriate for acquisition; (c) negotiate a contract acceptable to Buyer for the acquisition of Property; (d) safeguard and protect any confidential or proprietary information that Buyer discloses to Buyer's Designated Agent; (e) disclose to Buyer any information known to Buyer's Designated Agent that would materially affect Buyer's decision to acquire the Property; and (f) assist Buyer, once a contract for acquisition is signed, in securing financing or other commitments or services as may be necessary to close the transaction.

7. **LIMITATIONS ON BUYER'S DESIGNATED AGENT'S DUTIES.** Buyer acknowledges and agrees that Broker's Designated Agent: (a) may enter into exclusive brokerage relationships with other buyers of Property and may show the same or similar Properties in which Buyer is interested to other prospective buyers that Buyer's Designated Agent represents; (b) is not an expert with regard to matters which could have been revealed through a survey, title search or inspection of the Property; the condition of Property or items within the Property; building products and construction techniques; the necessity or cost of any repairs to the Property; hazardous or toxic materials; termites and other wood destroying organisms; the tax and legal consequences of any acquisition; the availability and cost of utilities and community amenities; appraised or future value of the Property (or matters relating to financing for which Buyer is hereby advised to seek independent expert advice); and conditions off the Property which may affect the Property; (c) is not responsible for the accuracy of room dimensions, lot size, square feet, variances, zoning or use restrictions which may or may not be reflected in the Multiple Listing Service ("MLS") or other sources; (d) shall owe no duties to Buyer nor have any authority on behalf of buyer other than what is set forth in the Agreement; (e) may make disclosures as required by law; (f) may show Buyer Property which is listed in the MLS by Broker or Broker's Designated Agent; and (g) IS NOT OBLIGATED TO SHOW PROPERTIES THAT ARE FOR SALE BUT NOT IN THE MLS IN WHICH BROKER OR BUYER'S DESIGNATED AGENT PARTICIPATE, UNLESS REQUESTED TO DO SO BY BUYER IN WRITING, AND THE PROPERTY IS AVAILABLE FOR SHOWING BY BUYER'S DESIGNATED AGENT.

8. **BUYER'S DUTIES.** Buyer must (a) work EXCLUSIVELY with Buyer's Designated Agent to identify and acquire Property during the Term of this Agreement; (b) comply with reasonable requests of Buyer's Designated Agent to supply relevant financial information that may be necessary to permit Buyer's Designated Agent to fulfill its obligations under this Agreement; (c) be available upon reasonable notice and at reasonable hours to inspect Properties that are potentially appropriate for acquisition by Buyer; (d) identify to Buyer's Designated

Buyer Initials:_____ Buyer Initials:_____   Broker Initials:_____ Broker Initials:_____

Agent those specific Properties not in the MLS that Buyer would want to inspect; (e) otherwise cooperate with Buyer's Designated Agent in its efforts to fulfill its obligations under this Agreement; and (f) pay Broker, or cause seller's listing broker or seller to pay Broker, the Compensation set forth in Paragraph 3 of this Agreement.

9. <u>DISCLAIMER</u>. Buyer acknowledges and agrees that Broker and Buyer's Designated Agent are being retained solely as real estate professionals and NOT as attorney, tax advisor, surveyor, structural engineer, home inspector, environmental consultant, architect, contractor, or other professional service advisor. Buyer understands and agrees that such other professional service providers are available to render advice or services to Buyer, if desired, at Buyer's expense.

10. <u>INDEMNIFICATION OF BROKER</u>. Buyer hereby indemnifies and holds Broker and Buyer's Designated Agent harmless from and against any and all claims, disputes, litigation, judgments, costs, and legal fees arising from (i) misrepresentations by Buyer or other incorrect or incomplete information supplied by Buyer; (ii) earnest money handled by anyone other than Broker; and (iii) injuries to persons on the Property and/or loss or damage to the Property or any portions of the Property.

11. <u>ARBITRATION</u>. Any controversy or claim arising out of or relating to this Agreement, or the breach of this Agreement, shall be settled by arbitration in accordance with the rules of the Chicago Association of REALTORS, and judgment upon the award rendered by the arbitrator may be entered in any court having jurisdiction.

12. <u>LIMITATION ON BROKER'S LIABILITY</u>. Neither Broker nor Buyer's Designated Agent shall, under any circumstances, have any liability pursuant to this Agreement which is greater than the amount of the Compensation paid to Broker by Buyer or seller's listing broker or seller, as the case may be (and excluding any commission amount retained by the listing broker, if any).

13. <u>REAL ESTATE SETTLEMENT PROCEDURES ACT COMPLIANCE</u>. Buyer shall comply with the Real Estate Settlement Procedures Act of 1974, as amended ("Act"), if applicable, and furnish all information required for compliance with the Act.

14. <u>DUAL REPRESENTATION</u>. By checking "yes" and writing its initials below, Buyer acknowledges and agrees that Buyer's Designated Agent ("Licensee") may undertake a dual representation (represent both seller and buyer or landlord and tenant, as the case may be) in connection with any acquisition of Property. Buyer acknowledges and agrees that Buyer has read the following prior to executing this Agreement:

Representing more than one party to a transaction presents a conflict of interest since both parties may rely upon the Licensee's advice and the parties' respective interests may be adverse to each other. The Licensee will undertake the representation of more than one party to a transaction only with the written consent of ALL parties to the transaction. Any parties who consent to dual representation expressly agree that any agreement between the parties as to any terms of the contract, including the final contract price, results from each party negotiating on its own behalf and in its own best interest. Buyer acknowledges and agrees that (a) Broker has explained the implications of dual representation, including the risks involved, and (b) Buyer has been advised to seek independent counsel from its advisors and/or attorneys prior to executing this Agreement or any documents in connection with this Agreement.

WHAT A LICENSEE <u>CAN</u> DO FOR CLIENTS WHEN UNDERTAKING DUAL REPRESENTATION:

1. Treat all clients honestly. 2. Provide information about the property to the purchaser or tenant. 3. Disclose all latent material defects in the property that are known to the Licensee. 4. Disclose the financial qualification of Buyer to the seller or landlord. 5. Explain real estate terms. 6. Help the Buyer arrange for property inspections. 7. Explain closing costs and procedures. 8. Help the Buyer compare financing alternatives. 9. Provide information to seller or Buyer about comparable properties that have sold so both clients may make educated decisions on what price to accept or offer.

WHAT A LICENSEE <u>CANNOT</u> DO FOR CLIENTS WHEN UNDERTAKING DUAL REPRESENTATION:

1. Disclose confidential information that the Licensee may know about either client without that client's express consent. 2. Disclose the price the seller or landlord will take other than the listing price without the express consent of the seller or landlord. 3. Disclose the price the purchaser or tenant is willing to pay without the express consent of the purchaser or tenant. 4. Recommend or suggest a price the Buyer should offer. 5. Recommend or suggest a price the seller or landlord should counter with or accept.

Buyer acknowledges having read these provisions regarding the issue of dual representation. Buyer is not required to accept this Paragraph 14 unless Buyer wants to allow the Licensee to proceed as a dual agent ("Dual Agent") in this transaction. By checking "yes", initialing below, and signing this Agreement, Buyer acknowledges that it has read and understands this Paragraph 14 and voluntarily consents to the Licensee acting as a Dual Agent (that is, to represent BOTH the seller and purchaser or landlord and tenant, as the case may be) should it become necessary. (check one) _____ Yes _____ No _____ (Buyer initials) _____ (Buyer initials).

15. <u>NONDISCRIMINATION</u>. BROKER, ITS AGENTS AND EMPLOYEES AND BUYER'S DESIGNATED AGENT SHALL NOT ACT IN ANY WAY TO INDUCE OR DISCOURAGE BUYER FROM ACQUIRING A PARTICULAR PROPERTY BASED ON THE RACE, COLOR, RELIGION, NATIONAL ORIGIN, SEX, ANCESTRY, AGE, MARITAL STATUS, PHYSICAL OR MENTAL HANDICAP OR FAMILIAL STATUS (OR ANY OTHER CLASS PROTECTED BY ARTICLE 3 OF THE ILLINOIS HUMAN RIGHTS ACT) OF THE SELLER AND/OR BUYER. THE PARTIES TO THIS AGREEMENT AGREE TO COMPLY WITH ALL APPLICABLE FEDERAL, STATE AND LOCAL FAIR HOUSING LAWS.

Buyer Initials:_____ Buyer Initials:_____ Broker Initials:_____ Broker Initials:_____

16. MISCELLANEOUS PROVISIONS.

A. **Amendments.** No amendment or alteration of this Agreement shall be valid or binding unless made in writing and signed by the Broker, Buyer's Designated Agent and Buyer.

B. **Gender Neutral.** Where applicable in this Agreement, the singular form of any word shall include the plural and the masculine form shall include the feminine and neuter, and vice versa.

C. **Successors and Assigns.** This Agreement shall be binding upon and inure to the benefit of the heirs, executors, administrato successors and assigns of the parties.

D. **Days.** Any reference in this Agreement to "day" or "days" shall mean business days, not calendar days, including Monday, Tuesday, Wednesday, Thursday, and Friday, and excluding all official federal and state holidays.

BUYER INFORMATION: **BROKER INFORMATION:**

Buyer's Signature:_____   Managing Broker's Signature:_____
Buyer's Signature:_____   Date:_____ ("Effective Date")
Date:_____

Buyer's Name (print):_____   Broker Company Name (print):_____
Address:_____   Office Address:_____
City:_____ State:_____ Zip:_____   City:_____ State:_____ Zip:_____
Office Phone:_____   Office Phone:_____
Home Phone:_____   Cell Phone:_____
Cell Phone:_____   Fax:_____
Fax:_____   Email Address:_____
Email Address:_____

Buyer's Name (print):_____   Designated Agent Name (print):_____
Address:_____   Designated Agent Number:_____
City:_____ State:_____ Zip:_____   Office Address:_____
Office Phone:_____   City:_____ State:_____ Zip:_____
Home Phone:_____   Office Phone:_____
Cell Phone:_____   Cell Phone:_____
Fax:_____   Fax:_____
Email Address:_____   Email Address:_____

Buyer Initials:_____ Buyer Initials:_____   Broker Initials:_____ Broker Initials:_____

Residential Lease Agreement

THIS LEASE AGREEMENT is made and entered into this _____ day of _____, 20 ____, by and between _____ hereinafter referred to as "Landlord" and _____, hereinafter referred to as "Tenant".

1. Landlord leases to Tenant and Tenant leases from Landlord, upon the terms and conditions contained herein, the dwelling located at _____ for the period commencing on the _____ day of _____, 20 ___, and thereafter until the _____ day of _____, 20 ___, at which time this Lease Agreement shall automatically renew each year unless terminated in writing. *The Tenant is required to give the Landlord in writing a notice 1 month (30 days) in advance of his/her moving. Notice must be given on the first day of a month. If notice is given after the first day of the month, the 1 month (30 day) notice will not start until the following month.* **(The notice must be one full calendar month starting on the first day of a month.)** Rent may be increased at any time after first year and the securite deposit can not be used for rent.

2. Tenant shall pay as rent the sum of $ _____ per month, due and payable monthly, in advance, no later than 5:00 p.m. by the forth day of every month. Tenant further agrees to pay a late charge of $_____ for each day rent is not received after the forth of the month to the Landlord regardless of the cause, including dishonored checks, time being of the essence. An additional Service Charge of $_____ will be paid to Landlord for all dishonored checks.

3. As an incentive to Tenant to make rent payments **before the first of the month** and for being responsible for all *minor maintenance of the premises*, a pre-payment discount in the amount of **$_____** may be deducted from the above rental amount each month. **Said discount will be forfeited if Tenant fails to perform as stated above.**

4. Tenant agrees to use said dwelling as living quarters only for _____ adults and _____ children, namely:

   _____
   and to pay $50.00 each month for each other person who shall occupy the premises in any capacity.

5. Tenant agrees to accept the property in its current condition and to return it in "moving-in clean" condition, or to pay a special cleaning charge of $185.00 upon vacating the premises. The carpets are to be professionally cleaned. If you prefer that we have the carpets cleaned for you the charge will be billed to you. Carpet cleaning cost are in addition to cleaning charge.

6. PETS ARE NOT ALLOWED WITHOUT WRITTEN PERMISSION FROM LANDLORD. As additional rent, Tenant agrees to pay a non-refundable pet fee of $10.00 per month for each pet. All pets on the property not registered under this Lease shall be presumed to be strays and will be disposed of by the appropriate agency as prescribed by law. A Pet Agreement, if applicable, is attached hereto as Exhibit "B", and incorporated herein by reference. PET NAMES AND DESCRIPTION: _____

7. Tenant agrees not to assign this Lease, nor to sublet any portion of the property, nor to allow any other person to live therein other than as named in paragraph 4 above without first obtaining written permission from Landlord and paying the appropriate surcharge. Further, it is agreed that covenants contained in this Lease, once breached, cannot afterward be performed, and that unlawful detainer proceedings may be commenced at once, without notice to Tenant.

8. Should any provision of this Lease be found to be invalid or unenforceable, the remainder of the Lease shall not be affected thereby and each term and provision herein shall be valid and enforceable to the fullest extent permitted by law.

9. All rights given to Landlord by this Lease shall be cumulative to any other laws which might exist or come into being. Any exercise or failure to exercise by Landlord of any right shall not act as a waiver of any other rights. No statement or promise of Landlord or his agent as to tenancy, repairs, alterations, or other terms and conditions shall be binding unless reduced to writing and signed by Landlord.

10. Tenant will be responsible for payment of all utilities, garbage, water and sewer charges, telephone, gas, association fees or other bills incurred during the term of this Lease. Tenant specifically authorizes Landlord to deduct amounts of any unpaid bills from the Security deposit upon termination of this Agreement.

11. No rights of storage are given by this Agreement. Landlord shall not be liable for any loss of Tenant's property by fire, theft, breakage, burglary, or otherwise, nor for any accidental damage to persons or property in or about the leased premises resulting from electrical failure, water, rain, windstorm, etc., which may cause issue or flow into or from any part of said premises or improvements, including pipes, gas lines, sprinklers, or electrical connections, whether caused by the negligence of Landlord, Landlord's employees, contractors, agents, or by any other cause whatsoever. Tenant hereby agrees to make no claim for any such damages or loss against Landlord. <u>Tenant shall purchase renter's insurance.</u> _____ is to be named as additional Insured

IMPROVEMENTS TO PROPERTY - Any improvements to the property made by tenant inside or outside <u>*must not be removed without written permission from the property manger*</u>. This includes landscaping, scrubs, flowers, walkways, out buildings such as storage sheds and play-houses, etc. Any interior improvements the tenant may have made to the property must also remain. Improvements such as but not limited to the following are installation of ceiling fans, book shelves, shelving, light fixtures, etc.

12. Any removal of Landlord's property without express written permission from the Landlord shall constitute abandonment and surrender of the premises and termination by the resident of this Agreement. Landlord may take immediate possession, exclude Tenant from property and store all Tenant's possessions at Tenant's expense pending reimbursement in full for Landlord's loss and damages.
13. Landlord has the right of emergency access to the leased premises at any time and access during reasonable hours to inspect the property or to show property to a prospective tenant or buyer. In the event that the property is sold, the lease/rental agreement between Landlord and Tenant is canceled on the date the new owner takes possession of property. Tenant has thirty days to vacate the property or sign new lease with new owner at new owner's option.
14. Tenant agrees to pay a Security Deposit of $ _____ to bind Tenant's pledge of full compliance with the terms of this agreement. NOTE: SECURITY DEPOSIT MAY NOT BE USED TO PAY RENT! Any damages not previously reported as required in paragraph 25, will be repaired at Tenant's expense.
15. Release of the SECURITY DEPOSIT, at the Option of the Landlord is subject to the provisions below .

    A. The full term of the Agreement has been completed.
    B. No damage to the premises, buildings, grounds is evident.
    C. The entire dwelling, appliances, closets, and cupboards are clean and free from insects, the refrigerator is defrosted and clean, The range is to be clean including the racks and broiler pan, all windows are to be clean inside and outside, all debris and rubbish have been removed from the property, carpets have been commercially cleaned and left clean and odorless.
    D. All unpaid charges have been paid including late charges, visitor charges, pet charges, delinquent rents, etc. WATER BILL MUST BE PAID IN FULL AND COPY OF PAID FINAL BILL SENT TO LANDLORD.
    E. All keys have been returned.
    F. A forwarding address for Tenant has been left with the Landlord. Within thirty (30) days after termination of the occupancy, the Landlord will mail the balance of the deposit to the address provided by Tenant in the names of all signatories hereto; or at the Option of the Landlord will impose a claim on the deposit and so notify the Tenant.
    G. It is the tenant's responsibility to call, make arrangements, and be at residence to let meter readers in for final reading on gas, electric, and water. If Landlord has to do this, there is a $50 charge for each utility.

16. The acceptance by Landlord of partial payments of rent due shall not, under any circumstances, constitute a waiver of Landlord, nor affect any notice or legal proceeding in unlawful detainer theretofore given or commenced under state law. Acceptance of partial rent due or late payments does not create a custom nor constitute a continuing waiver of the obligation to pay on time. No payment by the tenant or receipt by the landlord of any amount of the monthly rent herein stipulated shall be deemed to be other than **_on account_** of the stipulated rent, nor shall any endorsement on any check or any letter accompanying such payment of rent be deemed an accord and satisfaction, but the landlord may accept such a partial payment without prejudice to his rights to collect the balance of such rent.
17. If Tenant leaves said premises unoccupied for 15 days while rent is due and unpaid, Landlord is granted the right hereunder to take immediate possession thereof and to exclude Tenant therefrom; removing all Tenant's property contained therein and placing it into storage at Tenant's expense.
18. Payment of rent may be made by check until the first check is returned unpaid. Regardless of cause, no additional payments may afterwards be made by check. Rent must then be made by cashier's check, money order or certified check.
19. Rent may be mailed through the United States Postal Service at Tenant's risk. Any rents lost in the mail will be treated as if unpaid until received by Landlord.
20. Tenant agrees, without protest, to reimburse Landlord for all actual and reasonable expenses incurred by way of Tenant's violation of any term or provision of this lease, including, but not limited to $10.00 for each Notice to Pay, Notice to Quit or other notice mailed or delivered by Landlord to Tenant due to Tenant's non-payment of rent, all court costs and attorney's fees and all costs of collection. Both Landlord and Tenant waive trial by jury and agree to submit to the personal jurisdiction and venue of a court of subject matter jurisdiction located in _____ County, State of _____. In such event, no action shall be entertained by said court or any court of competent jurisdiction if filed more than one year subsequent to the date the cause(s) of action accrued.
21. Tenant agrees to accept said dwelling and all of the furnishings and appliances therein as being in good and satisfactory condition unless a written statement of any objections is delivered to Landlord within three (3) days after resident takes possession. Tenant agrees that failure to file such statement shall be conclusive proof that there were no defects in the property. Tenant agrees not to permit any damage to the premises during the period of this agreement to woodwork, floors, walls, furnishings, fixtures, appliances, windows, screens, doors, lawns, landscaping, fences, plumbing, electrical, air conditioning and heating, and mechanical systems. Tenant specifically agrees that he will be responsible for, and agrees to pay for, any damage done by rain, wind, or hail caused by leaving windows open; overflow of water or stoppage of waste pipes, breakage of glass, damage to screens, deterioration of lawns and landscaping whether caused by drought, abuse or neglect. Tenant agrees not to park or store a motorhome, recreational vehicle or trailer of any type on the premises.
22. Tenant's obligations are as follows:

A. Take affirmative action to insure that nothing is done which might place Landlord in violation of applicable building, housing, zoning, and health codes and regulations.
B. Keep the dwelling clean and sanitary, removing garbage and trash as it accumulates, maintaining plumbing in good working order to prevent stoppages and leakage of plumbing fixtures, faucets, pipes, etc.
C. Operate all electrical, plumbing, sanitary, heating, ventilating, air conditioning, and other appliances in a reasonable, safe manner.
D. Assure that property belonging to Landlord is safeguarded against damage, destruction, loss, removal, or theft.
E. Conduct himself, his family, friends, guests, visitors in a manner which will not disturb others.
F. Allow the Landlord or his agent access to the premises for the purpose of inspection, repairs, or to show the property to someone else at reasonable hours, and to specifically authorize unannounced access anytime rent is late, or this Agreement is terminated or for pest control, maintenance estimates, serving legal notices, or emergencies.
G. Comply with all provisions of this Agreement, particularly with respect to paying the rent on time and caring for the property. Tenant warrants that he/she will meet the above conditions in every respect, and acknowledges that failure to perform the obligations herein stipulated will be considered grounds for termination of this Agreement and loss of all deposits.

23. No additional locks will be installed on any door without written permission from the Landlord. Landlord is to be provided duplicate keys for all locks so installed at Tenant's expense within 24 hours of installation of said locks.
24. Tenant agrees to install and maintain a telephone, and to furnish the Landlord the telephone number and/or any changes thereof within three (3) days of its installation.
25. In the event repairs are needed beyond the competence of the Tenant, Tenant is urged to contact the Landlord. Tenant is offered the discount as an incentive to make his own decisions on repairs to the property and to allow Landlord to rent the property without the need to employ professional management. Therefore, as much as possible, Tenant should refrain from contacting the Landlord or his agent except for emergencies, or for expensive repairs. Such involvement by the Landlord or his agent will result in the loss of the discount and/or deductible.
26. Tenant warrants that any work or repairs performed by him will be undertaken only if he is competent and qualified to perform it. Tenant will be totally responsible for all activities to assure that work is done in a safe manner which will meet all the applicable codes and statutes. Tenant further warrants that he will be accountable for any mishaps and/or accidents resulting from such work, and will hold the Landlord free from harm, litigation, or claims of any other person.
27. Tenant is responsible for all plumbing repairs including faucets, leaks, stopped up pipes, frozen pipes, water damage, and bathroom caulking.
28. Appliances or furniture in the unit at date of lease per the attached Exhibit "A", are loaned, not leased to Tenant. Maintenance of appliances or furniture is the responsibility of Tenant who will keep them in good repair.
29. Tenant is responsible for all glass, screen, and storm door repairs.
30. No money is to be deducted by Tenant from rent payment for any reason without express written permission of Landlord.
31. Regardless of assignment of responsibility, Tenant agrees to be responsible for the first $75.00 of any repair or maintenance required on the major systems of the property for the term of the lease. This deductible applies per occurrence.
32. Tenant accepts entirely the responsibility for recharging air conditioner compressor and the cleaning of furnace or replacement of furnace filters.
33. Smoke Detectors have been installed and are in operable condition in the following places.
_____ Tenant initials _____. From this time on you will be required to maintain the smoke detectors. Any new batteries are your responsibility. If you have any questions about the smoke detectors, you should call us promptly.

I/We , the undersigned, have personally checked the smoke alarms in the unit which is provided and find it/them to be in working order. I/We understand that the law requires me/us to maintain the alarm/s and keep fresh batteries in the mechanism. Tenants failure to do so absolves the Landlord, or agent from any responsibility for losses due to my/our non-compliance with the law or malfunction of the alarm.
Tenant signature _____ Date _____

34. NO WATER BEDS PERMITTED WITHOUT WRITTEN PERMISSION.
35. All parties agree that termination of this Agreement prior to termination date will constitute breach of the tenancy and all Security Deposits and one full month's rent shall be forfeited in favor of Landlord as liquidated damages plus you will be charged the cost of restoring the property to rental condition plus advertising and rent loss incurred until the new resident moves in. Your liability for rent loss is limited to thirty (30) days after restoration is complete.
36. Properties built before and during the late sixties and early seventies may have had lead based products and asbestos products used in them. These products were considered to be safe at the time they were used, just as the building products used today are considered safe for home construction. Only the test of time will show which products are or are not safe to use. Having read the above, the tenant signs the lease below with the full understanding that these conditions may be present in this property. The tenant and all parties associated with this

property relieves the owner, property manager, and any of his agents from any responsibilities for these conditions regardless of when or how these conditions were caused.

You also acknowledge receiving the EPA Booklet "Protect Your Family From Lead In Your Home"

X _____ _____
Tenant Signature Date

X _____ _____
Tenant Signature Date

37. From time to time, owner may be represented by an agent who will carry identification.
38. In this Agreement the singular number where used will also include the plural, the masculine gender will also include the feminine, the term Landlord will include, Owner or Lessor; and the term Tenant(s) will include Resident, Lessee or Renter.
39. Unless specifically disallowed by law, should litigation arise hereunder, service of process therefor may be obtained through certified mail, return receipt requested; the parties hereto waiving any and all rights they may have to object to the method by which service was perfected.
40. TENANT agrees to send all notices to Landlord or Property Manager in writing by certified mail, return receipt requested. This is the only form of notice permitted in a court hearing as evidence of notice given.
41. The Tenant was asked if he/she could speak, read and understand English. He/she was told that signing below would indicate that they understood what they were signing and that he/she did speak and read English.

YOU SHOULD READ AND UNDERSTAND THIS LEASE, IT IS A LEGAL AND BINDING CONTRACT.

Signing below means you have read the Lease, are in full agreement with it and have received a copy of the contract.

ACCEPTED THIS _____ DAY OF _____ 19 _____,

at _____.

(Address, City and State)

_____   _____
Tenant 1   Tenant 3

_____   _____
Tenant 2   Landlord, Property manager or Agent

EXHIBIT "A"

The following appliances and/or furniture are on loan to Tenant for the period of Tenant's rental agreement or lease on the following basis: Tenant agrees, by the signing of this agreement, that all appliances and/or furniture herein listed are accepted by Tenant, individually, as being in good working order or condition. Tenant agrees to maintain said appliances and/or furniture in good working order at his expense. If tenant fails to pay rent by the fifth day of the month, the landlord/manager or his representative may enter building and remove appliances or furniture belonging to Landlord without giving tenant advance notice.

APPLIANCES AND/OR FURNITURE

	Furniture Description	Appliance Number or Item	Condition	Location
1				
2				
3				
4				
5				
6				
7				

8				
9				
10				
11				
12				
13				
14				
15				
16				

Tenant: _____

Date: _____

EXHIBIT "B"

PET AGREEMENT

Date: _____ (Addendum to Lease Agreement)

This agreement is attached to and forms a part of the Lease Agreement dated _____ between _____, Landlord, and _____, Tenant(s).

Tenants desire to keep a pet named _____ and described as _____ in the dwelling they occupy under the rental agreement or lease referred to above, and because this agreement specifically prohibits keeping pets without the Landlord's permission, Tenants agree to the following terms and conditions in exchange for this permission:

1. Tenants agree to keep their pet under control at all times.
2. Tenants agree to keep their pet restrained, but not tethered, when it is outside their dwelling.
3. Tenants agree not to leave their pet unattended for any unreasonable periods.
4. Tenants agree to dispose of their pet's droppings properly and quickly.
5. Tenants agree to keep pet from causing any annoyance or discomfort to others and will remedy immediately any complaints made through the Landlord or his agent.
6. Tenants agree to get rid of their pet's offspring within eight weeks of birth.
7. Tenants agree to pay immediately for any damage, loss, or expense caused by their pet, and in addition, they will add $ _____ to their Security Deposit, any of which may be used for cleaning, repairs, or delinquent rent when Tenants vacate.
8. Tenants agree that Landlord reserves the right to revoke permission to keep the pet should Tenants break this agreement.
9. Tenant agrees to pay an additional $ _____ in rent per month per pet.

_____
TENANT

_____
LANDLORD

Total Real Estate Solutions!
http://www.totalrealestatesolutions.com

DISCLOSURE AND CONSENT TO DUAL AGENT DESIGNATED AGENCY

This document serves three purposes:

1. It discloses that a real estate licensee may potentially act as a disclosed dual agent who represents more than one party to the transaction.
2. It explains the concept of disclosed dual agency.
3. It seeks your consent to allow the real estate agent to act as a disclosed dual agent.

A LICENSEE MAY LEGALLY ACT AS A DUAL AGENT ONLY WITH YOUR CONSENT. BY CHOOSING TO SIGN THIS DOCUMENT, YOUR CONSENT TO DUAL AGENCY REPRESENTATION IS PRESUMED. BEFORE SIGNING THIS DOCUMENT, PLEASE READ THE FOLLOWING:

The undersigned designated agent(s) _____
(Insert name(s) of licensee(s) undertaking dual representation)
and any subsequent designated agent(s) may undertake a dual representation represent both the buyer (or lessee) and the seller (or lessor) for the sale or lease of property described as _____.
(List address of property, if known)

The undersigned buyer (or lessee) and seller (or lessor) acknowledge that they were informed of the possibility of this type of representation. The licensee(s) will undertake this representation only with the written consent of ALL clients in the transaction.

Any agreement between the clients as to a final contract price and other terms is a result of negotiations between the clients acting in their own best interests and on their own behalf. The undersigned buyer (or lessee) and seller (or lessor) acknowledge that the licensee(s) has explained the implications of dual representation, including the risks involved. The undersigned buyer (or lessee) and seller (or lessor) acknowledge that they have been advised to seek independent advice from their advisors or attorneys before signing any documents in this transaction.

WHAT A LICENSEE CAN DO FOR CLIENTS WHEN ACTING AS A DUAL AGENT

- Treat all clients honestly.
- Provide information about the property to the buyer (or lessee).
- Disclose all latent material defects in the property that are known to the licensee(s).
- Disclose financial qualifications of the buyer (or lessee) to the seller (or lessor).
- Explain real estate terms.
- Help the buyer (or lessee) to arrange for property inspections.
- Explain closing costs and procedures.
- Help the buyer compare financing alternatives.
- Provide information about comparable properties that have sold so that both clients may make educated decisions on what price to accept or offer.

WHAT A LICENSEE CANNOT DISCLOSE TO CLIENTS WHEN ACTING AS A DUAL AGENT

- Confidential information that the licensee may know about the clients, without that client's permission.
- The price the seller (or lessor) will take other than the listing price without permission of the seller (or lessor).
- The price the buyer (or lessee) is willing to pay without permission of the buyer (or lessee).

You are not required to sign this document unless you want to allow the licensee(s) to proceed as a dual agent(s), representing BOTH the buyer (or lessee) and the seller (or lessor) in this transaction. If you do not want the licensee(s) to proceed as a dual agent(s) and do not want to sign this document, please inform the licensee(s).

By signing below, you acknowledge that you have read and understand this form and voluntarily consent to the licensee(s) acting as a dual agent(s), representing BOTH the buyer (or lessee) and the seller (or lessor) should that become necessary.

_____   _____
Buyer or Lessee   Seller or Lessor

_____ _____
Date   Date

_____ _____
Buyer or Lessee   Seller or Lessor

_____ _____
Date   Date

_____ _____
Licensee   Licensee

_____ _____
Date   Date

DDA 1/98

Code of Ethics

The Code of Ethics of the National Association of Realtors® is subscribed to by all brokers and salespersons who are Realtors®. It has become so well accepted over the years that it is now part of the rules and regulations governing the conduct of real estate licensees in many states.

Under all is the land. Upon its wise utilization and widely allocated ownership depend the survival and growth of free institutions and of our civilization. REALTORS should recognize that the interests of the nation and its citizens require the highest and best use of the land and the widest distribution of land ownership. They require the creation of adequate housing, the building of functioning cities, the development of productive industries and farms, and the preservation of a healthful environment.

Such interests impose obligations beyond those of ordinary commerce. They impose grave social responsibility and a patriotic duty to which REALTORS should dedicate themselves, and for which they should be diligent in preparing themselves. REALTORS, therefore, are zealous to maintain and improve the standards of their calling and share with their fellow REALTORS a common responsibility for its integrity and honor.

In recognition and appreciation of their obligations to clients, customers, the public, and each other, REALTORS continuously strive to become and remain informed on issues affecting real estate and, as knowledgeable professionals, they willingly share the fruit of their experience and study with others. They identify and take steps, through enforcement of this Code of Ethics and by assisting appropriate regulatory bodies, to eliminate practices which may damage the public or which might discredit or bring dishonor to the real estate profession. REALTORS® having direct personal knowledge of conduct that may violate the Code of Ethics involving misappropriation of client or customer funds or property, willful discrimination, or fraud resulting in substantial economic harm, bring such matters to the attention of the appropriate Board or Association of REALTORS.

Realizing that cooperation with other real estate professionals promotes the best interests of those who utilize their services, REALTORS urge exclusive representation of clients; do not attempt to gain any unfair advantage over their competitors; and they refrain from making unsolicited comments about other practitioners. In instances where their opinion is sought, or where REALTORS believe that comment is necessary, their opinion is offered in an objective, professional manner, uninfluenced by any personal motivation or potential advantage or gain.

The term REALTOR has come to connote competency, fairness, and high integrity resulting from adherence to a lofty ideal of moral conduct in business relations. No inducement of profit and no instruction from clients ever can justify departure from this ideal.

In the interpretation of this obligation, REALTORS can take no safer guide than that which has been handed down through the centuries, embodied in the Golden Rules, "Whatsoever ye would that others should do to you, do ye even so to them."

Accepting this standard as their own, REALTORS pledge to observe its spirit in all of their activities, through associates or others, or via technological means, and to conduct their business in accordance with the tenets set forth below.

ARTICLE 1

When representing a buyer, seller, landlord, tenant, other client as an agent, REALTORS pledge themselves to protect and promote the interests of their client. This obligation to the client is primary, but it does not relieve REALTORS of their obligation to treat all parties honestly. When serving a buyer, seller, landlord, tenant or other party in a non-agency capacity, REALTORS remain obligated to treat all parties honestly.

ARTICLE 2

REALTORS shall avoid exaggeration, misrepresentation, or concealment of pertinent facts relating to the property or the transaction. REALTORS shall not, however, be obligated to discover latent defects in the property, to advise on matters outside the scope of their real estate license, or to disclose facts which are confidential under the scope of agency or non-agency relationships as defined by state law.

ARTICLE 3

REALTORS shall cooperate with other brokers except when cooperation is not in the client's best interest. The obligation to cooperate does not include the obligation to share commissions, fees, or to otherwise compensate another broker.

ARTICLE 4

REALTORS shall not acquire an interest in or buy or present offers from themselves, any member of their immediate families, their firms or any member thereof, or any entities in which they have any ownership interest, any real property without making their true position known to the owner or the owner's agent or broker. In selling property they own, or in which they have any interest, REALTORS shall reveal their ownership or interest in writing to the purchaser or the purchaser's representative.

ARTICLE 5

REALTORS shall not undertake to provide professional services concerning a property or its value where they have a present or contemplated interest unless such interest is specifically disclosed to all affected parties.

ARTICLE 6

REALTORS shall not accept any commission, rebate, or profit on expenditures made for their client, without the client's knowledge and consent.

When recommending real estate products or services (e.g., homeowner's insurance, warranty programs, mortgage financing, title insurance, etc.), REALTORS shall disclose to the client or customer to whom the recommendation is made any financial benefits or fees, other than real estate referral fees, the REALTOR or REALTOR's firm may receive as a direct result of such recommendation.

ARTICLE 7

In a transaction, REALTORS shall not accept compensation from more than one party, even if permitted by law, without disclosure to all parties and the informed consent of the REALTOR's client or clients.

ARTICLE 8

REALTORS shall keep in a special account in an appropriate financial institution, separated from their own funds, monies coming into their possession in trust for other persons, such as escrows, trust funds, clients' monies, and other like items.

ARTICLE 9

REALTORS, for the protection of all parties, shall assure whenever possible that all agreements related to real estate transactions including, but not limited to, listing and representation agreements, purchase contracts, and leases are in writing in clear and understandable language expressing the specific terms, conditions, obligations and commitments of the parties. A copy of each agreement shall be furnished to each party to such agreements upon their signing or initialing.

ARTICLE 10

REALTORS shall not deny equal professional services to any person for reasons of race, color, religion, sex, handicap, familial status, national origin, or sexual orientation.

REALTORS shall not be parties to any plan or agreement to discriminate against a person or persons on the basis of race, color, religion, sex, handicap, familial status, national origin, or sexual orientation.

REALTORS, in their real estate employment practices, shall not discriminate against any person or persons on the basis of race, color, religion, sex, handicap, familial status, national origin, or sexual orientation.

ARTICLE 11

The services which REALTORS provide to their clients and customers shall conform to the standards of practice and competence which are reasonably expected in the specific real estate disciplines in which they engage; specifically, residential real estate brokerage, real property management, commercial and industrial real estate brokerage, land brokerage, real estate appraisal, real estate counseling, real estate syndication, real estate auction, and international real estate.

REALTORS shall not undertake to provide specialized professional services concerning a type of property or service that is outside their field of competence unless they engage the assistance of one who is competent on such types of property or service, or unless the facts are fully disclosed to the client. Any persons engaged to provide such assistance shall be so identified to the client and their contribution to the assignment should be set forth.

ARTICLE 12

REALTORS shall be honest and truthful in their real estate communications and shall present a true picture in their advertising, marketing, and other representations. REALTORS shall ensure that their status as real estate professionals is readily apparent in their advertising, marketing, and other representations, and that the recipients of all real estate communications are, or have been, notified that those communications are from a real estate professional.

ARTICLE 13

REALTORS shall not engage in activities that constitute the unauthorized practice of law and shall recommend that legal counsel be obtained when the interest of any party to the transaction requires it.

ARTICLE 14

If charged with unethical practice or asked to present evidence or to cooperate in any other way, in any professional standards proceeding or investigation, REALTORS shall place all pertinent facts before the proper tribunals of the Member Board or affiliated institute, society, or council in which membership is held and shall take no action to disrupt or obstruct such processes.

ARTICLE 15

REALTORS shall not knowingly or recklessly make false or misleading statements about other real estate professionals, their businesses, or their business practices.

ARTICLE 16

REALTORS shall not engage in any practice or take any action inconsistent with exclusive representation or exclusive brokerage relationship agreements that other REALTORS have with clients.

ARTICLE 17

In the event of contractual disputes or specific non-contractual disputes as defined in Standard of Practice 17-4 between REALTORS (principals) associated with different firms, arising out of their relationship as REALTORS, the REALTORS shall mediate the dispute if the Board requires its members to mediate. If the dispute is not resolved through mediation, or if mediation is not required, REALTORS® shall submit the dispute to arbitration in accordance with the policies of the Board rather than litigate the matter.

In the event clients of REALTORS wish to mediate or arbitrate contractual disputes arising out of real estate transactions, REALTORS shall mediate or arbitrate those disputes in accordance with the policies of the Board, provided the clients agree to be bound by any resulting agreement or award.

The obligation to participate in mediation and arbitration contemplated by this Article includes the obligation of REALTORS (principals) to cause their firms to mediate and arbitrate and be bound by any resulting agreement or award.

DEED OF TRUST

DEFINITIONS

Words used in multiple sections of this document are defined below and other words are defined in Sections 3, 11, 13, 18, 20 and 21. Certain rules regarding the usage of words used in this document are also provided in Section 16.

(A) **"Security Instrument"** means this document, which is dated _____, _____, together with all Riders to this document.

(B) **"Borrower"** is _____. Borrower is the trustor under this Security Instrument.

(C) **"Lender"** is _____. Lender is a _____ organized and existing under the laws of_____. Lender's address is _____ _____. Lender is the beneficiary under this Security Instrument.

(D) **"Trustee"** is _____.

(E) **"Note"** means the promissory note signed by Borrower and dated _____, _____. The Note states that Borrower owes Lender _____ Dollars (U.S. $_____) plus interest. Borrower has promised to pay this debt in regular Periodic Payments and to pay the debt in full not later than _____.

(F) **"Property"** means the property that is described below under the heading "Transfer of Rights in the Property."

(G) **"Loan"** means the debt evidenced by the Note, plus interest, any prepayment charges and late charges due under the Note, and all sums due under this Security Instrument, plus interest.

(H) **"Riders"** means all Riders to this Security Instrument that are executed by Borrower. The following Riders are to be executed by Borrower [check box as applicable]:

- ☐ Adjustable Rate Rider ☐ Condominium Rider ☐ Second Home Rider
- ☐ Balloon Rider ☐ Planned Unit Development Ride ☐ Other(s) [specify] _____
- ☐ 1-4 Family Rider ☐ Biweekly Payment Rider

(I) **"Applicable Law"** means all controlling applicable federal, state and local statutes, regulations, ordinances and administrative rules and orders (that have the effect of law) as well as all applicable final, non-appealable judicial opinions.

(J) **"Community Association Dues, Fees, and Assessments"** means all dues, fees, assessments and other charges that are imposed on Borrower or the Property by a condominium association, homeowners association or similar organization.

(K) **"Electronic Funds Transfer"** means any transfer of funds, other than a transaction originated by check, draft, or similar paper instrument, which is initiated through an electronic terminal, telephonic instrument, computer, or magnetic tape so as to order, instruct, or authorize a financial institution to debit or credit an account. Such term includes, but is not limited to, point-of-sale transfers, automated teller machine transactions, transfers initiated by telephone, wire transfers, and automated clearinghouse transfers.

(L) **"Escrow Items"** means those items that are described in Section 3.

(M) **"Miscellaneous Proceeds"** means any compensation, settlement, award of damages, or proceeds paid by any third party (other than insurance proceeds paid under the coverages described in Section 5) for: (i) damage to, or destruction of, the Property; (ii) condemnation or other taking of all or any part of the Property; (iii) conveyance in lieu of condemnation; or (iv) misrepresentations of, or omissions as to, the value and/or condition of the Property.

(N) **"Mortgage Insurance"** means insurance protecting Lender against the nonpayment of, or default on, the Loan.

(O) **"Periodic Payment"** means the regularly scheduled amount due for (i) principal and interest under the Note, plus (ii) any amounts under Section 3 of this Security Instrument.

(P) **"RESPA"** means the Real Estate Settlement Procedures Act (12 U.S.C. §2601 et seq.) and its implementing regulation, Regulation X (24 C.F.R. Part 3500), as they might be amended from time to time, or any additional or successor legislation or regulation that governs the same subject matter. As used in this Security Instrument, "RESPA" refers to all requirements and restrictions that are imposed in regard to a "federally related mortgage loan" even if the Loan does not qualify as a "federally related mortgage loan" under RESPA.

(Q) **"Successor in Interest of Borrower"** means any party that has taken title to the Property, whether or not that party has assumed Borrower's obligations under the Note and/or this Security Instrument.

TRANSFER OF RIGHTS IN THE PROPERTY

This Security Instrument secures to Lender: (i) the repayment of the Loan, and all renewals, extensions and modifications of the Note; and (ii) the performance of Borrower's covenants and agreements under this Security Instrument and the Note. For this purpose, Borrower irrevocably grants and conveys to Trustee, in trust, with power of sale, the following described property located in the _____ of _____:
[Type of Recording Jurisdiction]   [Name of Recording Jurisdiction]

which currently has the address of _____
                                                            [Street]
_____, California _____ ("Property Address"):
     [City]   [Zip Code]

TOGETHER WITH all the improvements now or hereafter erected on the property, and all easements, appurtenances, and fixtures now or hereafter a part of the property. All replacements and additions shall also be covered by this Security Instrument. All of the foregoing is referred to in this Security Instrument as the "Property."

BORROWER COVENANTS that Borrower is lawfully seised of the estate hereby conveyed and has the right to grant and convey the Property and that the Property is unencumbered, except for encumbrances of record. Borrower warrants and will defend generally the title to the Property against all claims and demands, subject to any encumbrances of record.

THIS SECURITY INSTRUMENT combines uniform covenants for national use and non-uniform covenants with limited variations by jurisdiction to constitute a uniform security instrument covering real property.

UNIFORM COVENANTS. Borrower and Lender covenant and agree as follows:

1. Payment of Principal, Interest, Escrow Items, Prepayment Charges, and Late Charges. Borrower shall pay when due the principal of, and interest on, the debt evidenced by the Note and any prepayment charges and late charges due under the Note. Borrower shall also pay funds for Escrow Items pursuant to Section 3. Payments due under the Note and this Security Instrument shall be made in U.S. currency. However, if any check or other instrument received by Lender as payment under the Note or this Security Instrument is returned to Lender unpaid, Lender may require that any or all subsequent payments due under the Note and this Security Instrument be made in one or more of the following forms, as selected by Lender: (a) cash; (b) money order; (c) certified check, bank check, treasurer's check or cashier's check, provided any such check is drawn upon an institution whose deposits are insured by a federal agency, instrumentality, or entity; or (d) Electronic Funds Transfer.

Payments are deemed received by Lender when received at the location designated in the Note or at such other location as may be designated by Lender in accordance with the notice provisions in Section 15. Lender may return any payment or partial payment if the payment or partial payments are insufficient to bring the Loan current. Lender may accept any payment or partial payment insufficient to bring the Loan current, without waiver of any rights hereunder or prejudice to its rights to refuse such payment or partial payments in the future, but Lender is not obligated to apply such payments at the time such payments are accepted. If each Periodic Payment is applied as of its scheduled due date, then Lender need not pay interest on unapplied funds. Lender may hold such unapplied funds until Borrower makes payment to bring the Loan current. If Borrower does not do so within a reasonable period of time, Lender shall either apply such funds or return them to Borrower. If not applied earlier, such funds will be applied to the outstanding principal balance under the Note immediately prior to foreclosure. No offset or claim which Borrower might have now or in the future against Lender shall relieve Borrower from making payments due under the Note and this Security Instrument or performing the covenants and agreements secured by this Security Instrument.

2. Application of Payments or Proceeds. Except as otherwise described in this Section 2, all payments accepted and applied by Lender shall be applied in the following order of priority: (a) interest due under the Note; (b) principal due under the Note; (c) amounts due under Section 3. Such payments shall be applied to each Periodic Payment in the order in which it became due. Any remaining amounts shall be applied first to late charges, second to any other amounts due under this Security Instrument, and then to reduce the principal balance of the Note.

If Lender receives a payment from Borrower for a delinquent Periodic Payment which includes a sufficient amount to pay any late charge due, the payment may be applied to the delinquent payment and the late charge. If more than one Periodic Payment is outstanding, Lender may apply any payment received from Borrower to the repayment of the Periodic Payments if, and to the extent that, each payment can be paid in full. To the extent that any excess exists after the payment is applied to the full payment of one or more Periodic Payments, such excess may be applied to any late charges due. Voluntary prepayments shall be applied first to any prepayment charges and then as described in the Note.

Any application of payments, insurance proceeds, or Miscellaneous Proceeds to principal due under the Note shall not extend or postpone the due date, or change the amount, of the Periodic Payments.

3. Funds for Escrow Items. Borrower shall pay to Lender on the day Periodic Payments are due under the Note, until the Note is paid in full, a sum (the "Funds") to provide for payment of amounts due for: (a) taxes and assessments and other items which can attain priority over this Security Instrument as a lien or encumbrance on the Property; (b) leasehold payments or ground rents on the Property, if any; (c) premiums for any and all insurance required by Lender under Section 5; and (d) Mortgage Insurance premiums, if any, or any sums payable by Borrower to Lender in lieu of the payment of Mortgage Insurance premiums in accordance with the provisions of Section 10. These items are called "Escrow Items." At origination or at any time during the term of the Loan, Lender may require that Community Association Dues, Fees, and Assessments, if any, be escrowed by Borrower, and such dues, fees and assessments shall be an Escrow Item. Borrower shall promptly furnish to Lender all notices of amounts to be paid under this Section. Borrower shall pay Lender the Funds for Escrow Items unless Lender waives Borrower's obligation to pay the Funds for any or all Escrow Items. Lender may waive Borrower's obligation to pay to Lender Funds for any or all Escrow Items at any time. Any such waiver may only be in writing. In the event of such waiver, Borrower shall pay directly, when and where payable, the amounts due for any Escrow Items for which payment of Funds has been waived by Lender and, if Lender requires, shall furnish to Lender receipts evidencing such payment within such time period as Lender may require. Borrower's obligation to make such payments and to provide receipts shall for all purposes be deemed to be a covenant and agreement contained in this Security Instrument, as the phrase "covenant and agreement" is used in Section 9. If Borrower is obligated to pay Escrow Items directly, pursuant to a waiver, and Borrower fails to pay the amount due for an Escrow Item, Lender may exercise its rights under Section 9 and pay such amount and Borrower shall then be obligated under Section 9 to repay to Lender any such amount. Lender may revoke the waiver as to any or all Escrow Items at any time by a notice given in accordance with Section 15 and, upon such revocation, Borrower shall pay to Lender all Funds, and in such amounts, that are then required under this Section 3.

Lender may, at any time, collect and hold Funds in an amount (a) sufficient to permit Lender to apply the Funds at the time specified under RESPA, and (b) not to exceed the maximum amount a lender can require under RESPA. Lender shall estimate the amount of Funds due on the basis of current data and reasonable estimates of expenditures of future Escrow Items or otherwise in accordance with Applicable Law.

The Funds shall be held in an institution whose deposits are insured by a federal agency, instrumentality, or entity (including Lender, if Lender is an institution whose deposits are so insured) or in any Federal Home Loan Bank. Lender shall apply the Funds to pay the Escrow Items no later than the time specified under RESPA. Lender shall not charge Borrower for holding and applying the Funds, annually analyzing the escrow account, or verifying the Escrow Items, unless Lender pays Borrower interest on the Funds and Applicable Law permits Lender to make such a charge. Unless an agreement is made in writing or Applicable Law requires interest to be paid on the Funds, Lender shall not be required to pay Borrower any interest or earnings on the Funds. Borrower and Lender can agree in writing, however, that interest shall be paid on the Funds. Lender shall give to Borrower, without charge, an annual accounting of the Funds as required by RESPA.

If there is a surplus of Funds held in escrow, as defined under RESPA, Lender shall account to Borrower for the excess funds in accordance with RESPA. If there is a shortage of Funds held in escrow, as defined under RESPA, Lender shall notify Borrower as required by RESPA, and Borrower shall pay to Lender the amount necessary to make up the shortage in accordance with RESPA, but in no more than 12 monthly payments. If there is a deficiency of Funds held in escrow, as defined under RESPA, Lender shall notify Borrower as required by RESPA, and Borrower shall pay to Lender the amount necessary to make up the deficiency in accordance with RESPA, but in no more than 12 monthly payments.

Upon payment in full of all sums secured by this Security Instrument, Lender shall promptly refund to Borrower any Funds held by Lender.

4. Charges; Liens. Borrower shall pay all taxes, assessments, charges, fines, and impositions attributable to the Property which can attain priority over this Security Instrument, leasehold payments or ground rents on the Property, if any, and Community Association Dues, Fees, and Assessments, if any. To the extent that these items are Escrow Items, Borrower shall pay them in the manner provided in Section 3.

Borrower shall promptly discharge any lien which has priority over this Security Instrument unless Borrower: (a) agrees in writing to the payment of the obligation secured by the lien in a manner acceptable to Lender, but only so long as Borrower is performing such agreement; (b) contests the lien in good faith by, or defends against enforcement of the lien in, legal proceedings which in Lender's opinion operate to prevent the enforcement of the lien while those proceedings are pending, but only until such proceedings are concluded; or (c) secures from the holder of the lien an agreement satisfactory to Lender subordinating the lien to this Security Instrument. If Lender determines that any part of the Property is subject to a lien which can attain priority over this Security Instrument, Lender may give Borrower a notice identifying the lien. Within 10 days of the date on which that notice is given, Borrower shall satisfy the lien or take one or more of the actions set forth above in this Section 4.

Lender may require Borrower to pay a one-time charge for a real estate tax verification and/or reporting service used by Lender in connection with this Loan.

5. Property Insurance. Borrower shall keep the improvements now existing or hereafter erected on the Property insured against loss by fire, hazards included within the term "extended coverage," and any other hazards including, but not limited to, earthquakes and floods, for which Lender requires insurance. This insurance shall be maintained in the amounts (including deductible levels) and for the periods that Lender requires. What Lender requires pursuant to the preceding sentences can change during the term of the Loan. The insurance carrier providing the insurance shall be chosen by Borrower subject to Lender's right to disapprove Borrower's choice, which right shall not be exercised unreasonably. Lender may require Borrower to pay, in connection with this Loan, either: (a) a one-time charge for flood zone determination, certification and tracking services; or (b) a one-time charge for flood zone determination and certification services and subsequent charges each time remappings or similar changes occur which reasonably might affect such determination or certification. Borrower shall also be responsible for the payment of any fees imposed by the Federal Emergency Management Agency in connection with the review of any flood zone determination resulting from an objection by Borrower.

If Borrower fails to maintain any of the coverages described above, Lender may obtain insurance coverage, at Lender's option and Borrower's expense. Lender is under no obligation to purchase any particular type or amount of coverage. Therefore, such coverage shall cover Lender, but might or might not protect Borrower, Borrower's equity in the Property, or the contents of the Property, against any risk, hazard or liability and might provide greater or lesser coverage than was previously in effect. Borrower acknowledges that the cost of the insurance coverage so obtained might significantly exceed the cost of insurance that Borrower could have obtained. Any amounts disbursed by Lender under this Section 5 shall become additional debt of Borrower secured by this Security Instrument. These amounts shall bear interest at the Note rate from the date of disbursement and shall be payable, with such interest, upon notice from Lender to Borrower requesting payment.

All insurance policies required by Lender and renewals of such policies shall be subject to Lender's right to disapprove such policies, shall include a standard mortgage clause, and shall name Lender as mortgagee and/or as an additional loss payee and Borrower further agrees to generally assign rights to insurance proceeds to the holder of the Note up to the amount of the outstanding loan balance. Lender shall have the right to hold the policies and renewal certificates. If Lender requires, Borrower shall promptly give to Lender all receipts of paid premiums and renewal notices. If Borrower obtains any form of insurance coverage, not otherwise required by Lender, for damage to, or destruction of, the Property, such policy shall include a standard mortgage clause and shall name Lender as mortgagee and/or as an additional loss payee and Borrower further agrees to generally assign rights to insurance proceeds to the holder of the Note up to the amount of the outstanding loan balance.

In the event of loss, Borrower shall give prompt notice to the insurance carrier and Lender. Lender may make proof of loss if not made promptly by Borrower. Unless Lender and Borrower otherwise agree in writing, any insurance proceeds, whether or not the underlying insurance was required by Lender, shall be applied to restoration or repair of the Property, if the restoration or repair is economically feasible and Lender's security is not lessened. During such repair and restoration period, Lender shall have the right to hold such insurance proceeds until Lender has had an opportunity to inspect such Property to ensure the work has been completed to Lender's satisfaction, provided that such inspection shall be undertaken promptly. Lender may disburse proceeds for the repairs and restoration in a single payment or in a series of progress payments as the work is completed. Unless an agreement is made in writing or Applicable Law requires interest to be paid on such insurance proceeds, Lender shall not be required to pay Borrower any interest or earnings on such proceeds. Fees for public adjusters, or other third parties, retained by Borrower shall not be paid out of the insurance proceeds and shall be the sole obligation of Borrower. If the restoration or repair is not economically feasible or Lender's security would be lessened, the insurance proceeds shall be applied to the sums secured by this Security Instrument, whether or not then due, with the excess, if any, paid to Borrower. Such insurance proceeds shall be applied in the order provided for in Section 2.

If Borrower abandons the Property, Lender may file, negotiate and settle any available insurance claim and related matters. If Borrower does not respond within 30 days to a notice from Lender that the insurance carrier has offered to settle a claim, then Lender may negotiate and settle the claim. The 30-day period will begin when the notice is given. In either event, or if Lender acquires the Property under Section 22 or otherwise, Borrower hereby assigns to Lender (a) Borrower's rights to any insurance proceeds in an amount not to exceed the amounts unpaid under the Note or this Security Instrument, and (b) any other of Borrower's rights (other than the right to any refund of unearned premiums paid by Borrower) under all insurance policies covering the Property, insofar as such rights are applicable to the coverage of the Property. Lender may use the insurance proceeds either to repair or restore the Property or to pay amounts unpaid under the Note or this Security Instrument, whether or not then due.

6. Occupancy. Borrower shall occupy, establish, and use the Property as Borrower's principal residence within 60 days after the execution of this Security Instrument and shall continue to occupy the Property as Borrower's principal residence for at least one year after the date of occupancy, unless Lender otherwise agrees in writing, which consent shall not be unreasonably withheld, or unless extenuating circumstances exist which are beyond Borrower's control.

7. Preservation, Maintenance and Protection of the Property; Inspections. Borrower shall not destroy, damage or impair the Property, allow the Property to deteriorate or commit waste on the Property. Whether or not Borrower is residing in the Property, Borrower shall maintain the Property in order to prevent the Property from deteriorating or decreasing in value due to its condition. Unless it is determined pursuant to Section 5 that repair or restoration is not economically feasible, Borrower shall promptly repair the Property if damaged to avoid further deterioration or damage. If insurance or condemnation proceeds are paid in connection with damage to, or the taking of, the Property, Borrower shall be responsible for repairing or restoring the Property only if Lender has released proceeds for such purposes. Lender may disburse proceeds for the repairs and restoration in a single payment or in a series of progress payments as the work is completed. If the insurance or condemnation proceeds are not sufficient to repair or restore the Property, Borrower is not relieved of Borrower's obligation for the completion of such repair or restoration.

Lender or its agent may make reasonable entries upon and inspections of the Property. If it has reasonable cause, Lender may inspect the interior of the improvements on the Property. Lender shall give Borrower notice at the time of or prior to such an interior inspection specifying such reasonable cause.

8. Borrower's Loan Application. Borrower shall be in default if, during the Loan application process, Borrower or any persons or entities acting at the direction of Borrower or with Borrower's knowledge or consent gave materially false, misleading, or inaccurate information or statements to Lender (or failed to provide Lender with material information) in connection with the Loan. Material representations include, but are not limited to, representations concerning Borrower's occupancy of the Property as Borrower's principal residence.

9. Protection of Lender's Interest in the Property and Rights Under this Security Instrument. If (a) Borrower fails to perform the covenants and agreements contained in this Security Instrument, (b) there is a legal proceeding that might significantly affect Lender's interest in the Property and/or rights under this Security Instrument (such as a proceeding in bankruptcy, probate, for condemnation or forfeiture, for enforcement of a lien which may attain priority over this Security Instrument or to enforce laws or regulations), or (c) Borrower has abandoned the Property, then Lender may do and pay for whatever is reasonable or appropriate to protect Lender's interest in the Property and rights under this Security Instrument, including protecting and/or assessing the value of the Property, and securing and/or repairing the Property. Lender's actions can include, but are not limited to: (a) paying any sums secured by a lien which has priority over this Security Instrument; (b) appearing in court; and (c) paying reasonable attorneys' fees to protect its interest in the Property and/or rights under this Security Instrument, including its secured position in a bankruptcy proceeding. Securing the Property includes, but is not limited to, entering the Property to make repairs, change locks, replace or board up doors and windows, drain water from pipes, eliminate building or other code violations or dangerous conditions, and have utilities turned on or off. Although Lender may take action under this Section 9, Lender does not have to do so and is not under any duty or obligation to do so. It is agreed that Lender incurs no liability for not taking any or all actions authorized under this Section 9.

Any amounts disbursed by Lender under this Section 9 shall become additional debt of Borrower secured by this Security Instrument. These amounts shall bear interest at the Note rate from the date of disbursement and shall be payable, with such interest, upon notice from Lender to Borrower requesting payment.

If this Security Instrument is on a leasehold, Borrower shall comply with all the provisions of the lease. If Borrower acquires fee title to the Property, the leasehold and the fee title shall not merge unless Lender agrees to the merger in writing.

10. Mortgage Insurance. If Lender required Mortgage Insurance as a condition of making the Loan, Borrower shall pay the premiums required to maintain the Mortgage Insurance in effect. If, for any reason, the Mortgage Insurance coverage required by Lender ceases to be available from the mortgage insurer that previously provided such insurance and Borrower was required to make separately designated payments toward the premiums for Mortgage Insurance, Borrower shall pay the premiums required to obtain coverage substantially equivalent to the Mortgage Insurance previously in effect, at a cost substantially equivalent to the cost to Borrower of the Mortgage Insurance previously in effect, from an alternate mortgage insurer selected by Lender. If substantially equivalent Mortgage Insurance coverage is not available, Borrower shall continue to pay to Lender the amount of the separately designated payments that were due when the insurance coverage ceased to be in effect. Lender will accept, use and retain these payments as a non-refundable loss reserve in lieu of Mortgage Insurance. Such loss reserve shall be non-refundable, notwithstanding the fact that the Loan is ultimately paid in full, and Lender shall not be required to pay Borrower any interest or earnings on such loss reserve. Lender can no longer require loss reserve payments if Mortgage Insurance coverage (in the amount and for the period that Lender requires) provided by an insurer selected by Lender again becomes available, is obtained, and Lender requires separately designated payments toward the premiums for Mortgage Insurance. If Lender required Mortgage Insurance as a condition of making the Loan and Borrower was required to make separately designated payments toward the premiums for Mortgage Insurance, Borrower shall pay the premiums required to maintain Mortgage Insurance in effect, or to provide a non-refundable loss reserve, until Lender's requirement for Mortgage Insurance ends in accordance with any written agreement between Borrower and Lender providing for such termination or until termination is required by Applicable Law. Nothing in this Section 10 affects Borrower's obligation to pay interest at the rate provided in the Note.

Mortgage Insurance reimburses Lender (or any entity that purchases the Note) for certain losses it may incur if Borrower does not repay the Loan as agreed. Borrower is not a party to the Mortgage Insurance.

Mortgage insurers evaluate their total risk on all such insurance in force from time to time, and may enter into agreements with other parties that share or modify their risk, or reduce losses. These agreements are on terms and conditions that are satisfactory to the mortgage insurer and the other party (or parties) to these agreements. These agreements may require the mortgage insurer to make payments using any source of funds that the mortgage insurer may have available (which may include funds obtained from Mortgage Insurance premiums).

As a result of these agreements, Lender, any purchaser of the Note, another insurer, any reinsurer, any other entity, or any affiliate of any of the foregoing, may receive (directly or indirectly) amounts that derive from (or might be characterized as) a portion of Borrower's payments for Mortgage Insurance, in exchange for sharing or modifying the mortgage insurer's risk, or reducing losses. If such agreement provides that an affiliate of Lender takes a share of the insurer's risk in exchange for a share of the premiums paid to the insurer, the arrangement is often termed "captive reinsurance." Further:

(a) **Any such agreements will not affect the amounts that Borrower has agreed to pay for Mortgage Insurance, or any other terms of the Loan. Such agreements will not increase the amount Borrower will owe for Mortgage Insurance, and they will not entitle Borrower to any refund.**

(b) **Any such agreements will not affect the rights Borrower has - if any - with respect to the Mortgage Insurance under the Homeowners Protection Act of 1998 or any other law. These rights may include the right to receive certain disclosures, to request and obtain cancellation of the Mortgage Insurance, to have the Mortgage Insurance terminated automatically, and/or to receive a refund of any Mortgage Insurance premiums that were unearned at the time of such cancellation or termination.**

11. Assignment of Miscellaneous Proceeds; Forfeiture. All Miscellaneous Proceeds are hereby assigned to and shall be paid to Lender.

If the Property is damaged, such Miscellaneous Proceeds shall be applied to restoration or repair of the Property, if the restoration or repair is economically feasible and Lender's security is not lessened. During such repair and restoration period, Lender shall have the right to hold such Miscellaneous Proceeds until Lender has had an opportunity to inspect such Property to ensure the work has been completed to Lender's satisfaction, provided that such inspection shall be undertaken promptly. Lender may pay for the repairs and restoration in a single disbursement or in a series of progress payments as the work is completed. Unless an agreement is made in writing or Applicable Law requires interest to be paid on such Miscellaneous Proceeds, Lender shall not be required to pay Borrower any interest or earnings on such Miscellaneous Proceeds. If the restoration or repair is not economically feasible or Lender's security would be lessened, the Miscellaneous Proceeds shall be applied to the sums secured by this Security Instrument, whether or not then due, with the excess, if any, paid to Borrower. Such Miscellaneous Proceeds shall be applied in the order provided for in Section 2.

In the event of a total taking, destruction, or loss in value of the Property, the Miscellaneous Proceeds shall be applied to the sums secured by this Security Instrument, whether or not then due, with the excess, if any, paid to Borrower.

In the event of a partial taking, destruction, or loss in value of the Property in which the fair market value of the Property immediately before the partial taking, destruction, or loss in value is equal to or greater than the amount of the sums secured by this Security Instrument immediately before the partial taking, destruction, or loss in value, unless Borrower and Lender otherwise agree in writing, the sums secured by this Security Instrument shall be reduced by the amount of the Miscellaneous Proceeds multiplied by the following fraction: (a) the total amount of the sums secured immediately before the partial taking, destruction, or loss in value divided by (b) the fair market value of the Property immediately before the partial taking, destruction, or loss in value. Any balance shall be paid to Borrower.

In the event of a partial taking, destruction, or loss in value of the Property in which the fair market value of the Property immediately before the partial taking, destruction, or loss in value is less than the amount of the sums secured immediately before the partial taking, destruction, or loss in value, unless Borrower and Lender otherwise agree in writing, the Miscellaneous Proceeds shall be applied to the sums secured by this Security Instrument whether or not the sums are then due.

If the Property is abandoned by Borrower, or if, after notice by Lender to Borrower that the Opposing Party (as defined in the next sentence) offers to make an award to settle a claim for damages, Borrower fails to respond to Lender within 30 days after the date the notice is given, Lender is authorized to collect and apply the Miscellaneous Proceeds either to restoration or repair of the Property or to the sums secured by this Security Instrument, whether or not then due. "Opposing Party" means the third party that owes Borrower Miscellaneous Proceeds or the party against whom Borrower has a right of action in regard to Miscellaneous Proceeds.

Borrower shall be in default if any action or proceeding, whether civil or criminal, is begun that, in Lender's judgment, could result in forfeiture of the Property or other material impairment of Lender's interest in the Property or rights under this Security Instrument. Borrower can cure such a default and, if acceleration has occurred, reinstate as provided in Section 19, by causing the action or proceeding to be dismissed with a ruling that, in Lender's judgment, precludes forfeiture of the Property or other material impairment of Lender's interest in the Property or rights under this Security Instrument. The proceeds of any award or claim for damages that are attributable to the impairment of Lender's interest in the Property are hereby assigned and shall be paid to Lender.

All Miscellaneous Proceeds that are not applied to restoration or repair of the Property shall be applied in the order provided for in Section 2.

12. Borrower Not Released; Forbearance By Lender Not a Waiver. Extension of the time for payment or modification of amortization of the sums secured by this Security Instrument granted by Lender to Borrower or any Successor in Interest of Borrower shall not operate to release the liability of Borrower or any Successors in Interest of Borrower. Lender shall not be required to commence proceedings against any Successor in Interest of Borrower or to refuse to extend time for payment or otherwise modify amortization of the sums secured by this Security Instrument by reason of any demand made by the original Borrower or any Successors in Interest of Borrower. Any forbearance by Lender in exercising any right or remedy including, without limitation, Lender's acceptance of payments from third persons, entities or Successors in Interest of Borrower or in amounts less than the amount then due, shall not be a waiver of or preclude the exercise of any right or remedy.

13. Joint and Several Liability; Co-signers; Successors and Assigns Bound. Borrower covenants and agrees that Borrower's obligations and liability shall be joint and several. However, any Borrower who co-signs this Security Instrument but does not execute the Note (a "co-signer"): (a) is co-signing this Security Instrument only to mortgage, grant and convey the co-signer's interest in the Property under the terms of this Security Instrument; (b) is not personally obligated to pay the sums secured by this Security Instrument; and (c) agrees that Lender and any other Borrower can agree to extend, modify, forbear or make any accommodations with regard to the terms of this Security Instrument or the Note without the co-signer's consent.

Subject to the provisions of Section 18, any Successor in Interest of Borrower who assumes Borrower's obligations under this Security Instrument in writing, and is approved by Lender, shall obtain all of Borrower's rights and benefits under this Security Instrument. Borrower shall not be released from Borrower's obligations and liability under this Security Instrument unless Lender agrees to such release in writing. The covenants and agreements of this Security Instrument shall bind (except as provided in Section 20) and benefit the successors and assigns of Lender.

14. Loan Charges. Lender may charge Borrower fees for services performed in connection with Borrower's default, for the purpose of protecting Lender's interest in the Property and rights under this Security Instrument, including, but not limited to, attorneys' fees, property inspection and valuation fees. In regard to any other fees, the absence of express authority in this Security Instrument to charge a specific fee to Borrower shall not be construed as a prohibition on the charging of such fee. Lender may not charge fees that are expressly prohibited by this Security Instrument or by Applicable Law.

If the Loan is subject to a law which sets maximum loan charges, and that law is finally interpreted so that the interest or other loan charges collected or to be collected in connection with the Loan exceed the permitted limits, then: (a) any such loan charge shall be reduced by the amount necessary to reduce the charge to the permitted limit; and (b) any sums already collected from Borrower which exceeded permitted limits will be refunded to Borrower. Lender may choose to make this refund by reducing the principal owed under the Note or by making a direct payment to Borrower. If a refund reduces principal, the reduction will be treated as a partial prepayment without any prepayment charge (whether or not a prepayment charge is provided for under the Note). Borrower's acceptance of any such refund made by direct payment to Borrower will constitute a waiver of any right of action Borrower might have arising out of such overcharge.

15. **Notices.** All notices given by Borrower or Lender in connection with this Security Instrument must be in writing. Any notice to Borrower in connection with this Security Instrument shall be deemed to have been given to Borrower when mailed by first class mail or when actually delivered to Borrower's notice address if sent by other means. Notice to any one Borrower shall constitute notice to all Borrowers unless Applicable Law expressly requires otherwise. The notice address shall be the Property Address unless Borrower has designated a substitute notice address by notice to Lender. Borrower shall promptly notify Lender of Borrower's change of address. If Lender specifies a procedure for reporting Borrower's change of address, then Borrower shall only report a change of address through that specified procedure. There may be only one designated notice address under this Security Instrument at any one time. Any notice to Lender shall be given by delivering it or by mailing it by first class mail to Lender's address stated herein unless Lender has designated another address by notice to Borrower. Any notice in connection with this Security Instrument shall not be deemed to have been given to Lender until actually received by Lender. If any notice required by this Security Instrument is also required under Applicable Law, the Applicable Law requirement will satisfy the corresponding requirement under this Security Instrument.

16. **Governing Law; Severability; Rules of Construction.** This Security Instrument shall be governed by federal law and the law of the jurisdiction in which the Property is located. All rights and obligations contained in this Security Instrument are subject to any requirements and limitations of Applicable Law. Applicable Law might explicitly or implicitly allow the parties to agree by contract or it might be silent, but such silence shall not be construed as a prohibition against agreement by contract. In the event that any provision or clause of this Security Instrument or the Note conflicts with Applicable Law, such conflict shall not affect other provisions of this Security Instrument or the Note which can be given effect without the conflicting provision.

As used in this Security Instrument: (a) words of the masculine gender shall mean and include corresponding neuter words or words of the feminine gender; (b) words in the singular shall mean and include the plural and vice versa; and (c) the word "may" gives sole discretion without any obligation to take any action.

17. **Borrower's Copy.** Borrower shall be given one copy of the Note and of this Security Instrument.

18. **Transfer of the Property or a Beneficial Interest in Borrower.** As used in this Section 18, "Interest in the Property" means any legal or beneficial interest in the Property, including, but not limited to, those beneficial interests transferred in a bond for deed, contract for deed, installment sales contract or escrow agreement, the intent of which is the transfer of title by Borrower at a future date to a purchaser.

If all or any part of the Property or any Interest in the Property is sold or transferred (or if Borrower is not a natural person and a beneficial interest in Borrower is sold or transferred) without Lender's prior written consent, Lender may require immediate payment in full of all sums secured by this Security Instrument. However, this option shall not be exercised by Lender if such exercise is prohibited by Applicable Law.

If Lender exercises this option, Lender shall give Borrower notice of acceleration. The notice shall provide a period of not less than 30 days from the date the notice is given in accordance with Section 15 within which Borrower must pay all sums secured by this Security Instrument. If Borrower fails to pay these sums prior to the expiration of this period, Lender may invoke any remedies permitted by this Security Instrument without further notice or demand on Borrower.

19. Borrower's Right to Reinstate After Acceleration. If Borrower meets certain conditions, Borrower shall have the right to have enforcement of this Security Instrument discontinued at any time prior to the earliest of: (a) five days before sale of the Property pursuant to any power of sale contained in this Security Instrument; (b) such other period as Applicable Law might specify for the termination of Borrower's right to reinstate; or (c) entry of a judgment enforcing this Security Instrument. Those conditions are that Borrower: (a) pays Lender all sums which then would be due under this Security Instrument and the Note as if no acceleration had occurred; (b) cures any default of any other covenants or agreements; (c) pays all expenses incurred in enforcing this Security Instrument, including, but not limited to, reasonable attorneys' fees, property inspection and valuation fees, and other fees incurred for the purpose of protecting Lender's interest in the Property and rights under this Security Instrument; and (d) takes such action as Lender may reasonably require to assure that Lender's interest in the Property and rights under this Security Instrument, and Borrower's obligation to pay the sums secured by this Security Instrument, shall continue unchanged. Lender may require that Borrower pay such reinstatement sums and expenses in one or more of the following forms, as selected by Lender: (a) cash; (b) money order; (c) certified check, bank check, treasurer's check or cashier's check, provided any such check is drawn upon an institution whose deposits are insured by a federal agency, instrumentality or entity; or (d) Electronic Funds Transfer. Upon reinstatement by Borrower, this Security Instrument and obligations secured hereby shall remain fully effective as if no acceleration had occurred. However, this right to reinstate shall not apply in the case of acceleration under Section 18.

20. Sale of Note; Change of Loan Servicer; Notice of Grievance. The Note or a partial interest in the Note (together with this Security Instrument) can be sold one or more times without prior notice to Borrower. A sale might result in a change in the entity (known as the "Loan Servicer") that collects Periodic Payments due under the Note and this Security Instrument and performs other mortgage loan servicing obligations under the Note, this Security Instrument, and Applicable Law. There also might be one or more changes of the Loan Servicer unrelated to a sale of the Note. If there is a change of the Loan Servicer, Borrower will be given written notice of the change which will state the name and address of the new Loan Servicer, the address to which payments should be made and any other information RESPA requires in connection with a notice of transfer of servicing. If the Note is sold and thereafter the Loan is serviced by a Loan Servicer other than the purchaser of the Note, the mortgage loan servicing obligations to Borrower will remain with the Loan Servicer or be transferred to a successor Loan Servicer and are not assumed by the Note purchaser unless otherwise provided by the Note purchaser.

Neither Borrower nor Lender may commence, join, or be joined to any judicial action (as either an individual litigant or the member of a class) that arises from the other party's actions pursuant to this Security Instrument or that alleges that the other party has breached any provision of, or any duty owed by reason of, this Security Instrument, until such Borrower or Lender has notified the other party (with such notice given in compliance with the requirements of Section 15) of such alleged breach and afforded the other party hereto a reasonable period after the giving of such notice to take corrective action. If Applicable Law provides a time period which must elapse before certain action can be taken, that time period will be deemed to be reasonable for purposes of this paragraph. The notice of acceleration and opportunity to cure given to Borrower pursuant to Section 22 and the notice of acceleration given to Borrower pursuant to Section 18 shall be deemed to satisfy the notice and opportunity to take corrective action provisions of this Section 20.

21. Hazardous Substances. As used in this Section 21: (a) "Hazardous Substances" are those substances defined as toxic or hazardous substances, pollutants, or wastes by Environmental Law and the following substances: gasoline, kerosene, other flammable or toxic petroleum products, toxic pesticides and herbicides, volatile solvents, materials containing asbestos or formaldehyde, and radioactive materials; (b) "Environmental Law" means federal laws and laws of the jurisdiction where the Property is located that relate to health, safety or environmental protection; (c) "Environmental Cleanup" includes any response action, remedial action, or removal action, as defined in Environmental Law; and (d) an "Environmental Condition" means a condition that can cause, contribute to, or otherwise trigger an Environmental Cleanup.

Borrower shall not cause or permit the presence, use, disposal, storage, or release of any Hazardous Substances, or threaten to release any Hazardous Substances, on or in the Property. Borrower shall not do, nor allow anyone else to do, anything affecting the Property (a) that is in violation of any Environmental Law, (b) which creates an Environmental Condition, or (c) which, due to the presence, use, or release of a Hazardous Substance, creates a condition that adversely affects the value of the Property. The preceding two sentences shall not apply to the presence, use, or storage on the Property of small quantities of Hazardous Substances that are generally recognized to be appropriate to normal residential uses and to maintenance of the Property (including, but not limited to, hazardous substances in consumer products).

Borrower shall promptly give Lender written notice of (a) any investigation, claim, demand, lawsuit or other action by any governmental or regulatory agency or private party involving the Property and any Hazardous Substance or Environmental Law of which Borrower has actual knowledge, (b) any Environmental Condition, including but not limited to, any spilling, leaking, discharge, release or threat of release of any Hazardous Substance, and (c) any condition caused by the presence, use or release of a Hazardous Substance which adversely affects the value of the Property. If Borrower learns, or is notified by any governmental or regulatory authority, or any private party, that any removal or other remediation of any Hazardous Substance affecting the Property is necessary, Borrower shall promptly take all necessary remedial actions in accordance with Environmental Law. Nothing herein shall create any obligation on Lender for an Environmental Cleanup.

NON-UNIFORM COVENANTS. Borrower and Lender further covenant and agree as follows:

22. Acceleration; Remedies. Lender shall give notice to Borrower prior to acceleration following Borrower's breach of any covenant or agreement in this Security Instrument (but not prior to acceleration under Section 18 unless Applicable Law provides otherwise). The notice shall specify: (a) the default; (b) the action required to cure the default; (c) a date, not less than 30 days from the date the notice is given to Borrower, by which the default must be cured; and (d) that failure to cure the default on or before the date specified in the notice may result in acceleration of the sums secured by this Security Instrument and sale of the Property. The notice shall further inform Borrower of the right to reinstate after acceleration and the right to bring a court action to assert the non-existence of a default or any other defense of Borrower to acceleration and sale. If the default is not cured on or before the date specified in the notice, Lender at its option may require immediate payment in full of all sums secured by this Security Instrument without further demand and may invoke the power of sale and any other remedies permitted by Applicable Law. Lender shall be entitled to collect all expenses incurred in pursuing the remedies provided in this Section 22, including, but not limited to, reasonable attorneys' fees and costs of title evidence.

If Lender invokes the power of sale, Lender shall execute or cause Trustee to execute a written notice of the occurrence of an event of default and of Lender's election to cause the Property to be sold. Trustee shall cause this notice to be recorded in each county in which any part of the Property is located. Lender or Trustee shall mail copies of the notice as prescribed by Applicable Law to Borrower and to the other persons prescribed by Applicable Law. Trustee shall give public notice of sale to the persons and in the manner prescribed by Applicable Law. After the time required by Applicable Law, Trustee, without demand on Borrower, shall sell the Property at public auction to the highest bidder at the time and place and under the terms designated in the notice of sale in one or more parcels and in any order Trustee determines. Trustee may postpone sale of all or any parcel of the Property by public announcement at the time and place of any previously scheduled sale. Lender or its designee may purchase the Property at any sale.

Trustee shall deliver to the purchaser Trustee's deed conveying the Property without any covenant or warranty, expressed or implied. The recitals in the Trustee's deed shall be prima facie evidence of the truth of the statements made therein. Trustee shall apply the proceeds of the sale in the following order: (a) to all expenses of the sale, including, but not limited to, reasonable Trustee's and attorneys' fees; (b) to all sums secured by this Security Instrument; and (c) any excess to the person or persons legally entitled to it.

23. Reconveyance. Upon payment of all sums secured by this Security Instrument, Lender shall request Trustee to reconvey the Property and shall surrender this Security Instrument and all notes evidencing debt secured by this Security Instrument to Trustee. Trustee shall reconvey the Property without warranty to the person or persons legally entitled to it. Lender may charge such person or persons a reasonable fee for reconveying the Property, but only if the fee is paid to a third party (such as the Trustee) for services rendered and the charging of the fee is permitted under Applicable Law. If the fee charged does not exceed the fee set by Applicable Law, the fee is conclusively presumed to be reasonable.

24. Substitute Trustee. Lender, at its option, may from time to time appoint a successor trustee to any Trustee appointed hereunder by an instrument executed and acknowledged by Lender and recorded in the office of the Recorder of the county in which the Property is located. The instrument shall contain the name of the original Lender, Trustee and Borrower, the book and page where this Security Instrument is recorded and the name and address of the successor trustee. Without conveyance of the Property, the successor trustee shall succeed to all the title, powers and duties conferred upon the Trustee herein and by Applicable Law. This procedure for substitution of trustee shall govern to the exclusion of all other provisions for substitution.

25. Statement of Obligation Fee. Lender may collect a fee not to exceed the maximum amount permitted by Applicable Law for furnishing the statement of obligation as provided by Section 2943 of the Civil Code of California.

BY SIGNING BELOW, Borrower accepts and agrees to the terms and covenants contained in this Security Instrument and in any Rider executed by Borrower and recorded with it.

Witnesses:

_____   _____ (Seal)
                                                                  - Borrower

_____   _____ (Seal)
                                                                  - Borrower

**SAMPLE MORTGAGE DOCUMENT
FOR LENDERS IN THE STATE OF FLORIDA AND IS NOT INTENDED FOR USE.**

This instrument was prepared by: **First name Last name, Street Address, City, State, Zip**

THIS MORTGAGE (herein "Instrument"), is made _____

between the Mortgagor/Grantor,__……. ....

(herein "Borrower"),and the Mortgagee, **lender name goes here**

whose address is ……………..**lender address goes here**………………(herein Lender").

Whereas, Borrower is indebted to Lender in the principal sum of …………. **thousand dollars ($…..,000.00)**

Dollars, which indebtedness is evidenced by Borrower's note of even date (herein "Note"), providing for monthly installments of principal and interest, with the full debt, if not paid earlier, due and payable on _**Month Day, Year**

TO SECURE TO LENDER (a) the repayment of the indebtedness evidenced by the Note, with interest thereon, and all renewals, extensions and modifications thereof; (b) the repayment of any future advances, with interest thereon, made by Lender to Borrower pursuant to paragraph 22 hereof (herein "Future Advances"). hereof; (c) the payment of all other sums, with interest thereon, advanced in accordance herewith to protect the security of this Instrument; and (d) the performance of the covenants and agreements of Borrower herein contained, Borrower does hereby mortgage grant, convey and assign to Lender the following described property located in

……………. County, Florida:

legal description goes here

Which has the address of__………………………………….., "Property Address"

TOGETHER with all buildings, improvements, hereditaments, appurtenances and tenements now or hereafter erected on the property, and all heretofore or hereafter vacated alleys and streets abutting the property, and all easements, rights, appurtenances, rents, royalties, mineral, oil and gas rights and profits thereof herein referred to as the "Property".

Borrower covenants that Borrower is lawfully seized of the estate hereby conveyed and has the right to mortgage, grant, convey and assign the Property that the property is unencumbered and that Borrower will warrant and defend generally the title to the Property against all claims and demands, subject to any easements and restrictions listed in a schedule of exceptions to coverage in any title insurance policy insuring Lender's interest in the Property.

Borrower and Lender covenant and agree as follows:

1. PAYMENT OF PRINCIPAL AND INTEREST. Borrower shall promptly pay when due the principal of and interest on the indebtedness evidenced by the Note, any prepayment and late charges provided in the Note and all other sums secured by this Instrument. In the event the agreed payment is less than the interest due then the excess unpaid interest shall be added to the principal.

2. FUNDS FOR TAXES, INSURANCE AND OTHER CHARGES. Borrower shall pay to Lender on the day monthly installments of principal or interest are payable under the Note, until the Note is paid in full, a sum (herein "Funds") equal to one-twelfth of (a) the yearly water and sewer rates and taxes and assessments which may be levied on the Property, (b) the yearly ground rents, if any, (c) the yearly premium installments for fire and other hazard insurance, rent loss insurance and such other insurance covering the Property as Lender may require pursuant to paragraph 5 hereof, all as reasonably estimated initially and from time to time by Lender on the basis of assessments and bills and reasonable estimates thereof. Borrower shall also pay to Lender an amount of $_...**00**_ per month to establish a fund to pay for major repair and/or maintenance items. Major items meaning those costing more than $500.

The Funds shall be held in an institution(s) the deposits or accounts of which are insured or guaranteed by a Federal or state agency. Lender shall apply the Funds to pay said rates, rents, taxes, assessments, insurance premiums and major maintenance/repair items so long as Borrower is not in breach of any covenant or agreement of Borrower in this Instrument. Lender shall not be required to pay Borrower any interest on the Funds. Lender shall give to Borrower, without charge, an annual accounting of the Funds in Lender's normal format showing credits and debits to the Funds and the purpose for which each debit to the Funds was made. The Funds are pledged as additional security for the sums secured by this Instrument. If at any time the amount of the Funds held by Lender shall be less than the amount deemed necessary by Lender to pay water and sewer rates, taxes, assessments and insurance premiums as they fall due, and for major repair/maintenance items Borrower shall pay to Lender any amount necessary to make up the deficiency within 30 days after notice from Lender to Borrower requesting payment thereof.

Upon Borrower's breach of any covenant or agreement of Borrower in this Instrument, Lender may apply, in any amount and in any order as Lender shall determine in Lender's sole discretion, any Funds held by Lender at the time of application (i) to pay rates, taxes, assessments and insurance premiums which are now or will hereafter become due, or (ii) as a credit against sums secured by this Instrument.

Upon payment in full of all sums secured by this Instrument, Lender shall promptly refund to Borrower any Funds held by Lender.

3. APPLICATION OF PAYMENTS. Unless applicable law provides otherwise, all payments received by Lender from Borrower under the Note or this instrument shall be applied by Lender in the following order of priority: (i)amounts payable to Lender by Borrower under paragraph 2 hereof ;(ii) interest payable on the Note; (iii) principal of the Note; (iv) interest payable on advances made pursuant to paragraph 8 hereof; (v) principal of advances made pursuant to paragraph 8 hereof; (vi) interest payable on any Future Advance, provided that if more than one Future Advance is outstanding, Lender may apply payments received among the amounts of interest payable on the Future Advances in such order as Lender, in Lender's sole discretion, may determine; (vii) principal of any Future Advance, provided that if more than one Future Advance is outstanding, Lender may apply payments received among the principal balances of the Future Advances in such order as Lender, in Lender's sole discretion, may determine; and (viii) any other sums secured by this Instrument in such order as Lender, at Lender's option, may determine; provided, however, that Lender may, at Lender's option, apply any sums payable pursuant to paragraph 8 hereof prior to interest on and principal of the Note, but such application shall not otherwise affect the order of priority of application specified in this paragraph 3.

4. CHARGES;LIENS. Borrower shall pay, when due, the claims of all persons supplying labor or materials to or in connection with the Property. Without Lender's prior written permission, Borrower shall not allow any lien inferior to this Instrument to be perfected against the Property.

5. HAZARD INSURANCE. Borrower shall keep the improvements now existing or hereafter erected on the Property insured by carriers at all times satisfactory to Lender against loss by fire, hazards included within the term "extended coverage", rent loss and such other hazards, casualties, liabilities and contingencies as Lender shall require and in such amounts and for such periods as Lender shall require. All premiums on insurance policies shall be paid in the manner provided under paragraph 2 hereof. All insurance policies and renewals thereof shall be in a form acceptable to Lender and shall include a standard mortgage clause in favor of and in form acceptable to Lender. Lender shall have the right to hold the policies, and Borrower shall promptly furnish to Lender all renewal notices and all receipts of paid premiums. At least thirty days prior to the expiration date of a policy, Borrower shall deliver to Lender a renewal policy in form satisfactory to Lender. In the event of loss, Borrower shall give immediate written notice to the insurance carrier and to Lender. Borrower hereby authorizes and empowers Lender as attorney-in-fact for Borrower to make proof of loss, to adjust and compromise any claim under insurance policies, to appear in and prosecute any action arising from such insurance policies, to collect and receive insurance proceeds, and to deduct therefrom Lender's expenses incurred in the collection of such proceeds; provided however, that nothing contained in this paragraph 5 shall require Lender to incur any expense or take any action hereunder. Borrower further authorizes Lender to apply the balance of such proceeds to the payment of the sums secured by this Instrument, whether or not then due, in the order of application set forth in paragraph 3 hereof accounting to the mortgagor for any surplus. In the event the mortgagor does not renew the insurance policy then mortgagee may obtain loss payee insurance coverage only, which cost shall be payable by the mortgagor. Failure to reimburse the mortgagee for the cost of this policy within 30 calendar days after being mailed a bill for it shall constitute default under the mortgage.

If the insurance proceeds are applied to the payment of the sums secured by this Instrument, any such application of proceeds to principal shall not extend or postpone the due dates of the monthly installments referred to in paragraphs 1 and 2 hereof or change the amounts of such installments. If the Property is sold pursuant to Paragraph 19 hereof or if Lender acquires title to the property, Lender shall have all of the right, title and interest of Borrower in and to such insurance policies and unearned premiums thereon and to the proceeds resulting from any damage to the Property prior to such sale and acquisition.

6. PRESERVATION AND MAINTENANCE OF PROPERTY Borrower (a) shall not commit waste or permit impairment or deterioration of the Property, (b) shall not abandon the Property, (c) shall restore or repair promptly and in a good and workmanlike manner all or any part of the Property to the equivalent of its original condition, or such other condition as Lender may approve in writing, in the event of any damage, injury or loss thereto, whether or not insurance proceeds are available to cover in whole or in part the costs of such restoration or repair, (d) shall keep the Property, including improvements, fixtures, equipment, machinery and appliances thereon in good repair and shall replace fixtures, equipment, machinery and appliances on the Property when necessary to keep such items in good repair, (e) shall comply with all laws, ordinances, regulations and requirements of any governmental body applicable to the Property, and (f) shall give notice in writing to Lender of and, unless otherwise directed in writing by Lender, appear in and defend any action or proceeding purporting to affect the Property, the security of this Instrument or the rights or powers of Lender.

7. USE OF PROPERTY. Property may be used only for purposes permitted by law.

8. PROTECTION OF LENDER'S SECURITY. If Borrower fails to perform the covenants and agreements contained in this instrument, or if any action or proceeding is commenced which affects the Property or title thereto or the interest of Lender therein, including, but not limited to, eminent domain, insolvency, code enforcement, or arrangements or proceedings involving a bankrupt or decedent, then Lender at Lender's option may make such appearances, disburse such sums and take such action as Lender deems necessary, in its sole discretion to protect Lender's interest, including, but not limited to, (i) disbursement of attorney's fees, (ii) entry upon the Property to make repairs, (iii) procurement of satisfactory insurance as provided in paragraph 5 hereof and may also (iv) declare all of the sums secured by this Instrument to be immediately due and payable without prior notice to Borrower, and Lender may invoke any remedies permitted by paragraph 19 of this Instrument.

Any amounts disbursed by Lender pursuant to this paragraph 8, with interest thereon at the rate stated in the Note, shall become additional indebtedness of Borrower secured by this Instrument.

9. INSPECTION. Lender may make or cause to be made reasonable entries upon and inspections of the Property.

10. CONDEMNATION. Borrower shall promptly notify Lender of any action or proceeding relating to any condemnation or other taking, whether direct or indirect, of the Property, or part thereof, and Borrower shall appear in and prosecute any such action or proceeding unless otherwise directed by Lender in writing. Borrower authorizes Lender, at Lender's option, as attorney-in-fact for Borrower, to commence, appear in and prosecute, in Lender's or Borrower's name, any action or proceeding relating to any condemnation or other taking of the Property, whether direct or indirect, and to settle or compromise any claim in connection with such condemnation or other taking. The proceeds of any award, payment or claim for damages, direct or consequential, in connection with any condemnation or other taking, whether direct or indirect, of the Property, or part thereof, or for conveyances in lieu of condemnation, are hereby assigned to and shall be paid to Lender.

Borrower authorizes Lender to apply such awards, payments, proceeds or damages, after the deduction of Lender's expenses incurred in the collection of such amounts, to payment of the sums secured by this Instrument, whether or not then due, in the order of application set forth in paragraph 3 hereof, with the balance, if any, to Borrower. Unless Borrower and Lender otherwise agree in writing, any application of proceeds to principal shall not extend or postpone the due date of the monthly installments referred to in paragraphs 1 and 2 hereof or change the amount of such installments. Borrower agrees to execute such further evidence of assignment of any awards, proceeds, damages or claims arising in connection with such condemnation or taking as lender may require.

11. BORROWER AND LIEN NOT RELEASED. From time to time, Lender may, at Lender's option, without giving notice to or obtaining the consent of Borrower, Borrower's successors or assigns or of any junior lienholder or guarantors, without liability on Lender's part and notwithstanding Borrower's breach of any covenant or agreement of Borrower in this Instrument, extend the time for payment of said indebtedness or any part thereof, reduce the payments thereon, release anyone liable on any of said indebtedness, accept a renewal note or notes therefor, modify the terms and time of payment of said indebtedness, release from the lien of this Instrument any part of the Property, take or release other or additional security, reconvey any part of the Property, consent to any map or plan of the Property, consent to the granting of any easement, join in any extension or subordination agreement, and agree in writing with Borrower to modify the rate of interest or period of amortization of the Note or change the amount of the monthly installments payable thereunder. Any actions taken by Lender pursuant to the terms of this paragraph 11 shall not affect the obligation of Borrower or Borrower's successors or assigns to

pay the sums secured by this Instrument and to observe the covenants of Borrower contained herein, shall not affect the guaranty of any person, corporation, partnership or other entity for payment of the indebtedness secured hereby, and shall not affect the lien or priority of lien hereof on the Property. Borrower shall pay Lender a reasonable service charge, together with such title insurance premiums and attorney's fees as may be incurred at Lender's option, for any such action if taken at Borrower's request.

12. FORBEARANCE BY LENDER NOT A WAIVER. Any forbearance by Lender in exercising any right or remedy hereunder, or otherwise afforded by applicable law, shall not be a waiver of or preclude the exercise of any right or remedy. The procurement of insurance or the payment of taxes or other liens or charges by Lender shall not be a waiver of Lender's right to accelerate the maturity of the indebtedness secured by this Instrument.

13. REMEDIES CUMULATIVE. Each remedy provided in this instrument is distinct and cumulative to all other rights or remedies under this Instrument, or afforded by law or equity and may be exercised concurrently, independently, or successively, in any order whatsoever.

14. ACCELERATION IN CASE OF BORROWER'S INSOLVENCY. If Borrower shall voluntarily file a petition under the Federal Bankruptcy Act, as such Act may from time to time be amended, or under any similar or successor Federal statue relating to bankruptcy, insolvency, arrangements or reorganizations, or under any state bankruptcy or insolvency act, or file an answer in an involuntary proceeding admitting insolvency or inability to pay debts, or if Borrower shall fail to obtain a vacation or stay of involuntary proceedings brought for the reorganization, dissolution or liquidation of Borrower, or if Borrower shall be adjudged a bankrupt, or if a trustee or receiver shall be appointed for Borrower or Borrower's property, or if the Property shall become subject to the jurisdiction of a Federal bankruptcy court or similar state court, or if Borrower shall make an assignment for the benefit of Borrower's creditors, or if there is an attachment, execution or other judicial seizure of any portion of Borrower's assets and such seizure is not discharged within ten days, then Lender may, at Lender's option, declare all of the sums secured by this Instrument to be immediately due and payable without prior notice to Borrower, and Lender may invoke any remedies permitted by paragraph 19 of this Instrument. Any attorney's fees and other expenses incurred by Lender in connection with Borrower's bankruptcy or any of the other aforesaid events shall be additional indebtedness of Borrower secured by this Instrument pursuant to paragraph 8 hereof.

15. TRANSFERS OF THE PROPERTY OR BENEFICIAL INTERESTS IN BORROWER; ASSUMPTION. On sale or transfer of (i) all or any part of the Property, or any interest therein, or (ii) beneficial interests in Borrower (if Borrower is not a natural person or persons but is a corporation, partnership, trust or other legal entity), Lender may, at Lender's option, declare all of the sums secured by this Instrument to be immediately due and payable, and Lender may invoke any remedies permitted by paragraph 19 of this Instrument.

16. NOTICE. Except for any notice required under applicable law to be given in another manner, (a) any notice to Borrower provided for in this Instrument or in the Note shall be given by mailing such notice by first class mail addressed to Borrower at Borrower's address stated below or at such other address as Borrower may designate by notice to Lender as provided herein, and (b) any notice to Lender shall be given by certified mail, return receipt requested, to Lender's address stated herein or to such other address as Lender may designate by notice to Borrower as provided herein. Any notice provided for in this Instrument or in the Note shall be deemed to have been given to Borrower or Lender when given in the manner designated herein.

17. SUCCESSORS AND ASSIGNS BOUND; JOINT AND SEVERAL LIABILITY; AGENTS; CAPTIONS. The covenants and agreements herein contained shall bind, and the rights hereunder shall inure to, the respective successors and assigns of Lender and Borrower, subject to the provisions of paragraph 15 hereof. All covenants and agreements of Borrower shall be joint and several. In exercising any rights here under or taking any actions provided for herein, Lender may act through its employees, agents or independent contractors as authorized by Lender. The captions and headings of the paragraphs of this Instrument are for convenience only and are not to be used to interpret or define the provisions hereof.

18. GOVERNING LAW; SEVERABILITY. This Instrument shall be governed by the law of the jurisdiction in which the Property is located. In the event that any provision of this Instrument or the Note conflicts with applicable law, such conflict shall not affect other provisions of this Instrument or the Note which can be given effect without the conflicting provisions, and to this end the provisions of this Instrument and the Note are declared to be severable.

19. ACCELERATION; REMEDIES. Upon Borrower's breach of any covenant or agreement of Borrower in this instrument, including, but not limited to, the covenants to pay when due any sums secured by this Instrument, Lender at Lender's option may declare all of the sums secured by this Instrument to be immediately due and payable without further demand and may

foreclose this Instrument by judicial proceeding and may invoke any other remedies permitted by applicable law or provided herein. Lender shall be entitled to collect all costs and expenses incurred in pursuing such remedies, including, but not limited to, attorney's fees, costs of documentary evidence, abstracts and title reports.

20. RELEASE. Upon payment of all sums secured by this Instrument, Lender shall release this Instrument. Borrower shall pay Lender's reasonable costs incurred in releasing this Instrument.

21. ATTORNEY'S FEES. As used in this instrument and in the Note, "attorney's fees" shall include attorney's fees, if any, which may be awarded by an appellate court.

22. RIDERS TO THIS INSTRUMENT. If one or more riders are executed by borrower and recorded together with this Instrument, the covenants and agreements of each such rider shall be incorporated into and shall amend and supplement the covenants and agreements of this instrument as if rider(s) were a part of this Instrument.

23. HAZARDOUS SUBSTANCES. Borrower shall not cause or permit the presence, use, disposal, storage or release of any Hazardous Substances on or in the Property. Borrower shall not do, or allow anyone else to do, anything affecting the Property that is in violation of any Environmental Law. The preceding two sentences shall not apply to the presence, use or storage on the Property of small quantity of Hazardous Substances that are generally recognized to be appropriate to normal residential uses and to maintenance of the Property.

Borrower shall immediately give Lender written notice of any investigation, claim, demand lawsuit or other action by any governmental or regulatory agency or private party involving the Property and any Hazardous Substance or Environmental Law of which Borrower has actual knowledge. If Borrower learns, or is notified by any govermental or regulatory authority, that any removal or other remediation of any Hazardous Substance affecting the Property is necessary, Borrower hall promptly take all necessary remedial actions in accordance with Environmental Law.

As used in this paragraph 23, "Hazardous Substances" are those substances defined as toxic or hazardous substances by Environmental Law and the following substances: gasoline, kerosene, other flammable or toxic petroleum products, toxic pesticides and herbicides, volatile solvents, materials containing asbestos or formaldehyde, and radioactive materials. As used in this paragraph 23, "Environmental Law" means federal laws and laws of the jurisdiction where the property is located that relate to health, safety and environmental protection.

In Witness Whereof, Borrower has executed this Instrument or has caused the same to be executed by its representatives thereunto duly authorized.

Signed, sealed and delivered in the presence of: _____

(Seal) -Borrower

_____

_____

(Seal) Borrower

_____

STATE OF FLORIDA

COUNTY OF_____ss:

I hereby certify that on this day, before me, an officer duly authorized in the state aforesaid and in the county aforesaid to take acknowledgements personally appeared

_____

to me known to be the person(s) described in who identified themself(ves) to be the persons described by means of _____ and who executed the foregoing instrument and acknowledged before me that _____executed the same for the purpose expressed.

Witness my hand and official seal in the county and state aforesaid this _____day of _____ 20___

(Seal)

_____

Notary Public

My Commission Expires_____

NOTE

FEBRUARY 28, 2011
[Date]

BETHESDA
[City]

MD
[State]

1234 MAIN STREET, BETHESDA, MD 20814
[Property Address]

C. BORROWER'S PROMISE TO PAY

In return for a loan that I have received, I promise to pay U.S. **$400,000.00** (this amount is called "Principal"), plus interest, to the order of the Lender. The Lender is **YOUR FAVORITE MORTGAGE CORPORATION**. I will make all payments under this Note in the form of cash, check or money order.

I understand that the Lender may transfer this Note. The Lender or anyone who takes this Note by transfer and who is entitled to receive payments under this Note is called the "Note Holder."

3. INTEREST

Interest will be charged on unpaid principal until the full amount of Principal has been paid. I will pay interest at a yearly rate of **5%**.

The interest rate required by this Section 2 is the rate I will pay both before and after any default described in Section 6(B) of this Note.

3. PAYMENTS

    (A) Time and Place of Payments

I will pay principal and interest by making a payment every month.

I will make my monthly payment on the 1st day of each month beginning on **APRIL 1, 2011**. I will make these payments every month until I have paid all of the principal and interest and any other charges described below that I may owe under this Note. Each monthly payment will be applied as of its scheduled due date and will be applied to interest before Principal. If, on **MARCH 1, 2041**, I still owe amounts under this Note, I will pay those amounts in full on that date, which is called the "Maturity Date."

I will make my monthly payments at **YOUR FAVORITE MORTGAGE CORPORATION'S MAILING ADDRESS** or at a different place if required by the Note Holder.

    (B) Amount of Monthly Payments

My monthly payment will be in the amount of U.S. **$2,147.29**.

E. BORROWER'S RIGHT TO PREPAY

I have the right to make payments of Principal at any time before they are due. A payment of Principal only is known as a "Prepayment." When I make a Prepayment, I will tell the Note Holder in writing that I am doing so. I may not designate a payment as a Prepayment if I have not made all the monthly payments due under the Note.

I may make a full Prepayment or partial Prepayments without paying a Prepayment charge. The Note Holder will use my Prepayments to reduce the amount of Principal that I owe under this Note. However, the Note Holder may apply my Prepayment to the accrued and unpaid interest on the Prepayment amount, before applying my Prepayment to reduce the Principal amount of the Note. If I make a partial Prepayment, there will be no changes in the due date or in the amount of my monthly payment unless the Note Holder agrees in writing to those changes.

5. LOAN CHARGES

If a law, which applies to this loan and which sets maximum loan charges, is finally interpreted so that the interest or other loan charges collected or to be collected in connection with this loan exceed the permitted limits, then: (a) any such loan charge shall be reduced by the amount necessary to reduce the charge to the permitted limit; and (b) any sums already collected from me which exceeded permitted limits will be refunded to me. The Note Holder may choose to make this refund by reducing the Principal I owe under this Note or by making a direct payment to me. If a refund reduces Principal, the reduction will be treated as a partial Prepayment.

2 BORROWER'S FAILURE TO PAY AS REQUIRED
B. Late Charge for Overdue Payments

If the Note Holder has not received the full amount of any monthly payment by the end of **15** calendar days after the date it is due, I will pay a late charge to the Note Holder. The amount of the charge will be **5%** of my overdue payment of principal and interest. I will pay this late charge promptly but only once on each late payment.

(B) Default

If I do not pay the full amount of each monthly payment on the date it is due, I will be in default.

(C) Notice of Default

If I am in default, the Note Holder may send me a written notice telling me that if I do not pay the overdue amount by a certain date, the Note Holder may require me to pay immediately the full amount of Principal which has not been paid and all the interest that I owe on that amount. That date must be at least 30 days after the date on which the notice is mailed to me or delivered by other means.

(D) No Waiver By Note Holder

Even if, at a time when I am in default, the Note Holder does not require me to pay immediately in full as described above, the Note Holder will still have the right to do so if I am in default at a later time.

(E) Payment of Note Holder's Costs and Expenses

If the Note Holder has required me to pay immediately in full as described above, the Note Holder will have the right to be paid back by me for all of its costs and expenses in enforcing this Note to the extent not prohibited by applicable law. Those expenses include, for example, reasonable attorneys' fees.

7. GIVING OF NOTICES

Unless applicable law requires a different method, any notice that must be given to me under this Note will be given by delivering it or by mailing it by first class mail to me at the Property Address above or at a different address if I give the Note Holder a notice of my different address.

Any notice that must be given to the Note Holder under this Note will be given by delivering it or by mailing it by first class mail to the Note Holder at the address stated in Section 3(A) above or at a different address if I am given a notice of that different address.

9. OBLIGATIONS OF PERSONS UNDER THIS NOTE

If more than one person signs this Note, each person is fully and personally obligated to keep all of the promises made in this Note, including the promise to pay the full amount owed. Any person who is a guarantor, surety or endorser of this Note is also obligated to do these things. Any person who takes over these obligations, including the obligations of a guarantor, surety or endorser of this Note, is also obligated to keep all of the promises made in this Note. The Note Holder may enforce its rights under this Note against each person individually or against all of us together. This means that any one of us may be required to pay all of the amounts owed under this Note.

9. WAIVERS

I and any other person who has obligations under this Note waive the rights of Presentment and Notice of Dishonor. "Presentment" means the right to require the Note Holder to demand payment of amounts due. "Notice of Dishonor" means the right to require the Note Holder to give notice to other persons that amounts due have not been paid.

10. UNIFORM SECURED NOTE

This Note is a uniform instrument with limited variations in some jurisdictions. In addition to the protections given to the Note Holder under this Note, a Mortgage, Deed of Trust, or Security Deed (the "Security Instrument"), dated the same date as this Note, protects the Note Holder from possible losses which might result if I do not keep the promises which I make in this Note. That Security Instrument describes how and under what conditions I may be required to make immediate payment in full of all amounts I owe under this Note. Some of those conditions are described as follows:

> If all or any part of the Property or any Interest in the Property is sold or transferred (or if Borrower is not a natural person and a beneficial interest in Borrower is sold or transferred) without Lender's prior written consent, Lender may require immediate payment in full of all sums secured by this Security Instrument. However, this option shall not be exercised by Lender if such exercise is prohibited by Applicable Law.

If Lender exercises this option, Lender shall give Borrower notice of acceleration. The notice shall provide a period of not less than 30 days from the date the notice is given in accordance with Section 15 within which Borrower must pay all sums secured by this Security Instrument. If Borrower fails to pay these sums prior to the expiration of this period, Lender may invoke any remedies permitted by this Security Instrument without further notice or demand on Borrower.

WITNESS THE HAND(S) AND SEAL(S) OF THE UNDERSIGNED.

_____(Seal)
Happy Homebuyer- Borrower

_____(Seal) -
Borrower

_____(Seal) -
Borrower

[Sign Original Only]

A. Settlement Statement (HUD-1)

B. Type of Loan

1. ☐ FHA	2. ☐ RHS	3. ☐ Conv. Unins.	6. File Number:	7. Loan Number:	8. Mortgage Insurance Case Number:
4. ☐ VA	5. ☐ Conv. Ins.				

C. Note: This form is furnished to give you a statement of actual settlement costs. Amounts paid to and by the settlement agent are shown. Items marked "(p.o.c.)" were paid outside the closing; they are shown here for informational purposes and are not included in the totals.

D. Name & Address of Borrower:	E. Name & Address of Seller:	F. Name & Address of Lender:

G. Property Location:	H. Settlement Agent:	I. Settlement Date:
	Place of Settlement:	

J. Summary of Borrower's Transaction

B. Gross Amount Due from Borrower	
C. Contract sales price	
102. Personal property	
103. Settlement charges to borrower (line 1400)	
104.	
105.	
Adjustment for items paid by seller in advance	
106. City/town taxes to	
107. County taxes to	
108. Assessments to	
109.	
110.	
111.	
112.	
120. Gross Amount Due from Borrower	
200. Amount Paid by or in Behalf of Borrower	
201. Deposit or earnest money	
202. Principal amount of new loan(s)	
203. Existing loan(s) taken subject to	
204.	
205.	
206.	
207.	
208.	
209.	
Adjustments for items unpaid by seller	
210. City/town taxes to	
211. County taxes to	
212. Assessments to	
213.	
214.	
215.	
216.	
217.	
218.	
219.	
220. Total Paid by/for Borrower	
300. Cash at Settlement from/to Borrower	
301. Gross amount due from borrower (line 120)	
302. Less amounts paid by/for borrower (line 220)	( )
303. Cash ☐ From ☐ To Borrower	

K. Summary of Seller's Transaction

2. Gross Amount Due to Seller	
3. Contract sales price	
402. Personal property	
403.	
404.	
405.	
Adjustment for items paid by seller in advance	
406. City/town taxes to	
407. County taxes to	
408. Assessments to	
409.	
410.	
411.	
412.	
420. Gross Amount Due to Seller	
500. Reductions In Amount Due to seller	
501. Excess deposit (see instructions)	
502. Settlement charges to seller (line 1400)	
503. Existing loan(s) taken subject to	
504. Payoff of first mortgage loan	
505. Payoff of second mortgage loan	
506.	
507.	
508.	
509.	
Adjustments for items unpaid by seller	
510. City/town taxes to	
511. County taxes to	
512. Assessments to	
513.	
514.	
515.	
516.	
517.	
518.	
519.	
520. Total Reduction Amount Due Seller	
600. Cash at Settlement to/from Seller	
601. Gross amount due to seller (line 420)	
602. Less reductions in amounts due seller (line 520)	( )
603. Cash ☐ To ☐ From Seller	

The Public Reporting Burden for this collection of information is estimated at 35 minutes per response for collecting, reviewing, and reporting the data. This agency may not collect this information, and you are not required to complete this form, unless it displays a currently valid OMB control number. No confidentiality is assured; this disclosure is mandatory. This is designed to provide the parties to a RESPA covered transaction with HUD-1 during the settlement process.

Previous edition are obsolete

L. Settlement Charges

700. Total Real Estate Broker Fees	Paid From Borrower's Funds at Settlement	Paid From Seller's Funds at Settlement
Division of commission (line 700) as follows :		
701. $ to		
702. $ to		
703. Commission paid at settlement		
704.		

800. Items Payable in Connection with Loan		
801. Our origination charge $ (from GFE #1)		
802. Your credit or charge (points) for the specific interest rate chosen $ (from GFE #2)		
803. Your adjusted origination charges (from GFE #A)		
804. Appraisal fee to (from GFE #3)		
805. Credit report to (from GFE #3)		
806. Tax service to (from GFE #3)		
807. Flood certification to (from GFE #3)		
808.		
809.		
810.		
811.		

900. Items Required by Lender to be Paid in Advance		
901. Daily interest charges from to @ $ /day (from GFE #10)		
902. Mortgage insurance premium for months to (from GFE #3)		
903. Homeowner's insurance for years to (from GFE #11)		
904.		

1000. Reserves Deposited with Lender		
1001. Initial deposit for your escrow account (from GFE #9)		
1002. Homeowner's insurance months @ $ per month $		
1003. Mortgage insurance months @ $ per month $		
1004. Property Taxes months @ $ per month $		
1005. months @ $ per month $		
1006. months @ $ per month $		
1007. Aggregate Adjustment -$		

1100. Title Charges		
1101. Title services and lender's title insurance (from GFE #4)		
1102. Settlement or closing fee $		
1103. Owner's title insurance (from GFE #5)		
1104. Lender's title insurance $		
1105. Lender's title policy limit $		
1106. Owner's title policy limit $		
1107. Agent's portion of the total title insurance premium to $		
1108. Underwriter's portion of the total title insurance premium to $		
1109.		
1110.		
1111.		

1200. Government Recording and Transfer Charges		
1201. Government recording charges (from GFE #7)		
1202. Deed $ Mortgage $ Release $		
1203. Transfer taxes (from GFE #8)		
1204. City/County tax/stamps Deed $ Mortgage $		
1205. State tax/stamps Deed $ Mortgage $		
1206.		

1300. Additional Settlement Charges		
1301. Required services that you can shop for (from GFE #6)		
1302. $		
1303. $		
1304.		
1305.		

1400. Total Settlement Charges (enter on lines 103, Section J and 502, Section K)		

Previous edition are obsolete

HUD-

**Recording Requested By and
When Recorded Mail to:**

_____

_____

_____

Recording Time, Book & Page

SOUTH CAROLINA GENERAL WARRANTY DEED

COUNTY: _____ TAX MAP NUMBER: _____

CITY: _____ DATE: _____

Grantor	Grantee

Enter in appropriate block for each party: name, address, and, if appropriate, character of entity, e.g. corporation, partnership, limited liability company

The designation Grantor and Grantee as used herein shall include the named parties and their heirs, successors and assigns and shall include singular, plural, masculine, feminine or neuter as required by context.

KNOW ALL MEN BY THESE PRESENTS, that Grantor, for and in consideration of the sum of _____ and _____/100 Dollars ($_____) paid by Grantee to Grantor, the receipt and sufficiency of which is hereby acknowledged, **SUBJECT TO** the matters set forth below, has granted, bargained, sold and released, and by these presents does grant, bargain, sell and release unto Grantee, the real estate (the "Premises") described as follows:

_____
_____
_____
_____
_____

A plat of the subject property is recorded in Plat Book _____ at Page _____.

Derivation: This being the same property conveyed to Grantor by Deed of _____ dated _____ and recorded _____ in the Office of the _____ for _____ County in Deed Book _____ at Page _____.

This conveyance is made **SUBJECT TO**: _____
_____

TOGETHER with all and singular, the rights, members, hereditaments and appurtenances to the Premises belonging or in any way incident or appertaining, including, but not limited to, all improvements of any nature located on the Premises and all easements and rights-of-way appurtenant to the Premises.

TO HAVE AND TO HOLD all and singular the Premises unto Grantee and Grantee's heirs successors and assigns forever.

And, **SUBJECT TO** the matters set forth above, Grantor does hereby bind Grantor and Grantor's heirs, successors and assigns, executors, administrators and other lawful representatives, to warrant and forever defend all and singular the

SC Bar Form:_____
Last Revised:_____

This form is a basic form intended for use only by South Carolina licensed attorneys. Use by others may constitute the unauthorized practice of law.

Premises unto Grantee and Grantee's heirs, successors and assigns against Grantor and Grantor's successors and against every person whomsoever lawfully claiming, or to claim, the same or any part thereof.

IN WITNESS WHEREOF, Grantor has caused this General Warranty Deed to be executed under seal this _____ day of _____, 20____.

SIGNED, SEALED AND DELIVERED
IN THE PRESENCE OF:

           GRANTOR:
           Signature of individual Grantor

_____   _____ (SEAL)
Witness #1   Type name: _____

_____   **Signature block for entity Grantor**
Witness #2

     Type name of entity _____

     By: _____ (SEAL)
     Signature of authorized signatory

     Type name of authorized signatory:_____

     Its: _____
     (Type capacity of signatory)

STATE OF SOUTH CAROLINA

COUNTY OF _____

Acknowledgment for Individual Grantor

I, a Notary Public for South Carolina, do hereby certify that _____, Grantor, personally appeared before me this day and acknowledged the due execution of the foregoing instrument.

Witness my hand and official seal this the _____ day of _____, 20____.

_____
Notary Public for South Carolina

My Commission Expires:

_____

STATE OF SOUTH CAROLINA

COUNTY OF _____

Acknowledgment for Entity Grantor

I, a Notary Public for South Carolina, do hereby certify that _____, Grantor, by _____
Its: _____, personally appeared before me this day and acknowledged the due execution of the foregoing instrument.

Witness my hand and official seal this the _____ day of _____, 20____.

_____
Notary Public for South Carolina

My Commission Expires:

_____

SC Bar Form:_____
Last Revised: _____

    This form is a basic form intended for use only by South Carolina licensed attorneys. Use by others may constitute the unauthorized practice of law.

SELLER'S REAL PROPERTY DISCLOSURE FORM

In accordance with Nevada Law, a seller of residential real property in Nevada must disclose any and all known conditions and aspects of the property which materially affect the value or use of residential property in an adverse manner *(see NRS 113.130 and 113.140).*

Date _____

Property address _____

Do you currently occupy or have you ever occupied this property? YES ☐   NO ☐

Effective October 1, 2011: A purchaser may not waive the requirement to provide this form and a seller may not require a purchaser to waive this form. *(NRS 113.130(3))*

Type of Seller: ☐Bank (financial institution); ☐Asset Management Company; ☐Owner-occupier; ☐Other: _____

Purpose of Statement: (1) This statement is a disclosure of the condition of the property in compliance with the Seller Real Property Disclosure Act, effective January 1, 1996. (2) This statement is a disclosure of the condition and information concerning the property known by the Seller which materially affects the value of the property. Unless otherwise advised, the Seller does not possess any expertise in construction, architecture, engineering or any other specific area related to the construction or condition of the improvements on the property or the land. Also, unless otherwise advised, the Seller has not conducted any inspection of generally inaccessible areas such as the foundation or roof. This statement is not a warranty of any kind by the Seller or by any Agent representing the Seller in this transaction and is not a substitute for any inspections or warranties the Buyer may wish to obtain. Systems and appliances addressed on this form by the seller are not part of the contractual agreement as to the inclusion of any system or appliance as part of the binding agreement.

Instructions to the Seller: (1) ANSWER ALL QUESTIONS. (2) REPORT KNOWN CONDITIONS AFFECTING THE PROPERTY. (3) ATTACH ADDITIONAL PAGES WITH YOUR SIGNATURE IF ADDITIONAL SPACE IS REQUIRED. (4) COMPLETE THIS FORM YOURSELF. (5) IF SOME ITEMS DO NOT APPLY TO YOUR PROPERTY, CHECK N/A (NOT APPLICABLE). EFFECTIVE JANUARY 1, 1996, FAILURE TO PROVIDE A PURCHASER WITH A SIGNED DISCLOSURE STATEMENT WILL ENABLE THE PURCHASER TO TERMINATE AN OTHERWISE BINDING PURCHASE AGREEMENT AND SEEK OTHER REMEDIES AS PROVIDED BY THE LAW *(see NRS 113.150).*

Systems / Appliances: Are you aware of any problems and/or defects with any of the following:

	YES	NO	N/A		YES	NO	N/A
Electrical System	☐	☐	☐	Shower(s)	☐	☐	☐
Plumbing	☐	☐	☐	Sink(s)	☐	☐	☐
Sewer System & line	☐	☐	☐	Sauna / hot tub(s)	☐	☐	☐
Septic tank & leach field	☐	☐	☐	Built-in microwave	☐	☐	☐
Well & pump	☐	☐	☐	Range / oven / hood-fan	☐	☐	☐
Yard sprinkler system(s)	☐	☐	☐	Dishwasher	☐	☐	☐
Fountain(s)	☐	☐	☐	Garbage disposal	☐	☐	☐
Heating system	☐	☐	☐	Trash compactor	☐	☐	☐
Cooling system	☐	☐	☐	Central vacuum	☐	☐	☐
Solar heating system	☐	☐	☐	Alarm system	☐	☐	☐
Fireplace & chimney	☐	☐	☐	owned.. ☐ leased.. ☐			
Wood burning system	☐	☐	☐	Smoke detector	☐	☐	☐
Garage door opener	☐	☐	☐	Intercom	☐	☐	☐
Water treatment system(s)	☐	☐	☐	Data Communication line(s)	☐	☐	☐
owned.. ☐ leased.. ☐				Satellite dish(es)	☐	☐	☐
Water heater	☐	☐	☐	owned.. ☐ leased.. ☐			
Toilet(s)	☐	☐	☐	Other _____	☐	☐	☐
Bathtub(s)	☐	☐	☐				

EXPLANATIONS: Any "Yes" must be fully explained. Attach explanations to form.

_____   _____
     Seller(s) Initials   *Buyer(s) Initials*

Nevada Real Estate Division
Replaces all previous versions

Property conditions, improvements and additional information: .... YES NO N/A

Are you **aware** of any of the following?:

1. **Structure:**
   (a) Previous or current moisture conditions and/or water damage? ...…... ☐ ☐
   (b) Any structural defect? .... ☐ ☐
   (c) Any construction, modification, alterations, or repairs made without
       required state, city or county building permits? ....…... ☐ ☐
   (d) Whether the property is or has been the subject of a claim governed by
       NRS 40.600 to 40.695 (construction defect claims)? ...….. ☐ ☐
   (If seller answers yes, FURTHER DISCLOSURE IS REQUIRED)

2. **Land / Foundation:**
   (a) Any of the improvements being located on unstable or expansive soil? ....…................ ☐ ☐
   (b) Any foundation sliding, settling, movement, upheaval, or earth stability problems
       that have occurred on the property? ....…........... ☐ ☐
   (c) Any drainage, flooding, water seepage, or high water table? ....….................... ☐ ☐
   (d) The property being located in a designated flood plain? .....…... ☐ ☐
   (e) Whether the property is located next to or near any known future development? .... ☐ ☐
   (f) Any encroachments, easements, zoning violations or nonconforming uses? .... ☐ ☐
   (g) Is the property adjacent to "open range" land? .... ☐ ☐
   (If seller answers yes, FURTHER DISCLOSURE IS REQUIRED under NRS 113.065)

3. **Roof:** Any problems with the roof? .... ☐ ☐
4. **Pool/spa:** Any problems with structure, wall, liner, or equipment... ☐ ☐ ☐
5. **Infestation:** Any history of infestation (termites, carpenter ants, etc.)? .... ☐ ☐
6. **Environmental:**
   (a) Any substances, materials, or products which may be an environmental hazard such as
       but not limited to, asbestos, radon gas, urea formaldehyde, fuel or chemical storage tanks,
       contaminated water or soil on the property? ....…................. ☐ ☐
   (b) Has property been the site of a crime involving the previous manufacture of Methamphetamine
       where the substances have not been removed from or remediated on the Property by a certified
       entity or has not been deemed safe for habitation by the Board of Heath? .... ☐ ☐

7. **Fungi / Mold:** Any previous or current fungus or mold? .... ☐ ☐
8. Any features of the property shared in common with adjoining landowners such as walls, fences,
   road, driveways or other features whose use or responsibility for maintenance may have an effect
   on the property? .... ☐ ☐
9. **Common Interest Communities:** Any "common areas" (facilities like pools, tennis courts, walkways or
   other areas co-owned with others) or a homeowner association which has any
   authority over the property? .... ☐ ☐
   (a) Common Interest Community Declaration and Bylaws available? .... ☐ ☐
   (b) Any periodic or recurring association fees? .... ☐ ☐
   (c) Any unpaid assessments, fines or liens, and any warnings or notices that may give rise to an
       assessment, fine or lien? .... ☐ ☐
   (d) Any litigation, arbitration, or mediation related to property or common area? .... ☐ ☐
   (e) Any assessments associated with the property (excluding property taxes)? .... ☐ ☐
   (f) Any construction, modification, alterations, or repairs made without
       required approval from the appropriate Common Interest Community board or committee? ..... ☐ ☐

10. Any problems with water quality or water supply? .... ☐ ☐
11. **Any other conditions** or aspects of the property which materially affect its value or use in an
    adverse manner? .... ☐ ☐
12. **Lead-Based Paint:** Was the property constructed on or before 12/31/77? .... ☐ ☐
    (If yes, additional Federal EPA notification and disclosure documents are required)
13. **Water source:** Municipal ☐ Community Well ☐ Domestic Well ☐ Other ☐
    If Community Well: State Engineer Well Permit # _____ Revocable ☐ Permanent ☐ Cancelled ☐
    Use of community and domestic wells may be subject to change. Contact the Nevada Division of Water Resources
    for more information regarding the future use of this well.
14. **Wastewater disposal:** Municipal Sewer ☐ Septic System ☐ Other ☐
15. This property is subject to a Private Transfer Fee Obligation? .... ☐ ☐

EXPLANATIONS: Any "Yes" must be fully explained. Attach explanations to form.

_____ _____   _____ _____
Seller(s) Initials   Buyer(s) Initials

Nevada Real Estate Division   Page 2 of 4   **Seller Real Property Disclosure Form**
Replaces all previous versions   **Revised 03/08/13   547**

Buyers and sellers of residential property are advised to seek the advice of an attorney concerning their rights and obligations as set forth in Chapter 113 of the Nevada Revised Statutes regarding the seller's obligation to execute the Nevada Real Estate Division's approved "Seller's Real Property Disclosure Form". For your convenience, Chapter 113 of the Nevada Revised Statutes provides as follows:

CONDITION OF RESIDENTIAL PROPERTY OFFERED FOR SALE

NRS 113.100 Definitions. As used in NRS 113.100 to 113.150, inclusive, unless the context otherwise requires:

1. "Defect" means a condition that materially affects the value or use of residential property in an adverse manner.
2. "Disclosure form" means a form that complies with the regulations adopted pursuant to NRS 113.120.
3. "Dwelling unit" means any building, structure or portion thereof which is occupied as, or designed or intended for occupancy as, a residence by one person who maintains a household or by two or more persons who maintain a common household.
4. "Residential property" means any land in this state to which is affixed not less than one nor more than four dwelling units.
5. "Seller" means a person who sells or intends to sell any residential property.

(Added to NRS by 1995, 842; A 1999, 1446)

NRS 113.110 Conditions required for "conveyance of property" and to complete service of document. For the purposes of NRS 113.100 to 113.150, inclusive:

1. A "conveyance of property" occurs:
(a) Upon the closure of any escrow opened for the conveyance; or
(b) If an escrow has not been opened for the conveyance, when the purchaser of the property receives the deed of conveyance.
2. Service of a document is complete:
(a) Upon personal delivery of the document to the person being served; or
(b) Three days after the document is mailed, postage prepaid, to the person being served at his last known address.

(Added to NRS by 1995, 844)

NRS 113.120 Regulations prescribing format and contents of form for disclosing condition of property. The Real Estate Division of the Department of Business and Industry shall adopt regulations prescribing the format and contents of a form for disclosing the condition of residential property offered for sale. The regulations must ensure that the form:

1. Provides for an evaluation of the condition of any electrical, heating, cooling, plumbing and sewer systems on the property, and of the condition of any other aspects of the property which affect its use or value, and allows the seller of the property to indicate whether or not each of those systems and other aspects of the property has a defect of which the seller is aware.
2. Provides notice:
(a) Of the provisions of NRS 113.140 and subsection 5 of NRS 113.150.
(b) That the disclosures set forth in the form are made by the seller and not by his agent.
(c) That the seller's agent, and the agent of the purchaser or potential purchaser of the residential property, may reveal the completed form and its contents to any purchaser or potential purchaser of the residential property.

(Added to NRS by 1995, 842)

NRS 113.130 Completion and service of disclosure form before conveyance of property; discovery or worsening of defect after service of form; exceptions; waiver.

1. Except as otherwise provided in subsection 2:
(a) At least 10 days before residential property is conveyed to a purchaser:
   (1) The seller shall complete a disclosure form regarding the residential property; and
   (2) The seller or the seller's agent shall serve the purchaser or the purchaser's agent with the completed disclosure form.
(b) If, after service of the completed disclosure form but before conveyance of the property to the purchaser, a seller or the seller's agent discovers a new defect in the residential property that was not identified on the completed disclosure form or discovers that a defect identified on the completed disclosure form has become worse than was indicated on the form, the seller or the seller's agent shall inform the purchaser or the purchaser's agent of that fact, in writing, as soon as practicable after the discovery of that fact but in no event later than the conveyance of the property to the purchaser. If the seller does not agree to repair or replace the defect, the purchaser may:
   (1) Rescind the agreement to purchase the property; or
   (2) Close escrow and accept the property with the defect as revealed by the seller or the seller's agent without further recourse.
2. Subsection 1 does not apply to a sale or intended sale of residential property:
(a) By foreclosure pursuant to chapter 107 of NRS.
(b) Between any co-owners of the property, spouses or persons related within the third degree of consanguinity.
(c) Which is the first sale of a residence that was constructed by a licensed contractor.
(d) By a person who takes temporary possession or control of or title to the property solely to facilitate the sale of the property on behalf of a person who relocates to another county, state or country before title to the property is transferred to a purchaser.
3. A purchaser of residential property may not waive any of the requirements of subsection 1. A seller of residential property may not require a purchaser to waive any of the requirements of subsection 1 as a condition of sale or for any other purpose.
4. If a sale or intended sale of residential property is exempted from the requirements of subsection 1 pursuant to paragraph (a) of subsection 2, the trustee and the beneficiary of the deed of trust shall, not later than at the time of the conveyance of the property to the purchaser of the residential property, or upon the request of the purchaser of the residential property, provide:
(a) Written notice to the purchaser of any defects in the property of which the trustee or beneficiary, respectively, is aware; and
(b) If any defects are repaired or replaced or attempted to be repaired or replaced, the contact information of any asset management company who provided asset management services for the property. The asset management company shall provide a service report to the purchaser upon request.
5. As used in this section:
(a) "Seller" includes, without limitation, a client as defined in NRS 645H.060.
(b) "Service report" has the meaning ascribed to it in NRS 645H.150.

(Added to NRS by 1995, 842; A 1997, 349; 2003, 1339; 2005, 598; 2011, 2832)

_____   _____   _____   _____
Seller(s) Initials   *Buyer(s) Initials*

NRS 113.135 Certain sellers to provide copies of certain provisions of NRS and give notice of certain soil reports; initial purchaser entitled to rescind sales agreement in certain circumstances; waiver of right to rescind.
   1. Upon signing a sales agreement with the initial purchaser of residential property that was not occupied by the purchaser for more than 120 days after substantial completion of the construction of the residential property, the seller shall:
      (a) Provide to the initial purchaser a copy of NRS 11.202 to 11.206, inclusive, and 40.600 to 40.695, inclusive;
      (b) Notify the initial purchaser of any soil report prepared for the residential property or for the subdivision in which the residential property is located; and
      (c) If requested in writing by the initial purchaser not later than 5 days after signing the sales agreement, provide to the purchaser without cost each report described in paragraph (b) not later than 5 days after the seller receives the written request.
   2. Not later than 20 days after receipt of all reports pursuant to paragraph (c) of subsection 1, the initial purchaser may rescind the sales agreement.
   3. The initial purchaser may waive his right to rescind the sales agreement pursuant to subsection 2. Such a waiver is effective only if it is made in a written document that is signed by the purchaser.
   (Added to NRS by 1999, 1446)

NRS 113.140 Disclosure of unknown defect not required; form does not constitute warranty; duty of buyer and prospective buyer to exercise reasonable care.
   1. NRS 113.130 does not require a seller to disclose a defect in residential property of which he is not aware.
   2. A completed disclosure form does not constitute an express or implied warranty regarding any condition of residential property.
   3. Neither this chapter nor chapter 645 of NRS relieves a buyer or prospective buyer of the duty to exercise reasonable care to protect himself.
   (Added to NRS by 1995, 843; A 2001, 2896)

NRS 113.150 Remedies for seller's delayed disclosure or nondisclosure of defects in property; waiver.
   1. If a seller or the seller's agent fails to serve a completed disclosure form in accordance with the requirements of NRS 113.130, the purchaser may, at any time before the conveyance of the property to the purchaser, rescind the agreement to purchase the property without any penalties.
   2. If, before the conveyance of the property to the purchaser, a seller or the seller's agent informs the purchaser or the purchaser's agent, through the disclosure form or another written notice, of a defect in the property of which the cost of repair or replacement was not limited by provisions in the agreement to purchase the property, the purchaser may:
      (a) Rescind the agreement to purchase the property at any time before the conveyance of the property to the purchaser; or
      (b) Close escrow and accept the property with the defect as revealed by the seller or the seller's agent without further recourse.
   3. Rescission of an agreement pursuant to subsection 2 is effective only if made in writing, notarized and served not later than 4 working days after the date on which the purchaser is informed of the defect:
      (a) On the holder of any escrow opened for the conveyance; or
      (b) If an escrow has not been opened for the conveyance, on the seller or the seller's agent.
   4. Except as otherwise provided in subsection 5, if a seller conveys residential property to a purchaser without complying with the requirements of NRS 113.130 or otherwise providing the purchaser or the purchaser's agent with written notice of all defects in the property of which the seller is aware, and there is a defect in the property of which the seller was aware before the property was conveyed to the purchaser and of which the cost of repair or replacement was not limited by provisions in the agreement to purchase the property, the purchaser is entitled to recover from the seller treble the amount necessary to repair or replace the defective part of the property, together with court costs and reasonable attorney's fees. An action to enforce the provisions of this subsection must be commenced not later than 1 year after the purchaser discovers or reasonably should have discovered the defect or 2 years after the conveyance of the property to the purchaser, whichever occurs later.
   5. A purchaser may not recover damages from a seller pursuant to subsection 4 on the basis of an error or omission in the disclosure form that was caused by the seller's reliance upon information provided to the seller by:
      (a) An officer or employee of this State or any political subdivision of this State in the ordinary course of his or her duties; or
      (b) A contractor, engineer, land surveyor, certified inspector as defined in NRS 645D.040 or pesticide applicator, who was authorized to practice that profession in this State at the time the information was provided.
   6. A purchaser of residential property may waive any of his or her rights under this section. Any such waiver is effective only if it is made in a written document that is signed by the purchaser and notarized.
   (Added to NRS by 1995, 843; A 1997, 350, 1797)

The above information provided on pages one (1) and two (2) of this disclosure form is true and correct to the best of seller's knowledge as of the date set forth on page one (1). **SELLER HAS DUTY TO DISCLOSE TO BUYER AS NEW DEFECTS ARE DISCOVERED AND/OR KNOWN DEFECTS BECOME WORSE** *(See NRS 113.130(1)(b)).*

Seller(s): _____ Date: _____

Seller(s): _____ Date: _____

BUYER MAY WISH TO OBTAIN PROFESSIONAL ADVICE AND INSPECTIONS OF THE PROPERTY TO MORE FULLY DETERMINE THE CONDITION OF THE PROPERTY AND ITS ENVIRONMENTAL STATUS. Buyer(s) has/have read and acknowledge(s) receipt of a copy of this Seller's Real Property Disclosure Form and copy of NRS Chapter 113.100-150, inclusive, attached hereto as pages three (3) and four (4).

Buyer(s): _____ Date: _____

Buyer(s): _____ Date: _____

_____   _____
Seller(s) Initials   *Buyer(s) Initials*

Appendix C

Final Exams

FINAL EXAM: I

1. A legal description using markers or monuments and ending at the same point as it began is:

   a. Government Rectangular Survey.
   b. Subdivision description.
   c. Metes and Bounds description.
   d. Recorded Plat description.

2. When husband and wife have acquired title to real property and then have the property statutorily divided equally is:

   a. condominium.
   b. chattel.
   c. cooperative.
   d. community property.

3. The required distance as established by zoning laws is called a:

   a. pre-emptive access.
   b. buffer zone.
   c. setback.
   d. variance.

4. A trade fixture is usually treated as:

   a. a fixture.
   b. an easement.
   c. personalty.
   d. real property.

5. Which of the following is NOT a characteristic of real property value?

   a. scarcity.
   b. permanence.
   c. use.
   d. transferability.

6. A cattle rancher constructs a fence around the perimeter of his ranch to confine his steer. The materials for construction are:

   a. personal property when purchased.
   b. personal property when constructed.
   c. real property when transported.
   d. None of these.

7. A tax that is assessed according to the value of the property's value is known as what kind of tax?

   a. transfer tax
   b. flat tax
   c. special assessment
   d. ad valorem

8. The clubhouse, pool, playground, and walking trails in a condominium project that are owned equally by all owners is:

   a. limited common elements.
   b. common areas.
   c. cooperative elements.
   d. community property.

9. Apartments are built between a commercial zoned district and an area zoned for single family, residential homes. The apartment complex is an example of:

   a. a redlined area.
   b. common areas.
   c. cooperatives.
   d. a buffer zone.

10. Economic policy to stimulate homeownership include all the following EXCEPT:

    a. allowing lower down payments.
    b. lowering the interest rates.
    c. requiring loan applicants to have better credit.
    d. reducing closing costs for first-time home buyers.

11. Mr. Smith and Mr. Jones acquire property with Smith owning ¼ and Jones ¾ of the property. The law will presume they hold the property as:

    a. Tenancy by the Entireties.
    b. Tenants in Common.
    c. Joint Tenants.
    d. Tenants in Severalty.

12. Any portion of the owner's property value above the loan payoff amount is called:

    a. debt ceiling.
    b. equity.
    c. surplus.
    d. escrow.

13. Clarence and Adrianna sold their home for $76,000 yielding a 12% profit. What was the initial purchase price of their property? (rounded)

    a. $66,880
    b. $67,860
    c. $84,025
    d. $85,120

14. Joseph and Lorraine are in escrow to purchase a new home for $296,000. If they put 5% down and have closing costs of 3% of the loan amount, how much cash must they produce to close? (rounded)

    a. $14,800
    b. $19,750
    c. $23,250
    d. $23,700

15. Property taxes are a result of:

    a. the market value multiplied by the assessment ratio.
    b. the market value multiplied by the tax rate.
    c. the assessed value multiplied by the assessment ratio.
    d. the assessed value multiplied by the tax rate.

16. A broker acting for both the buyer and the seller in the same transaction is usually considered a:

    a. transaction broker.
    b. dual agent.
    c. universal agent.
    d. cooperating broker.

17. Green Real Estate Co. and McCulley Brokerage enjoy a 65% market share combined. They were recently disciplined and fined for violation of anti-trust laws. More than likely, the brokers:

    a. were dealing in unlicensed exchange services.
    b. were undisclosed, dual agents.
    c. did not pay state and federal income taxes.
    d. were price fixing with respect to commission rates.

18. A 220' x 145' lot sold for $350 per front foot. What was the broker's commission with an 8% commission?

    a. $2,552
    b. $4,060
    c. $6,160
    d. $7,700

19. The BEST indication of an individual property's market value is:
    a. the listing agent's estimate from a market analysis.
    b. the appraiser's value after the reconciliation.
    c. the list price.
    d. the price agreed to between an informed buyer and seller.

20. For extra efforts that exceeded the Seller's expectations, a listing broker-salesperson can legally receive a performance bonus from:

    a. the seller.
    b. the buyer.
    c. the seller if paid to her by the title company.
    d. her broker.

21. The Income Approach is best suited for which of these properties?

    a. a single family residence
    b. a public airport
    c. an apartment complex
    d. a large vacant industrial building

22. The Cost Approach would be the best suited for which of these properties?

    a. a church
    b. a former, model home
    c. a 10 unit apartment building
    d. a car wash

23. A home with a few missing shingles and walls that are yellowed from age is suffering:

    a. curable functional depreciation.
    b. incurable physical depreciation.
    c. incurable environmental depreciation.
    d. curable physical deprecation.

24. An exclusive listing contract that exempts a commission to the broker if the owner makes the sale without the broker's aid is called an:

    a. open listing.
    b. exclusive-agency listing.
    c. exclusive-right-to-sell listing.
    d. option contract.

25. A mortgage clause that requires the loan must be paid in full when the property is sold is referred to as:

    a. the "Due on Sale" clause.
    b. the "Habendum" clause.
    c. the "Release" clause.
    d. the "Acceleration" clause.

26. An "Alienation" clause:

    a. requires the loan to be paid in full if the borrower is not a U.S. citizen.
    b. requires the loan to be paid in full when the lender declares it due.
    c. allows the lender to call the loan due if the borrower sells or transfers ownership.
    d. extends the lien of the mortgage to property owned by the borrower which is outside the United States.

27. The owner of a listed property suffered a heart attack and passed away while the listing contract was still in effect with the broker. The listing now:

    a. is binding on the owner's heirs for the remainder of the contract.
    b. remains valid.
    c. may be terminated because of the death of the principal.
    d. is binding only if the broker can still produce a ready, willing, and able buyer.

28. Which of these is FALSE regarding Adjustable Rate Mortgages?

    a. monthly payments may increase or decrease periodically.
    b. there is frequently a concessionary starting interest rate.
    c. in some, negative amortization can occur.
    d. the index plus the lifetime cap equals the interest rate.

29. Where the borrower is allowed possession of real property while paying off the loan against it is called:

    a. a pawn.
    b. a UCC 1 lien.
    c. a deed of trust.
    d. a hypothecation.

30. A special agent is:

    a. given complete authority to bind the client to a contract.
    b. has no authority to bind the client to any contract.
    c. is most likely doing property management.
    d. is limited by his broker to represent buyers only.

31. Seller Simmons needs to net $25,000 after the sale of his rental property. What must the sale price be if the selling costs include a 6.5% commission, a $119,000 loan payoff, and $4,200 in other expenses? (rounded)

    a. $144,000
    b. $148,200
    c. $158,500
    d. There is not enough information.

32. The lender charges a 1% loan origination fee and 1.5 discount points. If the purchase price is $84,500 and the loan is an 80% LTV, how much are the lender fees? (rounded)

    a. $2,960
    b. $2,365
    c. $1,690
    d. $1,270

33. A discount point:

    a. increases the lenders yield without increasing the stated note interest rate.
    b. Is 1% of the purchase price.
    c. profit to the mortgage broker.
    d. required to be charged by RESPA.

34. A broker working for the seller, under an exclusive right to sell listing, has what obligation to the buyer?

    a. none
    b. disclosure of confidential and public knowledge regarding the seller
    c. disclosure of latent defects, if any
    d. fair and honest dealing and disclosure of all material facts concerning the property

35. In a limited partnership:

    a. the number of investors is limited.
    b. all partners participate in running the business.
    c. general partners run the business.
    d. limited partners run the risk of unlimited liability.

36. An old IRS income tax lien on Russo's property is holding up the closing. This is because the lien is:

    a. a monetary charge that the purchaser must pay before closing can occur.
    b. an appurtenance tax that must be first satisfied.
    c. an encroachment.
    d. an encumbrance.

37. An agent is in the process of taking a listing when the seller announces that he does not want the property shown to any Vietnamese.

    a. The agent must advise the seller that this would be illegal for both the seller and the agent to do.
    b. The sales agent must not obey the client's instruction.
    c. If the seller insists, the agent must refuse the listing with this condition.
    d. All of these

38. *A* and *B* are joint tenants. *A* sells her share of the property to *C*. *B* and *C* are now:

    a. nothing, *A* cannot seller her share.
    b. joint tenants.
    c. tenants in common.
    d. tenants in severalty.

39. Mary and John are buying their first home from you and are relocating from out of state. They are interested in making an offer and ask about crime in the area. You should tell them:

    a. this is something they should research on their own, perhaps with the local police department.
    b. to call the Association of REALTORS for that information.
    c. only that information to which you have actual knowledge regarding crime in that area.
    d. All of these

40. You are writing an offer with your purchasers on an old ranch home built in 1963. You should be alerted that an additional federally mandated disclosure will be required in this transaction. It is:

    a. RESPA.
    b. Truth in Lending Act.
    c. Lead Based Paint disclosure.
    d. Fair Housing Act

41. *J* offers to buy *S*'s house at full price and *S* Accepts, changing the closing date from November 15th to December 1st.
    Do they have a contract?

    a. Yes.
    b. Yes, because they agreed on the price.
    c. No.
    d. No, because *S* made a counteroffer.

42. You are at the walk through at your seller's property. This transaction has been a harrowing experience and is finally going to close. The buyer and her agent are doing the walk through inspection and don't check the heat since it is 98° outside. Your seller whispers to you to please not mention the heating system does not work. What should you do?

    a. Follow your client's instructions in honoring your fiduciary duty.
    b. Explain to your seller you must disclose known defects to the customer.
    c. Do nothing as you should get advice from your broker first.
    d. Recommend to the buyer that she get a home warranty including air and heat.

43. Section 7 would be located in which quarter of its township?

    a. NW ¼
    b. NE ¼
    c. SE ¼
    d. SW ¼

44. Which of the following parcels is the largest?

    a. 4 sections
    b. 4 square miles
    c. one-ninth of a township
    d. 16 square miles

45. What is the major distinction between *fraud* and *misrepresentation*?

    a. the degree to which the client suffered a monetary loss.
    b. the consequences resulting from the agent's actions.
    c. intent.
    d. the sanction imposed by the Commission.

46. Could an unenforceable contract be performed?

    a. No, if it is unenforceable it is void.
    b. No, there was no meeting of the minds.
    c. Yes, the parties can agree to perform anyway.
    d. Yes, but only with a novation.

47. Reference to a plat map is used in the:

    a. government rectangular survey system.
    b. lot, block, and subdivision method.
    c. metes and bounds system.
    d. None of these

48. When Slate Building Supply delivered the Forte's building materials for the construction of their log cabin, and the Fortes do not pay, Slate may file a:

    a. mechanic's lien.
    b. deficiency judgment.
    c. lis pendens.
    d. construction lien.

49. Barnes employs Noble to make periodic runs to Cuba from Miami on his boat for the delivery of heroin. The employment agreement between Barnes and Noble is:

    a. valid, as there are no known laws regarding the delivery of heroin to Cuba.
    b. void, as this employment contract lacks an essential element of a contract.
    c. voidable, as Noble is not bound to perform.
    d. unenforceable, if it is a verbal agreement.

50. Eddy leaves his new car at the dealership to have the oil changed and the tires rotated. When the service writer accepted the car, the dealership and Eddy entered into:

    a. an executed contract.
    b. an implied contract.
    c. a unilateral contract.
    d. There is no contract.

51. Maquire instructs title to return Tomlinson's earnest money deposit who understands Maquire is putting the house back on the market. The parties have likely agreed to a:

    a. novation.
    b. assignment.
    c. rescission.
    d. subordination.

52. Which of the following is TRUE regarding a special warranty deed?

    a. The grantor is making additional warranties beyond those given in a warranty deed.
    b. The grantor retains a special interest in the ownership.
    c. The grantor is warranting that no encumbrances exist against the property.
    d. The grantor's warranties are limited to the time the grantor owned the property.

53. Who is typically the "Optionor?"

    a. the current owner of the property.
    b. the holder of a first right of refusal.
    c. a prospective buyer who wants time to decide.
    d. a tenant.

54. Jeff and Liz offer to buy Mike's house for $165,000 subject to their obtaining a new loan of $145,000 not to exceed 6% interest. What will happen if they cannot qualify for their loan?

    a. They will lose their deposit but are otherwise released from the contract.
    b. They will lose their deposit and are subject to damages if Mike sues.
    c. Their deposit will be applied to the purchase price and they will have to come up with the rest from another source.
    d. The contract is cancelled and they will get a return of their deposit.

55. You think you are buying 123 Willow Way, Unit #C. The Seller also owns 127 Willow Way, Unit #B and thinks that is the unit he is selling. Any agreement will be:

    a. in violation of Statute of Frauds.
    b. void due to mutual mistake.
    c. voidable due to mutual mistake.
    d. enforceable only upon the buyer.

56. The documented history of all the owners of a specific parcel of real estate is the property's:

    a. chain of title.
    b. certificate of title.
    c. title insurance policy.
    d. certificate of resale.

57. The deed is recorded in:

    a. the public records of the county where the buyer resides.
    b. the public records in the county the seller resides.
    c. the public records in the county where the property is located.
    d. the office of the Torrens registrar.

58. The fee charged by a mortgage broker to arrange a loan is a(n)

    a. loan processing fee.
    b. broker's commission.
    c. loan origination fee.
    d. prepayment cost.

59. Which of the following is FALSE regarding deed restrictions?

    a. They are called "restrictive covenants."
    b. They terminate when the grantee dies.
    c. They are often found in CICAs.
    d. They run with the land and bind future owners.

60. The clause in a deed of trust that allows the lender to call the loan due and payable immediately upon default is known as the:

    a. acceleration clause.
    b. assignment clause.
    c. foreclosure clause.
    d. due on sale clause.

61. A real estate loan with monthly payments that partially pay off the principal but requires a lump sum payment upon the final payment is called a(n):

    a. straight loan.
    b. balloon mortgage.
    c. fully amortizing loan.
    d. ARM

62. Adams applies for financing at North Star Credit to purchase a condominium.

    a. Adams is the mortgagee and North Star is the mortgagor.
    b. Adams is the beneficiary of the promissory note.
    c. North Star has legal title.
    d. None of these

63. Which is NOT covered by the Federal Fair Housing Act?

    a. Sexual Orientation
    b. Ethnicity
    c. National Origin
    d. Race

64. You pick up a couple at their hotel to show them homes. It is clear from their accent and general appearance that they are most likely Hispanic dissent. You show them only homes in areas of high Hispanic concentration.

    a. You are guilty of Redlining.
    b. You are guilty of Steering.
    c. You are guilty of Blockbusting.
    d. You have done nothing wrong.

65. Joe's lease with George was a 3-month term and Joe remains in possession and continues to make rent payments to George which George gladly accepts. What is the current tenancy between George and Joe?

    a. a periodic estate
    b. tenants in common
    c. an estate at sufferance
    d. a tenancy at will

66. A wheelchair bound person wants to rent an apartment. She may:

    a. demand a tenant on the first floor be evicted to allow her a first floor apartment.
    b. require the landlord to build her a ramp.
    c. rent only with evidence of adequate insurance to protect her against injury resulting from her status of handicap.
    d. make such alterations to the property as may be required to accommodate her handicap, but must restore the property on termination of her lease.

67. Tony's investor requires an 11% yield on any multi-family buildings he buys from Tony. Tony finds him a four-plex with a net operating income of $650 per unit per month. What is the highest most likely price Tony's investor would pay?

    a. $71,000
    b. $142,000
    c. $175,000
    d. $280,000

68. A property manager's primary obligation is to the:

    a. tenants.
    b. owners.
    c. lenders.
    d. CICA.

69. Which of the following would be considered a legal act by a lessor?

    a. charging a family with children a higher security deposit than is charged when there are no children
    b. refusing to allow a disabled person to install ramps and handrails in the landlord's property at the tenant's own expense
    c. refusing to rent to a lessee wishing to use the home as a house of worship
    d. refusing to sell a house to a person who has a history of mental illness

70. Dual agency is illegal in some states, while allowed in others only with disclosure and informed consent. Why is this so?

    a. Dual agency has inherent conflicts of interest.
    b. It is extremely difficult for one licensee to negotiate in the best interests of opposing clients in the same transaction.
    c. It is common for a licensee to breach a fiduciary duty in such a relationship.
    d. All of these

71. Contracts for the sale of real estate or for personal property over $500 must be in writing to be enforceable according to:

    a. statute of limitations.
    b. statue of liberty.
    c. statute of frauds.
    d. parol evidence rule.

72. As used in the real estate profession, the word "agency" describes:

    a. a mandatory part of the name of any company dealing in real estate transactions.
    b. the fiduciary relationship between an agent and a principal.
    c. the relationship between a real estate broker and the associated salespeople.
    d. the relationship between an agent and a customer.

73. With which type of income producing property would a GRM likely NOT be appropriate?

    a. shopping center
    b. free-standing office suite
    c. single family home
    d. a duplex

74. What law provided financing to all qualified Americans and prohibited discrimination in lending practices?

    a. ECOA
    b. RECD
    c. RESPA
    d. MGIC

75. Riparian rights pertain to the owner's rights to access of the water:

    a. when adjacent to large navigable lakes.
    b. along rivers or streams.
    c. regardless of the nature of the body of water.
    d. for oceanfront property.

76. Which of the following is commonly considered personal property?

    a. wood blinds
    b. closet shelving
    c. built-in barbeque
    d. portable spa

77. Which of these real estate descriptors is most likely required in your county for the recordation of real estate documents?

    a. street address.
    b. assessor's parcel number.
    c. valid legal description.
    d. MLS #

78. Seller Smithers is initiating a legal proceeding against Buyer Bronson to enforce the terms of the contract and complete the purchase as agreed. Smithers is pursuing a(n)

    a. an injunction.
    b. claim for liquidated damages.
    c. suit for specific performance.
    d. None of these

79. You are representing the seller. A contract is presented with the buyer's check for the required $5,000 earnest money, payable to the title company. The seller accepts the offer, all parties have signed, and escrow is opened. A few days later, you receive a call from the escrow officer telling you that the buyer's $5,000 check has been returned marked "Insufficient Funds." What should you do first?

    a. Contact the buyer immediately to get the check covered.
    b. Cover the check out of your own funds and then contact the buyer to pay you back.
    c. Notify the seller immediately of the bad check.
    d. First notify the buyer's agent to get a new check.

80. Which of the following BEST describes a voidable contract?

    a. a contract that has no legal effect and never had any from the very beginning
    b. an oral contract
    c. a contract that may be either enforced or declared void by one of the parties
    d. a contract that has been accepted but the acceptance has not been communicated to the offeror

81. RESPA requires:

    a. the borrow to receive a good faith estimate of loan closing costs within 3 business days of loan application.
    b. the use of the uniform settlement statement HUD-1.
    c. there be no undisclosed referral fees paid to the real estate professionals involved.
    d. All of these

82. Sam has an outstanding loan with Bank of America with a balance of $147,256. The interest rate is 4% and the P&I payments are $615 monthly on a fully amortizing loan. What will be the new balance after the next payment is made? (rounded)

    a. $147,680
    b. $147,256
    c. $147,132
    d. $146,766

83. What is the total square footage of the following floor plan?

    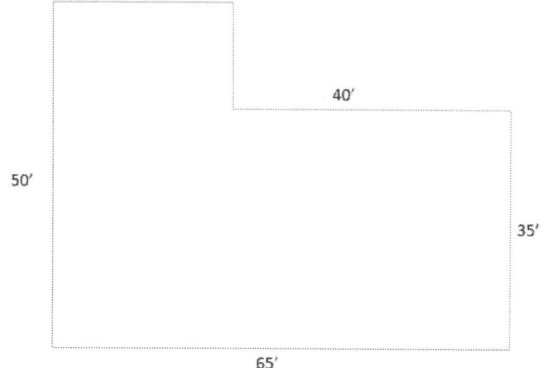

    a. 2,275
    b. 2,650
    c. 3,250
    d. 5,250

Appendix C: FINAL EXAMS page 12

84. The subject property has 4 bedrooms, 2 ½ baths, and a pool. The comparable, which sold for $320,000, has 4 bedrooms, 3 baths, and no pool. The appraiser uses the following data for making adjustments:

   One Bedroom $8,000
   One Bathroom $6,000
   ½ Bathroom $4,500
   Pool $18,000

   What adjustment would the appraiser make?

   a. adjust the subject upward $22,500
   b. adjust the subject downward $13,500
   c. adjust the comparable downward $22,500
   d. adjust the comparable upward $13,500

85. An eight unit apartment complex averages $725 per month per unit in rents collected after operating expenses. Jack's investor client is interested in purchasing the building, but requires a 12% return. What is the most Jack's investor would likely offer?

   a. $208,800
   b. $483,333
   c. $580,000
   d. $725,000

86. Wilkins' house is on the corner of a busy intersection where there have been many accidents. As a result, very few prospective buyers are interested in the home. Wilkins will suffer a loss in value due to:

   a. environmental obsolescence.
   b. physical depreciation.
   c. functional obsolescence.
   d. curable deterioration.

87. The county charges doc stamps at a rate of $3 per $1,000 of value, or any portion thereof. The sale price is $240,900 and closes on October 1st. What is the amount of the tax and to whom is it a debit?

   a. $723, debit to the seller.
   b. $723, debit to the buyer.
   c. $720, debit to the seller.
   d. $720, debit to the buyer.

88. On the 5th of the month, a Broker writes a check against his trust account to pay the rent for his office space. The broker could be disciplined by the licensing authority for:

   a. conversion.
   b. delinquent rental payments.
   c. failure to account.
   d. commingling.

89. The listing and selling firms agree to split an 8% commission equally on a $250,000 sale. The selling brokerage agent is paid on a 70% split with the firm retaining 30%. How much does the selling salesperson earn from the sale?

   a. $3,000
   b. $7,000
   c. $10,000
   d. $14,000

Appendix C: FINAL EXAMS page 13

90. Maximizing the owner's return on investment while preserving the value of the property are the primary duties of the:

    a. listing agent.
    b. selling agent.
    c. property manager.
    d. broker.

FINAL EXAM I - Answer Key

1. C
2. D
3. C
4. C
5. B
6. A
7. D
8. B
9. D
10. C
11. B
12. B
13. B
14. C
15. D
16. B
17. D
18. C
19. D
20. D
21. C
22. A
23. D
24. B
25. A
26. C
27. C
28. D
29. D
30. B
31. C
32. C
33. A
34. D
35. C
36. D
37. D
38. C
39. A
40. C
41. D
42. B
43. A
44. D
45. C
46. C
47. B
48. A
49. B
50. B
51. C
52. D
53. A
54. D
55. C
56. A
57. C
58. C
59. B
60. A
61. B
62. D
63. A
64. B
65. D
66. D
67. D
68. B
69. C
70. D
71. C
72. B
73. A
74. A
75. B
76. D
77. C
78. C
79. C
80. C
81. D
82. C
83. B
84. D
85. C
86. A
87. A
88. A
89. B
90. C

FINAL EXAM: II

1. A legal description including verbiage such as: "SANTA MARIA UNIT 17 PLAT BOOK 11 PAGE 126 LOT 13 BLOCK 16" is using which method of legal description:

    a. Government Rectangular Survey.
    b. Subdivision description.
    c. Metes and Bounds description.
    d. Recorded Plat description.

2. This form of ownership creates a corporation which owns the building and issues a proprietary lease to each stockholder.

    a. condominium.
    b. chattel.
    c. cooperative.
    d. community property.

3. If the local authority permits a different use than the zoned use for a particular property, they will issue:

    a. pre-emptive access.
    b. a buffer zone.
    c. a setback.
    d. a variance.

4. A leasehold improvement is usually treated as:

    a. a tenant improvement.
    b. an easement.
    c. personalty.
    d. real property.

5. Which of the following is NOT a characteristic of real property value?

    a. demand
    b. urgency
    c. scarcity
    d. transferability

6. A free standing, single car garage, is taken apart component by component and transported to be rebuilt at another location. While in transport, the materials are considered to be:

    a. personal property.
    b. real property.
    c. real estate.
    d. improvements.

7. The city of Santa Maria has levied a tax against all the homeowners whose property is adjacent to a new sewer line in the amount of $2,150. This type of tax is:

    a. an ad valorem tax.
    b. a flat tax.
    c. an encroachment.
    d. a transfer tax.

8. The clubhouse, pool, playground, and walking trails in a condominium project that are owned equally by all owners is:

    a. limited common elements.
    b. common areas.
    c. cooperative elements.
    d. community property.

9. As you look east from the Walmart shopping center, you will see the local high school, and further to the east, the start of residential homes. The high school is an example of:

    a. a redlined area.
    b. common areas.
    c. cooperatives.
    d. a buffer zone.

10. All of these would slow the economy and new home starts EXCEPT:

    a. requiring larger down payments.
    b. offering creative financing plans with higher loan to value ratios.
    c. requiring loan applicants to have better credit.
    d. eliminating first-time home buyer options.

11. Mr. Smith and Mr. Jones, are unrelated, and acquire property with Smith owning ½ and Jones ½ of the property. The parties could NOT hold title as:

    a. Tenancy by the Entireties.
    b. Tenants in Common.
    c. Joint Tenants.
    d. Tenants in Partnership.

12. Which of these is an example of a 90% LTV?

    a. $900,000 purchase price, $800,000 loan
    b. $100,000 loan, $15,000 down payment
    c. $5,000 down payment, $45,000 loan
    d. None of these.

13. Clem bought his four-plex a year ago for $170,000 and now suffers a 10% loss in selling the property. What did Clem sell it for?

    a. $163,000
    b. $153,000
    c. $187,000
    d. $171,700

14. Jed and Lori are closing on a ranch home for $129,000. If they obtain a 90% LTV loan and have closing costs of $2,750, how much cash must they produce to close?

    a. $10,150
    b. $12,900
    c. $15,650
    d. $17,450

15. The assessment ratio and equalization factor are used in calculating:

    a. the market value.
    b. the appraised value.
    c. the transfer tax.
    d. property taxes.

16. A broker who declares no fiduciary to either party and is only facilitating the sale is usually considered a:

    a. transaction broker.
    b. dual agent.
    c. single agent.
    d. cooperating broker.

17. Two of the largest brokerage firms in Silver City agree that one will only do business in the northern half and the other in the south. These brokers are violating what type of laws:

    e. NAR Code of Ethics.
    f. MLS rules.
    g. commingling.
    h. anti-trust.

18. A 90' x 145' lot sold for $350 per square foot. What was the broker's commission with a 7% commission? (rounded)

    a. $13,050
    b. $45,675
    c. $31,500
    d. None of these

19. The listing broker's commission is usually a percentage of the:

    a. list price.
    b. market value.
    c. agreed upon price.
    d. appraised value.

20. A listing broker-salesperson can legally receive a commission from:

    a. the seller.
    b. the buyer.
    c. the broker.
    d. All of these

21. The cost approach is best suited for which of these properties?

    a. a single family residence
    b. a municipal building
    c. an apartment complex
    d. a grocery store

22. The market data approach would be the best suited for which of these properties?

    a. a church
    b. a 40 unit apartment building
    c. a dry cleaners
    d. a duplex

23. A home built in the 1920's with a severely cracked foundation built on unstable soils was determined the slab is no longer safe or habitable. This home is suffering:

    a. curable functional depreciation.
    b. incurable physical depreciation.
    c. incurable environmental depreciation.
    d. curable physical deprecation.

24. A listing contract that protects the broker's commission even if the owner makes the sale without the broker's aid is called an:

    a. open listing.
    b. exclusive-agency listing.
    c. exclusive-right-to-sell listing.
    d. option contract.

25. Which of these mortgage clauses would typically be "triggered" in the event of the borrower's deficiency in making timely payments?

    a. "Due on Sale" clause
    b. "Habendum" clause
    c. "Release" clause
    d. "Acceleration" clause

26. A "Due on Sale" clause:

    a. prevents the transfer of title without first satisfying the loan.
    b. requires the loan to be paid in full when the lender declares it due.
    c. allows the lender to sell the loan to another mortgagee.
    d. requires the buyer of the mortgaged property to satisfy the loan upon purchasing.

27. A broker is said to have earned the commission when:

    a. the property is listed.
    b. the offer is accepted.
    c. a ready, willing, and able purchaser is procured.
    d. the transaction closes.

28. Which of these is TRUE regarding Adjustable Rate Mortgages?

    a. Monthly payments are level.
    b. There may never be a "teaser" rate.
    c. The index plus the lifetime cap equals the interest rate.
    d. The index plus the margin determines the rate.

29. Where the borrower is allowed possession of real property while paying off the loan against it is called:

    a. a pawn.
    b. a UCC 1 lien.
    c. a deed of trust.
    d. a hypothecation.

30. A general agent is:

    a. given complete authority to bind the client to any contract.
    b. has no authority to bind the client to any contract.
    c. given authority to bind the client to a contract within a predefined scope.
    d. is limited by his broker to represent buyers only.

31. The seller instructs her listing broker she wants to do a net listing. She must net $125,000 after the sale and must satisfy an $89,000 loan payoff and $4,200 in other expenses. What is the broker's commission is the property sells for $220,000 and the broker usually lists homes for 6%?

    a. $0
    b. $1,800
    c. $31,800
    d. There is not enough information.

32. The lender charges a 1.5% loan origination fee and 2 discount points. If the purchase price is $145,000 and the loan is an 85% LTV, how much are the lender fees? (rounded)

    a. $1,850
    b. $2,465
    c. $4,314
    d. $5,075

33. What is a discount point?

    a. 1% of the purchase price.
    b. A fee for brokering the loan.
    c. It is required to be charged by FNMA.
    d. It increases the lenders yield without increasing the stated note interest rate.

34. A broker, representing a buyer under a buyer representation agreement, has what obligation to the seller?

    a. none
    b. disclosure of confidential and public knowledge regarding the buyer
    c. disclosure of buyer's credit history
    d. fair and honest dealing and disclosure of all material facts concerning the property

35. In a general partnership:

    a. the number of investors is limited.
    b. all partners participate in running the business.
    c. there may be any number of unlimited partners.
    d. limited partners do not run the risk of unlimited liability.

36. An easement is considered:

    a. a lien.
    b. a tax.
    c. an encroachment.
    d. an encumbrance.

37. An agent, being told by his Latino buyers that they only wish to be shown homes in primarily Latino neighborhoods, does so in the selection of properties to preview. The agent:

    a. must obey the clients' instructions.
    b. would be guilty of redlining.
    c. would be guilty of steering.
    d. would be doing nothing wrong whatsoever.

38. A and B are tenants in common. A sells her share of the property to C. B and C are now:

    a. nothing, A cannot seller her share.
    b. joint tenants.
    c. tenants in common.
    d. tenants in severalty.

39. Mary and John are buying their first home from you and are relocating from out of state. They are interested in making an offer and ask about the quality of schools. You should:

    e. assure them the schools are excellent as this is merely an opinion.
    f. tell them to call the Association of REALTORS® for that information.
    g. this is something they should research on their own, perhaps with the school district.
    h. Any of these

40. This is found in insulation in residential and commercial buildings. Ingestion and inhalation present significant health hazards.

    a. lead
    b. radon
    c. formaldehyde foam
    d. EMFs

41. Section 31 would be located in which quarter of its township?

    a. NW ¼
    b. NE ¼
    c. SE ¼
    d. SW ¼

42. J makes an offer of $395,000 to buy K's house with K contributing $12,000 toward J's closing costs. K counters, accepting the $395,000 but not the contribution towards closing costs. While J contemplates the counter, K receives another offer at full price and terms which K then accepts. J is furious. Do J and K have a contract and does K have any obligation to J?

    a. No, because K didn't give J an opportunity to respond.
    b. No, because there has been no final acceptance nor communication.
    c. Yes, because K should have finished with J before proceeding with another offer.
    d. Yes, because they agreed on the price.

43. Your seller client instructs you not to mention to the buyer that the roof leaks above the master bedroom and he has concealed it with paint. What should you do?

    a. follow his instructions
    b. do nothing
    c. disclose it anyway as it is a material fact
    d. obtain a hold harmless agreement

44. Which of the following parcels is the smallest?

    a. tier
    b. township
    c. section
    d. range

45. What is the major distinction between *fraud* and *misrepresentation*?

    a. the degree to which the client suffered a monetary loss.
    b. the consequences resulting from the agent's actions.
    c. intent.
    d. the sanction imposed by the Commission.

46. Which of these would cause a contract to be declared void?

    a. not in writing
    b. one party was intoxicated at execution
    c. it is impossible to perform the duties
    d. competent parties

47. Reference to a Point of Beginning (POB) is used in the:

    a. government rectangular survey system.
    b. lot, block, and subdivision method.
    c. metes and bounds system.
    d. None of these

48. Which of these would be filed in the county records giving notice that litigation is pending concerning a property to prevent the property from being sold before the dispute is resolved?

    a. mechanic's lien.
    b. deficiency judgment.
    c. lis pendens.
    d. construction lien.

49. 14-year-old Johnny signs an employment agreement with the local newspaper to deliver newspapers. The agreement calls for Johnny to repay his bonuses received if he resigns prior to completing six months of employment. The employment agreement is:

    a. void.
    b. voidable.
    c. unenforceable.
    d. valid.

50. Who is typically the "Optionee?"

    a. a tenant
    b. the current owner of the property
    c. the lessor
    d. the holder of a first right of refusal

51. How many parties agree to a unilateral contract?

    a. 0
    b. 1
    c. 2
    d. it depends

52. An assignment of contract is permissible if:

    a. the contract is silent on the issue
    b. the contract contains verbiage allowing an assignment
    c. the parties agreed to a future assignment
    d. All of these

53. Which of the following is TRUE regarding a Grant, Bargain and Sale deed?

    a. The grantor is making additional warranties beyond those given in a General Warranty deed.
    b. The grantor is not making any warranties.
    c. The grantor's warranties are limited to the time the grantor owned the property.
    d. The grantor is offering the greatest number of warranties and covenants.

54. Fred and Betty offer to buy Sally's home with the only contingency being the qualification for a new loan. Subsequently, the buyers for Fred and Betty's home cannot qualify for the purchase and Fred and Betty cannot close. Which outcome is most likely?

    a. Their contract is cancelled and Fred and Betty will get a return of their deposit.
    b. They will lose their deposit and are subject to damages if Sally sues.
    c. Sally will be forced to wait until her buyers find another buyer who can close.
    d. Fred and Betty will have to close on Sally's home anyway.

55. A contract that is entered into by mutual mistake is:

    a. void.
    b. voidable.
    c. enforceable
    d. unenforceable.

56. The package typically provided by the seller of a home located in a CIC to the new purchaser containing all of the HOA rules and disclosures is:

    a. chain of title.
    b. certificate of title.
    c. title insurance policy.
    d. certificate of resale.

57. In order for a deed to be valid:

    a. it must be signed by the grantor.
    b. it must contain an identifiable grantee.
    c. it must contain a valid legal description.
    d. all of these

58. The lender's "commission" is the:

    a. loan processing fee.
    b. discount points.
    c. prepayment cost.
    d. loan origination fee.

59. Which of these would be found in the deed restrictions?

    a. the names of the parties
    b. limits on the grantee's use
    c. the consideration
    d. the type of deed to be utilized

60. The release clause in a deed of trust requires the mortgagee to execute a(n):

    a. satisfaction of mortgage.
    b. assignment of mortgage.
    c. subordination agreement.
    d. partial release.

61. A real estate loan with equal monthly payments where no portion of the payments is applied toward the reduction of principal is a(n):

    a. straight loan.
    b. RAM.
    c. fully amortizing loan.
    d. ARM.

62. Which party is also the lender in a financial transaction?

    a. the borrower
    b. the mortgagee
    c. the mortgagor
    d. the trustee

63. Which of these was first protected by the Federal Fair Housing Act?

    a. Ancestry
    b. Religion
    c. National Origin
    d. Race

64. Washoe Savings and Loans refuses to lend to home loan applicants who live in southeast Washoe because of the demographic composition of the applicants. The lender is guilty of:

    a. redlining.
    b. steering.
    c. blockbusting.
    d. racism.

65. Joe's lease with George ended October 31st yet Joe remains in the property without paying his rent. Which leasehold term best describes the current tenancy between George and Joe?

    a. periodic
    b. sufferance
    c. at will
    d. holdover

66. A wheelchair bound person is offered certain accommodations according to which law?

    a. FIRPTA
    b. ADA
    c. RESPA
    d. ECOA

67. Mary's investor demands a yield of at least 8.5% on any income producing buildings he buys from Jim. Jim locates a commercial building which produces net operating incomes of $135,000 per month, total. What is the highest most likely price Mary would pay?

    a. $19 million
    b. $9.6 million
    c. $1.6 million
    d. $1.4 million

68. Which of these is similar, if not the same, as a homeowners' association?

    a. CICA
    b. FHA
    c. HAO
    d. PUD

69. Which of the following would be considered an *illegal* act by a lessor?

    a. charging a family with dogs a higher security deposit than is charged when there are no pets
    b. requiring a person with a disability to pay higher rents because of the costs to modify the property for wheelchair access.
    c. refusing to rent to a lessee wishing to use the home as a house of worship
    d. refusing to sell a house to a person who has a history of drunkenness.

70. Some states prohibit a dual agency relationship while others will allow it, provided:

    a. the licensee informs the parties in writing of the dual agency relationship.
    b. the parties give their consent to the relationship
    c. the licensee is cautious about honoring the owed fiduciary duties to both parties
    d. All of these

71. Which of these would be required to be in writing according to the Statute of Frauds to be enforceable?

    a. the sale of a diamond pendant valued at $400
    b. an employment agreement between a school and a teacher
    c. a vacant lot worth $3,500
    d. the rental of a mobile home for 30 days totaling $250

72. As used in the real estate profession, the word "agency" describes:

    a. a mandatory part of the name of any company dealing in real estate transactions.
    b. the relationship between a real estate broker and the associated salespeople.
    c. the relationship between an agent and a customer.
    d. the fiduciary relationship between an agent and a principal.

73. A short-cut method for valuing real property includes *all but which* of the following?

    a. price per square foot method
    b. cost approach
    c. GRM
    d. GIM

74. The Equal Credit Opportunity Act prohibits discrimination in lending:

    a. based on receiving income from a public assistance program
    b. based on race, color, or national origin
    c. in mortgages, home improvement loans, or in the use of credit-based information
    d. All of these

75. Littoral rights pertain to the owner's rights to access of the water:

    a. when adjacent to large lakes, seas or oceans.
    b. along rivers or streams.
    c. regardless of the nature of the body of water.
    d. for non-navigable bodies of water.

76. Which of the following is commonly considered real property?

    a. curtains
    b. refrigerator
    c. unattached garage cabinetry
    d. chandelier

77. The descriptor for real property, similar to that of a social security number for a person, considered an "adequate" description is:

    a. street address.
    b. assessor's parcel number.
    c. lot, block, and subdivision.
    d. MLS number.

78. If the seller pursues the buyer's earnest money because the contract states it is forfeited upon breach by the buyer, the seller is seeking:

    a. an injunction.
    b. a claim for liquidated damages.
    c. suit for specific performance.
    d. a claim for punitive damages.

79. Your seller client has disclosed to you in confidence that the air compressor blew last night and the seller has an estimate of $4,500 to replace it. She tells you to keep this from the buyer as you are closing at the end of the week. You should:

    a. contact the buyer anyway to inform him of the damage.
    b. honor your duty of confidence as part of your fiduciary duties.
    c. do nothing as it is not your responsibility.
    d. inform your seller this information cannot be withheld and disclose it through the buyer's broker.

80. Which of the following BEST describes a valid contract?

    a. an oral or written agreement
    b. a contract that contains all five of the essential elements of a contract.
    c. a contract that is in writing and signed
    d. a contract that is NOT for an illegal purpose

81. Which of these laws require the borrower to receive a good faith estimate of loan closing costs within 3 business days of loan application?

    a. Truth in Lending
    b. RESPA
    c. ECOA
    d. Federal National Mortgages Act

82. Alice has a home loan with a balance of $414,600. The interest rate is 5.75% and the monthly P&I payments are $2,980 on a fully amortizing loan. What will be the new balance after the next payment is made? (rounded)

    a. $411,620
    b. $412,009
    c. $413,607
    d. $414,600

83. What is the total square footage of the following floor plan?

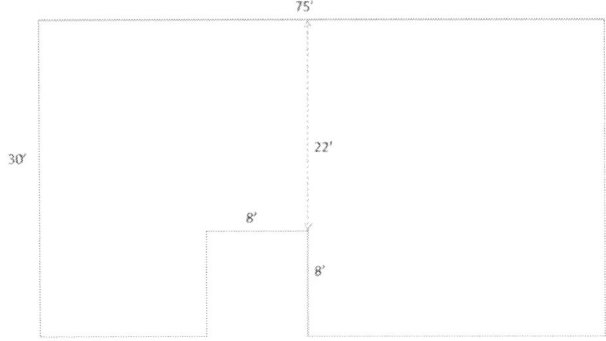

    a. 2,186
    b. 2,250
    c. 2,910
    d. There is not enough information.

84. The subject property is 3,200 square feet, has 5 bedrooms, and a pool/spa. The comparable, which sold for $415,000, is 2,750 square feet, has 4 bedrooms, and a pool. The appraiser uses the following data for making adjustments:

    Price per square foot: $125
    One Bedroom: $8,000
    Pool: $25,000
    Spa: $12,000

    What adjustments would the appraiser make?

    a. adjust the subject downward $20,000
    b. adjust the subject upward $76,250
    c. adjust the comparable upward $56,250
    d. adjust the comparable upward $76,250

85. A 90 unit apartment complex averages $850 per month per unit in rents collected after vacancies and bad debts with 31% operating expenses. Tony's investor client is interested in purchasing the building, but requires a 9.5% return. What is the most Tony's investor would likely offer? (rounded)

    a. $630,000
    b. $918,000
    c. $6.6 million
    d. $9.6 million

86. Which form of depreciation is *always* incurable?

    a. economic obsolescence
    b. physical depreciation
    c. functional obsolescence
    d. physical deterioration

87. The county charges doc stamps at a rate of $6.50 per $500 of value, or any portion thereof. The sale price is $148,900 and the home loan is for $134,500. What is the amount of the transfer tax and to whom is it a debit?

    a. $1,748.50, debit to the buyer.
    b. $1,930.50, debit to the seller.
    c. $1,937.00, debit to the seller.
    d. None of these

88. On the 5th of the month, a Broker writes a check against his trust account to pay the rent for his office space. The broker could be disciplined by the licensing authority for:

    a. conversion.
    b. failure to account.
    c. commingling.
    d. All of these

89. The listing and selling firms agree to split a 6% commission equally on a $520,000 sale. The listing agent is paid on a 65% split with the firm retaining 35%. How much does the selling salesperson earn from the sale?

    a. $10,140
    b. $15,600
    c. $31,200
    d. There is not enough information.

90. Which of these agents will most likely be a general agent?

    a. listing agent
    b. selling agent
    c. property manager
    d. broker

FINAL EXAM II - Answer Key

1.	D	24.	C	47.	C	70.	D
2.	C	25.	D	48.	C	71.	C
3.	D	26.	A	49.	B	72.	D
4.	D	27.	C	50.	A	73.	B
5.	B	28.	D	51.	C	74.	D
6.	A	29.	D	52.	D	75.	A
7.	B	30.	C	53.	D	76.	D
8.	B	31.	B	54.	B	77.	B
9.	D	32.	C	55.	C	78.	B
10.	B	33.	D	56.	D	79.	D
11.	A	34.	D	57.	D	80.	B
12.	C	35.	B	58.	D	81.	B
13.	B	36.	D	59.	B	82.	C
14.	C	37.	C	60.	A	83.	A
15.	D	38.	C	61.	A	84.	D
16.	A	39.	C	62.	B	85.	C
17.	D	40.	C	63.	D	86.	A
18.	D	41.	D	64.	A	87.	C
19.	C	42.	B	65.	B	88.	A
20.	C	43.	C	66.	B	89.	D
21.	B	44.	C	67.	A	90.	C
22.	D	45.	C	68.	A		
23.	B	46.	C	69.	B		

FINAL EXAM: III

1. To calculate the gross rent multiplier, one would divide the sales price of the property by the:

   a. net operating income.
   b. gross annual rent.
   c. number of square feet.
   d. gross monthly rent.

2. Which of the following are acceptable methods to calculate the replacement cost in the cost approach?

   a. unit in place
   b. quantity survey
   c. price per square foot
   d. all of these

3. Smith was successful in obtaining a judgment against Jones and recorded the judgment against Jones' property in the county records. Any potential buyer for Jones' property, whether checking the records or not, has been provided:

   a. prescriptive notice.
   b. constructive notice.
   c. actual notice.
   d. exculpatory notice.

4. A broker sloppily tells a purchaser that the appreciation rate in the neighborhood is one of the highest appreciation rates in the area without the facts to support the statement. The purchaser could rescind the agreement based on:

   a. fraud.
   b. misrepresentation.
   c. puffery.
   d. intentional deceipt.

5. A large percentage of homes built prior to 1978 are estimated to have potentially dangerous levels of lead. Because of this, some federal agencies, such as FHA:

   a. will not insure or guarantee these loans.
   b. requires testing and removal before approving loans on these properties.
   c. requires the buyer to acknowledge the possible existence of lead in the home.
   d. requires the seller to remediate any discovered lead contaminants before the transaction can close.

6. A purchase agreement that has not yet closed is considered to be:

   a. executed.
   b. executory.
   c. ostensible.
   d. voidable.

7. A fiduciary relationship exists between a broker and the broker's:

   a. client.
   b. customer.
   c. prospect.
   d. any of these

8. A seller may require an earnest money deposit in a transaction in order to:

   a. assure the buyer has sufficient cash to close the transaction.
   b. pay the broker a commission in the event the transaction does not close.
   c. show proof of the buyer's sincerity in fulfilling his contractual obligations.
   d. discontinue the presentation of future offers.

9. Buyer A made an offer to Seller B, which was not accepted. However, Seller B made a counteroffer to Buyer A which A signed and accepted. A's real estate agent delivered the acceptance to Seller B's agent. Meanwhile, Buyer A made an offer on Seller C's property which Seller C signed, accepted, and delivered to A. Which of the following is TRUE?

    a. only the contract between Buyer A and Seller B is valid.
    b. only the contract between Buyer A and Seller C is valid.
    c. both contracts are valid.
    d. neither contract is valid.

10. A buyer has a loan where the payments are interest only until the due date, at which time the full amount of the loan is due and payable. This is a(n):

    a. amortized loan.
    b. partially amortized loan.
    c. term loan.
    d. graduated payment mortgage.

11. A buyer and seller agree to a sale price of $100,000. The buyer is making application for an 80% LTV loan. Upon appraisal, the property is appraised at $90,000. What will be the required down payment for the buyer should the buyer which to proceed and assuming the sale price is not adjusted?

    a. $18,000
    b. $20,000
    c. $28,000
    d. none of these

12. A purchaser pledges her real property as collateral for the loan issued for her to purchase it and a lien is filed in favor of the lender. Who has legal title?

    a. mortgagee
    b. mortgagor
    c. vendor
    d. beneficiary

13. Mr. and Mrs. DeBernard leased a home for one year. The couple intends to move out at the end of the one year term. How much notice must the DeBernards give their landlord of their intent to terminate?

    a. 30 days
    b. 60 days
    c. 90 days
    d. no notice is required

14. When one owns shares of common stock in a corporation:

    a. one owns real property in common with other shareholders with respect to any real property held by the corporation.
    b. one is assured that the price of the stock will not decline when property values owned by the corporation decline.
    c. one owns a personal property interest.
    d. one can order the sale of any property owned by the corporation.

15. In front of a witness, Frank tells Penny he will pay $285,000 for her home located at 9906 Cherry Street. Penny tells Frank that is acceptable, and they shake hands. The contract is not enforceable because:

    a. the agreement is not in writing.
    b. there is no consideration.
    c. there is no discussion of earnest money.
    d. the closing date was not specified.

16. A formal appraisal will always be required when:

    a. the buyer wants to be assured of the property's worth.
    b. the lender will be selling the loan in the secondary market.
    c. the loan will require private mortgage insurance.
    d. the buyer is putting down less than a 20% down payment.

17. When a broker is placed into a relationship of trust and confidence with a client, the relationship is said to be one of a:

    a. fiduciary.
    b. brokerage.
    c. customer.
    d. client.

18. Due to antitrust laws, real estate brokers are prohibited from doing all of the following EXCEPT:

    a. dividing the market geographically and refraining from doing business in each other's territories.
    b. refusing to business with other brokers in the market.
    c. agreeing to set a standard commission of 7%.
    d. receiving commissions from both parties to a transaction.

19. The contract between the parties indicates that in the event the purchaser defaults on the contract, the seller is entitled to the $10,000 earnest money being held in trust by the broker. The $10,000 may be referred to as:

    a. punitive damages.
    b. liquidated damages.
    c. the settlement.
    d. a specific lien.

20. Broker Bob has produced buyers who are ready, willing, and able to meet the price and terms specified by the sellers. Under most listing agreements, Bob has earned his commission when:

    a. the transaction closes.
    b. the sellers accept the offer.
    c. the buyers qualify for the loan.
    d. the transaction is funded.

21. A benefit to the lender of a deed of trust rather than a mortgage is:

    a. a deed of trust eliminates community property issues.
    b. a deed of trust is less costly and easier to prepare.
    c. it is usually easier and quicker to foreclose.
    d. it is only a two-party instrument.

22. Terms such as "littoral," "riparian," and "prior appropriation" refer to:

    a. easements.
    b. land accretion.
    c. mineral rights.
    d. water rights.

23. The Federal Housing Administration functions similar to a(n):

    a. lending agency.
    b. insurance company.
    c. investment trust.
    d. mortgage company.

24. An easement can be created by all of the following EXCEPT:

    a. an assemblage of the properties.
    b. an agreement between the owners.
    c. the parties acting as if they have an agreement.
    d. a reservation in a deed.

25. An agreement where a seller agrees to sell, and a buyer agrees to purchase, is called a(n):

    a. novation.
    b. assumption.
    c. contract.
    d. agency.

26. The sellers ask their real estate salesperson to recommend a list price for their property. The salesperson's best response would be:

    a. to list the property 10% higher than the last sale in the neighborhood.
    b. to list the property at whatever price the seller wishes.
    c. to prepare a comparative market analysis to determine the property's current value.
    d. to order an appraisal.

27. A listing agreement is immediately terminated upon:

    a. the death of the salesperson.
    b. the death of the seller.
    c. the seller's divorce.
    d. the salesperson's relocation to another brokerage firm.

28. Lilly is applying for a new loan in the amount of $195,000. Her mortgage broker quotes her a rate of 5.5% for a 30-year loan (payment factor of 5.68 per thousand) or a rate of 6% on a 15-year loan (payment factor of 8.44 per thousand). What is the difference in the monthly payment between Lilly's two loan options?

    a. $276.00
    b. $389.90
    c. $411.50
    d. $538.20

29. Of the following, the best example of a buffer zone is:

    a. an apartment complex developed in between a neighborhood of single family homes and a shopping center.
    b. a new storage unit center opened between a townhouse community and a city park.
    c. a new home development being built in the middle of an office park and high rise apartments.
    d. a locals casino constructed between two single family neighborhoods.

30. Georgette is in default of her mortgage which contains an acceleration clause. Because of this clause, Georgette's lender has the right to:

    a. force Georgette from the home.
    b. seize all of Georgette's assets.
    c. demand the loan be paid immediately in full.
    d. file a loss claim with the private mortgage insurance company.

31. The closing of a property took place on July 16th. Property insurance for the full calendar year in the amount of $800 had already been paid in full. How much does the buyer owe the seller assuming a 360 day year where the seller pays for the day of closing?

    a. $222.22
    b. $364.44
    c. $400.00
    d. $435.55

32. Brown makes an offer on Stanton's property. Stanton responds by making a counteroffer to Brown. While Brown was considering the counteroffer, Stanton received an offer from Conti. Stanton can accept Conti's offer if:

    a. it is a better offer than Brown's offer.
    b. Stanton first withdraws his counteroffer to Brown.
    c. Brown rejects or counters Stanton's counteroffer.
    d. Conti is willing to be in a backup offer position.

33. The federal law that regulates a lender's advertising of credit terms is:

    a. ECOA.
    b. RESPA.
    c. the Fair Housing Act.
    d. Regulation Z.

34. Crops that require annual planting are considered to be:

    a. personal property.
    b. real property.
    c. improvements.
    d. fixtures.

35. Tom and Harriet are moving to a new city and wish to rent for a short while to determine where they would like to buy a home. Which type of lease agreement would best suit Tom and Harriet's needs?

    a. a one-year lease
    b. a month-to-month tenancy
    c. a lease option
    d. a lease purchase

36. Real estate broker commissions are determined by:

    a. the MLS.
    b. what is standard in the industry.
    c. agreements between brokers and their clients.
    d. the local association of REALTORS®.

37. Upon finalizing the closing, the escrowee must furnish the seller's social security number and the amount of the net proceeds to:

    a. FIRPTA.
    b. the Social Security Administration.
    c. HUD.
    d. the IRS.

38. The purpose of an Environmental Impact Statement (EIS) is to identify the anticipated effects of developing a new project as they pertain to:

    a. the safety and health of the public.
    b. the highest and best use of the land.
    c. zoning.
    d. the government.

39. Which of the following is FALSE regarding loan discount points?

    a. They reduce the borrower's interest rate.
    b. They can be paid for by the buyer or the seller.
    c. One point equals 1% of the selling price.
    d. They increase the lender's yield.

40. Driscoll wants to list his property with more than one real estate broker simultaneously. He can do this with which type of listing?

    a. open listing
    b. exclusive agency listing
    c. exclusive right to sell listing
    d. Driscoll cannot be listed with more than one broker at one time.

41. An offer is accompanied by a $5,000 earnest money check. The earnest money should be deposited in a trust account:

    a. at the broker's discretion.
    b. promptly according to state laws.
    c. in accordance with MLS rules.
    d. one day prior to the close of escrow.

42. A loan that is federally related requires that the appraisal be performed by a licensed or certified appraiser for residential properties with values in excess of:

    a. $150,000
    b. $250,000
    c. $325,000
    d. $418,500

43. A deed restriction on a property restricts the use of the property for the:

    a. present owner only.
    b. the current and future owners.
    c. future owners only.
    d. developer.

44. State usury laws:

    a. limit the fees lenders can charge when originating loans.
    b. prohibit competing mortgage brokers from collusion on setting interest rates.
    c. limit interest rates that may be charged on certain loans.
    d. govern the uses to which vacant land may be utilized.

45. A managing broker of a branch office may be held responsible for:

    a. all actions of all associated licensees of the firm.
    b. only those real estate related actions for which the managing broker is aware.
    c. all real estate related actions of all licensees whether the manager was aware or not aware.
    d. real estate related actions of only those licensees who are of employee status.

46. A lawsuit for inverse condemnation is initiated by the:

    a. government.
    b. land owner.
    c. tax payers.
    d. zoning board.

47. An African-American family of four qualified for a home priced between $350,000 and $375,000. The couple told the real estate agent they wanted a four bedroom home and asked to see a house that was listed in a predominantly Caucasian neighborhood. The licensee did not show the family the house because it was priced at $275,000 and had only three bedrooms. Did the salesperson act appropriately?

    a. Yes, because they could afford a much better home.
    b. Yes, because the salesperson should select which houses the buyers will see.
    c. No, because any qualified buyer should be allowed to see any home for which they are qualified.
    d. No, because the agent was steering the family toward African-American communities.

48. With a contract for deed, who holds fee ownership of the property?

    a. vendee
    b. vendor
    c. beneficiary
    d. mortgagor

49. A principal who authorizes an agent to conduct certain activities for a particular transaction has a:

    a. universal agency relationship.
    b. general agency relationship.
    c. specific agency relationship.
    d. real estate agency.

50. A home with a market value of $240,000 was assessed at 60% of its market value. If the tax rate is $16 per thousand, what are the monthly taxes the lender will require to be impounded?

    a. $2,304
    b. $3,065
    c. $3,840
    d. There is not enough information.

51. Economic characteristics of land include:

    a. location, scarcity, and durability.
    b. immobility, indestructibility, and uniqueness.
    c. subsurface, surface, and air rights.
    d. development, growth, recession, and recovery.

52. Timothy violated the restrictions placed on the property by the deed. The penalty for Timothy's violations could lead to:

    a. a forced sale of the property.
    b. an injunction, stopping his further use of the property.
    c. monetary penalties.
    d. the return of the property to the grantor.

53. The listing salesperson should himself verify:

    a. the integrity of the roof.
    b. whether there is toxic mold present.
    c. if there is radon gas in the home.
    d. the number of square feet of the house.

54. The government has the authority to adopt legislation to protect public health and safety, preserve order, and promote general welfare under:

    a. eminent domain.
    b. escheat.
    c. police powers.
    d. taxation.

55. Julie's listing with the sellers expired on January 7th. On January 11th, the sellers listed with another agent of a different firm. On January 12th, salesperson Karen contacted Julie asking for instructions on how to show the property. Julie should tell Karen:

    a. the seller keeps a spare key under the welcome mat.
    b. the house is no longer for sale.
    c. she will arrange for an appointment to show.
    d. she is no longer the listing agent.

56. A real estate broker and two of his partners agree to lend a developer the funds needed to build a townhouse project with the stipulation the broker has the exclusive right to list the townhouses for sale when the project is complete. This agreement is an example of a(n):

    a. exclusive right to sell.
    b. agency coupled with an interest.
    c. specific agency.
    d. option contract.

57. While showing the house on Franklin street, salesperson Mary tells the buyers, "This is the nicest house in the community." Mary's comments are considered:

    a. puffing.
    b. misrepresentation.
    c. fraud.
    d. steering.

58. The U.S. Government Rectangular Survey method of legal descriptions:

    a. includes a reference to plat map.
    b. both starts and ends with a point of beginning.
    c. is not generally found in the original 13 states.
    d. is not valid for use in deeds.

59. While listing their house for sale, the sellers tell the listing salesperson they require net proceeds of $20,000, have a mortgage to pay off of $185,000, and will agree to a 6.5% commission. What will the selling price need to be to accomplish the sellers' needs?

    a. $205,000
    b. $218,325
    c. $219,251
    d. There is not enough information.

60. Salesperson Janine lists the home of Mr. and Mrs. Erickson. Janine is classified as:

    a. a special agent.
    b. the seller's agent.
    c. a dual agent.
    d. the subagent of the seller.

61. In their will, husband and wife name their adopted son to be the heir for their primary residence. The husband and wife:

    a. cannot sell the residence to anyone without the written consent of the adopted son.
    b. cannot lease or sell the property.
    c. cannot alter their will and decide to leave the home to anyone else.
    d. may alter the will through a codicil or another will.

62. When showing a home to his purchasers, Ted is asked if the laundry room has a 220 outlet for their electric dryer to which Ted responds, "Yes, it does." After closing and moving into the property, the purchasers discover there is no 220 line but only a gas hook up. Which of these would best protect Ted and his broker from a financial loss?

    a. Education, Research, and Recovery Fund
    b. Home Warranty Policy
    c. Business Liability Insurance
    d. Errors and Omissions Insurance

63. Adams has obtained a judgment against Benson and Benson refuses to pay. What is the next step for Adams to seek payment?

    a. writ of execution
    b. lis pendens
    c. writ of attachment
    d. notice of default

64. With respect to the Truth in Lending Act, all of the following are "trigger terms" with the exception of:

    a. loan term.
    b. interest rate.
    c. prepayment penalties.
    d. down payment.

65. Which of the three approaches to value is most relevant to appraising a single family residence?

    a. cost approach
    b. market data approach
    c. income approach
    d. replacement approach

66. One of the benefits to purchasing a condominium rather than a detached, single family home is:

    a. there are more tax advantages of buying a condominium.
    b. condominiums are easier to resell.
    c. condominiums appreciate faster.
    d. condominiums are usually much more affordable.

67. A buyer wishes to purchase a property with an accompanying early occupancy agreement allowing the buyer to take possession of the property before closing. One of the best options for the buyer's salesperson is to:

    a. recommend the buyer and seller work that out on their own.
    b. to turn the matter over to the listing salesperson to handle.
    c. recommend the buyer have her attorney review the matter and construct such an agreement.
    d. talk to another agent in the firm for help.

68. The $66.33 sewer bill for July, August, and September will be available in early October. The parties are closing on the 31st of July. Using a 360 day year where the seller pays for the day of closing, what is the proration to be made at closing?

    a. credit the seller $22.11; debit the buyer $22.11
    b. credit the buyer $22.11; debit the seller $22.11
    c. credit the seller $44.22; debit the buyer $44.22
    d. credit the buyer $44.22; debit the seller $44.22

69. 16-year-old Audrey enters into a contract with a dance studio for ballet lessons. After two weeks of lessons, Audrey is dissatisfied with her instructor and wishes to cancel her contract. May she do so?

    a. Yes, because the contract is voidable.
    b. Yes, because the contract is void.
    c. No, because the contract is valid.
    d. No, because the contract is unenforceable.

70. A trade fixture is usually treated as:

    a. a fixture.
    b. an easement.
    c. personalty.
    d. real property.

71. A home with badly cracked and termite infested trusses is best described as suffering from:

    a. curable functional depreciation.
    b. incurable physical depreciation.
    c. incurable environmental depreciation.
    d. curable physical depreciation.

72. Where the borrower is allowed possession of the collateral while paying off the loan against it is called:

    a. a pawn.
    b. a UCC 1 lien.
    c. a deed of trust.
    d. a hypothecation.

73. An exclusive agency listing:

    a. allows the sellers to sell the property themselves without paying a commission.
    b. allows other brokers to advertise the property as their listing.
    c. forces the sellers to find all prospects through the exclusive agency broker.
    d. is illegal in most states.

74. You have listed a house built in 1976. What, if any, federally mandated disclosures are required in this transaction?

    a. nothing special other than the normal state disclosures
    b. location of known areas of seismic activity
    c. the Fair Credit Reporting Act disclosure
    d. the lead based paint disclosure and warnings

75. Your client needs $60,000 after paying off a mortgage of $289,000 and your commission of 6%. How much must the property sell for? (round up to nearest dollar)

    a. $371,277
    b. $379,940
    c. $369,950
    d. $349,000

76. A portion of Walter's building was inadvertently built on George's land. This caused an:

    a. accretion.
    b. avulsion.
    c. encroachment.
    d. easement.

77. For land to be taken by the government under its right of eminent domain, which of the following must apply?

    a. The taking must be for a public purpose.
    b. There must be a statutory dedication.
    c. This must be an adverse action.
    d. There must be constructive notice.

78. To create joint tenancy in the ownership of real estate, there must be equal unities of:

    a. grantees, ownership, claim of right, and possession.
    b. title, interest, encumbrance, and survivorship.
    c. possession, time, interest, and title.
    d. ownership, possession, heirs, and title.

79. Abel and Baker are joint tenants. Baker sells his interest to Charlie. What is the relationship of Abel and Charlie?

    a. They are joint tenants.
    b. They are tenants in common.
    c. There is no relationship because Baker cannot sell to Charlie.
    d. Abel owns a 2/3 interest and Charlie owns a 1/3 interest.

80. The clause in a mortgage instrument that would prevent the assumption of the mortgage by a new purchaser is a:

    a. due-on-sale clause.
    b. power-of-sale clause.
    c. defeasance clause.
    d. certificate of sale clause.

81. Under the community property laws of the state in which the couple live, all of the following apply to John and Mary Duncan EXCEPT:

    a. each may also own separate property.
    b. Mary may not convey community property without John's consent.
    c. John may also own community property with a person other than Mary.
    d. neither may encumber community property without the other's consent.

82. The south 1/2 of the SE 1/4 of the NW 1/4 of the NE 1/4 of Section 7 contains how many acres?

    a. 2.5
    b. 5
    c. 10
    d. 20

83. A mechanic's lien would be properly classified as a(n):

    a. equitable lien.
    b. voluntary lien.
    c. general lien.
    d. specific lien.

84. The mixing of trust funds with a broker's personal funds is:

    a. conversion.
    b. commingling.
    c. legal in most states.
    d. permitted in offices with fewer than three agents.

85. If a house sold for $80,000 and the buyer obtained a 90% LTV loan, how much money would the buyer pay for discount points if the lender charged 3 points?

    a. $2,400
    b. $2,328
    c. $2,160
    d. $240

86. A commercial lessee who pays some or all of the lessor's property expenses has a:

    a. gross lease.
    b. net lease.
    c. percentage lease.
    d. sublease.

87. If the potential gross rental income from a property is $20,000, the vacancy rate is 5 percent, and the additional income the landlord receives for providing laundry facilities and extra storage is $700, what is the effective gross income?

    a. $19,000
    b. $19,700
    c. $20,000
    d. $20,700

88. Carbon monoxide is *NOT*:

    a. easy to detect.
    b. a result of incomplete combustion.
    c. quickly absorbed in the body.
    d. a natural result of combustion.

89. Which deed has the greatest number of warranties?

    a. a Quit Claim Deed.
    b. a General Warranty Deed.
    c. a Bargain and Sale Deed.
    d. an Executor's Deed.

90. A lot that measures 300' X 300' is a little larger than what number of acres?

    a. 1 acre
    b. 2 acres
    c. 3 acres
    d. 4 acres

FINAL EXAM III - Answer Key

1.	D	24.	A	47.	C	70.	C
2.	D	25.	C	48.	B	71.	B
3.	B	26.	C	49.	C	72.	D
4.	B	27.	B	50.	A	73.	A
5.	C	28.	D	51.	A	74.	D
6.	B	29.	A	52.	D	75.	A
7.	A	30.	C	53.	D	76.	C
8.	C	31.	B	54.	C	77.	A
9.	C	32.	B	55.	D	78.	C
10.	C	33.	D	56.	B	79.	B
11.	C	34.	A	57.	A	80.	A
12.	B	35.	B	58.	C	81.	C
13.	D	36.	C	59.	C	82.	B
14.	C	37.	D	60.	D	83.	D
15.	A	38.	A	61.	D	84.	B
16.	B	39.	C	62.	D	85.	C
17.	A	40.	A	63.	A	86.	B
18.	D	41.	B	64.	C	87.	B
19.	B	42.	B	65.	B	88.	A
20.	B	43.	B	66.	D	89.	B
21.	C	44.	C	67.	C	90.	B
22.	D	45.	C	68.	B		
23.	B	46.	B	69.	A		

Appendix D
Glossary

1031 tax deferred exchanges allows investors to *exchange or trade* their property for other U.S. investment property and may be able to do so without having a current taxable event

abandonment may have occurred if the broker failed to actively market the property. This is really a revocation by the seller with the reason (none actually being required) being the broker has ceased to represent the property.

absentee owners live elsewhere from the subject property

abstract of title summarizes everything found in the public records which will include *recorded* encumbrances and liens. *Unrecorded* matters will not be noted as they will not be found.

acceleration clause allows the lender to call all payments due if the borrower defaults. This allows for a foreclosure of the entire outstanding balance. This clause "accelerates" the time for which payment is due to *now*.

acceptance of offer occurs when all parties agree to every detail of the last offer as submitted, no matter how small

accession refers to trade fixtures not removed by the tenant at the end of a commercial lease becoming the property of the landlord. This term also applies to the accretion of alluvial deposits.

accounting or accountability refers to the agent's receipt of money, property, or other things of value which belong to the client. The agent must account to the client for these items and must use great care in protecting the client's interests.

accretion is the increases in land due to where the action of water has added to the land

acknowledged means to be witnessed by a notary public

acre equals 43,560 square feet

actual eviction is the legal manner in which a landlord evicts the tenant

actual notice is accomplished by ***recording*** an interest with the county recorder's office. Recording puts the world at large of a recorded interest.

ad valorem tax is a tax levied based upon the property value

addendum is used If the parties discover a need to change or add terms after a contract has been signed

adjustable rate mortgage (ARM) has interest rates that fluctuate with the lender's cost of funds. The ARM has the following elements: index, margin, interval, cap, ceiling and floor, and sometimes a conversion feature.

adjusted basis is the original purchase price of an investment property plus any capital improvements made, less any depreciation previously taken

adjusted gross income*, or* ***effective gross income****,* is the income *actually collected or earned*. It is the gross scheduled income less the vacancies and bad debts.

administrator is a court-appointed individual who will oversee the distribution of a deceased's assets if there is no will

agency coupled with an interest refers to the agent having some legal right to, or an interest in, the property that is covered by the agency arrangement. If the agency is coupled with an interest, the agency usually cannot be revoked by the principal before the expiration of the interest. The interest gives the agent a level of legal power over any decisions about the principal's property.

agency describes the fiduciary relationship between the agent and the principal

agricultural real estate involves lands used for farming and cultivating crops, usually 10 or more acres

alienation clause (sometimes referred to as a ***due on sale clause***) informs the borrower, in advance, that the lender will not permit an assignment of the borrower's obligations under the note, or interest in the property, unless the lender is paid in full. As the name implies, the loan is due on sale – if there is a sale, the loan is due. ***Alienation*** refers to alienating oneself from the property.

alienation refers to "alienating" or separating one's self from the property. The most common example is deeding the property away after a sale has consummated.

all-inclusive deed of trust (or ***wrap around mortgage***) is a form of seller financing (purchase money mortgage) available only where there is no existing ***due on sale*** clause in the original mortgage document. The seller still owes on the original mortgage (the ***underlying mortgage***) and continues to make those payments. The buyer makes payments to the seller for the new amount financed as a purchase money mortgage.

allocation of customers occurs when several firms agree to divide markets and refrain from competing for customers. Brokers by internal policy may, however, allocate customers or markets into geographic areas where they plan to operate exclusively.

ALTA title insurance policy is a policy written to the standards of the American Land Title Association.

amenities are other factors that contribute to the subject property's value, in some instances, such as curb appeal, condition of exterior, nearby parks and shops, neighborhood condition, traffic or noise, and the school district.

Americans with Disabilities Act (ADA) is an anti-discrimination law that deals with physical workplace accommodations for disabled persons. The ADA prohibits discrimination in employment practices against persons with disabilities.

amortization is the pattern in which the principal of a loan is paid. With a level payment, fully amortizing loan, the amount of the payment remains the same over the life of the loan, however the components of principal and interest change with each payment. As the balance of the loan is reduced by payment of the principal, the amount for interest will decrease with each payment. This process causes the loan to pay off at the stated term.

annexation refers to converting personal property to real property through the method attachment

annual percentage rate (APR) is the finance charges to obtain the loan, expressed a percentage when applied to the unpaid balance of the loan

anticipation of change may be taking place in some parts of a community. The available uses for parcels may be changing. Local economic considerations may be affecting values. Anticipation of these changes can affect market value.

appraisal is the art of estimating a property's market value. It is an estimate by an appraiser of the current price which will most probably be paid in a market consisting of informed buyers and sellers who are acting under normal and rational motivations. Such a transaction should be at ***arm's length***, meaning there is no special pricing because of the relationship of the parties.

appraiser is an individual licensed or certified by a state authority who is educated in the field of valuation and is skilled in estimating the current value of property

appreciation is the increase in value

arm's length means there is no special pricing because of the relationship of the parties; the parties are at an arm's length distance from one another and negotiating in their own best interests

as is is used in many listings to communicate the fact that a property is being sold in its "known" present condition. It does not mean that a seller has been absolved of all responsibility relative to defects of which he or she is aware.

asbestos is found in insulation and in ceiling and floor tiles. Removal is very expensive, and inhalation of asbestos can lead to serious, often fatal lung disease.

assemblage and plottage comes into play when two or more parcels are legally combined into one (assemblage) and the resulting value is higher than the sum of the value of the individual parcels (plottage)

assessed value is the value derived after applying the ***assessment ratio*** to the ***market value***.

assessment is the levying of a tax

assessment ratio is an *artificial lowering* of the market value. The assessment ration is applied to the ***market value*** to determine the ***assessed value.***

assigned agency, also called ***designated agency,*** is utilized in some states where brokers are allowed to "designate" agents to represent clients. This could happen when one salesperson is designated to represent the seller and another is designated to represent the buyer in the same transaction.

assignment clause gives the borrower notice that the lender will likely be transferring the mortgage or deed of trust to another party sometime after the closing on the loan. As a mortgage or deed of trust is a contact, the lender wants to be sure there is no problem with the borrower if the lender assigns the contract to another investor or to the ***Secondary Mortgage Market.***

assignment of contract may occur when one party desires to assign his rights, obligations, and benefits under the contract to a third party. However that original party will remain liable for performance and obligations should the third party fail to perform. This is called ***secondary liability***. Contracts are freely and fully assignable unless prohibited in the agreement.

assumption clause describes under what circumstances, if any, the lender will allow another person to assume the mortgage or deed of trust

assumption of a mortgage means a person is acquiring property with an underlying loan and agrees to personally take over financial responsibility for the mortgage.

attestation in a deed is the notary public's swearing that the signing parties appeared before the notary, swore they were who they said they were, were authorized to sign the deed and did so as their free act, and actually signed the deed in the presence of the notary public

avulsion is the sudden removal of soil by an act of nature can cause a landowner's property to become much smaller very quickly

balloon loan amortizes at the stated interest rate and term, as if it were a fully amortizing loan, but requires an early payoff in a lump sum

bargain and sale deed contains an implied warranty of seisin. There are no written warranties and is only an implication that the grantor has title and the legal right to convey it.

base lines are the primary horizontal lines referenced when using the U.S. Government Rectangular Survey system

benchmark is a permanent reference mark, sometimes called a "brass cap," usually embedded in streets or sidewalks and used by surveyors as a reference point for elevations

beneficiary is the lender in a deed of trust

bequest is personal property given through a will

bilateral contracts are two-sided agreements where both parties are making promises and are undertaking performing those promises. One promise is given in exchange for another.

blanket mortgage will cover multiple parcels and is common in subdivision development financing. This loan will have a ***partial release clause*** allowing the builder to pull the parcel sold "out from under" the blanket mortgage.

blockbusting is the illegal attempting to create panic selling by creating a sales contract with a member of a protected class with the intent to use the sale to a protected class member as a method of inducing owners in the area to sell, before the neighborhood becomes too "mixed" or the homes lose value

boot is money or property added to make up the difference in value between two properties being exchanged in a 1031 deferred exchange

breach of contract occurs if either of the parties to a contract fails or refuses to perform any duties per the contract. The injured party has legal remedies available.

broker is an agent who agrees to represent the interests of the principal, and who agrees to let the broker exercise authority on behalf of the principal

broker price opinion is a tool to determine value as requested by a third party such as the lender in the case of foreclosure and by a relocation company in the event of an executive transfer that will result in a buyout. "BPOs" are generally performed by licensed real estate agents and brokers for a nominal fee. BPOs are normally more involved than a market analysis and less sophisticated than an appraisal.

brokerage is the matchmaking of people and bringing them together in a transaction of some kind

budget loans have payments of principal, interest, taxes, and insurance (PITI) and the mortgage insurance premium is included in the monthly payment

buffer zones are required separations between conflicting uses. They are often an area of land zoned for a use that smoothly *transitions* from one use to another.

building codes are enforced by requiring the builder to submit plans before construction can be commenced, and once the plans are approved, periodic inspections are conducted to be sure the construction is following the approved plans and is being done in a workman like manner

building permit has to be issued before construction can be commenced by the developer

bundle of rights include possession, control, enjoyment, exclusion, and disposition

business opportunities involves the sale or lease of existing businesses

buydown results when discount points are paid to buy the interest rate down and hence the name "discount" points

buyer brokerage agreement establishes an exclusive relationship where the buyer employs the broker to locate the desired property and to negotiate with the sellers on the buyer's behalf for the best available price and terms for a purchase (or a lease if a tenant representation agreement)

cap refers to the maximum the interest rate can change in any interval. This will be stated in the note and will not be changed for the life of the loan.

capital gain occurs when an asset is sold for more than its original cost basis. The *profit* realized may represent a capital gain. If the property is an investment property, the capital gain can probably be treated under the capital gain provisions in the tax code.

capital improvement is a major or significant improvement to investment property which will add value to the investment property and is of a durable nature and which will or is expected to last several years

capitalization rate, cap rate, desired rate of return, or ***return on investment***, is the yield to the investor for investing in the income property. This rate may be determined based on the current income and value of the property, or the rate the investor demands. This rate will be compared to alternate investments such as stocks, bonds, mutual funds, and anything the investor may have an interest in.

capitalization refers to estimating the value of property by dividing the net operating income by a desired rate of return (capitalization rate)

carbon monoxide (CO) is a colorless and odorless gas that occurs as a byproduct of burning certain types of fuels. It can pose a significant health hazard if not properly ventilated.

caveat emptor, translating to "buyer beware," refers to the buyer's obligation to discover all of the possible things wrong with a property before the purchase is consummated

ceiling and floor, sometimes called the ***lifetime cap***, the ceiling represents the maximum interest rate the borrower can be charged anytime during the life of the loan. Likewise, the ***floor*** represents the minimum interest rate the borrower will have to pay anytime during the life of the loan. This will be stated in the note and will not be changed for the life of the loan.

certificate of reasonable value (CRV) is the VA appraisal

chain of title is a history report making sure the title company can "link" each owner from the current owner all the way back to the first owner with no gaps (breaks) in the links

change and anticipation of change may be taking place in some parts of a community. The available uses for parcels may be changing. Local economic considerations may be affecting values.

chattel is another word for personal property

Civil Rights Act of 1866 (Reconstruction Act) provides that all persons born in the United States are declared to be citizens, regardless of race or color, and shall have the right to enter into contracts, to sue, inherit, acquire and dispose of property, and shall equally benefit from the law as do white citizens. Classes protected by this law are race and color.

client is the principal to whom the agent is expected to give advice and counsel during the period of agency

CLTA title insurance policy is a title policy written to the standards of the California Land Title Association

Code of Ethics and Standards of Practice are the rules by which all members of the National Association of REALTORS® agree to abide

codicil is a modification to a will

collateral is the real or personal property upon which the lien is given to secure the borrowing

commercial real estate involves income producing properties such as multi-unit dwellings, retail shopping centers, office buildings, etc.

common elements are components of the property, usually condominiums, that all owners benefit from and enjoy such as the club house, swimming pool, and other amenities. These are owned by all (***undivided interest***) of the condominium owners as *tenants in common.*

common interest communities (CICs) are often organized by a new home builder and set standards of behavior and living for a defined community. This is done through the establishment of **conditions, covenants & restrictions (CC&Rs)** that all homeowners agree to follow.

community property statutes create the possibility that a married couple may have property which belongs solely to the wife, or solely to the husband, or property which is held by them as community property. Community property is all property acquired by either the husband or the wife during the marriage and each spouse is presumed to own a 50% interest in the community property.

comparable sales approach or **market data approach** is the most common particularly for residential properties. The appraiser looks for properties which have sold recently, in close proximity, and comparable in features and amenities to the subject property.

comparables are recently sold properties that resemble the subject property but are not identical, and therefore some adjustments may be required

comparative market analysis (CMA) CMA is often prepared by a real estate agent when listing property for sale and may show current, available listings for sale, pending sales, closed sales, withdrawn listings, and expired listings

competent parties means all parties must be living, of lawful age, of sound mind, and mentally competent

Comprehensive Environmental Response, Compensation, and Liability Act (1980), CERCLA, established a *Superfund* to clean up hazardous waste sites and to collect the costs from certain responsible persons associated with the sites

condemnation is the process of *taking the property* under **eminent domain**, while the *payment for the property* is normally referred to as a **condemnation award**

conditional commitment is the FHA appraisal

conditional use permit (CUP) could grant a use in an area where there is not a specific zone in which it could otherwise be put. This often applies to a use, such as a hospital placed in a residential zone, for the betterment of the community.

conditions, covenants and restrictions (CC&Rs) placed by the developer of a restricted community creating certain conditions and restrictions on the property, including the creation of a Common Interest Community (CIC). These restrictions bind all future owners. The restrictions are usually managed by a homeowners' association (HOA), which often hires a property management company to enforce the restrictions.

condominium is, in reality, *a space in the building*, and the condo owner has ownership of only the internal walls, cabinets, fixtures, appliances, carpets, floors, etc.

confidentiality, as it pertains to the fiduciary duties, refers to the agent's obligation to keep confidential all information about the client which, if disclosed without the principal's permission, could hurt the principal's bargaining position

conformity refers to how consistent the subject property is with the other surrounding properties. If a property is significantly better than surrounding properties, its value will *regress* downward toward the value of the surrounding properties. If a property is significantly poorer than surrounding properties, the surrounding properties will tend to cause the subject property's value to *progress* upward as a result of the higher value of the surrounding properties.

consideration clause will be found in a deed reflecting one of these four types of consideration (anything of value) being offered

consideration may be money, anything of value, or just a statement that consideration exists, such as "for continued love and affection" or "for good and valuable consideration"

construction loan is a loan for construction purposes, usually a short term loan, two to five years depending on the length of time required, to build the project. It is considered *interim financing* until the builder can secure permanent financing to complete the project. The developer makes periodic *draws* against the maximum loan amount as construction progresses. The lender normally inspects each phase of construction to assure there is enough construction to serve as collateral. Normally the funds can only be used for construction of the project which is the collateral for the construction mortgage. This is considered a riskier loan and is priced accordingly. These are usually interest-only loans.

constructive eviction means the landlord has done, or failed to do, something that has had the effect of denying the tenant the use and enjoyment of the leasehold. Often this involves matters of landlord maintenance which has not been done. Changing the locks is a common scenario of an unlawful constructive eviction.

constructive notice is a legal principle that a party was actually given notice of an interest

Consumer Credit Protection Act, Truth-In-Lending Act, Regulation "Z" provide the consumer with complete and understandable credit information so the consumer can make informed credit decisions. The disclosures required by these laws are finance charges and the disclosure of the annual percentage rate.

contingency is a clause written into a contract stating some event must be completed before all of the duties of the contract can be or will be performed. Contingencies include new loan approval, sale of current residence, inspections to be conducted, etc. If the contingency is not fulfilled or waived, the contract is voidable.

contract for deed is a form of seller financing. In the contract for deed, sometimes called a **Land Contract**, the **vendor** (seller) retains *legal title* to the property but transfers e*quitable title* to the **vendee** (buyer). If the buyer does perform as required, then at the conclusion of performance, the seller is obligated to convey legal title to the buyer where it will join with the equitable title the buyer already holds.

contract is a voluntary agreement between informed and capable parties to do, or to refrain from doing, something which is legal to do, and which is supported by adequate consideration

contribution is what the market will pay for a feature or amenity. The value the feature or amenity *contributes* is not necessarily equal to its cost.

conventional loan is a loan that is neither FHA nor VA; made with *neither* federal government insurance nor guarantees

conversion gives the borrower the option of *converting* to a fixed rate mortgage at various periods during the loan. Usually, these are at 3 years, 5 years, and 7 years.

cooperating brokers refer to buyer brokers who work with (cooperate with) listing brokers to produce a buyer who is ready, willing, and able to purchase

cooperative apartments were created in major cities on the eastern seaboard when developers and investors realized that apartment and other buildings with residential potential would be far more profitable if the units could be sold rather than rented. The concept was created to form a corporation, which would own the building and sell shares of stock in the building, each share of stock entitling the owner to a **proprietary lease**.

corporation is a *legal person* meaning it can sue and be sued in court. A corporation consists of one or more shareholders who own stock in the corporation.

cost approach determines what it would cost to replace the subject property as if it were being built from the land up. Using informational sources available to the appraiser, the subject property is "rebuilt" on paper.

counteroffer is *any change,* no matter how small or large, made to the offer. A counteroffer rejects the offer as written, but modifies what terms and conditions must be changed to make the offer acceptable.

covenant (or ***warranty)*** is a promise by the grantor to the grantee concerning the title to the property, that some condition exists and will continue to exist, or, that a condition does not exist and never will.

curable depreciation/obsolescence has two (2) elements: that the depreciation can be cured (fixed or repaired), and that the added value to the property by curing the depreciation will be more than the cost to cure it

curtesy is a husband's legal interest, upon his wife's death, to property his wife has or acquired during their marriage

custom homes are where the builder has a buyer under contract to build a specific home that was designed and blueprinted by an architect

customer is a third party for whom a service is provided by the agent, but to whom the agent owes no fiduciary duties

datum is a permanent reference mark used by surveyors as a reference point for elevations

dedication is the act of turning over ownership to subdivision amenities such as streets, sidewalks, and green areas

deed is the only instrument used for the conveyance of title to land

deed of trust is a contract which creates a *monetary lien* against real property. Deeds of trust are most frequently used in the states west of the Rocky Mountains. In a deed of trust, there are three parties: the **trustor** (the borrower), the **trustee** (an independent third party chosen by the lender), and the **beneficiary** (the lender).

deed restrictions put certain restrictions on the future use of the property by including these limitations in the deed

defeasance clause requires the lender to issue a ***satisfaction of mortgage*** indicating the loan has been paid in full

defeasible fee (or ***fee simple defeasible*** or ***determinable fee)***, has an attached stipulation such as "for as long as" or "during" and provided that condition is not broken, the holder remains in title. Upon the occurrence of that designated event, title to the property **reverts** back to the former grantor.

deficiency judgment may be sought by the lender should the proceeds from a foreclosure sale or short sale, be insufficient to satisfy the loan

demand suggests that of the market does not want the property, it has little or no value. **Effective Demand** refers to the market having the capacity or ability to purchase the property. If the market lacks adequate purchasing power to buy the property, the property's value is greatly diminished.

depreciation is the reduction in value as a result of age, poor state of repair, poor design, etc. It is the loss in value for any reason. Buildings and improvements depreciate; land does not.

designated agency is another term for assigned agency

devise is real property given to a ***devisee*** through a will

disclosure is the agent's duty to keep the client informed (to disclose) of all material facts which may have any importance in matters where the agent is representing the client

discount point equals 1% of the loan amount. The IRS considers a point to be a form of interest paid upfront instead of over the term of the loan. Discount points are charged when there is a cost to receive a certain rate or to buy a rate down ("discount").

discount rate is the interest rate the Federal Reserve System charges its member banks. If the Federal Reserve Board of Governors feels inflationary pressures in the economy exist, they may decide to raise the discount rate, which would have the effect of making borrowing more expensive for business and consumers and in theory cooling the business economy and reducing inflationary pressure. The converse is also true. If the "Fed" thinks a little boost to the economy is needed, they might decide to reduce the discount rate making borrowing less expensive and encouraging consumers to spend more and for businesses to expand their operations, production and hiring.

dominant tenement enjoys the right to pass over the servient tenement's land

dower is a wife's legal interest, upon her husband's death, to property her husband has or acquired during their marriage

down zoning has occurred if uses a property already had are *taken away*. This may reduce the value of the property.

dual agency is a situation where one agent represents both buyer and seller. In some states, dual agency is not allowed. In others, it is allowed, but only with the expressed, informed consent of both represented parties. This is sometimes referred to as ***multiple-party representation***.

due diligence is that period of time, as granted in the purchase agreement, for the buyer to perform the inspections necessary to ensure that defects do not exist. For these reasons, many buyers perform a home inspection, a pest inspection, or any other inspections desired during this period. Contracts are usually contingent upon the results of these inspections allowing the buyer to cancel the contract without penalty.

due on sale clause (sometimes referred to as an ***alienation clause***) informs the borrower, in advance, that the lender will not permit an assignment of the borrower's obligations under the note, or interest in the property, unless the lender is paid in full. As the name implies, the loan is due on sale – if there is a sale, the loan is due. "Alienation" refers to alienating oneself from the property.

duty of further inquiry is part of the agent's duty to the principal. If the agent acquires information which would cause a reasonable person to ask some questions, the agent is expected to do so.

earnest money deposit is typically money that accompanies an offer to show the buyer's "earnestness" in completing the contract as it is often sacrificed upon a breach of contract

easement appurtenant is between owners of *neighboring* properties giving one owner a right of passage over the other owner's property

easement by necessity may come into play should a person find that he has purchased property which does not have ***ingress*** (entrance) or ***egress*** (exit) to the public way. This generally will involve court action and the court will seek to find the least intrusive method to give the landlocked property owner access to the public way.

easement by prescription is seldom seen in modern times, but arise through one party's conspicuous use of a portion of another's property to cross over. The use would have to have been for a "prescribed," long period of time, normally 21 years or longer (the time period varies by state); would have to be without the permission of the landowner; would have to be continuous; and would have to be "hostile" meaning contrary to the rights of the owner of the property being crossed.

easement in gross has only a servient tenement. The most common examples of an easement in gross are *utility easements*.

easement is the right of someone other than the owner to use part of a property for a specific purpose. Easements are typically recorded with the legal description, noted on a plat map, or otherwise part of the property records.

effective gross income, or *adjusted gross income*, is the income *actually collected or earned*. It is the gross scheduled income less the vacancies and bad debts.

egress (exit) to the public way

electromagnetic fields (EMFs) are fields generated by the movement of electrical currents, such as in power transmission lines

electronic contracting is a means by which agents can handle contracts by digital, or electronic methods. The **Uniform Electronic Transaction Act (UETA)** and the **Electronic Signatures in Global and National Commerce Act (E-Sign)** are the two federal laws that govern these activities.

emblements (or ***fructus industriales***) include fruit, vegetables, nuts, grasses, grains and other annually cultivated crops. These are considered personal property.

eminent domain means private property can be taken by the government, provided the tests of proof of a public use and payment of just compensation are met

enabling acts allow local governments decision-making authority for the individual circumstances of a community. This is mostly relevant to zoning.

encumbrance is defined as *a burden upon the title to the property,* even though great benefits may be derived by the owner as a result of the encumbrance

enforceable means a dispute between the parties will be heard in court and a judge will "enforce" the provisions of the contract

environmental impact statement (EIS) identifies the anticipated effects of developing a new project as they pertain to the safety and health of the public

Equal Credit Opportunity Act (ECOA) prohibits creditors from discriminating against credit applicants on the basis of race, color, religion, national origin, sex, marital status, age, or because an applicant receives income from a public assistance program

equalization factor may be applied to adjust for assessors who either tend to be high or low in their assessments

equitable title refers to the buyer's interests in the property while either in escrow or when making payments on a loan where the mortgagee is carrying the financing such as with a contract for deed. *Equitable title* or an *equitable interest* suggests the buyer has the property under contract and no one else does. The rights associated with equitable title vary from state to state.

equity loans, or home equity lines of credit (HELOC), may be done when the homeowner has a substantial amount of equity in the property and wishes to use that equity (by borrowing against it) for some other purpose. These loans are sometimes called ***open end mortgages*** as the loan is considered "open ended" for future advances from the lender usually to a pre-determined amount.

erosion removes land due to wind, rain, or flowing water and replaced it with water. The missing land no longer belongs to the landowner.

escalation lease is similar to an indexed lease, except that the tenant's lease payment is increased by the actual increases in the operating expenses of the property and not directly tied to an inflation index

escheat describes when a person dies with no will, and after a reasonable search, no heirs are found. The property will pass to the state by escheat.

escrow account is another term for a ***trust account*** established by a broker for the holding of the principal's funds until funding, such as with a buyer's earnest money deposit

escrow instructions is the escrowee's own document spelling out all the details of the transaction. Many times the purchase agreement also serves as escrow instructions.

escrow refers to the closing process as conducted by a third party called the escrowee

escrowee is an escrow company or agent, such as an attorney, who facilitates the close of escrow

estate at sufferance is the status of the parties where the term of the lease has expired and the tenant remains in possession without the landlord's consent. The tenant has no right to be there and is technically a trespasser. As the name implies, the landlord is "suffering" due to the tenant's continued presence in the property.

estate at will is an open-ended lease with no specific termination date and therefore, notice is required to terminate this lease. Should the parties have failed to specify the length of the notice period, the courts will require a "reasonable" notice be given.

estate for years is a type of lease has a definite starting and ending date. The term can be of any duration. No notice is required to terminate.

estate from period to period is a type of lease which has a stated *period of time* which will automatically renew for the same period over and over again until one party gives notice they no longer wish to continue

eviction is the lawful process of dispossessing a tenant who has either overstayed the lease term, or who is in breach of the lease, and eviction has been elected as a remedy by the landlord

exceptions and reservations clause is where the grantor will make the grant subject to any exceptions, encumbrances, or liens on title which will not be removed by the grantor. This clause is also where the grantor may create restriction or easements.

exclusive agency listing is a form of listing contract whereby the seller agrees to hire the broker on an exclusive basis, and agrees to pay a commission to the exclusive broker when the exclusive broker, or any other broker, produces a ready, willing, and able buyer at list price and terms or such other price and terms agreeable to the seller. The seller gives *exclusivity* to the broker and agrees that all other brokers must go through the exclusive broker. However, the seller may sell the property himself without owing a commission.

exclusive right to sell listing is a form of listing contract whereby the seller agrees to hire the broker on an exclusive basis and agrees to pay a commission to the exclusive broker when the exclusive broker, or any other broker, produces a ready, willing, and able buyer at list price and terms or such other price and terms agreeable to the seller. The seller gives *exclusivity* to the broker and agrees that all other brokers must go through the exclusive broker and further agrees that should the seller find a buyer on his own, he will still owe a commission to the exclusive broker.

executed contract is one that is fully and completely performed. "Executed," in a different context, can also mean that the contract has been fully signed by all parties.

executor the named individual in a will who will oversee the distribution of a deceased's assets

executory contract is not yet fully performed. For example, a 30 year mortgage is "executory" until the making of the last payment, if not paid off in full sooner. It is not "executed" until it is paid in full.

expressed agency occurs when a formal document is signed, binding the parties to an agency relationship. Once signed, a listing agreement, buyer's brokerage agreement, or similar document, creates an agency relationship. Note that "expressed" also means "using words" which includes verbal contracting.

expressed means the use of words, either written or oral, to show intentions of the parties to the contract

external/environmental/locational/economic obsolescence are four names all for the same thing. The property is located in an "environment" or in a "location" in which the market will penalize the value, such as the subject property being adjacent to a waste facility.

Fair Housing Act, formally known as Title VIII of the Civil Rights Act of 1968, protects four classes or classifications of Americans. Race and color from 1866 and in 1968 covered religion and national origin. Gender was added in 1974 and family status and disability were added in 1988.

farming is prospecting in a geographical area, staying in contact with all residents of a select neighborhood (the *farm*), providing information and real estate services

Federal Home Loan Mortgage Corporation (FHLMC "Freddie Mac") purchases qualified residential mortgages from the originators. Freddie Mac then issues a security to private investors which represents an undivided interest in the mortgages Freddie Mac owns. These securities contain a guarantee against loss to the investor. Freddie Mac deals in residential mortgages which *do not* contain U.S. government backed loans; these are the so called *conventional* mortgages.

Federal National Mortgage Association (FNMA "Fannie Mae") is a major warehouse underwriter of conventional loans as well as U.S. government insured (FHA) or guaranteed loans (VA).

Federal Trade Commission (FTC) is the primary enforcement body for truth-in-advertising claims, although a number of state agencies are also active in this regard. If real estate customers or clients have fallen victim to advertising violations, the law allows for the reporting of a complaint and remediation. Generally, truth-in-advertising laws require print, TV, magazine, newspaper, Internet, and other advertising to be truthful, non-deceptive, provable by evidence furnished by the advertiser, and fair.

fee simple absolute is the highest quality interest in real estate in that the holder has all the rights recognized by law. With an estate in fee simple, the estate runs forever and upon the death of the owner, the property is inheritable to the heirs. This is the ideal form of ownership.

FHA insured loans are loans made by private lenders who make the loan to a qualified borrower and the FHA *insures* the lender against loss on the loan. With the "full faith and credit" of the United States government standing behind the loan, private lenders are willing to make these loans, thereby meeting the needs of the home buying population and stimulating the economy.

fiduciary duties involve "trust and confidence" and are owed by the agent to the principal in the transaction, who may be the buyer, seller, lessor, or lessee of property. The six fiduciary duties are *care, obedience, loyalty, disclosure, accounting, and confidentiality* — often remembered by the acronym COLDAC.

financing is simply the borrowing of money. It may be borrowing from a private party or a professional lender. The borrowing may be unsecured (no collateral, only the credit worthiness of the borrower is considered), or the borrowing may be secured (real or personal property is given to assure repayment of the loan).

fixtures are items of personal property that have been permanently attached to land or a building, so that they become part of the real property

flat fee commissions are established in the listing contract as a specific amount, regardless of what the purchase price turns out to be

Foreign Investor in Real Property Tax Act (FIRPTA) applies to the sale of properties in the United States by foreign nationals or foreign corporations. At close of escrow, 10% of the gross sale price will be withheld and transmitted to the IRS.

fraud involves the intentional misrepresentation of a material fact. Fraud is also the intentional use of deceit, a trick, or some other dishonest means to take money, property, or a legal right from another person.

freehold translates to "ownership" and provides the bundle of rights of ownership for an indeterminable period of time, either based upon someone's lifetime or forever. Freehold estates may either be **Fee Simple Estates** or **Life Estates.**

fructus industriales (or **emblements**) include fruit, vegetables, nuts, grasses, grains and other annually cultivated crops. These are considered personal property.

functional depreciation is a loss in value because the property is out of style for the market place, or features of the property, although working properly, are inadequate for the property

funding fee is the up-front fee the VA charges the veteran buyer at close of escrow, but normally the veteran elects to roll the funding fee into the loan

general agency is a form of agency created in a general agency agreement, normally in writing, and often referred to as a **limited power of attorney** or a **general power of attorney**. A general agent has the authority to negotiate contracts and to bind the client to a contract, but only within specially designated and limited areas.

general lien is filed in order to collect on a judgment and creates a *general lien* against all of the property the judgment debtor owns in the jurisdiction

general partnership is a form of business ownership for profit. There is only one class of partners – general partners who have unlimited liability and participate in the decision-making process of the business.

general partner are members of a general partnership and may own equal or unequal ownership positions; however, all general partners are jointly and severally liable for the debts of the partnership

general warranty deed (also known as a **warranty deed,** or **grant, bargain, and sale deed**) is the most commonly used form of deed and it contains five (5) warranties (covenants)

good faith estimate of closing costs must be provided by the lender to the borrower within 3 business days from loan application reflecting the lender's best estimate of the loan and title costs associated with the closing. This is a requirement of RESPA.

good faith suggests that the licensee must always act in the client's best interests and carry out the principal's legal instructions within the scope of the authority provided by the principal

Government National Mortgage Association (GNMA "Ginnie Mae") provides a **mortgage backed security** which was completely backed by the "full faith and credit" of the United States government. This investment instrument allowed global investment capital to be funneled into the American housing market.

graduated lease is a lease where the tenant and the landlord have agreed that with the passage of time, the leased space will become more valuable and that the tenant's lease payment should increase. The lease provides the dates on which the tenant's lease payment will increase and the amount of the increase.

graduated payment mortgage is most often seen when interest rates are high and/or the borrower is not able to qualify at the higher interest rate. The lender makes the loan with a provision that the starting payments are lower than what would otherwise be required to pay the principal and interest on the loan. The borrower agrees to increase the payment amount each year for the next two or three years until reaching the required payment. During this time, the unpaid interest is added to the unpaid balance (***negative amortization***). This will result in an increase in the size of the loan balance until the agreed increase in payment is sufficient to amortize the loan.

grandfathering allows a non-conforming use to continue as the property's use existed before the zoning was put into effect

grant, bargain, and sale deed (also known as a ***warranty deed***, or ***general warranty deed***) is the most commonly used form of deed and it contains five (5) warranties (covenants)

grantee is the person to whom the conveyance is made through a deed

granting clause is found in a deed and states the nature and extent of the interest conveyed – *fee simple interest in . . .* , or *25% interest in . . .* , etc.

grantor is the person making the conveyance by a deed to the ***grantee***

gross lease is a type of lease where the tenant pays a fixed monthly rent and from those funds, the landlord pays the operating expenses of the property. This is most common in residential and small office leases.

gross rent multiplier (GRM) and ***gross income multiplier (GIM)***, are two alternate methods for assessing the value of income producing properties from a single family home to an industrial property. The GRM is used on smaller, residential property while the GIM is used on income producing real estate on a grander scale.

gross scheduled income, or ***potential gross income***, reflects the income the property *should have earned* had there not been vacancies or bad debts and before the operating expenses were calculated

ground lease is a lease of only the land where the tenant pays for and owns any improvements including buildings. This type of lease is commonly 99 years or a very long term.

group boycotting occurs when several businesses get together and agree to withhold their patronage or not use a particular organization, possibly an escrow company, or home warranty company, or lender

habendum clause may be included in the deed (not usually required) which says "to have and to hold from this day forward"

health codes provide for minimum standards regarding a wide variety of matters, ranging from food handling and preparation standards, to general sanitation standards, to various forms of signage like "Wash Your Hands Before Returning to Work," and other similar matters

highest and best use is the most profitable legal use for the property

home equity lines of credit (HELOC), also called "equity loans," may be done when the homeowner has a substantial amount of equity in the property and wishes to use that equity (by borrowing against it) for some other purpose. These loans are sometimes called ***open end mortgages*** as the loan is considered "open ended" for future advances from the lender usually to a pre-determined amount.

Homestead laws protect a homeowner's personal residence from certain creditors. The exemption offers virtually absolute protection from forced sale to meet the demands of creditors, except under special circumstances. By filing the homestead exemption in some states, property owners receive a reduction from the assessed value in the calculation of property taxes.

Housing for Older Persons Act (1995) outlines the requirements *for the persons who are 55 years of age or older* exemption established in the Fair Housing Act. This exemption applies to the familial status provisions of the Fair Housing Act, but does not exempt the housing from the other provisions of the law. This law states that communities can legally market themselves as "age-restricted" or "age-qualified," provided that 80 percent of the occupied units are occupied by at least one person who is 55 years of age or older.

HUD 1, also referred to as the ***Uniform Settlement Statement*** must be used for the closing according to RESPA. This is an easy to read form which details the amount of the closing costs and who is paying them.

hypothecation is the pledging of property as security for a debt but retaining possession and use of the property so long as the debt is being performed as agreed. Hypothecation is the most common form of secured lending arrangements.

implied means the actions of the parties demonstrate their intent. It looks like a contracting has occurred by the appearance of things (***ostensible***).

implied agency occurs when the parties involved "act like" or "imply" that an agreement has been reached. Once this occurs, an implied agency agreement has been created, though this may have been done accidently, inadvertently, or unintentionally.

impossibility suggests that if it is truly impossible for the parties to perform, the contract will be terminated by impossibility

impound accounts, also called ***escrow accounts***, are established to hold funds for the future payment of the borrower's property taxes and casualty insurance

income approach is based upon the value of an income producing property being a reflection of the investor's required rate of return by investing in real estate. This method is most commonly utilized to determine the value of an income producing property.

increasing and decreasing returns takes a look at whether or not the cost of making an improvement or repair adds more to the value than making the improvement or repair costs. If it does not, then the improvement or repair should not be made, unless the owner is doing it for reasons other than increasing the value of the property.

incurable depreciation/obsolescence dictates that the loss in value is either unfixable or not cost effective to make the repairs

independent contractor status is a tax status. The Internal Revenue Service (IRS) has agreed to allow real estate professionals to elect independent contractor status for tax purposes, even though they may legally be employees. In order to qualify for this treatment, agents must have a written employment agreement with the broker which states an agent will be treated as an independent contractor for tax purposes. As an independent contractor, agents are able to deduct those reasonable and necessary business expenses. This tax treatment often offers greater deductibility of operating expenses than if taxed as an employee.

index is the cost of funds indicator used by the lender. This may be the prime rate, the T-Bill rate, the 10-year treasury bond rate, the 11th district federal reserve funds rate, the London Interbank Offering Rate (LIBOR), or any other gauge or benchmark the lender and borrower choose. As the index rises or decreases, the interest rate will adjust accordingly.

indexed lease is one where the landlord ties the lease payment to an index for inflation, such as the Consumer Price Index (CPI), and as the index increases annually, so will the tenant's lease payment

industrial real estate includes industrial parks or lands

informed parties means there can be no fraud, no misrepresentation, and no duress. The parties are fully informed, aware of the conditions of the agreement, and consent to the terms.

ingress (entrance) to the public way

interest is the compensation paid by the borrower to the lender for the period during which the borrower has use of the lender's money

interval represents the frequency in which the interest paid by the borrower will change. Most ARMS have six month or one year intervals. The interval will be stated in the note and will not be changed to another period for the life of the loan.

intestate describes those who died without a will

involuntary alienation transfers are transfers by will upon death, foreclosure, adverse possession, condemnation, and erosion or avulsion (wearing away of the land)

joint tenancy could exist with two or more natural owners. The owners have four *unities of title*: equal right of access and possession, equal interests, acquired their title all at the same time, and acquired their title all in the same document (PITT).

judicial partition is a means of partition ordered by a court that may either declare a portion of the property to be owned separately by the partitioning party, or by a court-ordered sale where the property is ordered sold and the proceeds distributed based on the various percentages of ownership

land is defined as the surface of the earth, extending upward to infinity and downward to the center of the earth. It includes all things that are attached to the surface of the earth, like trees and shrubs, and the water that exists on and below the land. Land also includes the soil and minerals below the surface (termed the *subsurface*) and the air above the earth's surface (termed the *airspace*).

land contract, also called a **contract for deed,** is a form of seller financing. The **vendor** (seller) retains **legal title** to the property but transfers **equitable title** to the **vendee** (buyer). If the buyer does perform as required, then at the conclusion of performance, the seller is obligated to convey legal title to the buyer where it will join with the equitable title the buyer already holds.

latent defects are those defects that are not visible. These may be known or unknown to the seller or agent. If these are known, both the seller and the agent have a responsibility to reveal them.

law of decreasing returns means that the cost of making an improvement will NOT be covered by the added value to the property (*incurable*)

law of increasing returns means that the cost of making an improvement will be more than covered by the added value to the property (*curable*)

law/statute of descent and distribution applies when a person dies intestate. The state in which the property is located has laws to ensure that the real and personal property transfer to the decedent's heirs according to the state's formula. Essentially, the state is making a will for the decedent.

lead is found in plumbing pipes in older homes. Lead-based solder and lead-based seals could, over time, place harmful quantities of lead in the water.

lead-based paint can be found in homes built prior to 1978. Discovery was made that lead-based paint was often eaten by small children as they chewed on cabinet doors and trim. Lead-based paint, if ingested, can result in brain damage and death.

leaking underground storage tanks (LUST) are found in older gas stations and other facilities where gasoline and other petroleum products were stored in steel or iron underground tanks. The primary hazard is leaking and the contamination of ground water as the petroleum product leaches further into the soil.

lease option agreements start out as leases, but include an *option to purchase* by the expiration of the leasehold. The price and terms are negotiated up front.

lease purchase agreements start out as leases but include a *purchase agreement* that will go into effect by the expiration of the leasehold. The price and terms are negotiated up front.

leased fee means the landlord still owns the property, but has surrendered the rights of possession and use to the tenant

leasehold improvements are improvements or alterations to the leased space. Normally they are done at the *landlord's expense* and remain a part of the leased space as the landlord's property when the tenant vacates.

leasehold interest refers to the tenant's rights to the leased property, providing the right to possess and use the property

legacy is money given through a will

legal descriptions describe one parcel of property so well that it cannot be confused with another parcel

legal title is secured when the closing is completed, the deed transfers title from the seller to the buyer, and the deed is recorded

legality of object means the purpose underlying the contract must be legal

lessee is a party to a lease agreement and is the tenant

lessor is a party to a lease agreement and is the owner/landlord

license is the giving of permission by the landowner to allow another to come upon the land for specific purposes. The license is a privilege and is revocable.

lien theory states the ***mortgagor*** (borrower) retains legal and equitable title. The ***mortgagee*** (lender) has only a lien on the property as security for the debt. In order for the lender to take the property for sale, foreclosure proceedings must be initiated to obtain the legal title.

life estates are based upon the life of the owner or some other designated person. Life estates are not inheritable so it is necessary to pre-determine to whom title shall pass upon the passing of the named party.

limited liability company (LLC) is a business structure that is a hybrid of a corporation and a limited partnership

limited partnerships must have at least one general partner, and there may be any number of ***limited partners***. The general partners have the right to full participation in the activities of the partnership and are individually liable for the obligations and debts of the partnership. Limited partners have limited liability and do not partake in operating the business.

liquidated damages are those damages the contract pre-addressed that may be received in the event of default

lis pendens is placed in the public records and gives notice that litigation is pending concerning the property. Lis pendens tend to prevent the property from being sold before the dispute is resolved.

listing agreement is an employment contract between the seller of property and the real estate broker. It is important to note the contract is between the seller and the broker; not the salesperson.

littoral rights describe the rights of owners whose land borders large (commercially navigable) lakes, seas, and oceans

loan originators are those persons or businesses who *actually make* the loans in the primary market

loan to value ratio (LTV) is the ratio between the loan being made and the appraised value of the property given as collateral, or the purchase price, *whichever is less*

lot, block, and subdivision legal description involves the surveying of a plot of land and then divided into blocks and lots, streets, access roads, utility easements, parks, etc. Then, the blocks and lots are assigned numbers and letters. The resultant drawing is called a ***plat map*** or ***subdivision plat***.

margin represents the *profit and overhead* the lender wants to earn above the costs of funds. This will be stated in the note and will not be changed to another amount for the life of the loan. The margin is added to the index to calculate the interest rate.

market analysis is prepared by the real estate professional using the data in the *local **Multiple Listing Service™*** to estimate the value by examining sold listings, active listings, expired listings, and days on market.

market data or comparable sales approach is the most common particularly for residential properties. The appraiser looks for properties which have sold recently, in close proximity, and comparable in features and amenities to the subject property.

market value is the value of property today based on a probable price a seller would be willing to sell and a buyer would be willing to pay under normal conditions

marketable title means "good" title; good enough for an attorney to recommend the buyer accept

master plan allows each local government to develop a master plan for the community. The master plan should take into consideration the needs of the community, the location of various uses of land, the potential for conflict between uses, and the orderly growth of the community.

master planned communities develop plans that include recreation centers, parks, playgrounds, and other amenities, as well as reserved spaces for schools, churches, retail establishments, and other facilities. Many master planned communities are gated, so as to restrict access to residents.

material fact is a fact that would be important to a reasonable person in deciding whether to engage or not to engage in a particular transaction; or would affect the price paid. It is an important fact as distinguished from some unimportant or trivial detail.

mechanic's lien protects those persons who provide labor or materials to improve another's property. This lien is effective as of the date of first work or first delivery of materials, not the date it is filed in the public records.

metes and bounds legal description relies on a description of *metes* (distance and direction) and *bounds* (landmarks or boundary edges) to define the borders of a parcel of land. A metes-and-bounds description uses a ***point of beginning (POB)***, and then directions and linear measurements to define the borders of the property, finally returning to the POB.

mill is one-tenth of a penny or $1/1000^{th}$ of a dollar

misrepresentation can be negligent statements or just plain mistakes, and are considered "innocent" in nature. ***Negligent misrepresentations*** occur when a broker or agent should have known that a statement about a material fact was false. The broker's lack of awareness of the fact is no excuse. Also, the concept of negligent misrepresentation extends to situations where the broker or agent simply fails to do something or follow through as expected.

mixed use projects are uses of property that are different such as residential, retail, restaurant, office and medical/dental facilities

mold is a fungi that thrives on moisture. While some molds are benign or even beneficial, others can cause allergic reactions when inhaled or touched.

monetary encumbrance is a lien giving another the right to repossess or foreclose against real or personal property and to sell the property to pay that debt or obligation owed to the lienholder

mortgage bankers work as a "middle man" between mortgage brokers and the ultimate investors. Some mortgage bankers have funds of their own with which to fund the loan, but will normally then sell the loans they have created to liquidate capital to lend again. A significant difference between a mortgage banker and a mortgage broker is that bankers often *do* provide servicing for the loans after they are made. They service their own loans and provide this service for investors at an additional charge.

mortgage brokers are the *loan originators* most common in the market. The mortgage broker takes the application for the loan from the borrower, then "shops" the loan to find an investor who will make the loan and who will offer competitive terms. If a loan is made, the mortgage broker is paid a fee for services. Mortgage brokers do not provide loan servicing for the investor which would include collecting the loan payments, accounting tasks, handling escrow accounts for future payment of insurance, property taxes, etc. Once the loan is closed and funded, the job of the mortgage broker is essentially done.

Mortgage Insurance Premium (MIP) is paid by the borrower both in an up-front payment and also monthly for the life of the FHA loan. The amount, or percentage, for these two costs changes from time to time.

mortgage is a contract which creates a **monetary lien** against real property. Mortgages are most frequently used in the states east of the Rocky Mountains. Some think of mortgages as the "what if?" document where the question "what if the borrower stops making payments?" is addressed.

mortgagee is the lender who receives the mortgage from the borrower in exchange for the lender providing the financing

mortgagor is the borrower; the one giving the mortgage in exchange for receiving the loan

Multiple Listing Service (MLS)™ is available to members of the local association of REALTORS® in order to access data on member broker listings

multiple-party representation is another term for dual agency

mutual agreement or **mutual consent** to terminate a contract is where the parties decide they do not want to go forward and mutually agree that each should be released from the contract. By mutual agreement, the contract is terminated.

naked title is "bare" legal but with none of the benefits of ownership. This concept applies in a deed of trust where the trustee holds naked title and the beneficiary holds equitable title.

National Association of REALTORS® (NAR) is an organization, which has state-level and local associations under its national umbrella, and promotes a higher level of professionalism, integrity, and education than non-members

National Do Not Call Registry and federal legislation allows for consumers to add their phone numbers to a list managed by the Federal Trade Commission (FTC). Real estate agents may not call anyone on this list. Several exceptions should be noted.

natural person is a human being

negative amortization occurs when the unpaid interest is added to the unpaid balance. This will result in an increase in the size of the loan balance until the agreed increase in payment is sufficient to amortize the loan.

negotiable instrument refers to the promissory note meaning the lender may sell the note without consent from the borrower in order to liquidate the lender's funds

net lease is a lease where the tenant pays a *base rent* (fixed monthly rent) and in addition to the base rent, pays some, or all of the operating expenses of the property

net listing is a commission arrangement and is not permitted in many states as the arrangement inherently creates a conflict of interest between the broker and the client. In this situation, the broker's commission is anything in excess of the seller's desired net proceeds, payoff of liens, and closing costs.

net operating income is the gross scheduled income of the property minus the property's annual operating expenses and also minus the annual vacancies and bad debts the property experiences

non-conforming use (NCU) happens when a property is put to a given use where there are no zoning ordinances or zoning allowing it otherwise. Time passes and now the use does not "conform" with the current zoning.

non-natural person can be a corporation, a limited liability company (LLC), a partnership, or a limited partnership

note, or **promissory note,** is a legal document which creates and identifies the debt. The note is a contract and the equivalent of an I.O.U. It is the document which creates the debt between the borrower and the lender. It is the *evidence of the debt*.

novation is the substitution of a new *contract* for an old one

novation of parties is where a new *party* is substituted for an existing party

obsolescence is another term for depreciation; a loss in value

offer and acceptance is sometimes referred to as "mutual assent." This essential element of a contract shows there is a "meeting of the minds," that an offer was made and acceptance of that offer was reached.

offer is a proposed contract made by the offeror. Note that an offer becomes a contract when the offer has been accepted by the offeree and communication of that acceptance has been received by the offeror.

offeree is the party *receiving* the offer

offeror is the party *making* the offer

open listing is a listing contract whereby the seller agrees to pay a commission to *any* broker who procures a ready, willing, and able buyer at list price and terms, or such other price and terms agreeable to the seller. The seller gives *no exclusivity* to the broker, and the seller may sell the property himself without owing a commission to any broker. The seller may also have several open listings in effect.

operating expenses are costs associated with operating the building such as utilities, taxes, management fees, etc. and should not be confused with "debt service fees" which are incurred as a result of financing the original purchase of the property. When expressed as a percentage, they express a percentage of the effective/adjusted gross income.

operation of law refers to the fact that some contracts could be terminated by the courts or statutory prohibition

opinion of title is prepared by an attorney after reviewing the abstract of title and will render an opinion as to whether the title is **marketable** (good)

option contracts are between the owner of the property, the **optionor**, and a purchaser, **optionee,** who wants to have a period of time in which to decide on the purchase of the property. This is a unilateral contract in that the optionor has no obligation to perform until and unless the optionee decides to purchase. At that time, the optionor would complete the sale of the property to the optionee. The optionee must offer **option money**, better described as the agreed valuable consideration, in exchange for the option to purchase or not to purchase.

ordinary life estate calls for the title to the property to pass upon the death of the owner

ostensible means the actions of the parties demonstrate their intent. It looks like a contracting has occurred by the appearance of things (**implied**).

package mortgage provides financing for both the real estate and the personal property that goes with it. Common examples are loans that cover major appliances like refrigerators, washers and dryers, window treatments, equipment, furniture, etc. that are all included in the purchase price.

Parol Evidence Rule states that verbal words and representations will not be binding nor overrule any written agreements

partial release clause, found in a blanket mortgage, allows the builder to pull the parcel sold "out from under" the blanket mortgage

partition means to divide out an interest where there are multiple owners

patent defects (an archaic term, but still used in construction), are accessible, un-hidden, visible defects

percentage lease exists when the tenant pays a *base rent* plus a percentage of the gross business income, normally less any payment for returned goods. The philosophy is the landlord's location, anchor tenants, and marketing contributes to the overall business income of the tenant. This lease may be gross or net.

performance is the most desirable outcome of a contract. The parties perform all of their duties and receive all of their rights as agreed.

personal property is defined as all property which can be owned by an owner but does not fit the definition of real property. One important definitional difference is that personal property can be moved.

physical depreciation is a loss in value because the property is in a bad state of repair, or some of the components of the property are nearly worn out

physical partition is a means of partition done by agreement of the owners where a legal description for the agreed upon portion of the property is created and deeded out to the partitioning party by the remainder of the owners

Planned Unit Development (PUD) is a combination of housing, recreational amenities, and commercial uses all in one "planned development"

plat map (or **subdivision plat**) is used in the lot, block, and subdivision legal description method. The map shows the subdivision location and the boundaries of all individual lots.

plottage and assemblage comes into play when several smaller parcels are assembled into one large parcel, often resulting in the larger parcel having a greater value than the sum of the values of the individual smaller parcels. This increase in value is called p**lottage** and the act of bringing the parcels together is called a**ssemblage**.

point equals 1% of the loan amount. The IRS considers a point to be a form of interest paid upfront instead of over the term of the loan. Discount points are charged when there is a cost to receive a certain rate or to buy a rate down ("discount").

point of beginning (POB) is the starting point and the ending point in a metes and bounds legal description

police powers represents the government's right to regulate for the benefit of the general health and welfare of its citizens. Traditionally, police powers describe those activities of the state which regulate real estate such as the enacting of zoning regulations, building codes, health and safety regulations, traffic laws, and family law.

potential gross income, or *gross scheduled income,* reflects the income the property *should have earned* had there not been vacancies or bad debts and before the operating expenses were calculated

pre-approval demonstrates the borrower's ability to qualify subject to conditions being satisfied. Often done in the form of a pre-approval letter, this document strengthens the buyer's position as the buyer negotiates a purchase agreement with the seller.

prepayment clause informs the borrower under what circumstances the lender will accept payment, in whole or in part, before the due date. In some cases, the lender is happy to have the loan paid off sooner than planned such as when opportunities exist to use the capital at a higher yield. But should the lender not want the loan prepaid, such as when such opportunities do not exist, the issue will be addressed in the prepayment clause.

prepayment penalties are financial penalties assessed against the borrower and associated with loans that are paid off early, before the end of the term

pre-qualification is an interview, in person or by phone, between the lender and the borrower. The lender will typically obtain consent and run a credit report to look for red flags. Calculations as to debt to income ratios and debt to housing expense ratios are done.

price per front foot is a method to determine value, similar to the price per square foot method. Whenever land dimensions are given, the *first* dimension is always the front footage – that border of the property which is adjacent to the road frontage.

price per square foot is useful in determining a property's fair market value. Looking at your comparables, divide the sale price by the living area square footage for each comp, and calculate an average price per square foot. Then, apply that figure to the square footage in the subject property.

price-fixing is the act of agreeing to set prices or fees at a predefined level, as opposed to allowing markets and market forces to set them. This is illegal. Real estate brokers must independently set commission rates for their own companies, and they must never discuss these with other brokers in an attempt to arrive at a standard fee.

primary market represents those persons or businesses who *actually make* the loans. This primary market is often called the *loan originators*.

prime rate is the interest rate charged by banks to their most creditworthy customers (usually the most prominent and stable business customers)

principal delegates authority to the agent to represent the principal's interests in a transaction. The principal is obligated by contract to compensate the agent and not hinder the agent's ability to fulfill the agent's fiduciary obligations. Another definition of *principal* pertains to financing where the principal portion of the payment reduces the loan balance.

principal meridians are the primary vertical lines referenced when using the U.S. Government Rectangular Survey system

prior appropriation means that someone, often the government, has *already taken* and reserved the water rights for themselves and can sell or lease those rights separately

priority refers to the order in which liens were recorded. The priority of liens will determine which lien gets paid off first, then second, etc. in the event of a foreclosure. Note that tax liens also take a first priority position regardless of the date of recording.

private mortgage insurance was created to encourage lenders to lend at loan-to-value ratios above 80%. Given that a lender would loan only 80% without any further assurances, "PMI" provides insurance against loss on that portion of the loan above 80%.

probate is a formal judicial process that ensures that assets are distributed properly. Probate accomplishes three things: confirms that a particular will is valid if there is a will, adds up or accounts for all of a decedent's assets, and identifies the people who will receive the assets.

processing is performed by the processors who will verify all information provided to the loan officer, order the appraisal as well as title documentation, flood certifications, insurance, verify employment and asset account information, obtain any missing documentation, and lock the rate prior to underwriting

procuring cause means to be the cause of the chain of events that caused the sale

profits are the giving of permission by the landowner to allow another to come onto the land for the limited purpose of removing crops, timber, soil, etc. Here the person receiving *profits* is neither a trespasser, nor a license holder, and has no easement. He is there for a very limited purpose which can be revoked at any time.

progression implies if a property is significantly poorer than surrounding properties, the surrounding properties will tend to cause the subject property's value to ***progress*** upward as a result of the higher value of the surrounding properties

promissory note is a legal document which creates and identifies the debt. The ***note*** is a contract and the equivalent of an I.O.U. It is the document which creates the debt between the borrower and the lender. It is the *evidence of the debt*.

property management agreement is a contract between the owner and a broker/property manager which should specify both the owner's and the property manager's duties, responsibilities, and under what conditions the property manager has the authority to make decisions or sign a contract

property management means to handle the management of the owner's income property, maximizing the owner's return on investment while also protecting the value of the property itself. Many owners do not wish to take on the day-to-day activities and hassles associated with being a landlord and hire property managers to perform those functions on the owner's behalf.

property tax is a state tax, collected locally, based upon the assessed value of the real estate (land + improvements)

proprietary lease is utilized in a cooperative and gives each owner of the corporation a lease to occupy his or her unit

prospecting is the marketing of yourself in order to attract real estate clients to doing business with you

public land use controls include environmental protection laws, subdivision regulations, and zoning

puffing or ***puffery*** is the exaggeration of a property's benefits such as "This home has the best curb appeal on the block." Puffing is legal because it is based on individual opinions, but agents must make sure that none of their comments or statements about real estate can be treated as fraudulent.

punitive damages go above and beyond liquidated damages and may be sought to "punish" the breaching party and compensate the injured party

pur autre vie, translates to "for another's life." This life estate dictates that title to the property, that the life tenant enjoys, shall transfer to another individual upon the death of some other named person.

purchase money mortgage is any portion of the purchase price which the seller "carries" (finances). In real estate, the owner of the property being sold may be in the position to act as the lender.

quit claim deed offers no warranties at all. The grantor is *quitting* any claim the grantor may have to the property, but does not assert that there is any claim at all. This deed is often used to remove liens and encumbrances from title, to surrender community property claims, or to clear *clouds on the title*.

radon is an odorless, colorless, radioactive gas produced naturally by the radioactive materials in the ground. It represents another environmental hazard and has been linked to lung cancer.

range lines are imaginary lines vertically parallel to the principal meridians when using the U.S. Government Rectangular Survey system

ranges are strips of land, 6 miles apart, running vertically parallel to the principal meridian when using the U.S. Government Rectangular Survey system

real estate is defined as the land, plus all *improvements*, which are the man-made artificial things attached to the land. Notice the term *artificial* describes the man-made things that we know as buildings, fences, driveways, swimming pools, etc.

Real Estate Settlement Procedures Act (RESPA) requires lenders to inform the parties to a covered real estate transaction what the closing costs and charges are, and which costs they pay for

real property consists of physical land, the natural features, the man-made improvements to the land, and, the bundle of rights of ownership of real property.

REALTOR® is a member of the professional organization the *National Association of REALTORS® (NAR)*. Note the word REALTOR® is always put in all capital letters followed by the registered trademark symbol. Also note REALTOR® is pronounced "REAL-TOR®" (real tore) and not "REAL-A-TOR®" (real a ter).

reconciliation uses a "weighted average" giving the appraiser a method of expressing confidence in the results given by the application of the various approaches. It boils the three values derived from the three approaches down to one final number.

recording fees represent a state established charge for the recording of documents in the public records of the county

recording is the filing of important documents with the county recorder's office thus providing **actual notice**

redlining is the illegal act by a lender who refuses to lend in an area because it is populated with members of a protected class

regression implies if a property is significantly better than surrounding properties, its value will **regress** downward toward the value of the surrounding properties

Regulation Z requires lenders to disclose true costs of obtaining credit

rejection of offer simply says "no," and by doing so, has rejected the last offer, without counteroffering. An offeree should be aware that a rejection does not obligate the offeror to do anything whatsoever. religion, national origin, marital status, or source of income.

remainderman will take the title to the property as a fee simple estate upon the death of the life tenant

replacement cost represents the theoretical building of a substantially similar property, using currently available materials and construction techniques

reproduction cost would be used if the building were so unique that using available materials and techniques would not produce a substantially similar building

rescission occurs when either party decides to call off the contract and return the earnest money deposit to the buyer. This is a complete reversal of the contract, putting everyone back to where they were before the contract.

reserve requirements fluctuate should the Federal Reserve determine that the amount of available money in the system is either creating inflationary pressures on the economy, or is insufficient to sustain desired economic growth, reserve requirements may be adjusted.

residential real estate is usually defined as four or fewer residential units

reverse annuity mortgage (RAM) *is* designed mainly for older homeowners who own their homes free and clear, or who have very large equities, but who do not wish to sell or cash out the equity in their homes in one lump sum. The RAM lender will pay to the RAM borrower an agreed upon sum each month. In effect, the RAM borrower is drawing out equity in the home monthly.

reversionary interest belongs to the person to whom the property will revert (the original owner) in a life estate

revocation is a legal remedy available to the seller when the buyer defaults. The seller *revokes* the contact and *retains* the earnest money deposit.

right of first refusal is a scenario where the holder of the right of first refusal has the right to match any offer made on a property

right of survivorship means that upon the death of one of the joint tenants, the share of the deceased joint tenant is divided equally among all of the *surviving* joint tenants

riparian rights are common-law rights granted to owners along the course of a river or stream

rule of reason places an obligation on all of us to conduct ourselves as the "reasonable person" would, and to always act in a reasonable fashion. Ultimately, it is often the judge or jury who tells us, after the fact, if our conduct was reasonable.

sale leaseback is an arrangement whereby the buyer and seller agree to a leasehold, the seller remains in possession of the sold property under agreed upon lease terms, and compensates the buyer for that possession. This is ideal for an investor who is purchasing the property as an income producing property as the seller becomes the tenant.

satisfaction of mortgage is issued by the lender indicating the loan has been paid in full

scarcity is the extent to which the supply in the marketplace will have an influence on the value. If there are vast numbers of similar properties, any one property's value is greatly diminished. Likewise, if there are few or no such properties, the value will increase.

secondary liability comes into play under an assignment of a contract. When one party desires to assign his rights, obligations, and benefits under the contract to a third party, he may generally do so, however that original party will remain "secondarily liable" for performance and obligations should the third party fail to perform.

secondary market represents those persons or businesses who actually *fund* the loan. This group is where the *lenders* go to get the funds to lend.

sections are described when using the U.S. Government Rectangular Survey system. There are 36 sections in a township. Each section measures 5,280 feet on a side (one mile) and contains 640 acres of land.

separate property is property owned by an individual prior to a marriage or acquired after the marriage by gift or by inheritance. It remains the sole and separate property of the party owning it.

services of real estate brokerage are commonly described as buying, selling, leasing, exchanging, negotiating, offering, auctioning, and appraising for another person, for compensation. If an individual is performing any of these services of real estate, for compensation, or even for the expectation of being compensated, a real estate license from the state where the property is located is required.

servient tenement serves the dominant tenement allowing the dominant tenement the right of passage

setback is the required distance between structures

settlement is another term for the closing of a real estate transaction

Sherman Antitrust Act is among the federal laws pertaining to antitrust legislation. Violations of this act can range to $1 million for individuals and $100 million for corporations.

short sale of a property occurs when a property is sold for less than loan balances owed

single agency is the typical, agency relationship used in real estate. One agent represents the seller and another agent represents the buyer, in most cases. Every client who enters into an agency agreement with a broker has the right to know that in a single transaction, the agent exclusively represents only his side of a transaction.

special agency is a form of agency most often used in real estate. Special agency is created in an agreement, often in writing. The special agent represents the client and has all of the fiduciary duties, but has no authority to bind the client to anything. The role of the special agent is simply to represent the interests of the client, but the special agent must allow the client to make the final decision whether or not to be contractually bound.

special assessments are levied against properties for special improvements, such as sidewalks, street lights, landscaping of public areas, and other such improvements. The special assessment is charged against the properties which *directly benefit* from the improvements.

special warranty deed is used by executors, trustees and universal or general agents of the grantor. The only warranty created with the special warranty deed is the *warranty against undisclosed encumbrances*.

speculative homes ("spec homes") are new homes where the builder "speculates" what the market will do by completing a small number of homes without buyers under contract

sphere of influence is all the people you know and an excellent source of business

spot zoning represents the zoning authority's decision to rezone a small area in a zone different from the surrounding parcels

Statute of Frauds requires all real estate contracts, except short-term leases (less than 1 year), to be in writing. All other contracts where the amount in controversy exceeds $500 must also be in writing to be enforceable. "Enforceable" means a dispute between the parties will be heard in court and a judge will "enforce" the provisions of the contract.

Statute of Limitations is a legal limit to the time frame under which the injured party can legally sue the breaching party and this limit varies from state to state

steering is the illegal showing of properties to a prospective buyer or tenant only in areas of the market which are predominantly of the same ethnicity as the prospect

stigmatized property is a term that applies when a property become "defamed" because of some event that has occurred at the property or nearby, or because of the presence of some negative factor in the local area

straight loan, (also called a *term loan* or an *interest only loan*) is a scenario where the borrower pays only interest during the life of the loan. At the end of term, the entire principal balance is paid off in full. There is no amortization.

subagent is a person to whom agency has been delegated, always by an agent who is responsible to a principal and always with the permission of the principal. Subagents assist in carrying out client-based functions on behalf of the principal. Note that subagents from the same company have the same fiduciary duties and responsibilities as the original agent.

subdivision plat (or *plat map*) is used in the lot, block, and subdivision legal description method. It is required by most municipalities of a developer, who wishes to subdivide the large parcel into lots. The map clearly identifies the "lay of the land" identifying individual parcels, lot sizes, streets, utilities, and other information as required for approval.

subdivision regulations contain regulations such as street widths, provisions for sidewalks and street lights, drainage provisions, lot size, house size, house styles, roof material, exterior finishes, and a host of other matters required for the specific subdivision

subject property is the property for which the value is being appraised

subject to has two applications in real estate. In a wrap-around mortgage, the buyer purchases the property from the seller "subject to" the existing mortgage but does not assume personal liability for it. The other application is synonymous with *contingency.*

subordination agreement is an agreement between two lien holders to swap priority position

substitution and the *principle of substitution* is based on the likelihood that the market will not pay substantially more for one property over another if the properties are substantially the same

suit for damages is a legal remedy to either party for breach of contract on the part of the other party. A suit for damages will require the defaulting party to pay the other for any actual costs associated with the hardship.

suit for specific performance is a legal action which will require the defaulting party to perform all duties as specified in the contract

suit to quiet title is a court action taken if it is discovered there is a gap in title and will often involve the use of a *quit claim deed*

Superfund Amendment and Reauthorization Act (1986), SARA, clarified regulations regarding hazardous waste and limited liability for some parties, including innocent landowners and real estate brokers

supply and demand affects the value of the subject property. High Demand + Low Supply = Higher Values. Low Demand + High Supply = Lower Values.

survey is a study performed by a surveyor which determines property boundary lines. A survey will also uncover any violations of setbacks or encroachments.

tenancy by the entireties has the four unities of title found in joint tenancy, with the additional requirement that the parties *must be married*. Thus, there would be only two parties in a tenancy by the entireties situation but are treated as one legal person.

tenant in severalty exists when there is only one owner. The title to the property has been "severed" from all others. This form of ownership is available to natural and non-natural persons.

tenants in common could exist when there are two or more owners. There is only one ***unity of title***, the right of equal access and possession.

term loan, (also called a "straight loan" or an ***interest only loan***) is a scenario where the borrower pays only interest during the life of the loan. At the end of term, the entire principal balance is paid off in full. There is no amortization.

testate describes those individuals who have died with a will. They are said to have died testate.

testator is the person who made the will and died testate

tie-in agreements involve agreements to sell customers one product or service only if they purchase another product. Usually the sale of a desirable product is tied into the purchase of a less desirable product.

tiers are strips of land, 6 miles apart, running horizontally parallel to the base line when using the U.S. Government Rectangular Survey system

time is of the essence simply put, means that if a specific time period is set out in the contract, in which one of the parties is to do something, and has not done it when the allotted period of time expires, the other party may declare a breach

timeshare is the right to use and occupy a residential unit on a periodic recurring basis, according to an arrangement among the other owners. In most timeshare projects, the timeshare buyer purchases a right to use a unit (the actual room or suite where the persons will stay) for a week.

title is synonymous with *ownership* of real property. It means *ownership* of real property and includes the bundle of rights plus a ***deed*** to the land which serves as evidence of ownership.

title theory states the ***mortgagor*** (borrower) gives the ***mortgagee*** (lender) ***legal title*** and retains ***equitable title***. Legal title is returned to the mortgagor upon full payment of the debt.

townhomes may appear to be single family dwellings which are physically attached to adjacent structures. Each townhome is usually two- or three stories and typically sits on its own parcel of land. The owner of the townhome owns the land upon which the structure sits and also owns other common property (pools, tennis courts, parks, etc.) in the townhome project as a tenant in common with the other owners in the development.

township lines are imaginary lines horizontally parallel to the base lines when using the U.S. Government Rectangular Survey system

townships are formed by the intersection of the ranges and tiers when using the U.S. Government Rectangular Survey system. Each township contains 36 sections.

tract homes are built in a subdivision which typically has a few models from which purchasers can choose to have the builder construct on their behalf

trade fixtures are generally items of personal property that are installed in such a fashion as to make them a fairly permanent part of the leased space

transaction* or *transactional broker is a strategy used in some states to deal with dual agency concerns. A transaction broker is an agent without fiduciary duties but who handles the transaction from start to finish. Those states adopting the transaction broker approach take the position that the real estate professionals represent the transaction and not the parties to the transaction.

transfer taxes, sometimes referred to as *conveyance taxes*, *revenue stamps*, *documentary stamps*, or *deed stamps,* are a *state* tax, collected locally, based upon the value of real property when it is sold. It is normally paid by the seller at closing and is based upon a declaration of value.

transferability applies in that the property must be able to be sold (transferred) from one owner to another. If the property cannot be sold due to restrictions on its ownership, such as a burden on title, the property's value is greatly diminished.

trigger term is any term of the financing and "triggers" the need to disclose *all* credit terms – all or none.

trust account is another term for an ***escrow account*** established by a broker for the holding of the principal's funds until funding, such as with a buyer's earnest money deposit

trust is a device where one person transfers real property to another person for the benefit of a third, with the understanding that the real estate asset (and possibly other assets as well) will be used to care for the trustor.

trustee is an independent third party chosen by the lender and to whom the power of sale is granted in a deed of trust

trustor is the borrower in a deed of trust. The term is also used to describe the individual or business entity (e.g., a corporation, LLC, etc.) who transfers the property to the ***trustee*** within a trust.

U.S. Government Rectangular Survey System lays an imaginary grid of horizontal and vertical lines across the country and references the subject property within that grid

underwriting is the final review and decision making process pertaining to granting the loan

undivided interest applies when there is more than one owner to a property. The parties are said to hold *undivided interests* meaning that no owner can claim a specific physical portion of the property as belonging to that owner only. Multi-party ownership deals with *interests in* rather than *physical portions* of the property.

unenforceable contract appears to be valid, but if there is a disagreement between the parties in the performance of duties and the receipt of rights, the courts will not get involved in a resolution.

Uniform Residential Appraisal Report (URAR) is the standard format of a written appraisal as required by many institutions

Uniform Residential Landlord Tenant Act (URLTA) provisions were created to clarify, standardize, and modernize the rights and responsibilities of tenants and landlords in the United States

Uniform Settlement Statement (***HUD 1***) must be used for the closing according to RESPA. This is an easy to read form which details the amount of the closing costs and who is paying them.

Uniform Standards of Professional Appraisal Practice (USPAP) establishes the quality control standards applicable for real property, personal property, intangibles, and business valuation appraisal analysis and reports

unilateral means "one sided." Often taking the form of an option contract, a unilateral contract is binding on one party should the other party elect to perform under the agreement. It is one sided in that the party with the option does not ever have to perform.

unity of title is a condition of ownership which is common to all who hold title to the property. The more unities there are, the more the owners have in common (in their ownership) with each other. The four unities of title are time, title, interest, and possession.

universal agency is a form of agency created in a written ***unlimited power of attorney*** which grants the agent the authority to do anything the clients could do for themselves. Universal agency authorizes binding the client to contracts and authorizes the sale or other disposition of real and personal property.

up zoning takes place if additional uses are *added* to those already available for a property. This normally adds value to the property.

urea formaldehyde foam insulation (UFFI) has been used as an insulation in residential and commercial buildings. Ingestion and inhalation present significant health hazards.

usury refers to maximum interest rates lenders can charge on certain loans as established by the state. To the extent that the interest charged exceeds the statutory amount, it is referred to as *usurious* and cannot be collected. Not all states have such provisions.

utility implies that property must be useful in the eyes of the market. If the real estate is not useful (not good for anything) it has little or no value.

vacancies and bad debts are those losses to the gross income the owner incurred due to units being vacant for any length of time and for rents that should have been, but were not, collected. When expressed as a percentage, they reflect a percentage of the gross scheduled income.

valid contract contains visible evidence of all five essential elements of a contract (competent parties, offer and acceptance, legality of object, informed parties, and consideration) and is therefore binding and enforceable on all parties.

variance is a request for some leeway in using a parcel which violates the zoning regulations

vendee is a buyer

vendor is a seller

vesting clause states the vesting option selected by the grantee such as *in severalty,* as *a tenant in common,* as *joint tenants with right of survivorship,* etc.

Veteran's Administration (VA) guaranteed loans are not normally made by the VA. Loans are made through private lenders. The VA may fund the loan if there is no available lender. The VA does not set interest rates on VA loans. The interest is determined by the lender to be competitive in the market.

void agreement lacks any one or more of the essential elements of a contract and has no legal effect. It is not binding on the parties.

voidable contract appears to be valid but may be disaffirmed because it is missing competent parties (legal capacity) such as a minor, or is missing voluntary, informed parties such as a contract executed under misrepresentation, fraud, or duress. In a voidable contract, the party suffering the legal disability has the right to void the contract, provided it is done within a reasonable time.

voluntary alienation usually involves a deed where the owner voluntarily transfers his title to another person

warranty (or ***covenant***) is a promise by the ***grantor*** to the ***grantee*** concerning the title to the property, that some condition exists and will continue to exist, or, that a condition does not exist and never will

warranty against undisclosed encumbrances is a covenant in a deed that claims the grantor has disclosed to the grantee all encumbrances on the property, if any

warranty deed (also known as a ***general warranty deed,*** or ***grant, bargain, and sale deed***) is the most commonly used form of deed and it contains five warranties (covenants).

warranty of further assurances is a covenant in a deed where the grantor promises that should a claim of superior title be made, the grantor will defend against the claim and defeat it.

warranty of quiet enjoyment promises the grantee will be able to enjoy ownership of the property without hearing anyone make a valid claim of superior title or right to the property

warranty of seisin is a covenant in a deed that states the grantor owns the property and has the right and power to convey the property

warranty of title forever is a deed covenant where the grantor promises that should another party be able to establish a superior claim to the title, the grantor will pay back to the grantee the purchase price (the *money back guarantee*)

wrap around mortgage (or ***all-inclusive deed of trust***) is a form of seller financing (purchase money mortgage) available only where there is no existing ***due on sale*** clause in the original mortgage document. The seller still owes on the original mortgage (the ***underlying mortgage***) and continues to make those payments. The buyer makes payments to the seller for the new amount financed as a purchase money mortgage.

writ of attachment has the effect of preventing the transfer of assets until the lawsuit is concluded

writ of execution is utilized to assist in the collection of a judgment. The court will issue the writ of execution to the sheriff, which directs the sheriff to seize all property of the defendant in the jurisdiction, sell it, and apply the proceeds against the judgment.

zoning establishes what uses are available for each parcel of land. The categories of uses generally found in zoning ordinances are agricultural, residential, commercial, industrial, and governmental.

Made in the USA
Charleston, SC
29 August 2015